D1084355

UP IN THE AIR?

Up in the Air?

*The Future of Public Service Media
in the Western Balkans*

Edited by
Tarik Jusić, Manuel Puppis, Laia Castro Herrero,
and Davor Marko

Central European University Press
Budapest–New York

©2021 by the editors

Published in 2021 by
Central European University Press

Nádor utca 9, H-1051 Budapest, Hungary
Tel: +36-1-327-3138 or 327-3000
E-mail: ceupress@press.ceu.edu
Website: www.ceupress.com

ISBN 978-963-386-401-2 (hardback)
ISBN 978-963-386-402-9 (ebook)

Library of Congress Cataloging-in-Publication Data

Names: Jusić, Tarik, editor. | Puppis, Manuel, 1977- editor. | Castro
Herrero, Laia, editor.
Title: Up in the air? : the future of public service media in the Western
Balkans / edited by Tarik Jusić, Manuel Puppis, Laia Castro Herrero,
and Davor Marko.
Description: New York : Central European University Press, 2021. |
Includes bibliographical references and index.
Identifiers: LCCN 2021002751 (print) | LCCN 2021002752 (ebook) |
ISBN 9789633864012 (hardback) | ISBN 9789633864029 (pdf)
Subjects: LCSH: Public broadcasting—Balkan Peninsula. | Mass
media--Political aspects—Balkan Peninsula.
Classification: LCC HE8689.7.P82 U65 2021 (print) |
LCC HE8689.7.P82 (ebook) | DDC 384.5409496--dc23
LC record available at https://lccn.loc.gov/2021002751
LC ebook record available at https://lccn.loc.gov/2021002752

Contents

PART I: WESTERN BALKAN MEDIA SYSTEMS

PART II: COMPARATIVE PERSPECTIVES

List of Tables

List of Figures

Preface and Acknowledgments

The countries of the Western Balkans share a unique history. Yet there is little comparative research about their media systems, media policies and media organizations, including the transformation and prospects of public service broadcasting (PSB). This gap is exactly why we, together with scholars from the respective countries, started a research project investigating the regulation and operation of PSB in Albania, Bosnia and Herzegovina, Croatia, Kosovo, Montenegro, North Macedonia, and Serbia. Moreover, we invited scholars from all over Europe to think about PSB and media policy in the region. This book is the result of our work. Taking a comparative perspective, it provides a comprehensive overview of the role, prospects, and challenges of PSB in the Western Balkans and tries to make a contribution to our understanding of the transformation of media systems and media democratization in a region that took a distinct path of development with outcomes that differ from other post-communist states.

Aside from our research partners and the authors contributing to this book, we would like to thank the Swiss National Science Foundation (SNSF) for its generous support through the SCOPES program aimed at facilitating scientific co-operation between Eastern Europe and Switzerland. The SNSF not only supported our comparative research project but also awarded a valorization grant.

Moreover, we would like to thank CEU Press for their support throughout the publication process.

Belgrade, Fribourg, Prague, Sarajevo and Zurich, May 2020

CHAPTER 1

Challenges and Prospects of Public Service Broadcasting in the Western Balkans

Laia Castro Herrero, Tarik Jusić, Davor Marko,
and Manuel Puppis

. Introduction

The institutionalization of public service broadcasting (PSB) has been a fundamental element of the media policy paradigm in Western Europe since World War Two (van Cuilenburg and McQuail 2003). In contrast, the idea of PSB is relatively novel in the post-communist countries of Albania, Bosnia and Herzegovina, Croatia, Kosovo, Montenegro, North Macedonia, and Serbia. These Western Balkan countries could only start their democratization processes, including the transformation of their media systems, at the end of the 1990s and early 2000s, as a consequence of protracted armed conflicts in most of the countries that emerged from the dissolution of Yugoslavia and entrenched authoritarian regimes across the region. One of the key elements of their transformation has been an attempt to set up media systems that follow the Western European model characterized by a coexistence of commercial and public broadcasting.

Such a transformation was primarily based on a *mimetic* approach that attempted to mirror Western European legal frameworks and institutional arrangements (Jakubowicz and Sükösd 2008; Splichal 2001), mainly in connection with the European Union's (EU) conditionality mechanisms, like in the cases of Albania, Croatia, Montenegro, North Macedonia, and Serbia, or outright international intervention into media systems, like in the cases of post-war Bosnia and Herzegovina, and Kosovo (see Irion and Jusić 2018). However, in most, if not all cases, the attempted transposition of Western institutional models was, at best, only a half-hearted effort as ruling elites tried to preserve existing institutional arrangements and power relations while, at the same time, ticking boxes on the wishlists of international democratization agents in exchange for positive evaluations, political privileges, and financial support. At worst, the introduction of more democratic institutional forms and practices was met with fierce resistance and subversion.

As was the case in Central and Eastern European (CEE) countries in the early 1990s, the institutional transformation in the Western Balkans resulted in *atavistic* public service broadcasting systems colonized by political parties and state authorities (see Bajomi-Lázár 2014; Irion and Jusić 2018). To this day, PSB in the region suffers from highly politicized and monolithic structures that are resistant to change and primarily reflect the narrow agendas of political elites rather than any kind of broader public interest. As a consequence, the transformation of former state broadcasters into genuine PSB organizations across the Western Balkans has suffered significant setbacks, resulting in dysfunctional institutional arrangements and the loss of legitimacy that is most visible in the ever-widening distance between their programming and audience interests and demands (see Bašić-Hrvatin 2002; Bašić-Hrvatin, Thompson and Jusić 2008; Dragomir et al. 2005; Irion and Jusić 2018).

While the media systems of CEE countries have rightly received continuous attention by media, communication, and policy scholars, the same cannot be said for the Western Balkan countries, however. Despite the importance of understanding the similarities and differences of their media systems for both research and policymaking, studies on media transformation, media policy, and PSB in the region are rare, especially when it comes to comparative studies. This omission is striking given the unique historical and societal background the Western Balkan countries share.

This book thus attempts at filling an important gap in contemporary research by providing a comprehensive overview of the role, prospects, and challenges of PSB in the Western Balkans. As such it makes not only a valuable contribution to our understanding of the transformation of media systems and media democratization in general but also provides insights into a region that took a distinct path of development with outcomes that differ from other post-communist states. Beyond offering an in-depth analysis of individual media systems and their media policy, this volume takes a comparative perspective, mapping out the similarities and differences across Western Balkan media systems. Conceptualized in such a way, we hope that it can contribute to academic and policymaking debates about the regulation and organization of PSB in both the analyzed region and other media systems undergoing transformation.

In what follows, this introductory chapter will outline the theoretical background of our comparative study of PSB in the Western Balkans and the key characteristics of the transformation of PSB in post-communist countries. Next, the research questions and methods will be discussed before summarizing the main results of the comparative study. The chapter ends with reflections on the future of PSB in the Western Balkans.

Challenges and Prospects for Public Service Broadcasting in the Context of Democratization

Public Service Broadcasting and Shifting Media Policy Paradigms

After the end of World War Two, media policy in Western Europe has been following a *public service paradigm*, as van Cuilenburg and McQuail (2003, 191) labeled it, that "was dominated by sociopolitical rather than economic or national strategic concerns." The general idea behind the decision to set up PSB instead of licensing commercial broadcasters was that due to its non-commercial organization and public funding it could serve the public interest by meeting the communication needs of democratic societies, among them universality of geographic coverage, diversity, balanced information, and serving minorities (McQuail 2005).

In most countries, PSB held a monopoly until the 1980s when private commercial radio and television were finally authorized, leading to today's dual broadcasting systems (Donders, Pauwels, and Loisen 2013). This commercialization of broadcasting led to intense debate about the role of PSB in a multi-channel environment (Jarren et al. 2001) and culminated in the question of whether it even has a future (Siune and Hultén 1998). Yet the "dualization" of broadcasting was a sobering experience: given the limited interest of commercial broadcasters in news and current affairs, politicians generally accepted that PSB was their last, best hope for achieving public interest goals or at least, even if only for their self-interest, steady political coverage (Donges and Puppis 2003). Besides, PSB organizations proved their capability to reinvent themselves. Societal changes and increasing competition forced PSB organizations to adapt their programs and to put an emphasis on their legitimation. Many of them opted for what can be labeled a compensation strategy that is trying to cater to their audiences "without falling into the trap of commercialism" (Hultén and Brants 1992, 118). Considering that PSB has the remit to not simply focus on audiences of interest to advertisers but to cater for all societal groups, Syvertsen calls them the only remaining mass media (Syvertsen 1999).

In retrospect, "dualization" seems innocuous compared to digitization, which continues to fundamentally change the context of media policy in Europe. The digitization of media production and distribution, and especially the transition from broadcast to broadband brought about by the internet, inevitably challenges existing regulation and policy paradigms, raising questions regarding the legitimacy and the remit of PSB in the digital age. As PSB organizations "have increasingly embraced the Internet and the new opportunities it opens for service delivery" (Herzog and Karppinen 2014, 416–417), fierce debates regarding their role in society, the scope of their mission, and whether they should be allowed to evolve from public service broadcasting to public service media (PSM) have intensified (d'Haenens et al. 2008; Iosifidis 2007; 2010; Lowe and Bardoel 2007). Their entitlement to serve citizens with a broad range of programming irrespective of distribution technology tends to be contested, not least by publishers that aim at protecting their online ventures (Lowe and Berg 2013). Private media also filed complaints at the European level, leading to the introduction of so-called public value tests to ensure the compliance of public funding with EU state aid rules (Donders 2012; Donders and Moe 2011). The vested interests of commercial media organizations are only one source of criticism, however. In several Western European countries, PSB is confronted with severe budget cuts, political pressure mainly by right-wing governments, and changes to the traditional license fee funding model that might lead to more dependence from policymakers (Schweizer and Puppis 2018). At the same time, some scholars criticize PSB for having a relationship too intimate with elites that effectively undermine its ability to hold power to account (Freedman 2019). While the time of taking for granted the need for PSB might be over, the idea is still powerful in a platform society characterized by a crisis of commercial media and the growing importance of search engines, social networks, and video sharing services for communication in the public sphere. Practitioners and scholars alike thus rethink the role of PSB in a personalized media environment.

Public Service Broadcasting in Post-Communist Europe

While PSB has been a cornerstone of media policy in Western Europe, it simply did not exist in former communist countries where state-controlled broadcasters enjoyed an undisputed monopoly position. On their way to democracy, these countries underwent a rapid transformation that not only required a complete change of their political systems but also involved—at least formally—the setup of media systems that are independent from the state and politics.

Most research on the transformation of media systems of post-communist countries focuses on Central and Eastern European (CEE) countries. Studies show that the transformation of media systems involved a policy transfer from "the West" to "the East." This process of diffusion can be conceptualized as *mimetic isomorphism* (DiMaggio and Powell 1991; Radaelli 2000), meaning that media policy from countries that were perceived to be more successful or legitimate was imitated (Jakubowicz and Sükösd 2008; Splichal 2001). Although the Western European public service media policy paradigm was being undermined by commercialization and digitization processes, it was still perceived as a role model for former communist countries to follow. More specifically, this included exporting Western European institutional arrangements, such as public service broadcasting and dual media systems to the new democracies in "the East." The aim was to allow the operation of private media and to reorganize former state-controlled broadcasters into PSB organizations.

This mimetic approach was based on slightly naïve presumptions about the possibilities of policy transfer and did not take sufficiently into account that favorable political and journalistic cultures would require time to develop (Jakubowicz and Sükösd 2008). In many media development programs, the local context and specifics of the countries in which the processes of democratization were taking place were mostly neglected (Irion and Jusić 2014). It soon became apparent that the applicability of Western policy models and media institutions to CEE countries was limited. Scholars claim that what happened can be explained with an atavistic orientation in media policy-making—which is understood as "unwillingness of new power elites to give up all control of, or ability to influence, the media" (Jakubowicz 2008, 112). A lack of resources, highly politicized institutions, self-censorship among journalists, and nationalistic and populist discourses ran counter to any successful and profound media reform. As Splichal (2001) noted, both structural regulation—licensing, financing, media ownership regulation—and content regulation were failing across the CEE region. The power elites, both old and new, while ostensibly accepting the mimetic orientation, in most cases sought to cling to whatever elements of the old command system they could still maintain. Elite continuity from the former regimes to the new democracies favored negotiated revolutions and hindered institutional transformations (Sparks 1998).

The result of efforts to embark on policy transfer in such "disabling environments" (Jakubowicz and Sükösd 2008, 10) were media landscapes that combine the elements of both mimetic and atavistic media policy orientations (Jakubowicz 2008, 113). Where atavistic trends are more entrenched, public institutions are largely colonized by political parties and state authorities, media owners are embedded in clientelistic networks and higher levels of political media parallelism are to be found. According to Jakubowicz (2008), the extent to which specific features of atavistic or mimetic orientation were present in different countries depends on the level of consolidation of democracy: the more liberal the country, the more dominant was the mimetic orientation, whereas the more illiberal countries leaned towards atavistic orientations, with authoritarian countries clinging to an atavistic media policy approach with limited or no media freedom allowed. The mimetic orientation, supported through the considerable leverage of the EU accession process and influence of the Council of Europe as well as major state and non-state aid agencies and donors did indeed produce notable results in terms of introduction of legal and institutional arrangements for the development of PSB. The strongest impact was among the CEE states that were the first to acquire EU membership status, and success was most limited in countries where EU accession aspirations were not yet met (Jakubowicz 2008, 116). Nevertheless, once countries joined the EU, its leverage diminished. In several cases, such as Hungary and Poland, the ruling elites did their best to roll back the guarantees for the independence of PSB and regain control over such valuable political and financial assets. Consequently, the formal transformation to PSB in many cases resulted in little more than a legitimacy façade for former state broadcasters whose operation is still contingent on which way the political wind is blowing. Studies suggest that reforming institutions through conditionality does not correspond with successful institutional change (Shirley 2005). Indeed, scholars point out that "one of the largest challenges for development efforts is the lack of an enabling environment that allows independent media to develop .... Funding agencies and intermediary implementation agencies face legacies of undemocratic structures, politicians, and traditions, which make the creation of enabling laws and policies difficult or impossible" (Price, Davis Noll and De Luce 2002, 57).

In the end, existing research on CEE countries emphasizes that post-communist countries cannot be understood without taking their past into account and that their media systems are hybrids featuring elements of preceding regimes and democratic governance. As Voltmer suggests, "[g]iven the continuity of organizational structures, personnel, and practices, we have to factor in the particular features of the preceding authoritarian regime as a determinant of the emerging media system in new democracies" (Voltmer 2012, 236). The results of almost 20 years of transformation of media in CEE are "disheartening, in some cases even devastating," as we witness the "new trend of 'repoliticization' of public service media with intensified political pressures and diminishing editorial independence" (Voltmer 2013, 155).

While the transformation of post-communist media systems in CEE countries and the Southeastern European (SEE) countries of the Western Balkans show many commonalities (Zielonka and Mancini 2011), there are also important differentiators. First, media systems in the Western Balkans are heavily shaped by a context of weak post-conflict and at times inoperative *minimalist states* (Bieber 2011). Second, there are deep ethnic cleavages within and between the countries in the region. The transformation of state broadcasters into PSB organizations has therefore been highly idiosyncratic in nature. Third, the nature of PSB transformation has also been influenced by a plethora of international state and non-state actors, that have in many cases not only provided ideas and funding but have frequently pushed for solutions without much concern for local inputs or broader contextual constraints. This also gave the concept of mimetic media policy orientation significantly different meaning than it was in the case of CEE countries since many introduced reforms did not have sufficient local support that would ensure sustainable transposition of imported institutional models (see Irion and Jusić 2018). Fourth, the protracted nature of the EU integration processes—except for Croatia that became an EU member in 2013—and the oftentimes lacking complicity and skepticism of local political elites with the European project provide a significantly different backdrop for media policy in the Western Balkans than it was the case in CEE countries. Last but not least, all Western Balkan countries qualify as small media systems that are characterized, for example, by a small audience and advertising markets, which is expected to have consequences for the viability of media organizations and the objectives of media policy (Lowe and Nissen 2011; Puppis 2009).

Given these differences between the two regions, investigating the transformation of Western Balkan media systems promises to provide important insights. Nevertheless, there is little research on these media systems, their media policy, and their PSB organizations. Although important, the previous studies about PSB in the Western Balkans have been few and disconnected and have not provided a systemic analysis of the development and transformation of PSB in the region.

The 2005 study *Television Across Europe* that analyzed 20 EU members, candidates, and potential candidates—including Albania, Bosnia and Herzegovina, Croatia, Montenegro, North Macedonia, and Serbia—have found that:

[i]n transition countries, public service broadcasting often suffers in particular from a lack of professionalism, an enfeebled sense of mission, a lack of
viable funding, political interference with its governing bodies, and low public
awareness of public service television's distinctive role. Consequently, in these
countries, little is expected from public service broadcasting. (Dragomir et al.
2005, 54)

Although the transformation into PSB organizations has been completed in
transitional SEE countries, the introduced changes were rather more formal
than substantial, since the state retained its close control of these broadcasters.

Such a predicament of PSB in the Western Balkans has been confirmed in
other studies as well. Studies published in a recent edited volume about international media assistance in the Western Balkans (Irion and Jusić 2018) show how
difficult is the task of establishing PSB in the newly democratized SEE countries, especially those that have recently suffered traumas of war, ethnic hatred
and systemic breakdown of governance (Thompson 2018). Consequently, PSB
organizations in the Western Balkans "fulfill their mandate or mission weakly,
by and large. They are more or less politically captured, underfunded, demor-
alized, and held, for the most part, in middling to low esteem by the public"
(Thompson 2018, 193). The underlying causes for such a dire situation have to
do with the weak implementation of laws, financial dependence on the government, strong clientelism, and weak incentives among ruling elites for supporting
the genuine reforms of public broadcasters in the region. The situation is particularly difficult in the countries that have strong centrifugal drives due to deep
ethnic cleavages, such as Bosnia and Herzegovina, Kosovo, and, to an extent,
North Macedonia, with their complex consociational power-sharing constitutional frameworks that translate into the ineffective institutional arrangements
for PSB as well (see for example Bašić-Hrvatin and Thompson 2008; Jusić and
Palmer 2008). Given the range of challenges, it is not surprising that the majority of the countries in the Western Balkans also faced significant problems and
delays in the digital switchover process and had mixed results when it comes to
the digitization of public broadcasters (Schlossberg 2014).

The most recent insights from the IREX Media Sustainability Index 2019
show little or no progress when it comes to operational consolidation, professionalization, independence from political interference, and democratization of PSB
in the Western Balkans (IREX 2019). In line with the argumentation of Sandra
Bašić-Hrvatin, we may say that all of the above indicates that "a broad social
and political consensus on how to democratize the communication sphere"
(Bašić-Hrvatin 2002, 21–22), and in particular how to transform PSB, was lacking, resulting in superficial reforms and legal and institutional arrangements that
put interests of ruling elites before those of citizens.

While these studies provide important first insights, a comparative study
that provides a broad and yet systematic overview of PSB and media systems in
the Western Balkans is sorely missing.

Research Questions, Methods, and Structure of the Book

The research presented in this edited volume aims at offering a comprehensive overview of the development and current status of PSB in the region and to investigate the differences and similarities between the analyzed media systems.

To better understand its organization, remit, funding, performance, and relationship to politics, we first ask the question of how public service broadcasting in the Western Balkans is currently regulated and operated. More specifically, we are interested in the institutional and organizational setup of PSB, the scope of its mission for both traditional broadcasting and new digital services, as well as its formal and de-facto independence in light of financial constraints and political influence on both management and editorial decision-making. By addressing the aforementioned issues, we also provide insights as to what adds to successful transformations of state broadcasters into truly independent PSB organizations.

Second, we ask the question of which contextual factors help in explaining the current status and performance of public service broadcasting. In particular, we investigate the context under which new media policies for PSB were adopted, such as the political structures of the countries under scrutiny, the actors involved in policymaking, and pressures to comply with the EU *acquis communautaire*. Also, we take the structure of the media market and the position of PSB in economically weak and small media systems into account.

To provide answers to these research questions, a so-called descriptive or "simple" comparison aiming at a systematic analysis of similarities and differences of the media systems under investigation was performed (Puppis and d'Haenens 2012). The analyzed media systems included Albania, Bosnia and Herzegovina, Croatia, Kosovo, Montenegro, North Macedonia, and Serbia. Although the Western Balkans is a rather coherent region in terms of crucial social, political, and economic features, there are important differences between the individual countries and their media systems that offer some variation. First, out of seven countries covered by this study, only Croatia is an EU member since 2013, while four have obtained candidate status (Albania, Montenegro, North Macedonia, and Serbia). Overall, each country is in a different phase regarding the adoption of EU standards, with significant implications for the way their media systems operate. As an example, Croatia completed the transition to digital television already in 2012, and, like in Serbia, media organizations (including PSB) are taking steps towards media convergence at a more rapid pace than the rest of the countries in the region. Second, their path toward democratization has been tainted by the traumas of violent conflict in different ways and to different extents. After the fall of Yugoslavia, a number of its former republics experienced extensive military conflicts during the 1990s and early 2000s—Croatia (1991–1995), Bosnia and Herzegovina (1992–1995), Serbia and Kosovo (1998–2000)—with devastating consequences in loss of human lives, millions of refugees, destroyed infrastructure and plummeting productivity. North Macedonia went through a brief violent episode in 2001 that was stopped by a prompt international intervention and follow-up political agreement (Dimitrijevska-Markoski and Daskalovski 2008), while only Albania and Montenegro managed to completely avoid military conflicts in their territories. These different scenarios inevitably produced different starting points and different sociopolitical and economic contexts for the transformation of these societies, including the democratization of their media systems. Most notably, two countries that were most severely devastated by the wars—Bosnia and Herzegovina, and Kosovo—have limited sovereignty due to their formal status of international semi-protectorate as a consequence of international peacekeeping involvement in each of them (see relevant chapters on Bosnia and Herzegovina and Kosovo in Irion and Jusić 2018). Third, although all of the analyzed countries are multi-ethnic, only three of them—Bosnia and Herzegovina, Kosovo, and North Macedonia—have consociational power-sharing arrangements. These power-sharing arrangements ensure that none of the ethnic groups can rule alone to avoid majorization and protect the fragile peace, while at the same time making decision-making processes extremely cumbersome and ineffective, particularly in the case of Bosnia and Herzegovina. In such a context, mass media including PSB have been unable to facilitate communication across deep political cleavages, and are more often than not prone to solidify and deepen social divisions and conflicts (Sarajlić and Marko 2011).

Regarding methods of data collection and data analysis, this comparative study made use of documents and expert interviews that were then analyzed using qualitative methods. For the document analysis (Bowen 2009; Reh 1995; Karppinen and Moe 2012; 2019) policy documents, laws, and regulations, as well as official statistical bulletins, annual and financial reports of PSB organizations, minutes of parliamentary proceedings, and relevant secondary sources, were collected. The expert interviews (Bogner and Menz 2009; Van Audenhove and Donders 2019) with managers, editors, and journalists from PSB organizations as well as independent experts, academics, and other media professionals were carried out during 2015 and 2016. The empirical work was carried out by scholars in the respective countries.

The first part of the book presents these analyses of the individual Western Balkan media systems, namely of Albania (Chapter 2 by Blerjana Bino), Bosnia and Herzegovina (Chapter 3 by Nidžara Ahmetašević and Tea Hadžiristić), Croatia (Chapter 4 by Davor Marko), Kosovo (Chapter 5 by Naser Miftari), Montenegro (Chapter 6 by Nataša Ružić), North Macedonia (Chapter 7 by Snežana Trpevska and Igor Micevski), and Serbia (Chapter 8 by Davor Marko). Following the theoretical and methodological frameworks outlined above, all the chapters feature a similar structure and provide answers to the two above-mentioned research questions. The analysis of each country is broken down into three sections each of which with a thematic focus namely, (a) legal aspects conditioning the regulation of PSB, (b) financial challenges and PSB funding models, and (c) digitalization trends and technological developments impacting the future of PSB.

The second part of the book offers a comparative analysis of similarities and differences as well as common challenges and setbacks in the development of PSB across the region. The authors focus on cross-cutting issues that affect media policy and PSB in all countries in the region, complementing the country chapters. While Péter Bajomi-Lázár deals with the danger of increasing politicization of PSB (Chapter 9), Zrinjka Peruško discussed the historical context that helps explaining similarities and differences in PSB development in the Western Balkans (Chapter 10). Gregory Ferrell Lowe considers the mission, values and characteristic changes that are essential for PSB organizations in the region to be fully transformed (Chapter 11) and Michal Głowacki shows how organizational structures and procedures affect the functioning of PSB (Chapter 12). The issues of commercialization and program quality are addressed in a chapter by Marko Milosavljevič and Melita Poler Kovačič (Chapter 13). Digitization and subsequent policy-making prospects are touched upon by Sally Broughton Micova (Chapter 14) and Kenneth Murphy (Chapter 15) in their respective contributions. Finally, Barbara Thomass accounts for and summarizes the current state and future perspectives of PSB in the region of the Western Balkans (Chapter 16).

Before proceeding to the chapters dealing with individual media systems and cross-cutting issues, the remainder of this section provides an overview of the main results of the study.

Regulation and Operation of Public Service Broadcasting in the Western Balkans

The results of the research presented in this volume demonstrate that several common features are shared across the Western Balkan countries when it comes to the regulation and operation of PSB organizations. Four main sets of shared characteristics play a fundamental role in shaping the way how these broadcasters operate. First, political capture and instrumentalization severely undermine their de-facto independence. Second, PSB organizations across the region face financial constraints and pressures. Third, these broadcasters struggle to live up to their remit, particularly in the context of the growing importance of the internet. Finally, the strained relationship with their audiences additionally undermines PSB's legitimacy.

Political Capture, Clientelism and Instrumentalization

The regulation concerning public service broadcasting has been characterized by weak enforcement and permanent changes. Furthermore, the evidence presented in the country chapters shows that achievements at the formal level—such as formal compliance with the EU rules—do not guarantee the de-facto independence of PSB organizations and the fulfillment of their remit in practice. Frequent regulatory changes and the weak implementation of laws result in legal uncertainty and regulatory chaos, opening up numerous possibilities for political interference.

Hence, the most striking characteristic in all the media systems analyzed is a high level of political control over PSB organizations. These broadcasters have been politicized and instrumentalized by ruling elites and their parties, which use weak public institutions to advance their own political and financial agenda. In particular, the politicization of PSB materializes through the appointment of their supervisory boards and budget allocation. The instrumentalization of these politically "colonized" broadcasters ultimately takes various forms that effectively transfer public resources like well-paid positions, program production funds, or advertising contracts to party clients (see Chapter 9 by Bajomi-Lázár in this volume).

Consequently, many of the PSB organizations in the region do not enjoy editorial freedom, are under direct political control, cannot challenge ruling elites, and are not trusted by citizens (see Chapter 11 by Lowe in this volume). The situation is similar in all the Western Balkan countries. For example, clientelism determines the governance of PSB in Albania (see Chapter 2 by Bino in this volume). And in Montenegro, where one party ruled the country for almost 30 years, we find close political allegiance between ruling elites and PSB (see Chapter 6 by Ružić in this volume). In Bosnia and Herzegovina, the two PSB organizations at the level of the two entities are politically subordinated to the respective incumbent parties (see Chapter 3 by Ahmetašević and Hadžiristić in this volume). In Croatia, following their electoral victory in 2015, the conservative Croatian Democratic Union government dismissed the entire management and editorial board of HRT and appointed persons more in tune with party politics (see Chapter 4 by Marko in this volume).

Such a situation has consequences for the editorial independence of PSB. Pro-government bias is the norm rather than the exception. For instance, in many countries, there are frequent examples of explicit political propaganda in current affairs programs. As emphasized by Bajomi-Lázár, PSB organizations in the Western Balkans serve private interests at the detriment of the public good (see Chapter 9 by Bajomi-Lázár in this volume).

Financial Constraints and Commercial Pressure

Except for Albania and Croatia, limited funding is also among the core problems of PSB in the Western Balkans. From their inception, most of these broadcasters suffered from financial constraints, and the funding models of some of these broadcasters have virtually collapsed in several countries. For instance, in Bosnia and Herzegovina, the collection of the license fee is extremely inefficient and PSB is heavily indebted (see Chapter 3 by Ahmetašević and Hadžiristić in this volume). In Kosovo, the collection of the subscription fee through the Kosovo Electric Corporation has been ruled as unconstitutional, thus making RTK dependent on quarterly allocations from the state budget (see Chapter 5 by Miftari in this volume). In most of the other Western Balkan countries (Montenegro,

North Macedonia, and Serbia) the license fee has been abolished and funding is provided from the state budget, but still does not guarantee the optimal coverage of operational costs of some of these broadcasters, as is the case with North Macedonia (see Chapter 7 by Trpevska and Micevski in this volume). As a consequence, PSB in these countries has become even more vulnerable to governmental interference in their daily operations. In contrast, Albania and Croatia have a stable model of license fee funding in place.

Inadequate funding from the license fee or state budgets makes PSB in the Western Balkans highly dependent on advertising income, which in most cases constitutes a significant part of revenues. However, given the strong link between private corporations and large public companies and political and other interests, heavy reliance on advertising exposes PSB to additional avenues of external pressures, opening another front for political and financial influence over their operations.

By extension, advertising funding also has consequences on the possibility of PSB to fulfill its remit. In all the analyzed countries, there is a tradeoff between public service-oriented programming and commercial content, at the expense of the former. Instead of producing diverse quality content, PSB in the region rather puts its scarce resources into commercial and more entertainment-oriented programming, which allows them to compete with private broadcasters for advertising revenues. To keep their programs popular, they produce more entertainment and reality programs while at the same time decreasing the amount of news and current affairs programming, documentaries, and especially children, minority, cultural and drama programs, thus negatively affecting the overall quality of their content (see Chapter 13 by Milosavljević and Poler Kovačič in this volume). As an example, the Federal RTV in Bosnia and Herzegovina, one of the three members of the PSB system in the country, generates a significant part of its revenues from commercial sources (see Chapter 3 by Ahmetašević and Hadžiristić in this volume), while in Croatia HRT commercialized its content by introducing popular formats like casting shows to compete with private TV stations (see Chapter 4 by Marko in this volume).

Despite these attempts to keep its programs popular, PSB is struggling to attract substantial audiences. Except for Montenegro and Serbia, PSB in the countries of the Western Balkans has a low audience share, especially among young users who are spending their time online and rely less on television than older generations (see Chapter 9 by Bajomi-Lázár in this volume).

There seems to be a vicious cycle at play here: as PSB does not have adequate resources to produce quality content and ensure stabile operations, they commercialize their programming, thus further reducing resources for public service content. By so doing, these broadcasters become entangled in competition with commercial broadcasters which they cannot possibly win, consequently leading towards further erosion of their public service function, their ratings, and their public support.

In sum, financial constraints make PSB organizations vulnerable to a multitude of external pressures, leaving their management without sufficient financial resources to govern their operations independently, let alone strategically (see Chapter 16 by Thomass in this volume).

Changing Remit, Changing Organization

Another important characteristic of the Western Balkan countries is the lack of consensus about core values and the "rules of the game" regarding the mission, aims, and status of PSB (see Chapter 10 by Peruško in this volume). As a result, most PSB organizations in the region lack a clear mandate, independent and professional governance structures, a strategic outlook, editorial independence, and stable funding. In none of the Western Balkan countries do we find effective means of oversight of the operation of PSB, its compliance with regulation, and the fulfillment of its remit.

Moreover, PSB organizations in most Western Balkan countries have not adapted well to the growth of internet use and the move to online platforms by its audiences, thus missing new opportunities for the production and distribution of public service content. They mostly treat websites as an add-on to traditional broadcasting and have failed to develop effective ways of delivering content through third-party platforms, such as search engines, social networks, or video sharing services. Consequently, PSB is rarely considered to be among primary online sources of information. Except for Croatia and Serbia, PSB still operates within an outdated paradigm of traditional broadcasting (see Chapter 12 by Głowacki in this volume).

The main reason for the failure to adapt to shifting audience preferences and technological trends has to do with outdated technology and belated digitization of most of the PSB organizations in the region. Only Croatia completed the transition to digital television in 2012, before the deadline for EU member states. Nevertheless, most other countries in the region, except for Bosnia and Herzegovina, were able to catch up and PSB was at the center stage of digital switchover, contributing to the successful introduction of DTT but somehow failed to capitalize on such an advantaged position when it came to increasing their audience reach and improving programming (see Chapter 14 by Broughton Micova, Chapter 3 by Ahmetašević and Hadžiristić, and Chapter 5 by Miftari in this volume).

One aspect that contributes to a possible explanation for such a situation is that PSB across the region fell victim to organizational inertia in terms of the persistence of "path-dependent organizational rigidities" that condition how "business as usual" is done, typical for organizations with longer traditions (see Chapter 12 by Głowacki in this volume). This is exemplified in top-down approaches to management, vertical organizational structures, and a silos culture with a separation between radio, TV and online activities, and poor integration of newsrooms and production processes. Such an organizational setup in effect reduces adaptivity and capacity to change. Thus, these organizations are less capable to move from the old broadcasting paradigm to the age of online platforms and converged media (see Chapter 12 by Głowacki and Chapter 14 by Broughton Micova in this volume). This is the case with most Western Balkan PSB organizations except for the Croatian HRT, which strategically embraced the above-mentioned challenges and started to reorganize to integrate its production to cope with digitization (see Chapter 4 by Marko in this volume).

Strained Relationship with Audiences

PSB organizations across the region include very few mechanisms for interaction with citizens. In several countries (Croatia, Montenegro, North Macedonia, Serbia) civil society groups and professional associations are entitled to nominate candidates for the managing or consultative bodies (such as program councils) but the final decision regarding their appointment lies with political representatives and procedures are usually not fully transparent. For instance, in the case of Bosnia and Herzegovina, the national level broadcaster (BHRT) and the broadcaster of the Federation of Bosnia and Herzegovina entity (RTVFBiH) have no established program councils, while the role of the program council of the broadcaster of the Republika Srpska entity (RTRS) is limited to an advisory role (see Chapter 3 by Ahmetašević and Hadžiristić in this volume).

Only three (Albania, Croatia, Montenegro) out of ten analyzed PSB organizations have established specialized bodies to regularly contact, collect, and analyze feedback from viewers about their programming and operations. For example, in Croatia HRT established in 2011 an autonomous and independent body subordinated to the program council whose mandate is to communicate with the audience (see Chapter 4 by Marko in this volume). Another example is Albania where the Council for Viewers and Listeners has the task to hold RTSH accountable to its publics (see Chapter 2 by Bino in this volume). Given the lack of genuine two-way communication with citizens, political capture, and biased reporting, as well as the failure to provide compelling content, it is no wonder that PSB organizations are not highly regarded among the audience in Western Balkan countries.

Contextual Dynamics and the Public Service Broadcasting in the Western Balkans

The predicament of public service broadcasting in the Western Balkan countries can only be fully understood by taking contextual dynamics into account. While there are important differences between the analyzed media systems, results show that three broad sets of factors decisively affect the development of PSB across the region: weak political institutions, protracted EU accession processes, and the peculiarities of small media systems.

Weak Political Institutions

The level of consolidation of democracy and the weakness of political organizations and institutions heavily compromises the independence of PSB. In Chapter 10 Peruško identifies political conditions necessary for the successful establishment of PSB in the Western Balkans. She demonstrates a link between the level of consolidation of democracy and the successful development of public service broadcasting in the region. First, the countries scoring worst in the Economist Intelligence Unit (EIU) Democracy Index 2017 (Albania, Bosnia and Herzegovina, Montenegro, North Macedonia) also have significant problems with the establishment of PSB (Economist Intelligence Unit 2018). Second, the scores from the World Bank Political Stability Index closely correspond with the problems of PSB (World Bank n.d.). For example, inefficient state agencies and institutions have been recognized as one of the major obstacles in the introduction of DTT (Digital Terrestrial Television, see Chapter 15 by Murphy in this volume), while a weak public administration and an underdeveloped rational-legal authority,[1] plays a significant role in the unsystematic implementation of media regulation.

The weak public institutions closely correspond with the nature of political parties that are largely seen as weak and unstable, meaning that they have few members and resources, are barely institutionalized, and party loyalty is low. As such, the political parties act as cartels that colonize weak state institutions and PSB organizations in order to consolidate their positions by exploiting the captured resources (see Chapter 9 by Bajomi-Lázár in this volume). Since the weak civil society (Mišić Mihajlović and Engeli 2019) and declining support from international donors (Irion and Jusić 2018) are not able to counteract such negative trends, the only serious challenge to pervasive capture of the state institutions and the media comes from the conditionality mechanisms of the EU accession process as described in the following section.

The Influence of the European Union

Similar to CEE countries, the transformation of media systems and the creation of PSB organizations in Western Balkan countries were pursued to formally satisfy the requirements for accession to the EU. After all, Europeanization—the influence of the EU on domestic policies, including media policy—is not limited to member states but affects non-member states as well, either due to their membership aspirations or because of their geographical location and the importance of the common market for their economies (Schneider and Werle 2007; Sciarini, Fischer and Nicolet 2004; Puppis 2012). Given that EU membership became a key political aspiration for many governments in the Western Balkans, a far-reaching process of Europeanization started to take place within the first decade of the 2000s (Freyburg and Richter 2010; Schimmelfennig and Sedelmeier 2005). Thus, the EU played and still plays an important role in the democratization of SEE media systems.

Although previous research shows that post-accession countries show an increased capacity of law enforcement and the ability to tackle compliance problems due to the legacy of pre-accession conditionality (Sedelmeier 2011), recent

---

[1] One of the key characteristics of countries with a rational-legal authority is that their administrative apparatus has a significant degree of autonomy from various interest groups, parties, and individuals. They count on a system of recruitment of public civil servants based on merit and formal rules and free from outside interference. See for example Hallin and Mancini (2004).

setbacks in media freedom in EU member states like Hungary or Poland make it plausible that EU influence on media systems' democratization is bigger before accession when its leverage is at its peak. As shown for CEE, the prospect of full membership creates pressure for adaptation to EU policies and the whole *acquis communautaire*, as well as compliance with democratic principles (Schimmelfennig and Sedelmeier 2004). Yet once a country achieves membership, the EU has only very limited possibilities to push for respect towards fundamental principles of democracy, human rights, and the rule of law.

Nevertheless, the degree to which the EU has influenced political and media reforms in the Western Balkans has been very much contingent on cost-benefit analyses by local political leaders in the face of pre-accession EU conditionality. Aside from high adoption costs, the promise of EU membership in some countries is undermined by a lack of credibility of the EU's reward system, due to shifting EU priorities, continuously changing requirements, and the lack of clear deadlines for membership status, thus making the promise of EU membership a moving target. This is particularly the case in Kosovo where the lack of international recognition compromises the country's chances to become an EU member. It is also the case for some other countries in the region such as Albania or North Macedonia, due to a potentially changing EU enlargement policy which recently delayed the start of entry talks and negotiation processes for such countries (Emmott, Guarascio and Pennetier 2019; Irish and Emmott 2020).

Political socialization and national identity issues in Western Balkan countries also impact political elites' opportunities and motivations to cooperate and comply with EU integration imperatives. As an example, EU requirements and actions during the EU accession process were not questioned in Croatia as long as such reforms did not threaten socially accepted boundaries of national identity (Freyburg and Richter 2010), especially when it came to dominant interpretations of the sensitive issues linked to the 1991–1995 military conflict.[2] Similarly, local political elites acted as veto players when reforms implied addressing the contested nature and cohesion of states in Montenegro, Bosnia and Herzegovina, or Serbia, hindering the adoption of crucial institutional reforms (Bieber 2011), despite relatively broad societal support for joining the EU.[3] Against this background, local governmental and political elites' complicity with the EU project becomes a crucial factor to ensure media reforms' compliance with EU legislation, with the latter being an effective replacement in absence of domestic rules. Most importantly, the willingness of political elites to identify with the EU project can determine the extent to which the EU can be a driving force of overall political and media systems' democratization processes in the region.

---

[2]   As Freyburg and Richter (2010) noted, media reforms did not hinder the ability of the Croatian government to intervene when journalists raised politically sensitive issues linked to the 1991–1995 conflict.

[3]   See, for example, the data on attitudes on EU membership among the population of the Western Balkan countries by the Regional Cooperation Council (2019).

Peculiarities of Small Media Systems

The current status of PSB is not only the result of political and cultural factors but also of economic ones. All the Western Balkan countries feature small media systems due to their limited population size that ranges between 600,000 in Montenegro to approximately 7 million in Serbia. Media systems of small states feature some peculiarities, namely small audience and advertising markets, a shortage of resources, political and financial dependence, and vulnerability (Meier and Trappel 1992; Puppis 2009). In the Western Balkans, this is further exacerbated by generally rather poor economic performance characterized, in most cases, by the lack of economic growth, low competitiveness, high levels of unemployment, and insufficient investment (see World Bank 2019).

Consequently, media markets in the region are underdeveloped, ranging from approximately EUR 10 million of total advertising revenues in Montenegro to approximately EUR 300 million in Croatia, which is still relatively small compared to most CEE countries (IREX 2018; 2019). Such a situation affects the operation of both commercial and public media. While poor economic conditions limit the extent to which sufficient funding for PSB could be provided from the state budget or collected through license fees, at the same time small advertising markets prevent the development of sustainable alternative sources of funding. In such a context, PSB organizations are in a permanent state of resource shortages which makes them vulnerable to both government pressures and influence from commercial interests that are often linked to ruling political parties (see Chapter 9 by Bajomi-Lázár in this volume). Consequently, PSB organizations end up being caught in an iron grip of political and financial dependence on government, political, and economic interests, which translates into politically biased reporting coupled with overt commercialization of their programs (see Chapter 13 by Milosavljević and Poler Kovačič in this volume).

Conclusion

The research presented in this book demonstrates that the transformation of former state broadcasters in Western Balkan countries—Albania, Bosnia and Herzegovina, Croatia, Kosovo, Montenegro, North Macedonia, and Serbia—into genuine PSB organizations so far has either failed or produced largely unsustainable results. Despite comprehensive and prolonged institutional reforms, retrograde processes are underway, and we witness the restoration of elements of state broadcasting, with hybrid outcomes and atavistic orientation firmly taking ground across the region. More often than not, these institutions have been colonized by political parties, and are instrumentalized to serve private interests rather than the public interest. In effect, the majority of PSB organizations in the Western Balkans are characterized by a high level of politicization, financial insecurities coupled with commercial pressures, weak accountability mechanisms, and a slow adjustment to digital developments.

As we have seen, there are numerous contextual explanations as to why the transformation of Western Balkan media systems was less successful than initially expected. Incomplete democratization resulting in weak political institutions is only one part of the story. Another has to do with the character of media markets in the region that feature small audiences, insignificant advertising markets, and financial and political vulnerability.

Path dependence and organizational inertia are also important factors in understanding why the mimetic policy transfer mostly failed. Decisions taken in the past and practices that have gained society-wide acceptance, combined with political and economic factors, have had a lasting effect on the advance of media systems across the Western Balkans (see Chapter 10 by Peruško in this volume), thus steering the development of PSB organizations along paths set much earlier in the era of authoritarian rule and state-controlled broadcasting. As a consequence, mimetic transplantation often resulted in PSB only in name, so that the transforming countries ended up with inadequate media policies and often dysfunctional, hybrid institutional arrangements, which exert a strong atavistic orientation and are caught in a permanent state of crisis as demonstrated in practically all chapters of this volume (in particular, see Chapter 11 by Lowe, Chapter 9 by Bajomi-Lázár, and Chapter 10 by Peruško).

Cultural and systemic changes take much longer than the transformation of individual organizations. Historical trajectories and earlier institutional arrangements make for contexts that are different from the countries where the public service media policy paradigm originates. The absence of a consensus about the purpose, remit, and value of public service broadcasting, the presence of polarized pluralism, as well as weak journalistic professionalism are additional factors that need to be considered.

Against this background, it does not come as a surprise that citizens' distrust and apathy towards domestic political and media systems is a trend spread across SEE countries (Kurspahić 2003; Tworzecki and Semetko 2012; Splichal 2001). To this day, the level of trust in the media is lower in most countries of the Western Balkans than in EU member states, despite citizens recognizing the importance of PSB for democracy (EBU 2018; European Commission 2017). Low levels of (public and private) media trust in the region also go hand in hand with a widespread belief that PSB is not free from political interference, especially in countries such as Bosnia and Herzegovina, Croatia or Montenegro (Fabijanić and Sittig 2019). Therefore, a strained relationship between PSB organizations and their audiences across the region is one of the most profound structural challenges that stand in the way of their successful reform.

Thus, it is safe to say that the basic preconditions necessary for the development of PSB in Western Balkan countries are still missing. Moreover, we have to note that in recent decades the very concept of PSB that was supposed to be transferred to the new democracies of the Western Balkans has been challenged in the older democracies in Western Europe as well, not least because of digitization and neoliberal tendencies in policy-making. The legitimacy of public service broadcasters to become public service media that cater to citizens on all available platforms has increasingly come under scrutiny. This puts a big question mark on the prospects of the public service media policy paradigm in the Western Balkans as well.

It has become very clear that the idealistic view that PSB can be easily institutionalized in the Western Balkans and contribute to political debates and functioning democracies has been too naïve. Yet which is the right way forward?

The pessimistic (or even fatalistic) view put forth by Péter Bajomi-Lázár is that the very idea of public service broadcasting in Western Balkan (and in CEE) countries has failed, cannot be saved, and should be abandoned. Instead of investing in failing institutions, media policy should focus on new platforms and infrastructure (see Chapter 9 in this volume). Still, content to be used, shared, and discussed on "new" media needs to be funded and produced as well. While there is a need to keep pace with digital developments, it is our view that the idea behind PSB and a working organization that embodies it remains of great societal value.

However, it is also true that PSB in the Western Balkans cannot properly operate and fulfill their remit as long as the countries are not fully working democracies. Therefore, instead of going from the idealistic directly to the pessimistic view, we propose to manage our expectations and be more realistic about the possibilities and challenges for media democratization and PSB in the region. For instance, Lowe suggests that non-institutionalized forms of public service provision in media are perhaps the only feasible way for guaranteeing the "arm's length condition" given the extent of media capture in the region (see Chapter 11 in this volume). Another possible way, as suggested by Murphy (see Chapter 15 in this volume), might be incremental progress, especially concerning the strategic use of new technologies and digitization, which might help strengthen PSB in the specific broadcast and networked context in the region of the Western Balkans. In other words, the digital transition provides an opportunity to reposition public service broadcasting within a digital media infrastructure.

It is important to remember that transformations take time. Strengthening public service broadcasting requires political change first as the role, the possibility to develop into public service media, and the level of public funding are decided by media policymakers. A change of media policy and institutionalizing truly independent public service media require building a society-wide consensus about the role of media in a democracy. Organizing stakeholders and promoting media reform movements may create pressure from below to overcome path dependencies. Civil society organizations, journalists, and academics together can play a vital role here. Whether such initiatives will be successful despite new authoritarian tendencies across Europe remains to be seen.

References

Bajomi-Lázár, Péter. 2014. *Party Colonisation of the Media in Central and Eastern Europe.* Budapest/New York: CEU Press.

Bašić-Hrvatin, Sandra, and Mark Thompson. 2008. "Public Service Broadcasting in Plural and Divided Societies." In *Divided They Fall: Public Service Broadcasting in Multiethnic States*, edited by Sandra Bašić-Hrvatin, Mark Thompson and Tarik Jusić, 7–40. Sarajevo: Mediacentar. https://www.academia.edu/28197065/Divided_They _Fall_Public_Service_Broadcasting_in_Multiethnic_States_ed.

Bašić-Hrvatin, Sandra, Mark Thompson, and Tarik Jusić, eds. 2008. *Divided They Fall: Public Service Broadcasting in Multiethnic States.* Sarajevo: Mediacentar. https://www.academia.edu/28197065/Divided_They_Fall_Public_Service_Broadcasting_in_Multiethnic_States_ed.

Bašić-Hrvatin, Sandra. 2002. *Serving the State or the Public: The Outlook for Public Service Broadcasting in Slovenia.* Ljubljana: Mirovni inštitut. https://www.mirovni-institut.si/wp-content/uploads/2014/08/serving_the_state_or_the_public.pdf.

Bieber, Florian. 2011. "Building Impossible States? State-Building Strategies and EU Membership in the Western Balkans." *Europe-Asia Studies* 63, no 10 (November): 1783–1802.

Bogner, Alexander, and Wolfgang Menz. 2009. "The Theory-Generating Expert Interview: Epistemological Interest, Forms of Knowledge, Interaction." In *Interviewing Experts*, edited by Alexander Bogner, Beate Littig and Wolfgang Menz, 43–80. Basingstoke: Palgrave Macmillan.

Bowen, Glenn A. 2009. "Document Analysis as a Qualitative Research Method." *Qualitative Research Journal* 9, no 2 (August): 27–40.

d'Haenens, Leen, Helena Sousa, Werner A. Meier, and Josef Trappel. 2008. "Public Service Broadcasting," special issue, *Convergence: The International Journal of Research into New Media Technologies* 14, no. 3 (August).

DiMaggio, Paul J., and Walter W. Powell. 1991. "The Iron Cage Revisited: Institutional Isomorphism and Collective Rationality in Organization Fields." In *The New Institutionalism in Organizational Analysis*, edited by Walter W. Powell and Paul J. DiMaggio, 63–82. Chicago/London: University of Chicago Press.

Dimitrijevska-Markoski, Tamara, and Zhidas Daskalovski. 2008. "Assisting Media Democratization after Low-Intensity Conflict: The Case of Macedonia." In *Media Constrained by Context: International Assistance and the Transition to Democratic Media in the Western Balkans*, edited by Kristina Irion and Tarik Jusić, 133–158. Budapest/New York: CEU Press.

Donders, Karen, and Hallvard Moe, eds. 2011. *Exporting the Public Value Test: The Regulation of Public Broadcasters' New Media Services Across Europe.* Göteborg: Nordicom.

Donders, Karen, Caroline Pauwels, and Jan Loisen, eds. 2013. *Private Television in Western Europe: Content, Market, Policies.* Basingstoke/New York: Palgrave Macmillan.

Donders, Karen. 2012. *Public Service Media and Policy in Europe.* Basingstoke: Palgrave Macmillan.

Donges, Patrick, and Manuel Puppis. 2003. "Die Zukunft des öffentlichen Rundfunks. Eine Einleitung." In *Die Zukunft des öffentlichen Rundfunks. Internationale Beiträge aus Wissenschaft und Praxis* [The future of public service broadcasting. International contributions from academia and practice], edited by Patrick Donges and Manuel Puppis, 9–28. Köln: Halem.

Dragomir, Marius, Dušan Reljić, Mark Thompson, and Andreas Grünwald. 2005. "Overview." In *Television Across Europe: Regulation, Policy and Independence*, edited by Open Society Institute, 13–184. Budapest: Open Society Institute. https://www.opensocietyfoundations.org/publications/television-across-europe-regulation-policy-and-independence.

Economist Intelligence Unit. 2018. *Democracy Index 2017: Free Speech Under Attack*. Accessed May 4, 2020. https://www.eiu.com/public/topical_report.aspx?campaignid=DemocracyIndex2017.

Emmott, Robin, Francesco Guarascio, and Marine Pennetier. 2019. "France Under Fire for 'Historic Error' of Blocking Balkan EU Hopefuls." *Reuters*, October 18. Accessed May 4, 2020. https://uk.reuters.com/article/uk-eu-summit-balkans/france-under-fire-for-historic-error-of-blocking-balkan-eu-hopefuls-idUKKBN1WX1CX.

European Broadcasting Union. 2018. *Market Insights: Trust in Media 2018*. Geneva: EBU.

European Commission. 2017. *Standard Eurobarometer 88. Public Opinion in European Union. Annex*. Brussels: European Commission. http://ec.europa.eu/commfrontoffice/publicopinion/index.cfm/ResultDoc/download/DocumentKy/81142.

Fabijanić, Darija, and Hendrik Sittig, eds. 2019. *A Pillar of Democracy on Shaky Ground: Public Service Media in South East Europe*. Berlin: Konrad-Adenauer-Stiftung. https://www.kas.de/en/web/medien-europa/single-title/-/content/new-book-a-pillar-of-democracy-on-shaky-ground-public-service-media-in-south-east-europe.

Freedman, Des. 2019. "'Public Service' and the Journalism Crisis: Is the BBC the Answer?" *Television & New Media* 20, no. 3 (March): 203–218.

Freyburg, Tina, and Solveig Richter. 2010. "National Identity Matters: The Limited Impact of EU Political Conditionality in the Western Balkans." *Journal of European Public Policy* 17, no. 2 (March): 263–281.

Hallin, Daniel C., and Paolo Mancini. 2004. *Comparing Media Systems: Three Models of Media and Politics*. Cambridge/New York: Cambridge University Press.

Herzog, Christian, and Kari Karppinen. 2014. "Policy Streams and Public Service Media Funding Reforms in Germany and Finland." *European Journal of Communication* 29, no. 4 (May): 416–432.

Hultén, Olof, and Kees Brants. 1992. "Public Service Broadcasting: Reactions to Competition." In *Dynamics of Media Politics. Broadcast and Electronic Media in Western Europe*, edited by Karen Siune and Wolfgang Truetzschler, 116–128. London/Newbury Park/New Delhi: Sage.

Iosifidis, Petros, ed. 2010. *Reinventing Public Service Communication: European Broadcasters and Beyond*. Basingstoke/New York: Palgrave Macmillan.

——. 2007. *Public Television in the Digital Era: Technological Challenges and New Strategies for Europe*. Basingstoke: Palgrave Macmillan.

IREX. 2019. *Media Sustainability Index 2019: The Development of Sustainable Independent Media in Europe and Eurasia*. Washington, DC: IREX. https://www.irex.org/sites/default/files/pdf/media-sustainability-index-europe-eurasia-2019-full.pdf.

——. 2018. *Media Sustainability Index 2018: Tracking Development of Sustainable Independent Media around the World*. Washington, DC: IREX. https://www.irex.org/sites/default/files/pdf/media-sustainability-index-europe-eurasia-2018-full.pdf.

Irion, Kristina, and Tarik Jusić, eds. 2018. *Media Constrained by Context: International Assistance and the Transition to Democratic Media in the Western Balkans*. Budapest/New York: CEU Press.

———. 2014. "International Assistance and Media Democratization in the Western Balkans: A Cross-National Comparison." *Global Media Journal* (German Edition) 4, no. 2 (November).

Irish, John, and Robin Emmott. 2020. "Macron Opens Door to North Macedonia, Albania EU Accession talks." *Reuters*, February 15. Accessed May 4, 2020. https://www.reuters.com/article/us-germany-security-macron-balkans/macron-opens-door-to-north-macedonia-albania-eu-accession-talks-idUSKBN2090DM.

Jakubowicz, Karol, and Miklós Sükösd. 2008. "Twelve Concepts Regarding Media System Evolution and Democratization in Post-Communist Societies." In *Finding the Right Place on the Map: Central and Eastern European Media Change in a Global Perspective*, edited by Karol Jakubowicz and Miklós Sükösd, 9–40. Bristol/Chicago: Intellect.

Jakubowicz, Karol. 2008. "Finding the Right Place on the Map: Prospects for Public Service Broadcasting in Post-Communist Countries." In *Finding the Right Place on the Map: Central and Eastern European Media Change in a Global Perspective*, edited by Karol Jakubowicz and Miklós Sükösd, 101–124. Bristol/Chicago: Intellect.

Jarren, Otfried, Patrick Donges, Matthias Künzler, Wolfgang Schulz, Thorsten Held, and Uwe Jürgens. 2001. *Der öffentliche Rundfunk im Netzwerk von Politik, Wirtschaft und Gesellschaft* [Public service broadcasting in a network of politics, economics and society]. Baden-Baden/Hamburg: Nomos.

Jusić, Tarik, and L. Kendall Palmer. 2008. "The Media and Power-Sharing: Towards an Analytical Framework for Understanding Media Policies in Post-Conflict Societies. Public Broadcasting in Bosnia and Herzegovina." *Global Media Journal* (Polish Edition) 1, no. 4 (December): 110–139.

Karppinen, Kari, and Hallvard Moe. 2012. "What We Talk about When We Talk about Document Analysis." In *Trends in Communication Policy Research: New Theories, Methods and Subjects*, edited by Natascha Just and Manuel Puppis, 177–193. Bristol/Chicago: Intellect.

———. 2019. "Texts as Data I: Document Analysis." In *The Palgrave Handbook of Methods for Media Policy Research*, edited by Hilde Van den Bulck, Manuel Puppis, Karen Donders and Leo Van Audenhove, 249–262. Cham: Palgrave Macmillan.

Kurspahić, Kemal. 2003. *Zločin u 19:30. Balkanski mediji u ratu i miru* [Prime time crime. Balkan media in war and peace]. Sarajevo: Mediacentar.

Lowe, Gregory Ferrell, and Christian E. Berg. 2013. "The Funding of Public Service Media: A Matter of Value and Values." *International Journal on Media Management* 15, no. 2 (May): 77–97.

Lowe, Gregory Ferrell, and Christian S. Nissen, eds. 2011. *Small Among Giants: Television Broadcasting in Smaller Countries*. Göteborg: Nordicom.

Lowe, Gregory Ferrell, and Jo Bardoel, eds. 2007. *From Public Service Broadcasting to Public Service Media: RIPE@2007*. Göteborg: Nordicom.

McQuail, Denis. 2005. *McQuail's Mass Communication Theory*. 5th ed. London/Thousand Oaks/New Delhi: Sage.

Meier, Werner A., and Josef Trappel. 1992. "Small States in the Shadow of Giants." In *Dynamics of Media Politics: Broadcast and Electronic Media in Western Europe*, edited by Karen Siune and Wolfgang Truetzschler, 129–142. London/Newbury Park/New Delhi: Sage.

Mišić Mihajlović, Snežana, and Jens Engeli. 2019. "Why is the Space for Civil Society in the Balkans Shrinking?" *Helvetas Mosaic*, March. Accessed May 4, 2020. https://

www.helvetas.org/en/eastern-europe/about-us/follow-us/helvetas-mosaic/article/March2019/why-is-the-space-for-civil-society-in-the-Balkans-shrinking.

Price, Monroe E., Bethany Davis Noll, and Daniel De Luce. 2002. *Mapping Media Assistance*. Oxford: Programme in Comparative Media Law & Policy. https://repository.upenn.edu/asc_papers/62/.

Puppis, Manuel, and Leen d'Haenens. 2012. "Comparing Media Policy and Regulation." In *Handbook of Comparative Communication Research*, edited by Frank Esser and Thomas Hanitzsch, 221–233. London/New York: Routledge.

Puppis, Manuel. 2009. "Introduction. Media Regulation in Small States." *International Communication Gazette* 71, no. 1–2 (February): 7–17.

———. 2012. "Between Independence and Autonomous Adaptation: The Europeanization of Television Regulation in Non-EU Member States." *Communications* 37, no. 4 (August): 393–416.

Radaelli, Claudio M. 2000. "Policy Transfer in the European Union: Institutional Isomorphism as a Source of Legitimacy." *Governance* 13, no. 1 (December): 25–43.

Regional Cooperation Council. 2019. *Balkan Public Barometer*. Accessed May 4, 2020. https://www.rcc.int/seeds/results/2/balkan-public-barometerv.

Reh, Werner. 1995. "Quellen- und Dokumentenanalyse in der Politikfeldforschung: Wer steuert die Verkehrspolitik?" In *Politikwissenschaftliche Methoden* [Methods of political science], edited by Ulrich von Alemann, 201–259. Opladen: Westdeutscher Verlag.

Sarajlić, Eldar, and Davor Marko, eds. 2011. *State or Nation? The Challenges of Political Transition in Bosnia and Herzegovina*. Sarajevo: Center for Interdisciplinary Postgraduate Studies.

Schimmelfennig, Frank, and Ulrich Sedelmeier. 2004. "Governance by Conditionality: EU Rule Transfer to the Candidate Countries of Central and Eastern Europe." *Journal of European Public Policy* 11, no. 4 (August): 661–679.

———. 2005. "Introduction: Conceptualizing the Europeanization of Central and Eastern Europe." In *The Europeanization of Central and Eastern Europe*, edited by Frank Schimmelfennig and Ulrich Sedelmeier, 1–28. Ithaca: Cornell University Press.

Schlosberg, Justin. 2014. "Digital Media in the EU Enlargement Countries." In *Mapping Digital Media: Global Findings*, edited by Marius Dragomir and Mark Thompson, 239–252. New York: Open Society Foundations. https://www.opensocietyfoundations .org/publications/mapping-digital-media-global-findings.

Schneider, Volker, and Raymund Werle. 2007. "Telecommunications Policy." In *Europeanization: New Research Agendas*, edited by Paolo Graziano and Maarten Vink, 266–280. Basingstoke: Palgrave Macmillan.

Schweizer, Corinne, and Manuel Puppis. 2018. "Public Service Media in the 'Network' Era. A Comparison of Remits, Funding, and Debate in 17 Countries." In *Public Service Media in the Networked Society: RIPE@2017*, edited by Gregory F. Lowe, Hilde Van den Bulck and Karen Donders, 109–124. Göteborg: Nordicom.

Sciarini, Pascal, Alex Fischer, and Sarah Nicolet. 2004. "How Europe Hits Home: Evidence from the Swiss Case." *Journal of European Public Policy* 11, no. 3 (February): 353–378.

Sedelmeier, Ulrich. 2011. "After Conditionality: Post-Accession Compliance with EU Law in East Central Europe." *Journal of European Public Policy* 15, no. 6 (February): 806–825.

Shirley, Mary M. 2005. "Institutions and Development." In *Handbook of New Institutional Economics*, edited by Claude Menard and Mary M. Shirley, 611–638. Dordrechts: Springer.

Siune, Karen, and Olof Hultén. 1998. "Does Public Broadcasting Have a Future?" In *Media Policy: Convergence, Concentration and Commerce*, edited by Denis McQuail and Karen Siune, 23–37. London/Thousand Oaks/New Delhi: Sage.

Sparks, Colin. 1998. *Communism, Capitalism and the Mass Media*. London/Thousand Oaks/New Delhi: Sage.

Splichal, Slavko. 2001. "Imitative Revolutions Changes in the Media and Journalism in East-Central Europe." *Javnost/The Public* 8, no. 4 (November): 31–58.

Syvertsen, Trine. 1999. "The Many Uses of the 'Public Service' Concept." *Nordicom* 20, no. 1 (January): 5–12.

Thompson, Mark. 2018. "Looking for Shortcuts? Assistance to—and Development of—Public Service Broadcasting in Bosnia-Herzegovina, Serbia, Kosovo, Macedonia, and Albania." In *Media Constrained by Context: International Assistance and the Transition to Democratic Media in the Western Balkans*, edited by Kristina Irion and Tarik Jusić, 189–214. Budapest/New York: CEU Press.

Tworzecki, Hubert, and Holli A. Semetko. 2012. "Media Use and Political Engagement in Three New Democracies: Malaise versus Mobilization in the Czech Republic, Hungary, and Poland." *The International Journal of Press/Politics* 17, no. 4 (July): 407–432.

Van Audenhove, Leo, and Karen Donders. 2019. "Talking to People III: Expert Interviews and Elite Interviews." In *The Palgrave Handbook of Methods for Media Policy Research*, edited by Hilde Van den Bulck, Manuel Puppis, Karen Donders and Leo Van Audenhove, 179–197. Cham: Palgrave Macmillan.

van Cuilenburg, Jan, and Denis McQuail. 2003. "Media Policy Paradigm Shifts. Towards a New Communications Policy Paradigm." *European Journal of Communication* 18, no. 2 (June): 181–207.

Voltmer, Katrin. 2012. "How Far can Media Systems Travel? Applying Hallin and Mancini's Comparative Framework outside the Western World." In *Comparing Media Systems Beyond the Western World*, edited by Daniel C. Hallin and Paolo Mancini, 224–245. Cambridge: Cambridge University Press.

——. 2013. *The Media in Transitional Democracies*. Cambridge/Malden: Polity Press.

World Bank. n.d. *Worldwide Governance Indicators*. Accessed May 4, 2020. https://info.worldbank.org/governance/wgi/Home/Reports.

——. 2019. Rising Uncertainties: *Western Balkans Regular Economic Report No.16*. Washington, DC: International Bank for Reconstruction and Development/The World Bank. http://documents.worldbank.org/curated/en/643781570478210132/pdf/Rising-Uncertainties.pdf.

Zielonka, Jan, and Paolo Mancini. 2011. *Executive Summary: A Media Map of Central and Eastern Europe*. Oxford: Department of Politics and International Relations. https://de.scribd.com/document/161146265/Zielonka-Jan-and-Paolo-Mancini-2011-A-Media-Map-of-CEE-Summary-Politicisation-of-the-State.

PART I

WESTERN BALKAN MEDIA SYSTEMS

CHAPTER 2

Public Service Media in Albania: RTSH's Reforming Struggles[1]

Blerjana Bino

Introduction

Following the collapse of the communist regime in the early 1990s, contemporary Albania has been undergoing a series of economic, social, and political transformations. Such encompassing transformations affect, among other things, the role of media in society and the democratic processes. This is particularly true in the case of public service broadcasting (PSB), which, in principle, has the potential to contribute to democratic advancements in post-communist countries. This chapter aims to overview the current developments and prospects of the Albanian Radio and Television (RTSH) by analyzing policy and regulation, market and financing models, digitalization, and relations to audiences. Significant processes within the political and socio-economic context in Albania are also accounted for including post-communism, democratization, EU accession, liberal reforms, and the free market, as well as new social and cultural trends.

The research is relevant both in terms of contextual media policy developments in Albania and for its contribution to the field in general. First, the research is significant in terms of policy developments since it provides a comprehensive analysis of the current state and future perspectives of RTSH. This comes at a time when there is a growing interest in media developments regarding the digitalization and an intense proliferation of information and communication technologies (ICTs). Besides, debates on the future of PSB are important in light of the democratic processes in Albania and its EU accession. PSB reinvention and repositioning need to respond to the contemporary social, cultural, political, and economic developments in Albania. Media and democratization as a research topic is relatively underexplored in Albanian media studies, which corresponds with the claim of Rupnik and Zielonka that mass media remains one of the most poorly understood factors in the new democracies of the former

---

[1] The analysis of public service broadcasters in Albania has been conducted for the period until the end of 2017 and this chapter is based on a working paper co-authored by Blerjana Bino and Besart Kadia (2017).

Eastern Bloc (Rupnik and Zielonka 2013, 14), while public service broadcasting is neglected as a topic of research. Additionally, Voltmer (2006, 1) points out that mass media has been largely ignored by mainstream democratization research even though media plays a paramount role in the democratic processes. Following Hallin and Mancini's note that research on Eastern European media systems is still in the process of emergence, and lacking original research (Hallin and Mancini 2013, 16), this study aims to contribute to the systematic and comparative analysis of PSB and media systems in the Western Balkans.

RTSH is the oldest audiovisual broadcaster in Albania. The history of RTSH dates back to 1938 with the establishment of Radio Tirana, followed by the establishment of the Albanian Television (TVSH) in 1960. From 1993, RTSH also broadcasted through satellite and used to be an important source of information for Albanians living and working abroad in the early 1990s. Since the first news bulletin in 1963 until the collapse of the communist regime, RTSH was totally under the control of the state, i.e., the Communist Party. RTSH was the only electronic media available in Albania, with a simultaneous ban on all foreign channels. In the first years of post-communism, RTSH maintained its monopoly over the media market in Albania until 1995, when the commercial television market started to emerge.

The transformation of RTSH from a state-owned media to a public service broadcaster has been challenging for many reasons such as internal settings of RTSH as a media organization and the broader media landscape in Albania. Additionally, the process is impacted by the redefinition of PSM at the European level. Furthermore, a thorough and constructive debate regarding the role, relevance, and future developments of RTSH has been limited. It is naïve at best to assume that RTSH can be detached from politics in a country like Albania with a high level of politicization and continuous confrontation between political parties. It is also not realistic to expect journalists to adhere to the normative standards of journalistic professionalism in isolation from the conditions in which they work. For RTSH to fulfill its remit of serving the public interest and to survive in a fiercely competitive media market, the transformation into Public Service Media (PSM) is a viable option but calls for a remodeled relationship with audiences and an embrace of the opportunities offered by digitalization. This will enable more transparency and accountability, and a higher quality of programming, as well as attract audiences and increase the overall profile and performance of RTSH.

The chapter is organized as follows: The next section provides a comprehensive overview of the major features of the media landscape in Albania and a brief background to the establishment of RTSH. The subsequent section provides the research findings followed by critical discussions in relation to the conceptual framework. Finally, an elaboration on the future perspectives of RTSH's development leads the way to the chapter's concluding remarks.

Policy and Legislative Framework

The media landscape in Albania seems to be in a process of perpetual open-ended transformation. This started after the collapse of the communist regime and continues currently with the attempt to respond to contemporary societal developments. The current media landscape in Albania can be characterized as *clientelistic*, which implies a system that is marked by a subtle and symbiotic interdependence and interrelation amongst media, politics, and business. Various economic and political pressures, a lack of transparency of ownership, inadequate labor relations and working conditions, ethical and quality concerns, relatively limited professionalism, limited sustainability, and coping with digitalization and online media realities are some of the pressing matters currently faced by media in Albania (Londo 2014, 54). These features of the Albanian media landscape are in line with the theoretical model of "hybrid media" systems in new democracies (Voltmer 2006). It combines liberal ideas of a free and de-regulated press, the liberalization of the media market, and the flourishing of various commercial audiovisual outlets, with the legacy of the communist past and contextual local factors such as the high level of politicization and the experience of transition and democratization. Thus, the development of media in Albania in the past two decades has not been linear; rather, it echoes a dynamic and diverse media landscape.

The media legislative and policy processes have reflected daily political confrontations and vested business interests, rather than being guided by the core principles and normative media functions in new democracies. The symbiotic interrelation amongst media, politics, and businesses is reflected first and foremost in delays and deadlocks in media legislation. The Albanian Constitution, introduced in 1998, guarantees freedom of expression, but the media scene is poorly regulated. Audio-visual media legislation has undergone several changes in the last decade. Adopting European standards on media legislation and policy remain driving forces despite the problems in media development in the country. Assistance by international actors has been provided and the EU integration processes have also served as a key factor towards the improvement of media legislation (European Commission 2015). For example, discussions on the new law on audiovisual media began in 2008 but was not approved until March 2013. Also, the Strategy for a Digital Switchover was drafted in 2005 but was approved only in May 2012. The EU Report on Albania for 2019 noted that the implementation of media legislation and policies remains a challenge in Albania (European Commission 2019). First, the work of the regulatory body (AMA) has frequently been hindered by political deadlock and difficulties in electing its members. In December 2018, the government announced a package of amendments to the Law on Audiovisual Media and the Law on Electronic Communications, and a public consultation on these amendments was held in January 2019. Second, the delay in digital switchover is another concern, as the deadline of June 2015 was not met and was postponed several times until

September 2019. As a result of legal uncertainty, informality in the media sector has flourished. The legal framework and policy of the media in Albania has not paved the way for media development, but rather it has responded slowly to the existing, rapid advancements of the surrounding media landscape in Albania.

Studies have also demonstrated that the media landscape in Albania is characterized by political parallelism (Londo 2016), as well as mutual and close relations between the political and media systems (Mancini and Zielonka 2012, 381). This is primarily evident in the case of media content and bias, media funding and advertising as well as in the career paths of journalists, shaped by their political affiliations. Divisions and polarization can be traced in the processes of news selection, framing, tone of coverage, and selection of sources of information. The political agenda predominates over standards of media professionalism in news coverage and topics of public interest, also leading to self-censorship. Albanian media exhibit external pluralism. There is a wide range of media outlets reflecting different perspectives and interests. However, coverage and access vary from one kind of media to another and it is hard to identify features of internal media pluralism.[2] Besides, media funding and advertising are also dependent to a large extent on the media relations with the government and powerful political actors. What is more, an increasingly popular trend in Albania is the move of media professionals from journalism towards governmental positions (Halo et al. 2015).

Media Market: From Mainstream to Alternative Media

The media market in Albania is weak, small, and fragmented, far from being consolidated, and thus in a state of perpetual transformation (see Table 2.1). According to the Media Sustainability Index in 2019, the Albanian press "has felt the impact of the paralyzing political warfare that continued throughout 2018" (IREX 2019), but for the print media, the market entry remains free, open, and equal. The readership rates in Albania are relatively low due to inadequate print distribution infrastructure, a weak subscription system, high prices, competition from audiovisual media, and more recently from online media platforms. The exact figures of readership levels in Albania are debatable due to a lack of reliable data (Halo et al. 2015).

In terms of audiovisual media, there is a dual broadcasting system, with RTSH as the public service broadcaster, and a thriving private media. There are also limited and not certified data on broadcast audiences (Reporters Without Borders and BIRN Albania 2017). According to Freedom House, there is a trend

---

[2]   Based on insights from interviews.

of decline in independent media ratings in recent years. For example, in 2016 Freedom House reported that the independent media rating continued to remain at 4.25, representing a decline from 4.00 back in 2015 (Freedom House 2016). The Nation in Transit report in 2018 highlights that a "number of structural problems continued to beset the Albanian media, including self-censorship and the intimate connections between politics, business, and media" (Kajsiu 2018). Albania has dropped a total of seven places in the Reporters Without Borders 2019 World Press Freedom Index. These structural problems offset the positive trend established by the increasing number of online media outlets offering more diverse and independent information.

Table 2.1: Media Outlets in Albania

Type of media in Albania	Number of media operators
National daily newspapers	26
Monthly magazines	36
Quarterly publications	69
Public service broadcaster	1
National commercial TV channels	6
Local TV channels	48
Public service radio	1
National commercial radios	2
Local radios	56
Commercial multiplex	2
Online media	More than 650

Source: AMA (2019)

The dynamics of the online media market and digital processes in Albania are difficult to evaluate due to the lack of credible and systematic data and research. However, the growth in Internet access and ICTs in Albania, at least in urban areas, is omnipresent. First, almost all media outlets have their websites, and some provide mobile app versions. The websites also include live coverage of events and allow audiences to participate with comments on news articles and reports. The sites also include blogs and galleries, thus increasing the participatory aspect. Second, a large number of other online media platforms have emerged, mainly news, entertainment, sports, culture, and lifestyle sites (Londo 2012, 11). Hence, there is a diversity of information and content provided to and created by the public. As a consequence, online media in Albania, as elsewhere, has the potential to contribute to democratization through participatory, open, and multi-way communicative spaces (Londo 2012, 12). However, concerns about the quality of information and impact persist (European Commission 2019). Concerns persist over the approval of the new package of media law amendments in December 2019 aimed at regulating online media and introducing anti-defamation measures. The president vetoed these amendments in January 2020 and currently, the Venetian Commission is scrutinizing the amendments and providing recommendations to the government on how to align them with European and international standards, particularly regarding online media regulation.

The third type of media, in addition to commercial and public media, is that of alternative media, also referred to as community media, citizen media, critique, or radical media (Londo 2014). A study shows that alternative media in Albania for marginalized communities confirm that the sector is immature, new, prolific, uncertain, and evolving (Bino 2017). With the proliferation of ICTs, the alternative media are increasingly accessible and diverse in their purpose. They represent a participatory communication medium that could be employed by various groups to access the media landscape that otherwise cannot do so. However, the regulatory framework in Albania does not yet recognize them as a third pillar of the media system in addition to public and private media.

The small size of the market hinders media financial sustainability, and as a result, media ownership and transparency of media funding remain controversial issues. The cross-subsidization of the media by other businesses of their owners, owners' relations to politics, allegations of politically-allocated state advertising, and the influence of big commercial advertisers have all led to doubts about media standards and editorial independence (Londo 2014, 53). The size of the media market in Albania cannot be accurately assessed due to a lack of public data on media funding. Media outlets in Albania are not profitable businesses on their own and thus cannot ensure their financial sustainability. As argued by various media experts, "most media are supported by other businesses owned by the media's main shareholders, or through clientelism with government and political parties, which display a strong tendency to use these media as a tool to promote and protect their interests" (Londo 2015, 11).

As such, the media market is also characterized by fuzzy ownership (Mancini and Zielonka 2012, 380). For instance, the use of the media by their owners to gain political capital is a common phenomenon. Also, the model of ownership is that of media owners with interests in other businesses, no media expertise, and limited transparency of funding and with the aim of political engagement or using the media as a tool to court political actors and exchange mutual benefits. In this vein, the major challenge of media in Albania is clientelism, which directly influences media professionalism, its independence and the quality of the information provided to the public, and thus the role of the media in society.

Regulatory Framework of PSB in Albania

One of the central and most challenging reforms of the media system in Albania has been the reform of the state broadcaster to a public service broadcaster. Initially, the regulatory framework in Albania was set up in 1998, when the Law No. 8410 on Public and Private Radio and Television was adopted and then reformed with the law in 2013, which is the current regulatory framework. Law No. 8410 was the first law that regulated licensing of national and local private media, media content, and the implementation of the regulatory body, the National Council of Radio and Television (KKRT).

Albania had its first private TV station in 1996, two years before the law was implemented. KKRT started to operate in 2000, five years after the emergence of commercial television in Albania, and as such it was limited in its effort to regulate the existing dynamic and diverse media market. KKRT's task was to oversee the law compliance of broadcasters, guaranteeing fair competition and proposing, in cooperation with other legal authorities, new legislation for further media development (Law No. 8410). KKRT faced major challenges that relate to political parallelism of the media, the politicization of the state, the polarized political system, and the weakness of the rule of law and civil society (Law No. 97/2013). The main shortcomings of the Law of 1998 relate to its inadequacy to accommodate major changes related to technology improvements and developments in the electronic media services, as well as Albania's commitments under the Stability Association Agreement with the EU (European Commission 2015).

As a result, legal changes were initiated in 2016 for a new regulatory framework for audiovisual media in Albania including RTSH, which were finalized in 2013 with the adoption of the new Law No. 97/2013. The Law on Audiovisual Media of 2013 established the legal ground for the public service broadcaster's operation in Albania. RTSH is defined as a public provider of media services that offers audiovisual broadcasting that is free and easily accessible for the entire population. The law sets the PSB remit and its specific objectives of the operation (Article 91 and Article 118, Law No. 97/2013). The new law is in line with the EU legislation, a harmonization process that is ongoing.

KKRT was transformed into the Authority on Audiovisual Media (AMA 2016). AMA has seven board members, including a deputy director and director. The five board members are elected by parliament and are required to have at least ten years of experience in media, economics, or other regulatory agencies. The new members of the AMA and its new chair were appointed in 2014. The opposition disputed the election process in court, alleging that it did not follow the correct legal procedures. The AMA's work was hampered by the absence of its members nominated by the opposition from meetings, which was resolved in December 2015 (European Commission 2015). The AMA approved its 2017–19 strategic action plan in March 2017. The funding of the AMA has been doubled, and it has changed its structure to focus more strongly on supervisory and inspection activities to identify illegal broadcasting (European Commission 2019, 26).

The AMA's activities are subject to parliamentary oversight by the Committee on Education and Public Information Means.

These media transformation processes have been supported largely with funding and expertise from the international community—Organization for Security and Co-operation in Europe (OSCE), Council of Europe, EU, the US Embassy, the British Embassy, and the British Council (Londo 2013). To support the PSB reform, in particular, the European Broadcasting Union (EBU) together with the local PSB organization, RTSH, and the OSCE Presence in Albania signed a Memorandum of Understanding in 2015 to support and reform the PSB organization in the country (OSCE Presence in Albania 2015). In 2019, the OSCE Presence in Albania received funding from the EU to continue to support the transformation of RTSH. International assistance, especially legal expertise focused on drafting and adopting legislation, was particularly helpful for the Albanian media.

Governance of RTSH: Political Relations and Transparency

According to the Law on Audiovisual Media from 2013, the three main governing bodies of RTSH are the Steering Council, the Director-General, and the Administration Board (Law No. 8410). The Steering Council is the highest governing body, the Director-General is in charge of the daily management and the Administration Board is an advisory board to the Director-General on financial and administrative issues, but not related to programming and content.

Article 94 of the 2013 Law regulates the process of the Steering Council members' election (RTSH 2015). Its 11 members are directly elected by the parliament with a 5-year mandate and hold the right to be re-elected. The procedure foresees that media organizations, civil society, and academic bodies propose all candidates. The law requires that the majority in Parliament supports 5 members of the RTSH Council, and the opposition should support the other 5. The 2013 Law requires that the chairman be elected by the support of at least 7 members of the Steering Council.

However, in practice, the transformation and reform of RTSH remain a work in progress, while its relation to political actors hinders its independence and overall performance. This is evident in the deadlock regarding the selection of the management bodies of RTSH (Steering Council and Director General), politically biased content that corresponds to the interests of the incumbent government, and relatively limited transparency and accountability to the public (Londo 2015). For instance, the OSCE Presence in Albania considered the ballots in parliament for the election of the RTSH Steering Council in May 2015 as "politically motivated" and that "after initial attempts to elect the top management, the new Council has again become stalemated along party lines" (Mejdini 2015). The Steering Council is suspected of being composed of members whose political affiliation overweighs their professional credentials and integrity. Furthermore, the ODIHR Election Observation Mission Final Report 2019 noted that "dependence on the state budget and politicization of RTSH management raise concerns about the impartiality of the public broadcaster" (OSCE ODIHR, 2019, 16).

There are indications that "even though the law requires individuals with extensive experience in media and related fields, with high integrity and professionalism, and the representation of various groups from civil society, in essence, the members of the Steering Committee are influenced by and linked to certain political parties and they will obey the party's orders in decision-making."[3] Furthermore, political clashes in the parliament led to delays in electing the Director-General for about two years. Consequently, in April 2016 the government amended the law (Law no. 97/2013) and the Steering Council elected a new Director-General by a simple majority. Controversies followed regarding the new director, who had previously served as chief editor of the official ruling party newspaper and with alleged close ties to the family of the incumbent prime minister (European Broadcasting Union 2016).

Additionally, the governing body's structure and interrelations, as well as the lack of transparency, affect the RTSH performance. RTSH media professionals argue that "the uncertainty in legislation over the years, the delays in approval of laws and bylaws as well as the overlapping of competencies between the governing bodies of RTSH create bewilderment in the daily work of RTSH staff and thus hamper its normal functioning."[4] For instance, the Administration Board, which is supposed to be a consultative body on financial and management affairs, has also served in practice as a decision-making body, particularly during the absence of an elected Director-General. What is more, RTSH operations have been disrupted by high profile court cases whereby managers and a former Director-General have also been accused of alleged corruption and mismanagement of funds (Londo 2013).

Moreover, the audit of RTSH performance by the High State Control Office in 2015 found that the governing body's decisions are made available neither to the RTSH staff nor to the public (High State Control 2015). Currently, RTSH has published financial report overviews for 2014, 2015, 2017, and 2018 and the Parliamentary Committee on Education and Mediums of Public Information has published reports of hearings with RTSH governing bodies in 2016, 2017 and 2018 (Parliamentary Committee on Education and Mediums of Public Information 2017). Moreover, the audit also found scattered and uncoordinated communication between governing bodies and internal departments at RTSH (High State Control 2015). The Union of RTSH employees is rarely active and the Council of Viewers and Listeners does not have the capabilities to hold RTSH accountable. While the law may envisage the accountability of RTSH to the public, in practice the mechanisms do not achieve their aim.

At present, RTSH only partially fulfills the requirement of the public service broadcaster to be accountable to the public through a board of representatives of the society at large and selected in an independent, open, and transparent

---

3   Interview with media scholar 1, Tirana, April 2015.
4   Quote from an in-depth interview with the RTSH media professional, Tirana, May 2015.

manner. Although the law allows for a wide range of associations to propose members for the Steering Council, in practice the election of members reflects the political positions and preferences of the key political actors. This also refers to the development of internal capabilities at RTSH to build partnerships with the private sector, other media stakeholders, and above all the public (diverse publics). A positive development in this regard has been the introduction of a program portfolio of RTSH and its channels such as the arts, sports, music, etc.

Public Interest for a Public Broadcaster: Living up to its Remit

Two main phases with distinct features can be pointed out in terms of journalistic professionalism in RTSH. The first phase is related to the period from the fall of the communist regime in 1992 to 2000, characterized by the privileged position of RTSH on the market since private outlets had not been established. The challenge was to transform RTSH from a tool of propaganda into a medium for information and entertainment for all citizens by introducing new editorial policies, new programs, and focusing more on an informative function. At that time RTSH played a crucial role in the promotion of the political opposition in Albania. Hence, it ended up positioning itself as the mouthpiece of the new government formed by the first opposition party in Albania, the Democratic Party, in 1992. The second phase happened in the late 1990s and early 2000s, with the introduction of the new law on media that liberalized the market. The establishment of new commercial media attracted human resources away from RTSH, which further resulted in a decrease in RTSH's public influence and an increase in political interference from the government.

Albanian Radio and Television played a crucial role in the democratization of the country from 1991–1998.[5] RTSH had a pool of media professionals, programs, and technology in place as well as its legacy as the only broadcaster in the country for more than 35 years. It also served as a platform for the professional development of key journalists and public figures, who started their career at RTSH and then moved on to private media. During this period, RTSH attempted to adapt to the new political and social landscape of the country and opened up to new professional codes. However, at this time there was clear political parallelism, i.e., RTSH was an instrument of the political party in power and has been constantly criticized for this up until today. Also, the relatively limited diversity, quantity, and quality of programming hindered the positioning of RTSH in the new media landscape in Albania. What is more, commercial media opened up to other sources of information and working practices, while RTSH mainly used official sources of information, thus offering limited quality and diversity of content to the public. Thus, RTSH performed

---

[5]   Interview with a policymaker and a media professional, April and May 2015.

as a closed medium, a platform to give voice to the officials of the government more than to the public, civil society, experts, and others. RTSH also tried to diversify its program portfolio and include more entertainment programming, but it did not ensure a high impact and audience reach.[6]

The improvement of the legislation and its adjustments in line with the EU 's Audiovisual Media Services Directive (AVMSD) did not change the PSB organization's practice or make it operate more independently. The impasse and boycott of the process of selecting the Steering Council members and the Director-General of RTSH is a clear indicator of political affiliations and pressure put on editorial independence and professionalism. What is more, the AMA, the regulator that oversees the compliance of RTSH with the law, still lacks appropriate professional and technical capacities to ensure it performs its duty to full capacity.[7] Additionally, RTSH staff integrity has also been debatable, considering the normal practice of political appointment of staff in RTSH that echoes the rotation of political parties in government, not taking into account their professional profiles and their media experience or interest.[8]

The failure to establish editorial independence of the PSB organization in Albania is not only a result of the political pressures and symbiotic relations with the government but also of an embedded culture within the institution to serve the government. Although there might have been no direct indications, "the news and current affairs department at RTSH has adapted its tone and frame to serve the interests of the government and the political party in power. This is obvious in cases immediately after the general parliamentary elections when there is a political rotation, which is reflected in the news and current affairs coverage of RTSH."[9] The news coverage bias towards the government and lack of editorial independence fall short of meeting the public remit of RTSH and have been criticized particularly during election campaigns.

A thorough and constructive debate in the public sphere(s) in Albania regarding the relevance, transformation, role, and future developments of PSB has been missing. As witnessed by an interlocutor, "there is a neglect of RTSH and the public interest in media with no leading political, academic or public figure advocating for the merits of public service media in Albania and thus for ensuring that the public interest is a fundamental element of RTSH functioning and performance."[10] The situation of engagement of civil society and media associations has improved with their participation in the consultation processes of media laws. Particularly, the Albanian Media Institute is a major actor in civil society regarding media and public communication, with a large number of publications and studies on media developments in Albania. Other organizations focusing on investigative and quality journalism have had positive developments in the media market in Albania. The public mission and interest in the media, particularly in the case of RTSH, should drive the policy process.

---

6   Interview with the former Director-General of RTSH, Tirana, May 2015.
7   Interview with media scholar 1, April 2015, Tirana.
8   Interview with the former Director-General of RTSH, Tirana, May 2015.
9   Interview with media scholar 2, Tirana, June 2015.
10 Interview with media scholar 1, Tirana, April 2015.

The research confirms what has been suggested previously by media scholars and professionals, that there is the need for a strategy on media development, led by the public interest and contemporary changes in society and serving as a guide for future legislation and policy. Nonetheless, there is still no initiative announced in this regard.

The Funding Model: From Mismanagement to Substantial Reforms

The Albanian Law on Audiovisual Media prescribes that RTSH may obtain funding from the license fee, advertising, services to third parties, sponsoring, and the state budget (Law No. 97/2013). The law also clarifies that state funding should be used only for programs aired via satellite for Albanian compatriots living outside of Albania, important projects that would improve and introduce new technology to RTSH, the state symphonic orchestra and other artistic events of international importance (Law No. 97/2013/Article 114). The law specifies that no media outlet, including the PSB organization, can attract more than 30% of all private advertising (Albanian Media Institute 2014). There are relatively limited reliable data on how advertising is distributed in the Albanian media. The lack of transparency and biased decision-making regarding public spending on advertising means that the media in Albania serve the interests of those who sponsor the advertising rather than the public.

The funding of the RTSH is not an issue. Namely, the total revenue of the PSB organization in Albania has increased significantly from EUR 7 million in 2006 to 16.4 million EUR in 2014 and to EUR 21 million in 2017 (RTSH 2018). As set out in the Law of 2013, RTSH financing is relatively autonomous, but its sustainability for a long time remained dependent on the rate of license fee collection and advertising revenue. Compared to the EU average, Albanian PSB has a very small, almost insignificant market share of the advertising market. Inefficiency in collecting the license fees and decreased funding from the state budget has put financial pressure on the broadcaster, also slowing down the preparations for digital switchover (Lani 2013). However, the situation has improved with the high collection rate of the electricity bill, which includes the RTSH fee. For example, the RTSH annual financial report for 2017 highlights that the balance sheet is positive and that RTSH has managed an efficient budget in terms of income and spending (RTSH 2018, 1).

In Albania, the license fee is paid monthly by households, together with their electricity bill. Figures from RTSH's annual report show that the license fee has become an important source of income for PSB in Albania, accounting for 52% of total income in 2017 as compared to 40.5% of total income in 2013 and only 8% in 2006 (RTSH 2018, 1). RTSH state funding accounts for 38% of the total income in 2017; 3% comes from advertising revenue and 7% from other sources. The monthly amount for the license fee has been doubled since 2011, from EUR 4.5 to 9, and there have been calls recently for it to increase even further (Albanian Media Institute 2014). However, RTSH's position on the advertising market is considered to be weak even though it covers 98% of the territory. Nevertheless, there seems to be a consensus amongst policymakers and journalists that the current financing mechanism is effective and generates enough income to cover RTSH objectives.

Even though the budget of the public broadcaster seems to have improved through the years, there are still uncertainties regarding its future operations, taking into account the digital switchover. Experts suggest that the PSB organization in Albania cannot foresee its budget in advance and therefore cannot counteract the pressures on its independence (Nyman-Metcalf 2009). The High State Control audit of RTSH in 2015 found that the lack of an internal budget plan and framework for the implementation of the digital switchover strategy and the digital age have led RTSH to mismanagement of both funds and projects with higher costs and curtailed efficiency, thus hindering the return on investments (High State Control 2015).

Furthermore, the same report highlights the mismanagement of the human resources budget, which constitutes the second-largest share of expenditure (35%), following the investments in digital networks in 2016. Some of the reported issues are the enlarged administration with duplicate departments and personnel, frequent unjustified changes in the organizational structure and remuneration scheme, and an overcrowded workforce (High State Control 2015). As a consequence, RTSH approved new internal regulations for the organizational structure and human resource management in early 2017 following the approval of the new statute in December 2016 (Parliamentary Committee on Education and Mediums of Public Information 2017). While the approval of these fundamental documents marks progress for RTSH, the rapid implementation of the digitalization process requires an essential reformation of the overall operations of RTSH, coupled with a business model that addresses the challenges of the digital age.

Digitalization and Technological Innovation of RTSH

Despite the expressed political consensus for the digital switchover, it has become a contested issue in Albania. The complex business interests and pressures, its questionable independence, the legal disputes, and the slow digitalization of PSB are some of the factors hindering the entire digital switchover process. The Government of Albania adopted the National Strategy on the Transition from Analogue to Digital Broadcasting in 2012. The strategy provides the main objectives and principles of the transition and formulates the role of the state and the relevant structures of the state administration in the creation of the conditions for the transition to the digital system. The transition to digital broadcasting was to be achieved through the digital islands' method, i.e., by allotment up to full coverage of the country's territory, with a total of 11 allotments.

The regulatory authority, policymakers, and legislators in Albania have not only lagged behind the actual media developments in the country, particularly in the case of digital broadcasting but have also hindered the process itself. The first commercial digital multiplex, DigitAlb, started operating in 2004 when neither the regulator nor other lawmakers had yet discussed or issued regulations on digital broadcasting (Londo 2012, 11). What is more, the regulatory authority has not been able to perform adequately in the process of the digital switchover, due to problems in its constitution, functioning, independence, and accountability. The rotation of power after the June 2013 elections in Albania brought once more to the fore the debate on the election of the key management of the media regulatory authority. The Parliamentary Committee on Education and Public Information Mediums could not agree for many months on the validity of the term of the AMA chair and election of its AMA members. This has negatively impacted the digital switchover process, as it is one of the reasons that impedes the AMA from deciding on granting licenses for commercial multiplexes.

Another reason relates to the political independence of AMA and its members. AMA drafted the Regulation "On the Licensing of Digital Networks and their Programs, According to the Procedure of a Beauty Contest," and issued a public notification for taking part in the selection procedure, according to the beauty contest principle, for granting 3 private national digital networks. However, this process of awarding new digital frequencies to private operators has been characterized by delays, impasse, and court cases. Digital broadcasting has been a reality in Albania since 2004 with the introduction of DigitAlb and later on with Tring, but this has been outside of the legal framework as the companies offering digital broadcasting had no licenses. In this light, the process of awarding new digital frequencies in 2015 was merely an attempt to legalize an already existing and functioning reality. The tender opened by AMA for the award of the digital frequencies to private providers has been marred by accusations of conflicts of interest, including the AMA chair.[11]

RTSH was assigned the leading role in the digitalization process. As the strategy outlines "the public broadcaster—RTSH—creates, exploits and operates the national digital network based on the contract stipulated with AMA." (Council of Ministers of the Republic of Albania 2012, 11). With the digital switchover, the remit of RTSH is reaffirmed as to offer free-to-air informative, didactic, and entertainment programs to users spread over the country regardless of their geographic position. Therefore, RTSH will offer free public programs as

---

[11]   It claims that it favors a media conglomerate comprising the broadcasters DigitAlb, Super Sport, and Top Channel over their competitors, Media Vizion—which owns Vizion Plus TV—and Tring TV. However, AMA and the Minister for Innovation and Public Administration argue that this is a false accusation and that the tender war was lawful. This investigation was originally published on Reporter.al, the award-winning online publication of the Balkan Investigative Reporting Network in Albania.

well as conditional access programs. Additionally, the existing local broadcasters will be transferred to the RTSH digital networks and will pay a differentiated fee to RTSH for this service based on the "digital islands" approach. The regulator and the PSB organization are supposed to cooperate as part of the digital switchover (Council of Ministers of the Republic of Albania 2012). After this transition period, the digital network license is to be given by an open competition warranting an equal, objective, and non-discriminatory treatment. AMA, on its initiative or with the request of interested subjects, will open the competition process, taking into consideration the frequency plan and the availability of the free frequencies for digital broadcasting. However, if the independence and accountability of the regulatory body are still in question after the transition, as it is today, then the process is undermined.

RTSH has fallen short of adhering to its role regarding the digital switchover. The strategy envisages that after building two networks through an international tender, RTSH would serve as a host for existing regional and local broadcasters. In parallel with this, it was planned that the AMA would license private operators—the three private networks—to complete the process, as will be explained below. However, all these processes have been significantly delayed and thus the switchover deadline of June 2015 was not met and was postponed to September 2019. The delay in electing Steering Council members and the deadlock over the election of a new director have also affected the ability of RTSH management to approve the documents needed to proceed with the digital switchover process (Londo 2012, 12). Apart from the limited functionality of the Steering Council and the consequent delays, a major problem in the process of digitalization of RTSH has been the legal dispute over the tender for the digital switchover of its two networks.

The Strategy for the Digital Switchover allocated two national frequencies to the public broadcaster, out of eight assigned to Albania. The tender was carried out amid the objection of the opposition that it was not appropriate to undertake projects of such a scale immediately before the election period. The digitalization tender for RTSH held in May 2013 was contested in court. Thus, the process was delayed by the legal challenges to the public broadcaster's tender and by the AMA's procedures to license private broadcasters. The process restarted in March 2015, when the government signed a contract for EUR 21.5 million with the German company Rohde & Schwarz to construct two networks for RTSH.[12] The delay in building the digital networks has affected not only RTSH, but also local broadcasters that are supposed to be hosted on these networks, and

---

[12]   It should be noted that there have been troubles with the company that won the tender to build the digital network in Albania, which has reduced political collaboration concerning this issue. The Ministry for Innovation invited tenders for the construction of the transmission network for the public broadcaster RTSH in 2013. In June 2013, the Albanian government awarded and then canceled the right of Rohde & Schwarz to build the network. A legal battle ensued between the Albanian state and the German company Rohde & Schwarz. However, the Ministry for Innovation in Albania retreated from its initial objective to cancel the tender and awarded it to the German company for EUR 21.5 million in March 2015. This legal battle has delayed the building of the digital networks by two years and the contract with the firm is the same as that signed in June 2013.

ultimately the entire digital switchover process. The construction of the two digital networks started in July 2015, with the first phase to be completed during the summer of 2016, covering at least 85% of the population with a digital signal, while the second phase, completed over the summer of 2017, will cover at least 96.5% of the population with a digital signal.

The digital switchover process encompasses the issues of access and affordability, which are addressed in the strategy, but the implementation is far from appropriate. The strategy provides for public and outreach activities, including a call center, a public campaign, and organization of public events to spread awareness. In reality, there has been almost no discussion in the media regarding the digital switchover. Discussions and hearing sessions in Parliament have been reported mainly by the media following the interest that each company has in the digital switchover.[13] However, there has been no in-depth program or discussion organized beyond brief and biased news reporting. This discussion has been seen as more of internal development within the media companies or the public broadcaster, rather than a process that will affect every citizen. The digital switchover has not even been discussed in the academic sphere. The only exception was a media campaign for decoders which started in June 2016, that was linked to the economic interests of changing the decoders in each household. The new deadline set by the AMA for the digital switchover process was September 2019. The infrastructure to access digital broadcasting is generally already in place. However, the AMA has postponed the deadline of the digital switchover in Tirana and Durres due to the scarcity of DVB-T2 digital decoders on the market and the associated public discontent. These events indicated a shortcoming in the AMA's role in the management of the process as well as a lack of public awareness about the digital switchover (European Commission 2019).

Remit in the Digital Age: Towards Innovative Digital Presence and Audience Relations

The digital age, characterized by a ubiquitous proliferation of ICTs, a plethora of media platforms, programs, services, and an abundance of information and digital networks, calls into question the relevance of public service media. If PSM are to sustain their role and legitimacy in contemporary society, surely, they need to handle the challenges and opportunities represented by the rapid rise of digital media (Sehl et al. 2016). Two key issues can be outlined here: (i) expansion of multimedia to effectively deliver public service media content online across multiple platforms; and (ii) remodeled relations to audiences allowing for participation in and through the media and prompt responsiveness to ever-changing audiences' needs and preferences.

---

[13] For example, the coverage of Top Media vs. Tring TV, having opposite interests in the process.

Despite delays, the digitalization process has enabled RTSH to invest substantially in digital technology for media production, management, and broadcasting. RTSH now has an online presence through its official website, broadcasts in high definition as well as streaming some of its channels online. Since 2012, RTSH has started to build an infrastructure of digital transitions, a program packet with 4 channels such as RTSH HD, RTSH Sport, RTSH Music, and RTSH Art in Standard Definition format (SD). RTSH is now investing in new studios and employing new staff. The RTSH digital presence is relatively limited but is showing potential for growth. For example, the online updates are delayed for more than 24 hours, there are few followers on RTSH online social media profiles such as Facebook, Twitter, and YouTube accounts, and the RTSH website does not offer any possibilities for user-generated content.

Moreover, this expansion has not been carried out in synchrony with the Digital Switchover Strategy and RTSH still lacks an integrated strategic plan for the digital area (Oktrova 2015). In 2015 the High State Control reported that RTSH had not developed fundamental documents and processes for the digital era and, more specifically, there was no Strategy for the Management of Technological Transformation/Digitalization 2015–2020, no working group for drafting the RTSH Development Strategy, no approved action plan regarding digitalization phases, no risk management and no corresponding budget plan framework, as well as no Marketing Plan for the Digital Switchover (Oktrova 2015). The basic approach was that of ad hoc actions and considering digitalization only as a technological upgrade. A positive step was taken in early 2017 with the initiation of the drafting of the RTSH Development Strategy (Oktrova 2015). This process needs to be open and transparent with proper consultations within the Council of Viewers and Listeners, regulatory bodies, a respective parliamentary committee, civil society, experts, and the public. Currently, the public broadcaster RTSH has a new internal structure that reflects the digital switchover process.

In addition to a technology upgrade, RTSH has also introduced new channels and programs. It has increased its coverage of education, entertainment, sports, culture, and socio-economic and international affairs, rather than political and current affairs. Also, RTSH is the only mainstream media that produces programs for ethnic, national, and linguistic minorities in Albania. RTSH has developed and approved editorial principles to guard against political interference.

However, the introduction of all channels as envisaged in the Digital Switchover Strategy is not completed and the regulatory framework requires public consultations, which have not yet been completed.[14] Moreover, no funds have been spent on an independent production in 2014 and 2015, but an open call for competition for independent production in science education was introduced at the beginning of 2017. This would allow for various groups to participate

---

[14] As per the Strategy, RTSH should have 12 channels, such as RTSH 2, RTSH Parliament, RTSH special topic, RTSH diversity, RTSH history, RTSH children, and RTSH film (not yet fully operative).

in RTSH media production and thus positively impact RTSH relations to audiences by helping to overcome low levels of social trust in RTSH (Halo et al. 2015). The advancements in programming both in quality and quantity call for improvements in processes of content production.

Currently, at RTSH, production, particularly of news, is structured primarily around broadcast, i.e., the format that is suitable for television and radio. The online news production is largely seen as separate, albeit with some degree of cooperation. For instance, there is limited integration and internal coordination among the various media production departments at RTSH. The Department of Digital Programming was established in 2015, but its coordination and communication with the Department of Structural Programming and Current Affairs is ineffective (High State Control 2015). The Department of WEB was introduced in late 2015 with the main duty to set up a suitable platform for online media and publish content in various formats—audio, text, photo, and video—provided by other departments. Currently, the logistics of producing media content for multiple online media platforms have yet to be developed. Reporting to a hearing with parliament, the Committee on Education and Mediums of Public Information, RTSH Director-General confirms the efforts towards reforming the current media production practices and moving towards the incorporation of digital media working practices.

The Challenges to the Future Development of PSB in Albania

For RTSH to successfully transform from state-owned broadcaster to a public service media, it needs to rebuild social trust by adhering to its remit and strengthen its relations with audiences. For this to happen, two components are of paramount importance: independence and professional autonomy guaranteed by law and safeguarded by the relevant supervisory and regulatory bodies as well as the public and civil society (for instance the proper functioning of the Council of Listeners and Viewers).

RTSH lacks *directionality*, i.e., the ability to set directions of change and innovation in the media market, for instance in creating or shaping media trends. For the future transformation of RTSH, it is thus paramount to set clear directions vis a vis other media stakeholders in the Albanian market and in response to the contemporary developments of the Albanian society.

Apart from the two phases already elaborated on in the previous sections, a future, third phase of development of PSB in Albania should seek to achieve three main goals. First, a rebalancing of the media market in Albania. This implies an increased audience and interest in the public broadcaster and not just private media. This would enable a new balance between public and private media in the market and therefore allow for more competition between media outlets, the better quality of content and programs, and higher standards of professionalism. Secondly, the transformation of RTSH would be an added value to the Albanian media market in light of the new information and communication technologies that have affected the audiovisual media. Third, this transformation would be in favor of the citizens of Albania, the real "owners" of the RTSH, who so far have only paid the bill without getting the benefits in return.[15]

The attempts to establish PSB in Albania come at a time when PSB itself is undergoing major transformations in pursuit of redefining its role in society and democracy. There is also no clear model of PSB and its future development in Europe that could be transplanted to Albania. What is more, the efforts to come up with a solution for the future of PSB in Albania are situated between two main current phenomena: on one hand, Albania, like other new democracies, is experiencing "democratic fatigue," and to some, it still seems vulnerable to political instability, which does not favor the transformation of PSB; on the other hand, the EU as the guarantor of democratization in Albania is under unprecedented economic, financial, and democratic crisis (Rupnik and Zielonka 2013, 2). This is an issue of concern considering that the EU and other international actors have pushed forward the agenda for the transformation of PSB in Albania.

The potential risks and dilemmas that come with the transformative processes of the RTSH require the establishment of capacities (structures and processes) that will mitigate risks and be capable of addressing the challenges in a rapidly changing media landscape. RTSH, based on its remit and specific objectives, should provide diverse programming for all interests and perspectives. For example, RTSH is the only audiovisual media that is offering programs for minorities through its regional centers.

Moreover, the development of a learning organization requires the reorganization of the internal procedures and workflow within the RTSH. With the digital services, the media production processes do not start with the development of a single program, but rather with a concept or idea that is then elaborated on in various media formats and platforms.

Conclusion

Despite noticeable progress, RTSH is adjusting its remit, operations, and performance at a reluctant pace. As a consequence, its speed of transformation is slower than the changes in the landscape in which it operates and the public it serves. Furthermore, its transformation is affected by contingency factors such as the political, economic, and socio-cultural context in Albania. Although lately, RTSH has carried out important organizational reforms—digitalization, a new

---

[15]   Interview with a policymaker and a media professional, April and May 2015.

statute, editorial principles, and a code of ethics—it is clear that internal organizational barriers also constrain RTSH's ability to seize the opportunities and tackle the challenges of digital media.

RTSH should overcome the current practices of perceiving digitalization as merely a technological upgrade and engage in the consolidation of substantial reformative processes encompassing its governance and operations, content production, human capital, and overall performance and status in the Albanian media landscape and society. This transformation largely depends on the success of expansion to online multimedia and the transformation of RTSH's relationship with audiences or diverse publics. Therefore, RTSH as PSM needs to reposition itself in a way that confirms its legitimacy and role in society, while at the same time reconnecting with its audiences.

This leads to the personalization of services for a fragmented and complex society through diverse and quality programming and the embrace of media convergence including multimedia platforms, integrated newsrooms, creativity, and innovation in programming, media production, and workflows. This strategy will then attract talent and contribute to quality programming and thus more audiences. The tasks are highly demanding and require substantial reforms of RTSH's organizational structure and culture to shift from traditional media production for broadcasting towards innovative production processes for integrated multimedia platforms.

The value and relevance of RTSH in Albania need to be discussed in a thorough public debate with the public interest at its center. The legitimacy of RTSH needs to be confirmed in the digital era and RTSH needs to strengthen its profile as a representative of public interest. The concept of public interest as the underpinning principle of RTSH needs to be unpacked and mechanisms developed to help it take center stage in media policy and RTSH performance. This is interlinked to the enhancement of the public interest in RTSH and more broadly in media integrity, freedom, and independence as cornerstones of democratization. Furthermore, civil society, academia, and media associations should play a more proactive role in advocating for the public interest in the media and holding AMA, RTSH, and relevant public bodies accountable.

References

Albanian Media Institute. 2014. *State, and Private Advertisement in Albanian Media: Report 2014.* Tirana: Albanian Media Institute.
AMA. 2016. "AMA: A Presentation." Accessed May 14, 2020. http://ama.gov.al/rreth-amas/.
Bino, Blerjana. 2017. *From Access to Empowerment: Countering Marginalisation of Roma Communities through Alternative Media in Albania.* Tirana: European University of Tirana. https://uet.edu.al/images/doktoratura/Blerjana_Bino.pdf.
——., and Besart Kadia. 2017. *The Prospect and Development of the Public Service Media: The Case of Albania.* Sarajevo: Analitika Center for Social Research. http://www.analitika.

ba/sites/default/files/publikacije/PSB%20Albania.pdf.

Council of Ministers of the Republic of Albania, 2012. *National Strategy on the Transition from Analogue to Digital Broadcasting.* Tirana: Council of Ministers.

European Broadcasting Union. 2016. "Albanian Public Service Broadcaster Radion Televizioni Shqiptar Elects new Director General." Accessed May 9, 2020. https://www.ebu.ch /news /2016/05/ebu-news-entry.

European Commission. 2019. *Albania 2019 Report.* Accessed January 20, 2020. https://ec.europa.eu/neighbourhood-enlargement/sites/near/files/20190529-albania-report.pdf.

——. 2015. *Albania 2015 Report.* Accessed January 20, 2020. https://ec.europa.eu/neighbourhood-enlargement/sites/near/files/pdf/key_documents /2015/20151110_report_albania.pdf.

Freedom House. 2016. *Nations in Transit 2016.* Washington, DC: Freedom House. https://freedomhouse.org/sites/default/files/FH_NIT2016_Final_FWeb.pdf.

Hallin, Daniel C., and Paolo Mancini. 2013. "'Comparing Media Systems' between Eastern and Western Europe." In *Media Transformations in the Post-Communist World: Eastern Europe's Tortured Path to Change*, edited by Peter Gross and Karol Jakubowicz, 15–32. Lanham/Boulder: Lexington Books.

Halo, Adela, Dorarta Hyseni, Dorian Matlija, and Theodoros Alexandridis. 2015. *A Blind Eye on the News: Self-censorship in the Albanian Media.* Tirana: Balkan Investigative Reporting Network. https://birn.eu.com/wp-content/uploads/2017/05/Report-on-self-censorship-in-the-Albanian-media.pdf.

High State Control. 2015. *Report on the Performance of the Albanian Radio and Television 2014–2015, Audit Performance Report.* Tirana: High State Control. http://www.klsh.org.al/web/performanca_e_radio_televizionit_shqiptar_1485.pdf.

IREX. 2019. *Albania: Media Sustainability Index 2019.* Washington, DC: IREX. https://www.irex.org/sites/default/files/pdf/media-sustainability-index-europe-eurasia-2019-albania.pdf.

Kajsiu, Blendi. 2018. *Nations in Transit 2018.* Washington, DC: Freedom House. https://freedomhouse.org/country/albania/nations-transit/2018.

Lani, Remzi, ed. 2013. *Balkan Media Barometer Albania 2013.* Tirana: Friedrich-Ebert-Stiftung. https://library.fes.de/pdf-files/bueros/albanien/10892.pdf.

Ligj Nr. 97/2013, për mediat audiovizive në republikën e shqipërisë [The law no. 97/2013 on audiovisual media in the Republic of Albania], *Official Gazette* 37/13.

Ligji Nr. 8410 për radion dhe televizionin publik e privat në Republikën e Shqipërisë [Law no. 8410 on public and private radio and television], *Official Gazette* 24/98.

Londo, Ilda. 2016. "Albania: When Market Runs Ahead of the Legislation." In *Time Zero of the Digital Switchover in SEE*, edited by Center for Independent Journalism, 10–16. Bucharest: Center for Independent Journalism. http://www.mc.rs/upload/documents /projekti/regionalna%20saradnja/Time-%20Zero.pdf.

——. 2015. *Monitoring EU Guidelines in Albania: Regulator and PSB Exposed to Political Power Relations.* Ljubljana: Peace Institute. http://mediaobservatory.net /sites/default/files/ Albania_Regulator%20and%20PSB%20exposed%20to%20political%20power%20 relations.pdf.

——. 2014. "Albania." In *Media Integrity Matters: Reclaiming Public Service Values in Media and Journalism*, edited by Brankica Petković, 51–119. Ljubljana: Peace Institute. https://www.media.ba/sites/default/files/media_integrity_matters _za_web_final_0. pdf.

——. 2013. *Limited Assistance for Limited Impact: International Media Assistance in Albania.* Sarajevo/Tirana: Albanian Media Institute/Analitika Center for Social Research.

https://www.analitika.ba/sites/default/files/publikacije/londo_i_-_rrpp_albania_wp02_3dec2013_final_for_publishing.pdf.

——. 2012. *Mapping Digital Media: Albania*. Open Society Foundations: London. https://www.opensocietyfoundations.org/sites/default/files/mapping-digital-media-albania-20120217.pdf.

Mancini, Paolo, and Jan Zielonka. 2012. "Introduction." *The International Journal of Press/Politics* 17, no. 4 (September): 379–387.

Mejdini, Fatjona. 2015. "Albanian TV in Deadlock Over New Chief." *BIRN Balkan Insight*, October 22. Accessed May 11, 2020. https://balkaninsight.com/2015/10/22/albania-in-limbo-over-public-tv-chief-10-21-2015/.

Nyman-Metcalf, Katrin. 2009. *Analysis of the Draft Albanian Strategy for Digital Switchover*. Vienna: OSCE. https://www.osce.org/albania/36196?download=true.

Oktrova, Mirela. 2015. *The Two-Folded Challenges of the Digital Process of the Public Service Broadcasting Service in Albania*. Tirana: Albanian Media Institute.

OSCE ODIHR. 2019. *Election Observation Mission Final Report*. Accessed May 14, 2020. https://www.osce.org/odihr/elections/albania/429230?download=true.

OSCE Presence in Albania. 2015. "OSCE Presence, European Broadcasting Union Join Forces to Help Transform Albania's Public Broadcaster." Accessed May 9, 2020. https://www.osce.org/albania/163191.

Parliamentary Committee on Education and Mediums of Public Information. 2017. *Evaluation of the RTSH Operations for 2016. Annual Report*. Tirana: The Parliament of the Republic of Albania. http://www.klsh.org.al/web/performanca_e_radio_televizionit_shqiptar_1485.pdf.

Reporters Without Borders and BIRN Albania. 2017. *Media Ownership Monitor Albania: Media Concentration*. Accessed May 5, 2020. http://albania.mom-rsf.org/en /findings/media-concentration/.

Reporters Without Borders. 2019. *2019 World Press Freedom Index*. Accessed May 13, 2020. https://rsf.org/en/ranking/2019.

RTSH. 2018. *Annual Financial Report 2017*. Accessed May 11, 2020. https://www.rtsh.al/wp-content/uploads/2018/03/Analiza-VJETORE-2017.pdf.

——. 2015. *Statuti i Radiotelevizionit Shqiptar (RTSH)* [RTSH statute]. Accessed May 11, 2020. https://www.rtsh.al/statuti-i-rtsh-se/.

Rupnik, Jacques, and Jan Zielonka. 2013. "Introduction: The State of Democracy 20 Years on: Domestic and External Factors." *East European Politics and Societies* 27, no. 1 (December): 3–25.

Sehl, Annika, Alessio Cornia and Rasmus Kleis Nielsen. 2016. *Public Service News and Digital Media*. Oxford: Reuters Institute for the Study of Journalism. https://reutersinstitute.politics.ox.ac.uk/sites/default/files/research/files/Public%2520Service%2520News%2520and%2520Digital%2520Media.pdf.

Voltmer, Katrin. 2006. "The Mass Media and the Dynamics of Political Communication in Processes of Democratization: An Introduction." In *Mass Media and Political Communication in New Democracies*, edited by Katrin Voltmer, 1–20. London: Routledge.

CHAPTER 3

The Future of Public Service Broadcasting in Bosnia and Herzegovina

Nidžara Ahmetašević and Tea Hadžiristić

Introduction

Since its creation, public service broadcasting in Bosnia and Herzegovina has struggled to fulfill its primary goals. Financial difficulties have brought the state broadcaster near the brink of collapse several times (Pelešević 2016), while state capture by political parties has politicized public service broadcasting (PSB) across the board (Voltmer 2013, 25) and increased its dysfunction.

Our research (see also Ahmetašević and Hadžiristić 2017) found that PSB in Bosnia and Herzegovina (BiH) has failed to secure a sustainable funding model, is not independent from the political sphere, does not fulfill its remit, and has failed to adopt new technologies crucial to its continued relevance and survival.

PSB is a victim of the political colonization of the media sphere, and weak, dysfunctional state institutions that suffer from the chronic disregard for the law demonstrated by ruling elites. At the same time, the ongoing debate about PSB in BiH is largely anachronistic and fails to capture the core challenges and to articulate much needed innovative policy solutions that would look beyond the now largely outdated, defunct model of PSB that was introduced in 2002.

Background

The end of socialism in South-Eastern Europe ushered in a period of transition which included transforming state broadcasters into PSB organizations to remove the media from direct state control. However, today, the media in much of the region do not play the role of a forum for public debate but are rather a tool of political elites and interest groups.

BiH's PSB organizations are examples of what Jakubowicz (2011, 215) calls Potemkin institutions, that are designed "to satisfy the requirement of external actors, such as international donors," which function only as de jure organizations and fail to fulfill their goals.[1] While public service broadcasting is part of the country's EU accession process, local political actors fail to engage genuinely with the process and indeed have little incentive to do so.

BiH is unique in the region, however, in that its political, economic, and social context is defined by the legacy of the 1992–1995 war in Bosnia and Herzegovina amid the violent breakup of Yugoslavia, the power-sharing state structures constructed in the aftermath of the war, and particularly dire economic circumstances. PSB was formally established in 2002 by the Office of the High Representative (OHR), an international body that is responsible for overseeing the peace treaty which ended the war in BiH (the OHR was envisioned in the Dayton Peace Agreement of 1995). PSB was made an official condition for signing the Stabilization and Association Agreement between the EU and BiH in 2005 (Jusić and Ahmetašević 2013, 40). Since then, the process has been in the hands of the political elites of BiH, which has arguably led to strife and stagnation.

BiH is dominated by political capture of the state; political elites most often belong to ethnically defined political parties, which purport to serve as "guardians" of national interest for their own groups. Ruling parties in BiH continue to demonstrate characteristics of what Mujkić calls "a democracy of ethnic oligarchies" (Mujkić 2007, 113), in which parties continually "provoke interethnic tensions and then present themselves as saviors of the state's various nations" (Jahić 2017). Divisions and disagreements among dominant political parties have repeatedly stalled the implementation of even the most basic reforms, including the implementation of laws pertaining to public service media. Freedom House's latest Nation in Transit report considers BiH a hybrid regime, caught in the transition between a consolidated democracy and authoritarianism, with declining scores in democracy, growing corruption levels, and independent media scores stagnating since 2011 (Jahić 2018). The 2020 Transparency International Corruption Perceptions Index found that the country has declined the most in the region, receiving the lowest score in the last 8 years. Alarmingly, Transparency International in BiH found that corruption has become an official policy on a state, entity, and cantonal level (Transparency International Bosnia and Herzegovina 2020).

In this context, PSB flounders against oligarchic interests, which have no endogenous incentive for empowering an independent PSB system. Deliberate backpedaling about PSB's proper implementation and development thus undermines its proper democratic and cohesive function. Likewise, parties face insufficient exogenous incentives for PSB reform. While functional PSB and free media are nominally conditions for EU accession, international actors such as the EU are, on the whole, unwilling to challenge political elites or demand accountability, exacerbating the stagnation and politicization of PSB (see Mujanović 2014). What is lacking is more robust support for democratization and civic action which would transform the very structure that sustains ethnopolitical elites and fails to incentivize support for a truly public and functioning PSB.

---

[1]   Voltmer (2013, 25) corroborates the politicization of the public media in post-communist settings: "In many new democracies of post-communist Eastern Europe, public service has been hijacked by political elites to serve their needs of controlling the public agenda."

Additionally, the imperiled economic situation has had negative consequences for public media, too. Bosnia and Herzegovina had one of Europe's highest unemployment rates for many years, though in recent years that number has improved somewhat, reaching 18.4% in 2019 (Jusić and Numanović, 2015; International Monetary Fund 2019). BiH is often ranked as one of the poorest countries in Europe by various metrics (Klix.ba 2016; see also World Bank n.d.). Some argue that within the complex governmental structure, partisan conflicts have "affected living conditions," with enormous debts growing "as budget funds were sunk in corruption or used to buy social peace at the expense of investment" (Jahić 2016). The World Bank estimates that various factors likepolitical and social turmoil, and lack of progress in making improvements to the business climate, have reduced economic growth rates (World Bank n.d.). Critics have pointed to rapid post-war privatization and deregulation as evidence of the predatory actions of local political elites whose pillage of state assets began during the war (Horvat and Štiks 2015, 2). Growing emigration and a low birth rate also contribute to a general population decline. Though it is almost impossible to identify with accurate how many people are emigrating, BIRN estimates that Bosnia will suffer a nearly 29% population decline in the 1989–2050 period (Judah 2019).

Unsurprisingly, assessments of the country's media have continuously declined in the last decade. Freedom House scores for Independent Media in BiH have stagnated since 2011 (Jahić 2016), and the IREX Media Sustainability Index shows a decline in the development of a sustainable media system since 2006 and stagnation in the past few years. The country's media system is considered to be "an unsustainable mixed system" and almost all indicators have been decreasing, though 2019 shows several very slight improvements (IREX 2019). This state of affairs seems to be corroborated by public opinion. Survey research conducted in 2019 shows that 88% of respondents in Bosnia and Herzegovina believe that public service media in the country is under political influence, the highest rate in Southeast Europe (Sittig and Fabijanić 2019).

BiH's media market is small, oversaturated, and faces declining revenues. Though the size of the radio and TV market is hard to establish due to fragmentation and a lack of reliable media market research, oversaturation has led to rapidly decreasing advertising revenues (Udovičić 2015) and increased competition between public and private media (IREX 2017). PSB organizations do, however, receive a large part of the media market revenues on the whole: the latest report by the Communications Regulatory Agency (CRA) finds that 70% of the total revenue of the electronic media market in 2012 (approximately 90 million of 156.5 million KM in total) in BiH went to public service broadcasters. A full 35.4% of the total marketing revenue of television, print, radio, and online marketing goes to PSB organizations, which is relatively large compared to other countries in Europe (CRA 2013).[2] PSB organizations are generally uninterested in accurately measuring audiences or using this information to improve programming, and measurements have been unreliable for at least half a decade (IREX 2017).

---

[2]   This remains the last analysis done on the broadcasting market by the Communications Regulatory Agency of Bosnia and Herzegovina.

PSB Organizations

The Public Broadcasting System of BiH includes one national and two entity broadcasters:[3]

- The state-level public broadcaster of BiH (BHRT), consisting of one television channel (BHT) and one radio channel (BH Radio 1).[4]

- Radio-Television of the Federation of Bosnia and Herzegovina (RTVFBiH), consisting of one TV channel (FTV) and two radio channels (Radio FBiH and Radio 202).[5]

- Radio-Television of the Republika Srpska (RTRS),[6] consisting of one TV channel and one radio channel (for more on the internal structure of PSB organizations, see Ahmetašević and Hadžiristić 2017).

The legally prescribed fourth unit, the Corporation, was modeled after the BBC, proposed by a consultancy team that was involved in the early process of transformation. The BBC model operates in "an internal market among PSB units, where all the services would be purchased between the units, thus making the production more cost-effective and the system more accountable" (Jusić and Ahmetašević 2013, 36). The involvement of BBC experts was part of the postwar international intervention spearheaded by the Office of the High Representative; local media experts were hardly consulted in the process.[7]

The Corporation is envisioned as an umbrella organization to manage equipment, set the development strategy, coordinate the technical and human potential of the three broadcasters, and collect all advertising revenues and license fees and distribute them among the broadcasters in accordance using a predefined formula.[8] However, it was never established, which has been blamed partly on obstruction by political parties, given that the establishment of the Corporation would have eventually led to the creation of a unified system, with minimal

---

3   Additionally, 74 local TV and radio stations that are funded through municipal and cantonal budgets but are not considered part of the PSB system. In total there are 4 cantonal TV stations, 8 municipality run TV stations, three cantonal and 59 municipality-run radio stations, plus a radio station in Brčko. Information from Helena Mandić, director of broadcasting at the Communications Regulatory Agency, interview with the author, March 2016.

4   BHRT website: http://www.bhrt.ba.

5   RTVFBiH websites: http://www.rtvfbih.ba/loc/ and http://www.federalna.ba.

6   RTRS website: http://rtrs.tv.

7   Esad Gotovuša, President of the Governing Board of the BHRT at the time of the fieldwork study for this paper, remembers his attempt to influence the BBC team and to draw their attention toward the existence of radio and TV stations at the cantonal and municipality level, proposing that all should be incorporated into one system. "I believe they did not want to bother with that. All they wanted was to move away from the socialist model we had. And they left these cantonal and municipality broadcasters to exist, up until today, as mere mouthpieces of the political option at a given time over the territory" (interview with the authors, April 2016).

8   The Corporation was never established although it is envisaged by the System Law 2005.

possibility for political or economic influence. However, resistance to its establishment is also present on the part of the entity-level broadcasters. Given the redistribution of earnings envisaged by the System Law of 2005 (which would be collected by the Corporation), it is neither in the interest of RTVFBiH nor of RTRS, who would both lose a significant segment of the revenues from advertising they earn through the transfers to BHRT.

Moreover, the Corporation would gain ownership of the equipment, which is also not in the interest of individual broadcasters, particularly those that are better equipped. In effect, the PSB system was never truly established in its envisaged form—instead, the three broadcasters act like competitors rather than partners who belong to the same organizational structure.

Regulation of PSB in BiH

The dysfunctional organizational structure described above is directly linked to the failure to implement the legal framework that was introduced in 2002 by the OHR. The regulatory framework for PSB in BiH, much of which was drafted by the international community in the postwar years in line with EU principles, was for a while considered innovative and exemplary in the region. Nevertheless, PSB laws have since not been modernized; the only changes that were adopted were those giving political parties more control over the PSB system. More importantly, the core elements of the legal framework have not been implemented a full 18 years since their adoption.

The initial set of laws imposed by OHR in 2002 was updated between 2005 and 2008 (Boev 2012). Today, the legal framework for PSB includes the following four laws:

- The Law on the Public Service Broadcasting System of BiH of 2005 (System Law) which regulates the structure and guiding principles of public broadcasters and relations between them, including the establishment and functions of the Corporation.[9]

- The Law on the Public Service Broadcasting of 2005 (BHT Law 2005) which regulates the public broadcaster at the state level.

- The Law on the Public Service Broadcasting of RS of 2006 (RTRS Law 2006) which regulates the public broadcaster of Republika Srpska.

- The Law on the Public Service Broadcasting of FBiH of 2008 (RTVFBiH Law) which regulates the public broadcaster of the Federation.

The System Law decreed that the broadcasters were to be independent in terms of program policy and finances, have the same legal status, and share resources

---

[9]   Enforcement of this law is questionable given the nonexistence of the corporation.

through the Corporation.[10] It also stated that these broadcasters should have a similar internal structure, and cooperate in terms of introduction of new technologies, digitalization, co-production, and advertising (System Law, Article 6). However, the law has effectively been rendered irrelevant. Consequently, only the three laws that regulate the individual broadcasters have been put into practice, in such a way that they operate as separate, competing broadcasting companies, while the PSB system was never fully established.

A brief analysis of the key elements of the legal framework demonstrates that BiH suffers from all ills democratizing societies in the region and Europe: incomplete implementation and constant changes of the laws and rules in accordance with the interests of ruling elites and other influential groups. There is a high level of informality present in the current implementation of the legal framework for PSB in the country, and selective implementation of only those provisions that are acceptable to particular influential interests, at the detriment of society as a whole.

PSB Funding Model

The very existence of PSB in Bosnia has been put into question recently due to extreme financial hardship and an inability to agree on a functional funding model. Revenues of PSB organizations (consisting of monthly license fee levied on all households, advertising revenues, and income from other sources such as rental of equipment) have been decreasing across the board and BHRT and RTVFBiH have been heavily indebted since at least 2011 (Musanovic 2011).

The redistribution of income among the three broadcasters which was envisioned by the legal framework simply does not occur in practice. The laws stipulate that 50% of advertising revenues and license fee income will be allocated to BHRT, while 25% will go to each entity broadcaster. In practice, RTVFBiH's advertising revenues far outweigh those of the other two broadcasters and it is simply not in their interest to redistribute these revenues to the other broadcasters. According to the CRA analysis of the broadcasting market in BiH in 2013, RTVFBIH earned 63% of advertising revenues within the PSB system, while BHRT and RTRS received only 19% and 18% respectively (CRA 2013). The failure to establish the joint Corporation means that there are no mechanisms for proper collection and management of PSB revenues.

The second problem has to do with the inability to collect license fees at a sustainable level. Collection rates have been dropping radically for the past two years (BHRT 2016, 16), in part due to inefficiencies in the collection as well as boycotts led by various political parties. The model of license fee funding collected

---

[10] A public service broadcasting corporation which was intended to coordinate the three distinct PSBs as well as "manage the equipment and the transmission network and be in charge of sales and advertising."

via landline telephone bills officially expired in June 2016,[11] and no proposed models (Smajić and Latal 2016) were implemented until August 2017, when the entire system was near collapse. In 2017, local political elites finally introduced a new model whereby the license fee will be collected alongside electricity bills (I. Č. 2017), yet Republika Srpska continues to collect fees through landline telephone bills, and fees are not collected at all in some areas of the Federation with Croat leadership (IREX 2018). At the same time, the Consumer Ombudsman for BiH has been warning that the model of collecting license fees through electricity bills does not comply with consumer protection laws, and the matter is unresolved (Zenica Info 2019). A 2019 European Commission report described the license fee collection model as inadequate (European Commission 2019).

Advertising revenues dropped in recent years, and there are also concerns that the way advertising revenues are allotted has less to do with actual viewership or audience data and more to do with the political interests of advertisers. Though PSB organizations rely mainly on public funding, there are worries that advertisers may have increasing control over the editorial line (IREX 2018). Ultimately, financial instability is a major factor leading to the compromised independence of the PSB in BiH.

Politicization

Institutional instability and financial woes make the PSB system in BiH vulnerable to direct political interference when it comes to the appointment of managing boards, editors, and even journalists. Observers of BiH's media system worry that politicians hold too much power over key nominations and dismissals of the managing boards of PSB organizations (Boev 2012). Formally, the independent CRA nominates the board members of BHRT and RTRS. However, the National Assembly of Republika Srpska has the power to reject CRA-nominated members without giving a concrete reason. In Federation BiH, RTVFBiH board members are not nominated by the CRA but by a parliamentary commission which also has the power to dismiss the Board of Governors (Hodžić 2015, 9; also see: U.S. Department of State 2015, 9).

The authors of the 2018 Alternative Analytical Report of BiH's application for EU membership conclude that media freedom and the working conditions of journalists "have deteriorated compared to the previous period, and there are great chances that the situation will further decline in the coming period, considering the upcoming election campaign." They also notice that the CRA "is more concerned with technical issues than media freedom, and journalists generally do not perceive it as a body that protects their interests," while the Director-General is elected by political line, and the institution can no longer be perceived as an independent body (Cvjetićanin, Dardić and Hadžimešić 2018).

---

[11]   A temporary model to begin with; the parliament failed to agree on a new model before it expired.

There are fears that in the case of RTVFBiH and RTRS, appointments are now completely in the hands of the legislative bodies on entity levels. Legally, board members cannot belong to a political party or hold legislative, executive, or judicial power,[12] though they are often people who are closely aligned to political parties. The latest IREX MSI report finds "politicization continues to poison appointments to managerial positions at the entity's public broadcasters" (IREX 2016, 20).

Political influence is discernible through links between political parties and appointments of editors and journalists. Political parties unofficially have their say in appointing editors.[13] For example, when the Social Democratic Party (SDP) was in the ruling coalition in the Federation (2010–2012), it obtained significant control over FTV. This culminated with a leaked video in 2012 in which the SDP party leader was seen giving clear instructions to an FTV editor about exactly how to present an issue in the primetime news, as the editor nodded along (Sarajevo-x.com 2012). This link was not denied by the SDP or FTV, while the editor in question kept his position as one of the editors of the primetime news. One of the most prominent journalists at FTV in this period was later the SDP candidate for the Presidency of BiH during the 2014 elections, demonstrating the tight links between political parties and journalists (Slobodna Bosna 2012). The Program Council, which should ultimately represent citizens in the co-creation of editorial policy has been marginalized in the RTRS and entirely maligned in RTVFBiH and BHRT.[14]

Overt political influence translates into editorial policy and programming, which can be seen in the scant airtime given to critical programming, analysis, and alternative voices. The 2015 Alternative Report on BiH's EU Progress warned of a worrying level of political influence over PSB (Gavrić, Cvjetićanin, and Hadžić, 2015), and the same report in 2019 spoke of biased election coverage by PSB organizations, particularly RTRS (Cvjetićanin 2019). The 2019 IREX report found that the lack of media coverage of civic protests by RTRS was indicative of the broadcaster's support of the ruling party, the SNSD. This favoritism was confirmed by the CRA monitoring of the broadcaster in 2017 (IREX 2019). Primetime news often uses political parties and officials as sources but does not invite those with different opinions to speak to the public. In effect, this gives politicians an almost unlimited space to express their views, without questioning their claims. Their spokespeople are given more airtime than necessary, and government press releases are broadcast directly, without reflecting on their content. This has the effect of narrowing "the range of opinion in both entities" (U.S. Department of State 2015), which in practice means that PSB organizations are not fulfilling their obligation to provide political pluralism. The U.S. Bureau of Democracy considers FTV politically dependent and biased, while RTRS is 'directly controlled' by the RS government and its ruling party,

---

[12] "Members in all three broadcasters cannot perform the functions within the legislative, executive or judicial power, nor can they hold membership in political parties (according to Rule 57/2011 on Public Radio and TV Broadcasters)" (Hodžić 2015, 9).
[13] Sanela Hodžić (interview with the authors, March 2016).
[14] Sanela Hodžić (interview with the authors, March 2016).

the SNSD (U.S. Department of State 2015). Local media analysts point to the large amounts of airtime provided for leading political parties in comparison to opposition voices as a key example of its use as a governmental mouthpiece.[15]

Socio-Cultural Aspects of PSB

The ethnic power-sharing arrangement of Bosnian politics is reflected in the managerial structures, staffing, and editorial principles of the PSB system, which are meant to ensure equal representation of the three constituent people and minorities. The CRA requires that public radio and TV stations establish Editorial Councils which should reflect the ethnic, cultural, and religious character of their audience (CRA 2011, Article 4). Programming is also legally meant to reflect the needs, languages, and cultures of all constituent peoples and minorities (IREX 2016), however, there are no "quotas for each of the constituent peoples and ethnic minorities" (Jusić and Palmer 2008, 132) and the legal framework does not contain a clear provision and obligation to offer programs related to national minorities (Marko 2013,132). The focus on the three constituent peoples has essentially edged out any regard for ethnic, religious, sexual and any other minorities. For example, the LGBT population is entirely ignored by public media (Tanić 2015), Roma are represented by the public broadcasters in a "sensationalist and biased" way, while ethnic minorities are underrepresented (IREX 2016, 20). In 2018, when Bosnia became part of the so-called Balkan route for migration to the EU, PSB turned once again into a propaganda tool, allowing local politicians to use hate speech while leaving out critical reporting on how the ongoing humanitarian crisis was handled by local institutions (Ahmetašević 2019; Buljubašić 2019).

The central topic of the last decade has been the continuous request by Croat political parties to establish a separate Croat-language public TV channel. A majority of prominent linguists agree that Bosnian, Croatian, and Serbian belong to the same dialect continuum and are mutually intelligible. To that end, a group of local NGOs, linguists, activists, and academics signed the Declaration of Common Language in 2017, which affirmed that Bosnian, Croatian, Montenegrin, and Serbian are regional variations of one common polycentric language (Milekić 2017). However, these linguistic differences have been commandeered by ethnonationalist political parties and have proven to be highly polarizing issues when it comes to PSB in the country (See Trudgill 2000; Kordić 2010; Ronelle 2006).

---

[15] By analyzing the RTRS prime-time news program, Gordana Katana notes that the leading political party in this entity dominates the program, while the president of this party remains the central figure of the prime-time news (interview with the authors, March 2016). Opposition parties in RS, led by the SDS, the main opposition party, often point to SNSD control over RTRS. Some parties publicly incite people to boycott the license fee (see Alternativna televizija 2014; Katana 2016).

Hence, the issue of the lack of Croatian-language coverage in the existing PSB channels has been consistently raised by dominant ethno-nationalist Croat political parties. Supporters of these initiatives submitted an appeal to the Constitutional Court of BiH "to assess the constitutionality of existing laws ... [but] the Constitutional Court repudiated this appeal as unfounded" (Halilović and Džihana 2012, 192). A recent draft law was proposed in 2016, suggesting the establishment of three state-wide public broadcasters, one in each language with state-wide coverage. This issue had quieted down in 2018 and 2019. In 2019, RTV Herceg Bosna was launched as a partial response to this demand, funded mainly by Croatian-majority municipalities and cantons in the Federation, the Republic of Croatia, and Croatian emigres in the United States. However, it has been plagued by issues such as low studio quality and has been unable to expand its coverage—it mainly broadcasts reruns of television shows, despite the public money that has funded the project (R. D. 2020).

This issue is significantly influencing the overall process of the creation of the PSB system and is closely linked with the boycott of payment of the monthly license fee by Croat political parties and their followers (see earlier section on financing) until this request is met. However, some of the analysts we spoke to conclude that this, like many other politicized issues in Bosnia, is not about providing better services for people, but rather is an excuse to exploit ethnic division for political gain and for nationalist political elites to remain in power.

Technological Innovations and Digitalization

The digitalization of public broadcasting in BiH has lagged behind the rest of Europe, which switched off analogue signals in 2015. Although the Strategy on Digital Switchover was adopted in 2009 and the first deadline for transition to a digital signal was set to 2011, implementation was delayed for years[16] after several failed public tenders for equipment. The first phase of installation was finally completed by the end of October 2016 (SRNA 2016), and a call for tenders for the second phase was put out in March 2017. The second phase involves the procurement, installation, and testing of equipment that would digitalize more hubs in BiH and connect the country with its neighbors—the job is meant to be finished by early 2018 (FENA 2017). By 2019 only the expansion of digital signal coverage in Sarajevo, Banja Luka, and Mostar had been completed (Andrijani 2019). Among the host of reasons for the delay was that all three PSB systems had to name a delegate for the commission that will procure the

---

[16]   Former secretary of the Digital Terrestrial Television (DTT) Forum, Emir Vajzović, told us that the strategy was well thought out, but that they encountered political difficulties: "Suddenly, new people were appointed to our working groups ... we felt like the main problem was that the entire bureaucratic apparatus suddenly started working to prevent our work" (interview with the authors, May 2016).

digital equipment necessary for the process, RTRS failed to do so (Džaferović 2019). The Communications Regulatory Agency then decided to sidestep this issue and granted a license to a new operator, "Multiplex C," that will allow all TV stations in BiH to broadcast using a digital signal (Šarenkapa 2019). This is meant to be operational in 2020, as all current licenses for PSB organizations and commercial TV stations are due to expire in April 2020, after which they will not be able to be renewed as analog broadcasters (Rupčić 2019).

The digitalization process was slowed by political obstructions and a lack of accountability by the elected leaders, said Emir Vajzović, former general secretary of the DTT Forum.[17] The lack of a joint corporation meant that equipment was in the possession of each broadcaster[18] and this fragmented the process. The institutionalized lack of accountability arguably created an atmosphere in which the benefits of digitalization were never clearly articulated or pushed for by ruling politicians. In sum, the failure of digitalization was the collateral damage of dysfunctional public institutions.

New media platforms, such as cable and Internet Protocol Television (IPTV), online media, and social media platforms are reaching BiH, with many private print magazines turning solely to online. In 2018, mobile phone penetration in BiH reached 98.01%, and internet penetration was 90.49% (CRA 2018).

However, television remains the main source of news in BiH—a 2016 EBU infographic demonstrated that Bosnians watch the most television in Europe—on average 5 hours and 4 minutes a day (European Broadcasting Union, 2016). Hence, PSB organizations in BiH still rely on the idea of a traditional public and use traditional channels to communicate with them. The focus on delayed digitalization has arguably distracted PSB organizations from questions of modernization in the domain of production, internal re-structuring, and the introduction of new forms of governance, use of a variety of new communication channels (including social media), introduction of new services, and online presence in general (Sehl, Cornia and Nielsen 2016, 5). Only RTRS has begun construction on a digital studio, and the trend of integrated newsrooms (which blur the distinction between media such as radio, TV, and online content) has not begun in Bosnia. All three broadcasters have only started investing in their online presence, although their websites are ranked quite low in the country. Meeting these challenges is crucial for the sustainability of PSB in the modern age, maintaining their appeal to youth, and enhancing their legitimacy as public institutions.

---

[17] Emir Vajzović (interview with the authors, May 2016).

[18] Former advisor to the Minister of Communications and Transport, Mehmed Agović, claimed that the RS insisted on owning the equipment, refusing "to accept any reform which they saw as undermining their entity's powers and empowering a state-level public broadcasting system" (interview with the authors, March 2016). Nevertheless, those at RTRS see the situation differently. Siniša Mihailović of RTRS said that when, some years ago, RTRS obtained digitalization equipment and tested it from the Kozara mountain, the CRA fined them (interview with the authors, April 2016).

Conclusion

The issue of the development of public broadcasting in BiH has not undergone a true public debate and as a result, lacks legitimacy. The attempt to import a foreign model has failed, while the lack of incentive for local elites to foster independent public media leads to politicization and selective implementation of laws, an unsustainable funding model, institutional inertia within public broadcasting institutions, and an inability for PSB organizations to adapt to new technological innovations. The malfunctioning of the PSB system mirrors the low levels of democratic values and practices in the country (Economist Intelligence Unit 2016). The lack of international pressure and low involvement of the EU in PSB in BiH means a lack of external incentives for local elites to foster independent public media. The internal governance of public media needs substantial reforms. With regards to the Council of Europe's recommendations (Council of Europe 2012), BiH's PSB must first obtain independence from the government if it is to serve its role properly.

The failed transformation of Bosnia's state broadcaster to public service broadcasting reflects the stagnation and "unfinished transition" plagued by state capture by ethno-nationalist political elites and crony capitalism (Berend and Bugarič 2015, 779). The ruling ethnic oligarchs who control the political parties render political influence over PSB pervasive at the legislative, managerial, editorial, and journalistic levels. Constructive conversations on the topic are avoided, and the main debates on PSB in the country center on political questions rather than those of how PSB can fulfill its remit, become financially sustainable and adapt to new modes of production and media.

At the same time, international actors such as the EU generally stop short of demanding accountability from local politicians, leaving the PSB organizations' compromised independence unchallenged. Many scholars consider that international interventions to create public service broadcasting result in institutions which are merely "forms without substance," what some authors refer to as "isomorphic mimicry": an imitation of Western models without their actual implementation (Berend and Bugarič 2015, 780).

Many of our interlocutors believe that there is no public dialogue (or consensus) on the role of PSB in BiH, nor a shared conceptualization of the public interest in general. The public sphere in BiH is considered plural only where ethnic identity is concerned. Other forms of difference and other bases for the creation of communities are marginalized and underrepresented. While this lack of pluralism means that citizens are exposed to a "highly limited range of viewpoints" in their media consumption, the decline of print media and the increasing turn to social media and online sources for news raises other worries, namely about the prevalence of misinformation (IREX 2019).

Many supporters of PSB underscore that the broadcasters' existence should never come into question, but generally avoid critical questions as to whether PSB as a whole fulfills its goal (Mediacentar Online 2016). The media critics we spoke to all agreed that the lack of public trust in PSB organizations and/or a lack of understanding of their importance is due to low-quality programming and perceived political dependence. According to viewership measurements, fewer citizens are watching BHRT than commercial TV stations. For example, in 2015, BHRT was in seventh place among nine measured public and commercial TV stations on the national level (Arnautović, 2016a; 2016b). There is no form of public value test which would evaluate the economic efficiency and social value of PSB organizations.

There is recognition on the part of BiH's PSB organizations that their internal governance needs substantial reforms. On the level of management, the politicized processes of appointment and dismissal seem to have severely limited PSB management's ability to maximize efficiency, hampered additionally by bloated workforces. Our field research confirmed that by and large, the internal culture of the PSB organizations is not defined by "transparency, openness, responsiveness, and responsibility" (Ahmetašević and Hadžiristić 2017, 13), but rather by self-censorship and unprofessionalism.

The unsustainability of the PSB system and its dependence on political decision-making makes it very difficult to predict its future. It is hard to imagine an optimistic scenario without a new, sustainable funding model, a collective deliberation on what and who PSB is for, political autonomy of PSB, internal restructuring (including more members on the System Board of PSBs, and selection of candidates based on expertise and professional experience rather than ethnicity), as well as more attention paid to this issue by EU enlargement actors. In the absence of these conditions, likely, BHRT will eventually have to stop emitting due to a lack of funding (the consequences for its 800 employees would likely be dire), and entity broadcasters will increasingly receive their funding from entity budgets, which could additionally imperil PSB's independence and further divide the broadcasters.

A collective deliberation on the value and remit of PSB in BiH is necessary for successfully achieving its aims in the future. Uncritically supporting the continued existence of PSB in its current form without questioning their function is not enough (Mediacentar Online 2016). Ending the "vicious cycle" of a lack of funding and political will require redefining the role of public broadcasting by listening not only to politicians but the voices of the public (Marko 2016).

References

Ahmetašević, Nidžara. 2019. "Mediji, političari i migranti: Jezik mržnje umjesto solidarnosti" [The media, politicians, and migrants: hate speech instead of solidarity]. *Mediacentar Online,* May 29. https://media.ba/bs/mediametar/mediji-politicari-i-migranti-jezik-mrznje-umjesto-solidarnosti.

Ahmetašević, Nidžara, and Tea Hadžiristić. 2017. *The Future of Public Service Broadcasting in Bosnia and Herzegovina.* Sarajevo: Analitika Center for Social Research. https://www.analitika.ba/sites/default/files/publikacije/psb_bih.pdf.

Alternativna televizija. 2014. "SDS: SNSD preuzeo kontrolu nad RTRS-om" [SDS: SNSD has taken control of RTRS]. *Alternativna televizija*, March 22. https://www. atvbl .com/sds-snsd-preuzeo-kontrolu-nad-rtrs-om.

Andrijani, Željko. 2019. "Digitalizacija u BiH: Podržavamo kompromisni prijedlog [Digitization in BiH: we support the compromise proposal]." *Večernji list,* May 21. https://www.vecernji.ba/vijesti/digitalizacija-u-bih-podrzavamo-kompromisni-pri-jedlog-1320654.

Arnautović, Aldin. 2016a. "A Decade of Failures: BHRT. Employee Surplus and Poor Results." *Mediacentar Online,* September 6. https://www.media.ba/en/magazin / decade-failures-bhrt-employee-surplus-and-poor-results.

——. 2016b. "A Decade of Failures: Public Broadcasting Service Owes Millions." *Medi-acentar Online,* September 2. https://www.media.ba/en/investigative-journalism/ decade-failures-public-broadcasting-service-owes-millions.

Berend, Ivan T., and Bojan Bugarič. 2015. "Unfinished Europe: Transition from Com-munism to Democracy in Central and Eastern Europe." *Journal of Contemporary History* 50, no. 4 (October): 768–785.

BHRT. 2016. "Izvještaj o radu i poslovanju Radiotelevizije Bosne i Hercegovine za 2015" godinu [Report on the functioning and performance of radio-television of Bosnia and Herzegovina in 2015]. Sarajevo: BHRT.

Boev, Boyko. 2012. *Analysis of the Laws Pertaining to the Public Service Broadcasting System of Bosnia and Herzegovina.* Vienna: Office of the OSCE Representative on Freedom of the Media.

Buljubašić, Belma. 2019. "Izvještavanje o migrantskoj i izbjegličkoj krizi u BiH: insinu-acije, rasizam i ksenofobija" [Reporting on the migrant and refugee crisis in BiH: insinuations, racism, and xenophobia]. *Mediacentar Online*, May 12. https://me-dia.ba/bs/magazin/izvjestavanje-o-migrantskoj-i-izbjeglickoj-krizi-u-bih-insinu-acije-rasizam-i-ksenofobija.

Council of Europe. 2012. *Recommendation CM/Rec(2012)1 of the Committee of Ministers to Member States on Public Service Media Governance.* Accessed May 11, 2020. https:// search.coe.int/cm/Pages/result_details.aspx?ObjectID=09000016805cb4b4.

CRA. 2018. *Godišnji Izvještaj Regulatorne Agencije za Komunikacije za 2018. godinu* [Yearly report of the Communications Regulatory Agency for 2018]. Sarajevo: CRA. https://docs.rak.ba//documents/b9be1646-a90f-4560-9bcc-0a1264735aa9.pdf.

——. 2013. *Analiza tržišta emitovanja u BiH* [Analysis of the broadcasting market in BiH]. Sarajevo: CRA. https://rak.ba/bs-Latn-BA/brdcst-market-analysis.

——. 2011. *Rule 57/2011 on Public Radio and Television Broadcasters,* Sarajevo: CRA.

Cvjetićanin, Tijana, eds. 2019. *2019 Alternative Report on the Application of Bosnia and Herzegovina for the European Union Membership: Political Criteria.* Sarajevo: Sara-jevo Open Center. https://eu-monitoring.ba/site/wp-content/uploads/2019 /04/ alternativni_eng-1.pdf.

Cvjetićanin, Tijana, Dragana Dardić, and Inela Hadžimešić, eds. 2018. *2018 Alternative Analytical Report on the Application of Bosnia and Herzegovina for the European Union Membership: Political Criteria.* Sarajevo: Sarajevo Open Center. http://eu-monitor-ing.ba/site/wp-content/uploads/2018/04/APR-ENG_2018_web-1.pdf.

Džaferović, Adem. 2019. "Ekonomski stručnjaci upozoravaju na gubitke koji se nanose državi stopiranjem procesa digitalizacije, a u Ministarstvu ukazuju na opstrukcije RTRS-a" [Economists warn of losses from delays in digitalization process, ministry points to RTRS obstruction]. *Oslobođenje,* March 20. https://www.oslobodjenje.ba /vijesti/bih/besmisleno-je-blokiranje-digitalizacije-442413.

Economist Intelligence Unit. *2016 Democracy Index 2015: Free Speech Under Attack.* Accessed May 4, 2020. https://www.eiu.com/public/topical_report.aspx?campaignid=DemocracyIndex2015.

European Broadcasting Union. 2016. *Europeans & Television: An Overview of TV Viewing Habits Across Europe.* Geneva: EBU.

European Commission. 2019. *Analytical Report Accompanying the Document Communication from the Commission to the European Parliament and the Council Commission Opinion on Bosnia and Herzegovina's Application for Membership of the European Union.* May 25. Brussels: European Commission. https://ec.europa.eu/ neighbourhood-enlargement/sites/near/files/20190529-bosnia-and-herzegovina-analytical-report.pdf.

FENA. 2017. "Objavljen međunarodni tender za drugu fazu digitalizacije RTV servisa u BiH" [International tender announced for the second phase of public broadcaster digitalization in BiH]. *Klix.ba,* March 16. https://www.klix.ba/ vijesti/bih/objavljen-medjunarodni-tender-za-drugu-fazu-digitalizacije-rtv-servisa-u-bih/170316125.

Gavrić, Saša, Tijana Cvjetićanin, and Inela Hadžić, eds. 2015. *Alternativni izvještaj o napretku 2015: politički kriteriji* [Alternative progress report 2016: political criteria]. Sarajevo: Sarajevo Open Center. https://eu-monitoring.ba/site/wp-content/ uploads/2015/07/Alternativni-izvještaj-o-napretku-BiH-2015.pdf.

Halilović, Mehmed, and Amer Džihana, eds. 2012. *Media Law in Bosnia and Herzegovina.* Sarajevo: Internews in Bosnia and Herzegovina.

Hodžić, Sanela. 2015. *Monitoring EU Guidelines in Bosnia and Herzegovina: Continuing Political Pressures and Obstructions.* Ljubljana: Peace Institute. https:// www.mirovni-institut.si/wp-content/uploads/2012/12/BiH-Continuing-political-pressures-and-obstructions.pdf.

Horvat, Srećko, and Igor Štiks. 2015. *Welcome to the Desert of Post-Socialism: Radical Politics after Yugoslavia.* London: Verso Books.

I. Č. 2017. "Od augusta naplata RTV takse uz račun za struju Elektroprivrede BiH" [From August monthly license fee to be collected with the electricity bill of Elektroprivreda BiH]. *Klix.ba,* August 1. https://www.klix.ba/vijesti/bih/od-augusta-naplata-rtv-takse-uz-racun-za-struju-elektroprivrede-bih/170722042.

International Monetary Fund. 2019. *World Economic Outlook Database.* October 2019. https://www.imf.org/external/pubs/ft/weo/2019/02/weodata/index.aspx.

IREX. 2019. *Media Sustainability Index 2019: Bosnia and Herzegovina.* Washington, DC: IREX. https://www.irex.org/sites/default/files/pdf/media-sustainability-index-europe-eurasia-2019-bosnia-herzegovina.pdf.

——. 2018. *Media Sustainability Index 2018: Bosnia and Herzegovina.* Washington, DC: IREX, 2018. Accessed on May 9, 2020. https://www.irex.org/sites/default/files / pdf/media-sustainability-index-europe-eurasia-2018-bosnia.pdf.

——. 2017. *Media Sustainability Index 2017: The Development of Sustainable Independent Media in Europe and Eurasia.* Washington, DC: IREX, https://www.irex.org/ sites/default/files/pdf/media-sustainability-index-europe-eurasia-2017-full.pdf.

——. 2016. *Media Sustainability Index 2016: The Development of Sustainable Independent Media in Europe and Eurasia.* Washington, DC: IREX. https://www.irex.org/sites/ default/files/pdf/media-sustainability-index-europe-eurasia-2016-full.pdf.pdf.

Jahić, Dino. 2018. *Nations in Transit 2018: Bosnia and Herzegovina.* Washington, DC: Freedom House. https://freedomhouse.org/sites/default/files/NiT2018_Bosnia. pdf.

———. 2017. *Nations in Transit 2017: Bosnia and Herzegovina.* Washington, DC: Freedom House. https://freedomhouse.org/sites/default/files/NiT2017_Bosnia.pdf.

———. 2016. *Nations in Transit 2016.* Washington, DC: Freedom House. https://freedomhouse.org/sites/default/files/FH_NIT2016_Final_FWeb.pdf.

Jakubowicz, Karol. 2011. "Public Service Broadcasting: Product (and Victim?) of Public Policy." In *The Handbook of Global Media and Communication Policy*, edited by Robin Mansell and Marc Raboy, 210–229. Oxford: Wiley-Blackwell.

Judah, Tim. 2019. "Bosnia Powerless to Halt Demographic Decline." *BIRN Balkan Insight*, November 21. https://balkaninsight.com/2019/11/21/bosnia-powerless-to-halt-demographic-decline/.

Jusić, Tarik, and L. Kendall Palmer. 2008. "The Media and Power-Sharing: Towards an Analytical Framework for Understanding Media Policies in Post-Conflict Societies: Public Broadcasting in Bosnia and Herzegovina." *Global Media Journal* (Polish Edition) 1, no. 4 (December): 110–139.

Jusić, Tarik, and Nidzara Ahmetašević. 2013. *Media Reforms Through Intervention: International Media Assistance in Bosnia and Herzegovina.* Sarajevo: Analitika Center for Social Research.

Jusić, Mirna, and Amar Numanović. 2015. *Flexible Labour in Inflexible Environment: Reforms of Labour Market Institutions in Bosnia and Herzegovina in Comparative Perspective.* Sarajevo: Analitika Center for Social Research.

Katana, Gordana, "RTRS: postupi po naredenju!" [RTRS: Do as ordered!]. *Analiziraj. ba*, February 27. https://analiziraj.ba/2016/02/27/rtrs-postupi-po-naredenju/.

Klix.ba. 2016. "Bosnia and Herzegovina the Fifth Poorest Country in Europe" [Bosna i Hercegovina peta najsiromašnija država u Evropi]. *Klix.ba*, February 22. https://www.klix.ba/vijesti/bih/bosna-i-hercegovina-peta-najsiromasnija-drzava-u-evropi/160221022.

Kordić, Snježana. 2010. *Jezik i nacionalizam* [Language and nationalism]. Zagreb: Durieux.

Law on Public Radio-Television Service of Bosnia and Herzegovina (BHT Law 2005) [Zakon o javnom radiotelevizijskom servisu Bosne i Hercegovine]. *Official Gazette of Bosnia and Herzegovina* 92/05.

Law on Public Radio-Television Service of Republika Srpska (RTRS Law 2006) [Zakon o Radioteleviziji Republike Srpske]. *Official Gazette of Republika Srpska* 49/06.

Law on Public Radio-Television Service of the Federation of Bosnia and Herzegovina (RTVFBiH Law 2008) [Zakon o Radioteleviziji Federacije BiH]." *Official Gazette of Federation of Bosnia and Herzegovina* 48/08.

Law on Public Radio-Television System of Bosnia and Herzegovina (System Law 2005) [Zakon o javnom radiotelevizijskom sistemu Bosne i Hercegovine]. *Official Gazette of Bosnia and Herzegovina* 78/05.

Marko, Davor. 2016. "Javni emiteri moraju radikalno preispitati svrhu svoga postojanja" [Public broadcasters must radically question their raison d'être]. *Mediacentar Online*, July 7. http://www.media.ba/bs/magazin-novinarstvo/javni-emiteri-moraju-radikalno-preispitati-svrhu-svoga-postojanja.

———, ed. 2013. *Informisanje na jezicima manjina na Zapadnom Balkanu: Sloboda, pristup, marginalizacija* [Informing in the languages of minorities in the Western Balkans: Freedom, access, marginalization]. Sarajevo: Media plan institut.

Mediacentar Online. 2016. "Postojanje BHRT-a ne smije biti upitno" [The existence of BHRT must not be put into question]. *Mediacentar Online*, June 3. https://www.media.ba/bs/magazin-novinarstvo/postojanje-bhrt-ne-smije-biti-upitno.

Milekić, Sven. 2017. "Post-Yugoslav 'Common Language' Declaration Challenges Nationalism." *BIRN Balkan Insight,* March 30. http://www.balkaninsight.com/en /article/ post-yugoslav-common-language-declaration-challenges-nationalism-03-29-2017.

Mujanović, Jasmin. 2014. "The *Baja* Class and the Politics of Participation." In *Unbribable Bosnia and Herzegovina: The Fight for the Commons,* edited by Damir Arsenijević, 135–144. Baden-Baden: Nomos.

Mujkić, Asim. 2007. "We, the Citizens of Ethnopolis." *Constellations: An International Journal of Critical and Democratic Theory* 14, no. 1 (March): 112–128.

Musanovic, Mirza. 2011. "Zašto tone televizija Federacije BiH" [Why FTV is sinking]. *Radio Feral,* February 13.

Pelešević, Elvir. 2016. "Bosnian and Herzegovinian Parliament Secures BHRT's survival … so far." *Eurovisionary,* June 15.

R. D. 2020. "TV Herceg-Bosne i pored 800 hiljada KM javnih sredstava na niskim granama" [TV Herceg-Bosna doing poorly even with 800,0000KM in public funds]. *Klix.ba,* February 5. https://www.klix.ba/vijesti/bih/tv-herceg-bosne-i-pored-800-hiljada-km-javnih-sredstava-na-niskim-granama/200205129.

Ronelle, Alexander. 2006. *Bosnian, Croatian, Serbian: A Grammar with Sociolinguistic Commentary.* Madison: University of Wisconsin Press.

Rupčić, Valentina. 2019. "Pomakli smo BiH sa sramotne pozicije posljednje zemlje u Europi bez pokrivenosti 4G mrežom" [We have moved BiH from the shameful position of being the last country in Europe without 4G network coverage]. *Večernji list,* October 14. https://www.vecernji.ba/vijesti/pomakli-smo-bih-sa-sramotne-pozicije-posljednje-zemlje-u-europi-bez-pokrivenosti-4g-mrezom-1359479.

Sarajevo-x.com. 2012. "Kako Zlatko Lagumdžija uređuje Dnevnik FTV-a" [How Zlatko Lagumdžija edits the FTV news]. *Klix.ba,* March 4. https://www.klix.ba/vijesti /bih/kako-zlatko-lagumdzija-uredjuje-dnevnik-ftv-a/120304013.

Šarenkapa, Almir. 2019. "RAK objavio poziv kojim deblokira proces digitalizacije" [CRA issues call which unblocks digitalization process]. *Oslobođenje,* June 24. https://www.oslobodjenje.ba/vijesti/bih/rak-objavio-poziv-kojim-deblokira-proces-digitalizacije-467735.

Sehl, Annika, Alessio Cornia, and Rasmus Kleis Nielsen. 2016. *Public Service News and Digital Media.* Oxford: Reuters Institute for the Study of Journalism. https://reutersinstitute.politics.ox.ac.uk/sites/default/files/research/files/Public%2520Service%2520News%2520and%2520Digital%2520Media.pdf.

Sittig, Hendrik, and Darija Fabijanić. 2019. *Strong Majority in South East Europe: Public Service Media are Important for Democracy Results of KAS Media Programme's Survey on the Significance of Public Service Media in Ten Countries of South East Europe.* Berlin: Konrad Adenauer Stiftung. https://www.kas.de/documents/252038 /4520172/Strong+Majority+in+South+East+Europe.+Public+Service+Media+Are+Important+for+Democracy.pdf/ade48621-51e4-c8e2-5f15-d70fddf-c272f?version =1.0&t=1572526295521.

Slobodna Bosna. 2012. "Bakir Hadžiomerović kandidat SDP-a za člana Predsjedništva BiH!" [Bakir Hadžiomerović is an SDP candidate for the BiH Presidency!]. *Slobodna Bosna,* July 12. https://www.slobodna-bosna.ba/vijest/15207/bakir_hadziomerovic _kandidat_sdp_a_za_chlana_predsjednistva_bih.html.

Smajić, Zekerijah, and Srećko Latal. 2016. "Broadcasters' Collapse Mirrors Bosnia's Own Decline." *BIRN Balkan Insight,* March 2. https://balkaninsight.com/2016/03/02 /broadcasters-collapse-mirrors-bosnia-s-own-decline-03-01-2016/.

SRNA. 2016. "Konačno Javni RTV servisi u BiH počeli emitovanje digitalnog signala" [Finally, public broadcasters in BiH begin to broadcast digital signals]. *Blic*, October 14. https://www.blic.rs/vesti/republika-srpska/konacno-javni-rtv-servisi-u-bih-poceli-emitovanje-digitalnog-signala/6creq0c.

Tanić, Dalibor. 2015. "Pozitivnija slika u BH. Medijiama o LGBT temama" [More positive picture of LGBT themes in Bosnian media]. *LGBT.BA,* July 20. https://lgbt.ba/pozitivnija-slika-u-bh-medijima-o-lgbt-temama/.

Transparency International Bosnia and Herzegovina. 2020. "BiH među zemljama koje najviše nazaduju u borbi protiv korupcije" [BiH among the countries backsliding the most in the fight against corruption]. *Transparency International Bosnia and Herzegovina*, January 23. https://ti-bih.org/english-bih-medju-zemljama-koje-najvise-nazaduju-u-borbi-protiv-korupcije/?fbclid=IwAR2vbfDSYloVt-Cl8-VX-zOkrCFduYQ1_CNa2QptueOC9WZvibpGlErDfMl0.

Trudgill, Peter. 2000. *Sociolinguistics*. London: Penguin Books.

Udovičić, Radenko. 2015. *Working Conditions for Journalists in Bosnia and Herzegovina: Journalists in a Gap Between Devastated Media and Legal Insecurity*. Bucharest: Center for Independent Journalism. https://www.media.ba/sites/default/files/working_conditions_bosnia_and_herzegovina_march_2015.pdf.

U.S. Department of State. 2015. *Country Reports on Human Rights Practices for 2015*. Washington, DC: U.S. Department of State. https://2009-2017.state.gov/j/drl/rls/hrrpt/humanrightsreport/index.htm.

Voltmer, Katrin. 2013. *Building Media Systems in the Western Balkans: Lost between Models and Realities*. Sarajevo: Analitika Center for Social Research. https://www.analitika.ba/sites/default/files/publikacije/voltmer_k_-_rrpp_building_media_-_wp10_-_3dec2013_final_for_publishing.pdf.

World Bank. n.d. *The Poverty and Equity Data Portal: Bosnia and Herzegovina*. Accessed May 11, 2020. http://povertydata.worldbank.org/poverty/country/BIH.

Zenica Info. 2019. "Već dvije godine Elektroprivreda BiH nezakonito naplaćuje RTV taksu od gradana" [Elektroprivreda BiH has been illegally charging RTV fees for two years]. *Zenica Info*, June 13. https://zenicainfo.ba/2019/06/13/vec-dvije-godine-elektroprivreda-bih-nezakonito-naplacuje-rtv-taksu-od-gradana/.

CHAPTER 4

The Future of Public Service Broadcasting in Croatia[1]

Davor Marko

Introduction

This chapter provides an analysis of the transformation of the former state-controlled Radio-Television of Zagreb into a public broadcaster, renamed to the Croatian Radio-Television (Hrvatska radiotelevizija, or HRT) after the first multi-party election in 1990. The case of the Public Service Broadcaster in Croatia is somewhat unique compared to other regional broadcasters. HRT's funding model has been considered as one of the most successful. HRT's license fee collection system has been continuously and systematically improved since the 1960s when it was first introduced. Albeit the level of editorial independence and financial sustainability of Croatian PSB has seen frequent oscillations at different points in time, HRT maintains its financial sustainability, and manages internal development by relying mostly on its own resources. Like other countries in the region, PSB in Croatia is under permanent political pressure, which derogated its editorial policy in recent years, while its programming has been commercialized and became less distinctive from content provided by HRT's commercial competitors.

The analysis provided within this chapter deals with several aspects of the HRT transformation. First, the chapter focuses on the development of regulation and PSB-related media policies. The second aspect outlined in the chapter is the status and the role of the PSB organization in Croatia, with special attention to PSB remit, funding model, formal and de-facto independence, market share, and the progress regarding technological innovations and digitalization. Finally, the chapter deals with the challenges to the PSB operation in Croatia, taking into account ongoing debates on the global level, as well as country-specific discussions.

The development of the regulatory and legal framework in Croatia has been influenced by the Europeanization processes taking place after 2000 and by political interference until Croatia became an EU member in 2013. Due to

---

[1]   The analysis of public service broadcasting in Croatia was conducted for the period until the end of 2017.

technological developments, commercialization, audience fragmentation and information abundance, the status, funding model and social role of PSB are highly contested (see Postman 1970 and Strate 2006). To evolve into a genuine public media, Croatian Radio-Television faces these challenges both internally and externally. This chapter briefly elaborates on these challenges taking into account research evidence and relevant theoretical contributions presented in the introductory chapter of this book.

PSB in Croatia: Background, Development, and Challenges

Croatian Radio-Television (HRT) is the legal successor to the Radio-Television of Zagreb that operated until May 26, 1956. Since the beginning of the 1990s, it was part of the Yugoslav Radio-Television (JRT), the state broadcasting system that coordinated the exchange of radio and television programs between former Yugoslav republics. JRT ceased to exist in 1992 and the war (1991–1995) prevented HRT from using its technological and human capacities to develop into a public service immediately.

During the 1990s, HRT was largely a party-controlled state broadcaster (Kurspahić 2003; Thompson 1995; Plevnik 2002). The ruling party, the Croatian Democratic Union (HDZ), imposed control over it and laid off almost a quarter of its employees, some of which because of their political or ethnical belonging (Građanska inicijativa 1993; Thompson 1995). In that period, there were no private TV stations with a significant share or influence at the national level, which left HRT in a monopolistic position (Kurspahić 2003). From 1990 to 2000, the law regulating HRT was changed six times, and five HRT general directors in this period, were party (HDZ) members (Car 2005, 67). The first systematic attempt to reform the HRT into public service came in 1998 when a group of editors and journalists from the HRT and other respectable media gathered around the so-called "Forum 21" movement, adopted a resolution in which they advocated for applying a series of normative criteria, corresponding with the Council of Europe recommendations (1999), as a necessary precondition for a HRT reform. However, the regime ignored these appeals (Car 2005, 65–66).

Following the political changes in 2000[2] and the liberalization of the political sphere, the introduction of new legal and regulatory frameworks and the establishment of the dual broadcasting system created the conditions for the substantial transformation of the HRT.

---

[2] In 2000, the conservative government led by the Croatian Democratic Union lost the elections for the first time since Croatian independence and the left-oriented Social-Democratic Party established a new ruling coalition.

From 2000 onward, extensive changes shaped the media scene in Croatia, further influencing the development and operation of the HRT. These included the full implementation of a dual system with commercial competitors that attracted increased attention of media audiences; a policy development process which was mostly created from the top (policy documents and laws were usually tailored by politicians, while the influence of media experts, NGOs, and other non-state actors were limited to consultative roles); frequent changes of legal solutions that resulted in decreased independence and autonomy of the PSB organization. The EU accession process significantly influenced the process of HRT development, speeding up some decisions, for example, state aid regulations. Permanent technological innovations and digitalization forced the HRT management to develop strategies and take an active role in restructuring its organization and production logic, and to follow the new trends of the market. Unfortunately, due to fragile institutional guarantees, the editorial policy of the PSB organization in Croatia has been significantly affected and its independence undermined as a result of political interference.

HRT broadcasts five television channels—HTV1 and HTV2 (offered throughout MUX 1), HTV3 (a channel specializing in culture and the arts), HTV4 (a 24-hour news channel), as well as one TV channel offered through satellite. It also has 3 radio channels with national coverage, 8 regional radio stations, and 2 international channels, Voice of Croatia (*Glas Hrvatske*) and the Croatian Channel for the diaspora.

The Agency for Electronic Media (AEM) and its service for monitoring are legally obliged to supervise HRT and implement the provisions of the audiovisual and radio programs through satellite, Internet, cable, and other means of transmitting.

Regulation of PSB in Croatia

The Law on Croatian Radio-Television 2010, in Article 3, defines the HRT as a public institution founded by the Republic of Croatia, and grants public broadcasting services independent status from any political or economic interest. Its basic activities include "production of radio, audiovisual and multimedia program, music production, providing audio and audiovisual media services, multimedia services and electronic publications as public services." The law was amended in 2012, introducing changes in the domain of the HRT governance and the mechanisms of its public control. Following the examples of some countries (the Royal Charter in the UK, for example), the Croatian Government and HRT managerial board signed an agreement that regulates the establishment of a service with a public mission and the financing of the programming obligations of the HRT under the law. The agreement also defines the type, scope, and content of public services that the HRT can provide.

The main governing bodies of the HRT are the General Director, the Directorate, Supervisory Board, and the Program Council (for an organizational chart see Figure 4.1). The General Director responsible for the entire PSB organization's operation is appointed by the Croatian Parliament by a majority of votes. The Supervisory Board, with 5 members (4 are elected in the Parliament and 1 represents HRT employees), controls the HRT operation. The HRT Directorate includes the Director-General, and heads of the working units within the HRT (Program, Production, Technology, and Management). The Program Council promotes and protects the public interest and oversights HRT programming. It has 11 members out of which 9 are appointed by the parliament, and 2 by HRT employees.

Figure 4.1: Organizational Chart of HRT

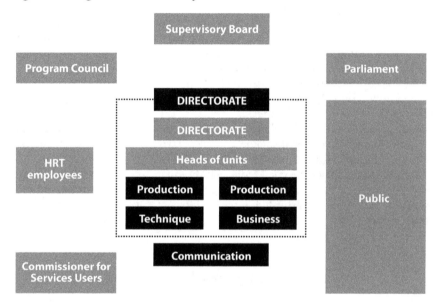

Source: Marko (2017)

Even though the law in 2010 was created and formulated to guarantee the political independence of the PSB organization, it did not meet expectations, and in practice, it caused the so-called "governance crisis" (Car and Andrijašević 2012, 89). Hence, the introduction of a new managerial/governance structure in 2012 made it easier for the parliamentary majority to influence the process of appointments of the main managerial bodies. The Parliament and its Committee on Media and Information are responsible for the selection of the Director-General, the appointment of 4 out of 5 members of the Supervisory Board, and for all 11 members of the HRT Program Council.

In order to be more transparent, and to strengthen its direct communication with the audience, HRT introduced the Commissioner for Consumers in 2011. The Law on HRT of 2010, Article 32, prescribes that the commissioner is "responsible for examining complaints and suggestions of viewers, listeners and other users of HRT services." As an autonomous and independent agent, the commissioner must submit reports to the HRT Program Council twice a year.

From 2011 this function has been performed by an experienced and retired radio journalist, who was re-appointed in 2015. According to commissioner records, there has been a drastic increase in the number of citizens who are contacting the commissioner. Most of these complaints concern inaccurate or incomplete information, while the use of the Croatian language and freedom of speech are in second place. It is followed by complaints that indicate political bias in journalistic reporting (Marko 2017).

Funding Model of PSB in Croatia

The current funding model for HRT has been considered as highly efficient. As a result of long-term, continuous, and systematic investments, HRT today has a functional, self-sustainable, information system to collect and manage data on each subscriber and to check the implementation of the Law on HRT when it comes to its financial aspect. The latest development of this model, between 2000 and 2010, was affected by the new EU state aid regulations and decisions, which resulted in a decreased amount of advertising in the PSB program. Before these changes, regulations allowed HRT to broadcast 12 minutes per hour, while now, during primetime, this is limited to 4 minutes per hour. It was concluded that that PSB should be funded through the license fee and limited commercial revenues (Marko 2017, 27–30).

Primary incomes for the HRT come from a monthly-based license fee (*pristojba* in Croatian) that each citizen who owns or possesses a receiving set (radio, television, or other devices) should pay. The law also regulates the distribution of collected funds—the largest portion goes for the TV and radio program production, while 30 percent is allocated to cover HRT operative costs (Law on Croatian Radio-Television 2010).

Beginning in 2000, when the model was updated, the share of funds collected through the license fee increased significantly, and has remained stable since 2010 (see Figure 4.2 and Table 4.1).

Figure 4.2: Total HRT Income and Income from the License Fee (2000–2014), in Million EUR

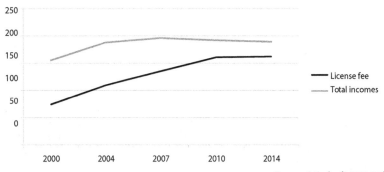

An important pillar of this funding model includes cooperation with law offices, public notaries, and state financial institutions. Cooperation with law firms started in 2003,[3] when the system of enforced payment was introduced. This system includes notification of non-paid service, and three stages of warnings before a law firm begins the enforcement process. Due to its internal information system, HRT is able to monitor the process and oversee its success. The process was additionally accelerated with the involvement of notaries who could quickly obtain final legal solutions. Additionally, cooperation with financial institutions such as the Financial Agency (FINA) enforced the final payment based on legal solutions. As a result of such enforcement efforts, in 2015 the collection rate of the license fee increased from 95% to 98% (Marko 2017, 27–30).

As part of its structure, HRT has the Service for the License Fee which reduced the number of employees from 71 (in 2003) to 63 (in 2011) but increased its costs mainly because workload per person significantly increased. At the same time, the number of subscribers increased from 1,145,725 to 1,210,727. Within the period of three years, HRT has established a more transparent and planned financial operation that contributed to the rationalization of its operation (HRT 2013a; HRT 2013b). As part of this process and internal restructuring, HRT reduced its number of employees from 3,360 to 2,926 (HRT 2015).

Table 4.1: Income and Expenses of HRT (2012–2015) in Million EUR

Year	Revenues	Expenses	Operative incomes
2015 (9 months)	142.6	123.2	19.4
2014	188.5	181.3	7.2
2013	186.5	181.6	4.9
2012	195.9	198.1	No information

Source: HRT (2013a; 2014; 2015)

---

[3] The first law firm that HRT established cooperation with in 2003, was Hanžeković and Partners, while in 2011 it started cooperation with several other law firms to make the process competitive, measuring their effectiveness and results. Each law office has the freedom to choose a notary firm to work with, while the HRT License Fee Department only monitors and follows the efficiency of their work.

Program Quality

Stakeholders in Croatia believe that HRT, besides its informative and educational role, is one of the most important places to demonstrate creative potentials and it is also a valuable resource in a symbolic, cultural, social, and economic sense. Nevertheless, there is a decreased satisfaction with the HRT program in the recent period.

Objections run from allegations of partisan reporting, a lack of flexibility in breaking-news situations, and excessively high monthly subscription fees. With the arrival of commercial networks—Nova TV in 1998 and RTL in 2003—HRT faced serious challengers and its management decided to compete and chase the ratings, albeit not with high quality programming but with popular programs (Car and Andrijašević 2012, 24–26). This resulted in two trends: The first is related to the "decrease in the share of the factual/information model that dominated the first decades of television broadcasting in Croatia," while the second denotes the rise of entertainment-oriented programming, affected mostly by commercial television after 2000 (Peruško and Čuvalo 2014).

Even the potential of two specialized channels (HTV3 for culture, and HTV4 as a news channel) that contributed to the plurality of content at HRT has not been fulfilled. Another contribution of HRT to content plurality is the production of minority programs. Content related to minorities has been regularly broadcasted in prime-time news and on HTV4, and in different TV shows. HRT also has a special page on its website with new regularly updated material related to minority groups (manjine.hrt.hr). Radio and television programs intended to inform national minorities are available on-demand as well (Kanižaj and Šalaj 2004; Kanižaj 2005; Car and Kanižaj 2010).

The HRT Program Council regularly organizes thematic sessions to evaluate program quality. This is considered as an important mechanism for assessing and discussing program quality.

Technological Innovations and Digitalization

The digitalization process in Croatia was initiated in 2002 when Transmitters and Communications Ltd. began broadcasting experimental programs in digital terrestrial technology (DVB-T) (Hajduk 2011, 151). Transmitters and Communications Ltd. was part of the HRT system until 2001, when the new Law on HRT established it as an independent legal entity of public status that could compete, along with other bidders, for the position of the multiplex operator. By 2006 Croatia was entirely covered by a digital signal, and the country met the international deadline three years in advance, in 2010.

Following the adoption of the Analogue to Digital Television Broadcasting Switchover Strategy in 2008 and subsequent discussion, Croatian authorities decided to establish a model that would be implemented in an obligatory date, and that would come with a regional (phased) switchover, MPEG-2 standard of compression, subsidies for equipment, and an information campaign (Car and Andrijašević 2013, 283). During the process of digitalization, Croatia was divided into nine digital regions in line with specific, mostly technical and geographic, criteria (Hajduk 2011, 158–160). This model was initially tested in one of the smallest digital regions of Istria, and due to initial success, the Croatian authorities applied it, step by step, in all other regions. The Croatian model of digital switchover has been acknowledged as a model of good practice internationally (Hajduk 2011, 152).

The most problematic issue related to the digitalization process concerns the selection of a compression format. The Republic of Croatia has opted for MPEG-2 (and not for MPEG-4, which was, for example, chosen in Serbia, and which is now in use in the EU). The subsequent discussion led towards the transition to the DVB-T2 system, and this was primarily driven by the fact that the system in place did not offer an efficient way of broadcasting in HD format, while multiplexes did not have enough capacity.[4]

In a digital era, three multiplexes are operating in Croatia, two with national coverage (MUX A and MUX B, with the DVB-T standard definition, and MPEG-2 compression format), and one that combines specialized low-budget programs of national broadcasters, for example, HTV4, a 24-hour news program, and programs of regional and local broadcasters (MUX D DVB-T, the standard definition, MPEG-2). Since 2009, the public company Transmitters and Communications Ltd. has been administering the operation of the multiplexes.

During the creation of multiplexes, it was discussed whether or not PSB should be awarded and manage a multiplex on its own. It was decided that general channels with national coverage would be allocated to MUX A (HRT1, HRT2, RTL, and Nova TV), specialized channels to MUX B, while MUX D was created to enable the broadcasting of specialized low-cost channels, as well as programs of regional and local TV stations. Some believe that HRT could better manage the multiplex if it were in a position to do it solely. For example, it could establish and run an experimental program in HD format.

Following the 2010 law provisions, HRT introduced the news channel HTV4, that was launched at the end of 2012, while HTV3, which started broadcasting in the same year, was not designed as a family channel (as it was envisioned by the law), but as a specialized channel for culture and the arts. Both were supposed to start earlier, but they did not, since HRT was poorly prepared for the process, which affected its efficiency. In addition to a lack of technical and financial resources, the HRT management also lacked a clear strategic orientation to take advantage of the process of transformation. Compared to the commercial

---

4   The alternative option is H.265, which supports 4K format.

TV stations on the market, HRT represents a large and inefficient organization, which is slowly moving towards a functional model adapted for digital production (Car and Andrijašević 2012, 32).

HRT also began an internal reorganization to adjust its structure and operation to meet new demands and production/distribution logic. In 2013 and until 2017, a new internal strategy was adopted, that resulted in the creation of several separate units, Business (joint activities), Production (the majority of people and journalists are included here), Technology (everything related to the technological aspect), and Programming (a relatively small number of people, mostly people from the Integrated Media Service, or IMS, usually staff that serves the informative program). IMS relates to the daily news, and the position of its editor is equivalent to the former editor of the informative program. Apart from daily news, the Production unit produces other types of programs that are not broadcasted on a daily basis. A newly established system unified television, radio, and the Web into a single, multiplatform system. At the moment of introduction, IMS included seven newsrooms and a newsdesk that produced 60 radio and 34 informative TV shows daily, as well as the online content (Marko 2017, 30–33).

While this research was conducted during December 2015, the big hall in the HRT premises (labelled as "television square") was adapted to serve the purpose of the integrated newsdesk. Not all sides within the broadcaster have been satisfied with these reforms. Members of the HRT Program Council criticized IMS for being inefficient, with an unclear structure, and overlapping duties and responsibilities, and with no significant contribution to the program quality and popularity (HRT 2014).

When it comes to digital production, HRT introduced the so-called "wide news system" in 2004, and slowly implemented it in its daily operation. In the process of digital production, HRT management faced an obstacle to establishing a new corporative culture and production logic. To overcome this obstacle, HRT strategically educated its staff, mainly with the support of the European Broadcasting Union (EBU).

HRT intensively uses online platforms and social networks to distribute its content and reach its audience. At the beginning of 2015, HRT completely redesigned its website to make it more user-friendly and to be more visually attractive and easier to browse. It is an interactive online platform that enables visitors to follow its programs live and on-demand. From 2013, HRT users have been able to download a mobile application for Croatian Radio, while in October 2015, HRT launched a new multimedia service (HRTi) which enables users to watch and listen to all 4 TV and 12 radio programs through mobile platforms (smartphones, desktop computers, tablets). This was a strategic decision of the HRT management in order to approach the young audience and match their information habits (HRT website). When it comes to social networks, HRT has several profiles on Facebook (among which HRT Vijesti is the most popular), a YouTube channel, and is also active on Twitter.

Discussion

The reform of the public broadcaster in Croatia has been marked by a combination of mimetic and atavistic orientations and a normative approach. A mimetic orientation refers to the fact that local media institutions have been modelled as imitations of successful institutions from the developed countries, while the atavistic orientation refers to the capture of public institutions, such as PSB, by local political elites. The Croatian case demonstrated the importance of local factors in influencing reforms and their outcomes. As a result, this led to the creation of a specific, 'hybrid' model. Croatian PSB was not fully imposed or transplanted from abroad—the country developed its model based on the already existing infrastructure, resources, and practices inherited partly from the socialist time and conditioned by war, economic uncertainties, and the political and ideological cleavages during the 1990s. Some elements of Western models were borrowed—successfully or less successfully (for example, the participatory model implemented by the Program Council), while others—such as the model of funding—have been developed independently relying mostly on local efforts (experiences, resources, and expertise). In the case of Croatian PSB, atavistic tendencies have been reflected through the lack of independence and failure to execute an autonomous editorial policy and produce programs that satisfy the larger portion of the media public in Croatia.

Public control, as another important feature of PSB, has been contested in the Croatian case. The inclusion of civil society representatives in the Program Council and enabling their appointment directly and outside of the parliament, has been considered as a necessary step towards the democratization of the Croatian PSB. International experts considered such a civic model of PSB governance as an important step for PSB development (Marko 2017, 39–40). This mostly targeted the normative level, neglecting the fact that, at the level of implementation, democracy in Croatia was still too premature to embrace successful solutions from developed countries. In the case of Croatian PSB, the proposed model of the so-called "civic" program council failed. As Peruško noted, since Program Council members "were not rooted in an actual social segment with durable interests, the influence of informal political powers filled the void naturally" (Peruško 2014, 246). In practice, such a Council proved to be inefficient due to the clash of many (not exclusively political or party-related) interests that prevented it from functioning properly and fulfilling its mission. This is another example that models and practices could not be simply borrowed and transplanted from one context to another, without taking into consideration the recipient's characteristics.

The case of the Croatian PSB shows that financial stability and independence does not necessarily lead to its institutional independence and editorial autonomy. Having the functional mechanism of license fee collection did not provide a sufficient basis for the HRT's independence from political influences. What has happened in practice is political colonization, which intensified after 2015 when a new government was elected, and which enables political parties to misuse the public funds to promote their exclusive political interests. Public polemics regarding the funding of PSB in Croatia have largely been related to the method of collection of funds, the amount of the monthly fee, and the program quality. As for the collection, the most discussed issue is related to enforcement through cooperation with law firms. This has been considered somewhat controversial and problematic because certain law companies developed a profitable business out of this, while the HRT management avoided publishing details on this cooperation until 2012.

As it is vulnerable to external political pressures and economic conditions, HRT is struggling to sustain its institutional independence, which has been highly challenged in the recent period. Constant changes of public laws and regulatory frameworks enable politicians to easily influence decisions on its management structure and editorial policy. The way the Croatian PSB operates within society, which is ideologically and politically divided, corresponds to the "polarized-pluralist model" developed by Hallin and Mancini (2004, 67–68), characterized by a high level of political parallelism, commentator journalism, a parliamentary or government model of PSB, instrumentalized by political parties. Political and ideological cleavages within HRT have led to permanent dissatisfaction with the staff and program of PSB, mostly at a personal level.

Reasons for dissatisfaction with the program quality vary from topic selection to the lack of professional approach, production quality, and a general lack of innovation. Critics can be categorized into two main groups. The first includes dissatisfaction with the balance provided within the PSB content. The main critical voices indicate the lack of social, political, cultural, religious, and minority viewpoints, while the last period has been marked with growing complaints about the obvious political bias within HRT's informative programs. Another strand of criticism relates to the program commercialization. The Croatian experience has demonstrated that, in the long run, competition with commercial stations for popularity usually results in a decrease in program quality, which is meant to be one of the essential strengths and trademarks of public broadcasters.

The Croatian PSB organization is not a leader when it comes to technological innovation, and it still lags behind commercial competitors in the country. A traditional and robust organizational structure, with many employees and a complex hierarchy, prevents Croatian HRT from developing a corporative culture that supports the establishment of a functional and efficient model for digital production and distribution.

At the level of decision making, HRT still maintains a rigid top-down decision-making process, with several mechanisms recently introduced to make it more open, transparent, and to enable regular communication with its public. The biggest challenge to establish an integrated, functional, and efficient system is the lack of resources and internal capacities, including the mindset of the people employed in this institution.

The digital switchover in Croatia opened up several issues and challenges that had to be addressed. The primary issue was how to respond to the new program obligations since HRT had to introduce specialized digital channels (one in the domain of culture, and the second a news channel) whose quality and influence still needs to be comprehensively assessed. The second issue is related to the system of production, which includes internal restructuring, creation of an integrated newsdesk and changing the logic of news production and distribution. Its webpage looks modern, it is popular and includes several tools for interaction (such as HRTi), but there is still space for further improvement to turn HRTi into a genuine online platform, combining different formats that attract audience attention and maintain high production quality and reliability in the terms of professional conduct and the PSB mission.

Conclusion

This chapter dealt with the transformation of Croatian Radio-Television into a public service broadcaster by taking into account the most prominent contextual factors that shaped this process, including the non-friendly environment during the 1990s and the political shift after 2000, the role of EU accession process, as well as effects of the market forces, competition, and political influences.

As most interlocutors for the study said, local politicians never gave up their influence over HRT. Considering it as a "post-election chase," local political actors perceived PSB as a tool for shaping public opinion. Once the process of EU accession was completed in July 2013, the EU's leverage decreased, and a re-politicization of the PSB unfolded (Marko 2017).

Both the state of Croatia and HRT embraced the process of digitalization strategically. Not only the technical aspect but the more essential aspect related to digital production and digital convergence were widely discussed and partly implemented in practice. Croatia entered the era of digital transmission earlier than the other Western Balkan states, and the state invested own resources to build a transmitting network to cover the majority of its geographical space with a digital signal. Croatian Radio-Television started to produce digitally in 2004, and it is slowly adjusting its internal structure and network of regional centers to the new production and distribution demands. Despite continuous education of its staff, HRT continuously struggled to establish a proper mindset among its staff. In this regard, HRT still needs to strategically address new consumption habits in Croatia and to develop its services accordingly.

There are many open questions that stakeholders in Croatia should discuss to create sound and feasible policy solutions for PSB. The transformation of HRT, including the provision of the news service and expansion to online platforms, was not challenged in Croatia as was the case in some other countries (Germany, Belgium, and the Netherlands, for example). In this regard, policymakers in Croatia enacted a promising legal frame for PSB to use the advent of new technologies and digitalization to make its services innovative and follow new trends without constraints. At the same time, such freedom can easily be a burden, especially accounting for the inefficient traditional structure and the lack of motivation and know-how to gear up the potential for innovations. HRT has to re-think internally how to employ all its capacities, technical, production, and human, and how to decide strategically on the main channels or platforms for its distribution. This is strongly connected with the second challenge, which is related to the audience.

To properly address the challenge of audience fragmentation, the public broadcaster needs to know who its public is, what their main concerns and interests are, and to develop regular ways to interact with them. In this regard, special focus should be put on the younger generations who use media content differently, i.e., in a more fragmented, non-linear way, consuming media predominantly through their smartphones, relying on social networks as news-feeds, and so forth.

References

Car, Viktorija. 2005. "Transformation from State to Public Service Television. Comparative Analyses of Croatian Public Service HRT and Slovenian Public Service RTV Slovenia." Master's thesis, University of Zagreb.

——, and Ivana Andrijašević. 2012. *Mapping Digital Media: Croatia*. Open Society Foundations: London. https://www.opensocietyfoundations.org/uploads/38713c2a-c2b6-429c-971c-68b925679b5e/mapping-digital-media-croatia-20120906.pdf.

——. 2013. "How We Survived Digital Television Broadcasting Switchover." *International Journal of Digital Television* 4 (3): 279–297.

Car, Viktorija and Igor Kanižaj. 2010. "Program za nacionalne manjine u hrvatskim televizijskim i radijskim programima" [Program for national minorities in TV and radio programs in Croatia]. *Međunarodne studije* 10, no. 3–4 (December): 86–115.

Council of Europe. 1999. *Resolution 1185: Honouring of Obligations and Commitments by Croatia*. Accessed May 13, 2020. http://www.assembly.coe.int/nw/xml/XRef/Xref-XML2HTML-en.asp?fileid=16696&lang=en.

Law on Croatian Radio-Television 2010. *Official Gazette of the Republic of Croatia* 137/10, 76/12 and 78/16.

HRT 2015. *Izvješće o poslovanju HRT za prvih devet mjeseci 2015* [Annual report for 2015]. Zagreb: HRT. https://www.hrt.hr/304024/organizacija/hrt-u-prvih-devet-mjeseci-ove-godine-nastavio-trend-pozitivnoga-poslovanja-6.

——. 2014. *Izvješće o poslovanju HRT za 2014* [Annual report for 2014]. Zagreb: HRT. https://www.hrt.hr/281673/hrt/hrt-u-2014-ostvario-najbolji-poslovni-rezultat-u-posljednjih-10-godina-28.

——. 2013a. *Izvješće o poslovanju HRT-a za 2013. godinu* [Annual Report for 2013]. Zagreb: HRT. https://www.hrt.hr/281676/organizacija/hrvatska-radiotelevizija-ostvarila-dobit-u-2013.

——. 2013b. *Strategija poslovanja i razvoja HRT-a* [Strategy of Business Operation and Development 2013–2017]. Zagreb: HRT. https://www.hrt.hr/uploads/media/Strategija_poslovanja_i_razvoja_HRT-a_2013.-2017.pdf.

Građanska inicijativa za slobodu javne riječi. 1993. *Annual Report*. Zagreb: Građanska inicijativa za slobodu javne riječi.

Hajduk, Damir. 2011. "Digitalizacija u Hrvatskoj" [Digitalization in Croatia]. In *Digitalno doba* [Digital era], edited by Nada Zgrabljić-Rotar, 139–165. Zadar: University of Zadar.

Hallin, Daniel C., and Paolo Mancini. 2004. *Comparing Media Systems: Three Models of Media and Politics.* Cambridge: Cambridge University Press.

Kanižaj, Igor. 2005. *Manjine između javnosti i stvarnosti* [Minorities between the public and reality]. Zagreb: Sveučilišna knjižara.

——, and Berto Šalaj. 2004. "Medijska slika manjina" [Media picture of minorities]. In *Javnost i mediji* [The public and the media], edited by Stojan Obradović, 30–40. Split: Stina.

Kurspahić, Kemal. 2003. *Zločin u devetnaest i trideset* [Crime at 7:30 pm]. Sarajevo: Mediacentar.

Marko, Davor. 2017. *The Future of Public Service Broadcasting in Croatia.* Sarajevo: Analitika Center for Social Research. http://www.analitika.ba/sites/default/files / publikacije/PSB%20Croatia.pdf.

Peruško, Zrinjka, and Antonia Čuvalo. 2014. "Comparing Socialist and Post-socialist television culture: Fifty Years of Television in Croatia." *Journal of European Television History and Culture* 3, no. 5 (June): 255–272.

Peruško, Zrinjka. 2014. "Great Expectations: On Experiences with Media Reform in Post-socialist Europe (and Some Unexpected Outcomes)." *Central European Journal of Communication* 72, no. 2 (Fall): 241–252.

Plevnik, Darko. 2002. *Rat i mir za Hrvatsku: Zapisi 1991–1995* [War and peace for Croatia: Records 1991–1995]. Zagreb: Nakladni zavod Matice Hrvatske.

Postman, Neil 1970. "The Reformed English Curriculum." In *High School 1980: The Shape of the Future in American Secondary Education*, edited by Alvin C. Eurich, 160–168. New York: Pitman.

Strate, Lance. 2006. *Echoes and Reflections: On Media Ecology as a Field of Study.* Cresskill, NJ: Hampton Press.

Thompson, Mark. 1995. *Kovanje rata* [Forging war]. Zagreb: Hrvatski helsinški odbor, Građanska inicijativa za slobodu javne riječi and ARTICLE 19.

CHAPTER 5

The Future of Public Service Broadcasting in Kosovo

Naser Miftari

Introduction

This chapter investigates the current position, role, and functioning of the Radio-Television of Kosovo (RTK). The chapter reflects on how RTK was established, analyzes the process of initial media policy adoption and the roles of various actors (such as the EU and local power elites) in the introduction of public broadcasting in Kosovo. By assessing the current situation, the chapter takes into account the regulatory, financial, technological, and socio-political trends that affect RTK's operation. In doing so, we conduct a detailed review of legislation related to RTK, such as research reports, documents, and official correspondence, and undertake interviews with interlocutors—media experts, RTK managers, and media consultants.

Before the declaration of independence in 2008, Kosovo was under the functional governance of the United Nations Mission in Kosovo (UNMIK). The mission was set in line with the UN Security Council Resolution 1244 from June 1999, to govern and establish the institutions of self-government in the post-conflict Kosovo. The development of the media sector was also covered under the UNMIK mandate and was carried out by the Organization for Security and Cooperation in Europe (OSCE), as one of the pillars of UNMIK. One of the major initiatives in the media sector taken by UNMIK was the establishment of the Radio-Television of Kosovo. This was done through the Memorandum of Understanding with the European Broadcasting Union (EBU) which enabled the RTK to start broadcasting in September 1999 (Thompson 2000).

What sets the Kosovo public broadcaster apart from the rest of the Western Balkans is that the RTK did not emerge as a result of the transformation of the former state broadcaster. During socialism, and prior to Kosovo's conflict in 1999, the Radio and Television Pristina (RTP) existed and was part of the larger broadcasting system with headquarters in Belgrade. Despite operating from the premises of the former state broadcaster, RTK did not claim to be a continuation of the RTP. On the contrary, RTK was promoted by UNMIK as a new entity and service (Thompson 2000). Nonetheless, from its inception in 1999 RTK started on an unclear and uncertain mandate, with no well-defined goals and faced with legal challenges related to the succession of the RTP including ownership claims over the premises of the former state broadcaster and the working rights claims by the former employees of the state broadcaster (Price 2000).

While in charge of the RTK between 1999–2001, EBU strived to set certain general standards. Here too the logic of the RTK development was driven by different approaches about the role of a public broadcaster in a post-conflict setting such as Kosovo (Borrink 2000). The international management and systematic monitoring played a role in how the RTK evolved until Kosovo declared its independence in 2008.[1] Following the declaration of independence, the RTK ownership was handed over to local actors. As the government became the principal source of the RTK's financing in the years that followed, the service gradually began to fall more and more under government influence.

Over the years, the need to address the vulnerable position of the RTK and ways to ensure its editorial independence have been voiced out in the EU's Kosovo progress reports (European Commission 2013, 2014 and 2015). From the EU perspective, nurturing the independence and financial sustainability of RTK is seen as a firm assurance that Kosovo will continue to have a universally accessible public forum where ideas, opinions, and political views are presented and debated. It is also a firm assurance that the diverse segments of Kosovo's multicultural landscape will feel represented. From the perspective of successive Kosovo governments, as long as Kosovo moves forward in the process of the EU integration, the government remains committed to upholding the independence and sustainability of RTK, as it committed itself before signing the Stabilization and Association Agreement (SAA) as a first important step towards the European integration process (Government of Kosovo 2012). However, as the process of the EU integration drags on, the likelihood of the RTK remaining an independent public broadcaster diminishes. While the RTK's editorial independence and sustainability are not related per se to the EU integration process, the absence of such prospects might diminish the aspiration for greater editorial independence. With such considerations in mind, this chapter proceeds to point out the challenges and strives to offer some insight regarding how RTK can manage to pass the threshold of consolidation and emerge as a strong public broadcaster in the future.

---

[1] In 2001, UNMIK established RTK as an independent public service broadcaster with a Board of Directors made up of local staff (UNMIK Regulation No. 2001/13). The decision formally ended the EBU's mandate over RTK. However, the mixed management of RTK continued. At that point, RTK hired Richard Lucas (ex-BBC manager) for another six months as an advisor to the new local Director-General. Later, following the March 2004 riots in Kosovo, international consultants were imposed back in RTK. From that time RTK had various direct monitors from OSCE or international consultants who advised RTK on editorial issues until 2006. Meanwhile, two international board members continued to sit on the RTK Board until 2008.

The Socioeconomic and Political Context

With a population of 1.8 million and a GDP/GNI per capita listed in the lower middle income, at USD 3,950 based on the indicators for 2017, Kosovo is making inroads towards consolidated democracy. Albanians are the largest ethnic group and make 91% of the Kosovo population. Other communities include Serbs (3.4%) and others (5.6%). The annual budget of Kosovo is close to USD 2 billion, yet Kosovo's economic wellbeing is still dependent on remittances from abroad. Its economic revitalization has been sluggish and foreign direct investments are still limited, while the unemployment rate stands at 26.5% (Statistical Agency 2017).

Kosovo is a parliamentary democracy with a multi-party proportional electoral system. The 120-member unicameral National Assembly, as the most important legislative, representative and oversight institution, elects the president, who serves a five-year term. The prime minister is nominated by the president and requires the assembly's approval. The central decision-making powers are vested with the government and the prime minister. However, as Kosovo's fragmented political system is susceptible to low policy consensus syndrome, the voting on relevant legislation, including media legislation, is often driven alongside political party lines. The legislation regarding Kosovo's public broadcaster is no exception to this pattern and it was reflected once again in the adoption of the most recent Law on Public Broadcaster in 2019.

Media System and Advertising Market

After the conflict in 1999, the dual media system was introduced in Kosovo. Based on the recent data, the number of licensed broadcasters in Kosovo is 197, with 20 TV stations, 82 radio stations, 37 cable operators, and 58 service providers that operate via cable service (Independent Media Commission 2015). The cable broadcasting has seen a surge in recent years. Of the 20 television stations that operate throughout Kosovo, three have Kosovo-wide coverage: the public broadcaster (RTK), and two commercial broadcasters (RTV21 and KTV). Eleven TV stations have regional coverage; six have local coverage, and one has a low power transmission. The size/value of the media market is close to EUR 30 million annually (Independent Media Commission 2013). Approximately 34%—or EUR 10 million—goes to the national broadcasters (TV and radio). RTK and its two national radio stations receive about one-third of the EUR 10 million.

Guiding Laws, Rules, and Regulations for RTK and its Management

RTK operates based on the Law on RTK that was adopted in 2012 and amended in 2019, as well as the RTK's Statute and Professional Standards and Ethical Principles of Journalism. Externally, 17 other laws influence the work principles and the day-to-day operation of RTK (Radio-Television of Kosovo 2015). Additionally, there are 16 house rules and sub-legal acts that regulate the internal functioning of the RTK, including the Regulation on Internal Organization, on Rights and Responsibilities, Regulation on Preventing Conflict of Interest, etc.

Based on an annual audit report from 2016, RTK had 745 full-time employees (Radio-Television of Kosovo 2016). The main governing bodies of the RTK are the RTK Board and General Director. The Board of RTK is comprised of 11 members and on a formal level, it is the main decision-making authority of RTK. In practice, however, the RTK Board is often sidelined by the RTK Director-General who engages in direct communication with the Kosovo Assembly, bypassing the RTK Board as the principal authority to engage in direct communication with the legislature.

Between the Director-General and the RTK Board stands RTK's Internal Auditor. The Director-General maintains the key responsibilities regarding the overall programming and managerial issues related to the operation of the public broadcaster. The Director-General is also the principal liaison between the RTK management and the Board of RTK (for an organizational chart see Figure 5.1). It is important to highlight that the Director-General operates with a cabinet, which consists of numerous associates and advisors, including the Internal Revision Representative, Manager for International Affairs, Manager for Projects and Developments, Manager for Archives, the Head of the Procurement Unit of the RTK and the Editor of the RTK Web. Based on RTK's Internal Regulation the Director-General can appoint additional members to this cabinet on an as-needed basis.

The Law on RTK 2012 recognizes RTK as the public broadcaster of Kosovo, a legal non-profit entity with the status of an independent public institution of particular importance. The Kosovo Assembly is considered the founder of RTK and as stipulated in the Law on RTK 2012 it must ensure RTK's institutional autonomy, as well as adequate financing for the execution of RTK's public service mission. The Law on RTK 2012 likewise stipulates that RTK's mission is informative, educative, cultural, and entertaining. Article 7 of the law which stipulates the obligations of RTK regarding content, channels, and services notes that promoting a culture of civic dialogue and providing a wide arena for public discussion, the realization of the constitutional rights of the Serb community and other communities regarding the provision of public information and distribution of the RTK content are some of the main duties that the broadcaster must fulfill.

RTK is additionally organized based on its Internal Organization Document that sets out the levels of management within RTK. In a nutshell, it is a top-down hierarchical structure. The Director-General, following the Law on RTK 2012, the Regulation on Internal Organization and other bylaws, organizes and manages

Figure 5.1: Organizational Chart of PSB in Kosovo

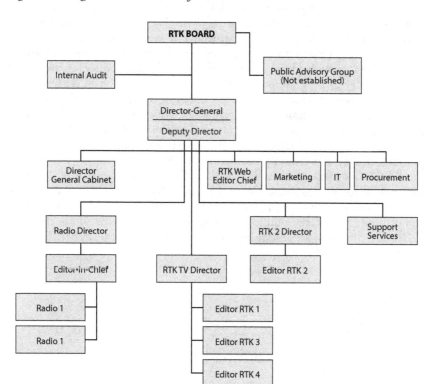

Source: Author's illustration.

the working process and operations within the RTK. The director is formally accountable to the board, issuing reports once a month. The board has the competencies to appoint and/or dismiss the Director-General of RTK based on Article 29, paragraph 2.6. Article 33 of the Law on RTK 2012 stipulates that the Director-General is appointed by 2/3 of the votes of the whole board, with a mandate of 3 years and with the possibility to be re-elected for another mandate. However, as noted, if on a formal level the RTK Board is the main decision-making authority, in practice, the board remains somewhat subordinate to the RTK management.

RTK Programming

Radio-Television of Kosovo operates four channels (European Broadcasting Union 2014) of which RTK 1, RTK 3, and RTK 4 are terrestrial and RTK 2 in Serbian, is broadcasted via cable. The most important channel is RTK 1 which is the central channel of RTK. The Serbian-language RTK 2 was launched in 2013 and is only available via cable. It does not reach all of the Kosovo Serb population, especially in the north of Kosovo. Since the IMC has not imposed its "must carry clause" for RTK throughout Kosovo, RTK has no terrestrial signal in northern Kosovo. Otherwise, RTK 2 has a staff of about 90, most of them local Kosovo Serbs, with 47 working full-time. Initially, it began with funds allocated to it from RTK's main budget line and an additional equipment grant of EUR 200,000 provided by the Kosovo Government. It produces an average of 10 hours a day of programming and it is the best reflection of RTK's efforts to being inclusive and accommodating. Content-wise, RTK 3 and RTK 4 broadcast primarily information and entertainment, education, science, and culture programs. Under its umbrella, RTK also has two radio stations, Radio Kosovo 1 and 2 and RTK web (rtklive.com). The website is perceived as growing in importance and it has had 8 staff members since 2015.

RTK is not a full member of the EBU as Kosovo is not yet part of the International Telecommunication Union. However, RTK enjoys a comprehensive service agreement with the EBU, and RTK has affirmed and pledged to adopt and promote EBU's core public service values of universality, independence, excellence, diversity, accountability, and innovation (European Broadcasting Union 2013).

RTK's Main Challenges: Sustainable Funding and Editorial Independence

The main challenges for RTK over the years are to ensure long-term and sustainable financing and preserve its editorial independence from political interference. However, in realizing these important objectives, RTK seems constrained, both from the inside as well as from the outside. Inside RTK, there has been a lack of willingness on the part of its management and board to be more assertive in seeking the re-introduction of the license fee or pursue greater editorial independence. Outside RTK, primarily in the political decision-making arena, generally, all political parties seem to have benefited from such a vulnerable position of RTK.

The decline of RTK's editorial independence has gone hand-in-hand with the shift in its financial dependence. The risk of compromising its editorial as well as financial independence began following the amendments to an earlier version of Law on RTK 2006 (Mustafa 2006). Particularly damaging to the prospect of sustainability of RTK was the decision to set a cap on the level of advertising revenues through Article 14 and the introduction of the Kosovo budget as a source of funding for RTK in Article 19 of the Law on RTK 2006. In later years, the introduction of the current Law on RTK 2012 further cemented and legitimized the formal political influence over RTK, particularly regarding the method of appointment of board members and consequently the RTK management.

Since 2010 RTK has seen a shift from being fully funded from the license fee (85%) and advertising revenues (15%) to becoming almost fully dependent (85%) on the state budget, as indicated in its annual and audit reports from 2010 until 2016. Between 2006–2009, before falling under the assembly control, RTK strived to achieve financial independence from the Kosovo budget, considering its dependence on the license fee as the most acceptable approach (Radio-Television of Kosovo 2006). During that time, it also reflected greater editorial independence and impartiality. If we look at the numbers, the license fee that was collected during those years by Kosovo Electric Corporation (KEK) ensured RTK's sustainability. However, the arrangement did not leave much space for political interference on RTK. Therefore, a year before its expiration, KEK decided to unilaterally terminate the contract with RTK, claiming that it was suffering losses (Institute for Advanced Studies 2011). Next, the Constitutional Court of Kosovo suspended the RTK license fee, considering its collection unconstitutional (Constitutional Court 2009). The management of RTK at that time saw this as a political effort to interfere with RTK ahead of the elections scheduled for 2007, as indicated in the RTK Annual Report. RTK also cited UNMIK's lack of support in favor of continuing the collection of the license fee, despite the recommendations of EBU (Radio-Television of Kosovo 2008). After KEK terminated the contract, it gave RTK six months to find an alternative solution. During the hiatus that ensued, the Kosovo Assembly dragged the matter and failed to adopt a new Law on RTK. Meanwhile, the suspension order from the Constitutional Court of Kosovo remained in effect. In the absence of an alternative solution to collect the license fee, in 2010 RTK ended being fully dependent on the Kosovo state budget.

Based on the Law on RTK 2012, apart from the assembly funding, RTK can be funded through the license fee, self-funding and through its economic activity, as well as through other sources of revenue including contracts with third parties, other program services, sponsorships and donations and in-house production and sale of programs. When the law was approved, it contained provisions that the assembly would allocate 0.7% of the Kosovo Budget for the next three years to finance RTK. It noted that the assembly had one year from the date of the publication of the Law on RTK 2012 in the *Official Gazette* (April 27, 2012) to find a solution for the long-term funding. However, the Kosovo Assembly has failed to meet its legal obligation to ensure RTK's financial independence, by failing to approve the re-introduction of the license fee, even seven years after the promulgation of the Law on RTK.

The method that the Kosovo Assembly has maintained since 2010 in financing RTK—by providing funding for its essential operations on a quarterly basis instead of a long-term commitment—has led RTK to feel financial instability and insecurity; has delayed the restructuring of the service, has delayed needed investments in technological upgrades and has kept the service in a state of perpetual crisis. Such a grim outlook has been detrimental to efficient business management, morale, productivity, and creativity within RTK. Under these conditions, RTK ended up accumulating losses over the years, and in 2017 had a negative balance of more than EUR 4 million.

2019 was set out as the tentative year for the re-introduction of the license fee for RTK following the discussions in recent years around the amendment of the Law on RTK 2012. In a recent development, amid resistance from the opposition on May 30, 2019, the assembly (with 55 votes in favor, 1 against and 5 abstaining) voted in principle in favor of the new draft of Law 06/L-097 on Kosovo's Public Broadcaster (Shefkiu 2019). It instructed the functional committees of the assembly to review the draft law and to present their recommendations in a timely manner. However, less than two months later, the Kosovo government resigned, and extra-ordinary elections were held in October 2019. The elections have produced a new government and it remains to be seen whether draft Law 06/L-097 on Kosovo's Public Broadcaster will move to a second reading in the Kosovo Assembly or it will be turned back to be revised by the new government. Among the proposed changes to the law was the clause that the license fee was to be introduced in 2019. Nonetheless, RTK could still receive 0.4% of the Kosovo Budget on an annual basis alongside the collection of the license fee. Other amendments relate to the procedures for the appointment of board members and of management, as well as ways to ensure greater public accountability of RTK.

Erosion of Editorial Independence

The provisions regarding RTK's independence are stipulated in Article 3 and its freedom to pursue an independent editorial policy is provided in Articles 18 and 23 of the current Law on RTK 2012. In terms of editorial independence, Article 18, paragraph 3 states that "RTK shall lead, develop and cultivate editorial policy with sound, positive, impartial, creative perspective, and civilizing, professional and humane content." On a formal level, its de facto independence is guaranteed. However, other provisions included in the same legislation enable Kosovo legislators to influence and determine the selection of board members and consequently senior management appointments within RTK, making it unlikely for professionals who are not affiliated with political parties to get these positions. As a result, the sustained editorial independence of the public broadcaster cannot be achieved in the given setup. To ensure such independence, the partisan process of board appointments and consequently of senior management within RTK must end. At present, the process of nomination of RTK Board members as stipulated in the Law on RTK 2012 is done within the Kosovo Assembly. During the processes of board and management appointments, the political affiliation and loyalties to political parties are routinely taken into account more than professionalism. Attention has been drawn to the issue of politically influenced board appointments in the European Commission's annual progress reports on Kosovo from recent years (2013, 2014 and 2015). It is unlikely that this situation will change unless the law is amended to provide for the introduction of a more depoliticized board and RTK management in the foreseeable future. Most recently the appointment of the new Director-General of RTK Mr. Ngadhnjim Kastrati on April 19, 2019, for a three-year mandate, was challenged by Kosovo opposition parties (Jusufi 2019). Nonetheless, the new Director-General assumed his role, and not long after he also received a congratulatory letter from the heads of EBU (Indeksonline 2019).

Based on Article 26 of the Law on RTK 2012, the board members are appointed by the Kosovo Assembly for terms lasting between 2 to 4 years. Procedurally, RTK announces the bid for new board members 90 days before the expiration of the mandate of old board members. Upon the review of all candidatures, the Ad Hoc Committee of the Assembly recommends to the Kosovo Assembly two candidates for each board position. The two candidates are then voted on in a future session of the assembly on the first-past-the-post principle. What usually happens is that the candidate that has the backing of the leading political parties gets selected and the apolitical professionals are left out. Such was the case in 2015 when new board members of RTK were up for election. Members of the assembly disregarded some of the more qualified candidates and voted for the ones with ties to political parties despite the suggestions of the OSCE addressed to the MPs to take into consideration the concerns of civil society and other institutional stakeholders upon deciding on board member candidatures and to strive to introduce a more apolitical board on RTK.[2]

Challenges as Opportunities: Digitalization, New Media, and Convergence

Kosovo authorities were not able to meet the deadline of June 2015 for the digital switchover as set forth by the International Telecommunication Union (ITU). Amid delays and mistakes in the process,[3] Kosovo's Independent Media Commission (IMC) put forward a strategy for the transfer to digital broadcasting. It contains guidelines on how the process should be carried out, stages of digitalization, as well as an action plan for the implementation of the strategy. However, despite being submitted for review to the Kosovo government, they have been slow in reviewing it.

---

[2] A copy of correspondence from the OSCE Head of Mission in Kosovo sent to the Kosovo Assembly in 2015.

[3] Initially, the Digitalization Strategy was drafted and submitted in 2012 for approval to Kosovo's government from a departing IMC Board without passing public discussion. As such, the strategy was considered in breach of the IMC Law and was returned to the IMC for further revision and completion. Likewise, several clauses in the law put forward by the Ministry of Economic Development were in breach of the Kosovo Constitution and were also removed when the law was approved.

Previously, the Law on Digitalization 2015 was approved and promulgated. Article 13 of the law entails that the public broadcaster is awarded the right for a multiplex with coverage of the entire territory of Kosovo, without conducting a public call procedure. It further stipulates that the public broadcaster shall use the multiplex for its channels and other non-commercial channels under conditions approved by the IMC. The law nonetheless was approved before the Strategy of Digitalization and as such certain clauses of the law could not be implemented.

There are questions about who will bear the cost of the switchover to a digital signal and the timeframe for the transition. The Strategy for Digitalization suggests that the Kosovo Assembly should bear these costs. However, it is not clear how this will be accomplished and whether there will be funds allocated at all in the 2018 budget towards this purpose. IMC proposed an estimated budget of EUR 20–25 million for financing the transition from analog to digital in the first stage. The strategy also highlights that RTK is entitled to one MUX, but it does not offer a clear timeline on when this might happen and how it will be technically achieved.

Meanwhile, in 2015, RTK received assistance from Japan's International Development Agency (JICA) in the amount of EUR 1.2 million for a project that ensured the internal digitalization of RTK's newsroom into an Integrated Media Service. From its end, the RTK management believes that it will be able to manage the switchover at a low cost, so long as it can reach quality agreements with Post and Telecom Kosovo (PTK)—the largest public communications entity to use its network, covering 95% of Kosovo's territory, for its digital signal. In turn, as per the plans of RTK's former general director, PTK will be allowed to introduce one or two channels into the multiplex, as it sees fit. However, to maintain the quality service, and to keep it in par with other public broadcasters in the region, RTK needs continuous financial support to ensure it meets the requirements for the digital switchover process. The financial support will ensure RTK remains competitive in the Kosovo media market and the international market geared principally towards members of the Kosovo diaspora through subscription rates for cable, given the capacities of RTK to broadcasts via satellite platforms to Western Europe and North America. So far RTK has under-utilized such potential that could become a principal revenue generator towards ensuring a financially self-sustainable RTK in the future.

In recent years, RTK has taken steps toward upgrading its online presence while updating its webpage and adding interactive features on the webpage. A quick data comparison of the online presence of Western Balkans broadcasters shows that RTKlive.com is successful to a certain degree in retaining online audiences and particularly the diaspora audience. RTK's 2015 annual report notes that its programs on YouTube have started to generate revenues for the RTK budget. RTK programs, albeit selectively, are also well promoted on the RTK Facebook page which has close to 300,000 likes, almost an equal number to Serbia's RTS, the largest broadcaster in the region. According to the same report, rtklive.com had between 76,400 and 142,350 visitors daily. The percentage of visitors from Kosovo is just above 40%, while 60% come from the Albanian diaspora. RTK's YouTube channel has 75,112 subscribers, which, based on some estimates, is the highest figure among all ten broadcasters from the region. However, it remains puzzling whether it will manage to maintain the pace or draw fresh audiences given the fragmented nature of the Kosovo public and the fact that RTK trails behind strong news portals in embracing new technologies.

Discussion

As Kosovo is still in the process of inner consolidation and facing challenges to accommodate its ethnic Serb minority within its institutional umbrella, the role of RTK remains crucial. The sources of funding, governance, the formula of the selection of the RTK Board and management, accountability and responsibility, the scope and utility of audits are all part of the debate related to the present and future of RTK. Yet it appears that there is neither much political willingness nor genuine public interest, to address such important challenges systematically. At the same time, there is little debate on the role of RTK in a new digital and technological environment, redefinition of its remit, audit processes, three-step tests and the possibility of revoking its license in the case of non-compliance, all these matters of importance for a genuine public broadcaster.

From the funding perspective, RTK has been almost entirely dependent on the state budget since 2010. While the license fee might be re-introduced in 2020, there remain uncertainties as to how this could work in practice. The shift in RTK funding since 2009 has also influenced the programming, making the RTK employees prone to becoming politicized. The analysis shows that the process of appointments of the members of the RTK's managing body favors political affiliation and party loyalty, rather than professionalism and expertise.

Our interlocutors draw attention to the fact that the problem of RTK is also the lack of diligent managers. According to EBU media advisor Mr. Boris Bergant: "even the most diligent (managers) are politically nominated and afraid to make problems with politics." For him, "the RTK management accepts the current system of funding and control because for them it is easier to be paid their salaries from the budget." He further notes that both the government and opposition consider the current setting as a good instrument to influence RTK and do nothing to change the situation. Hence, this situation demands that various actors, including civil society and media, overcome their narrow interest and push for a public service dependent on the public.[4]

There is a persistent assumption about the inherent pro-government bias of RTK and its management. The important question is whether RTK's reporting can overcome such bias? In conditions when many journalists and editors have their jobs at RTK in part due to their connections with politicians, this seems unlikely. Furthermore, in the present political setup in Kosovo where leading commercial broadcasters have tended to pursue a somewhat strong antagonist

---

4   Boris Bergant, EBU media advisor (Skype interview with the author, September 11, 2015).

approach to the coverage of government, RTK remained the only Kosovo-wide broadcaster through which the government was able to push forward its agenda.

The interlocutors interviewed for this research generally agree that the continued dependence on Kosovo budget funding leaves RTK vulnerable to political interference. This, in turn, increases the likelihood of compromising its editorial independence.

Recent efforts from RTK to put energies toward upgrading its online presence and improving its online appeal reflect a willingness on the side of the broadcaster to remain competitive with other commercial broadcasters in a multichannel environment. However, so long as the central question of funding of its core traditional operations remains pending, it seems unlikely that RTK will direct energies towards upgrading technologically or appeal harder on legislators to put more funding towards expanding its online platform.

Given the circumstances in which RTK is today, interlocutors see three scenarios related to the future of RTK. The first, and more idealistic one, is that a consensus might emerge within the political elite that a depoliticized public service broadcaster is in everyone's interest and a law on public broadcasting providing de facto and de jure guarantees on RTK's independence can be pushed forward with the introduction of a depoliticized board and management and full accountability to the Kosovo public.

The second scenario is that RTK continues to take on features of a state broadcaster common to those in authoritarian or semi-authoritarian regimes. In such a scenario we might witness the agonizing demise of RTK resulting in RTK losing ratings, credibility, and influence over time.

The third and most likely scenario, if nothing else changes, is that RTK will remain a somewhat powerful medium, yet still substantially dependent on state funding. Such a scenario would entail that RTK continues to receive funding from the Kosovo Assembly without a defined timeframe and is likely left without an alternative funding method, such as license fee. In such conditions, RTK would continue to be utilized for short-term gains from politics and politicians. This also means that RTK will remain essentially non-accountable to the Kosovo public while maintaining quasi-clientelist relations with whoever is in power.

The changes in the political landscape following the October 2019 election might bring a new perspective as to how RTK will operate in the future. Meanwhile, the transition toward the much desirable first scenario might happen only as a result of powerful political goodwill and increased pressure from the EU.

Conclusion

This chapter explored whether the context in which the Kosovo public broadcaster, RTK, is embedded provides a favorable environment for its prospects and continued development, and how it relates to the ongoing trends on the global and EU levels affecting the development of public service media. It took into account the situation in which the RTK operates, as a result of laws and policies adopted over the years to regulate the remit, position, and work of the public broadcaster. The findings from this research indicate that the external players including UNMIK (via OSCE) and the EBU were crucial in setting up and later consolidating the RTK through the introduction of the license fee model. Consequently, as Kosovo made some strides in the EU integration processes, the European Commission's Office in Kosovo became more assertive in pushing for a legal framework in line with the EU standards and directives.

The research emphasized that the issue of political interference in the RTK has intensified following "Kosovarization." The circumstances in which the RTK funding model evolved from the license fee based towards the fully budget-dependent, have made the RTK more vulnerable to political influence.

As Kosovo is still in the process of inner consolidation, the role of the RTK remains important in ensuring cohesion in a fragile and divided society. The country needs the public broadcasting service as a firm assurance that the diverse segments of Kosovo's multicultural society will feel represented.

As it is now, instead of being universally accepted as a true public service forum, the RTK lingers between the models of the state broadcaster and a weak replica of a public service media, sometimes seen as a mouthpiece of the government, sometimes of particular political parties and most times unable to serve a genuine public service role.

If Kosovo wants to move forward in the EU processes, a proper and sustainable system of funding for the RTK has to be considered and introduced. The license fee, as the prevailing model of financing that constitutes a direct relationship between citizens and the broadcaster, is the best option for realizing such a goal.

The future of the RTK, including its funding model and other guarantees of its institutional independence, is closely linked with the improvement of the political climate in Kosovo and the growing acceptance of institutional checks and balances. However, without a broad political consensus on the necessity of such independent public broadcasting, there is no certain future for the RTK. Such a consensus should be comprehensive enough to deal with the RTK's financial problems and long-term sustainability of the service while ensuring that it remains accountable and responsible. The nature and practicalities of such a consensus will also determine the future modernization of the RTK.

References

Borrink, Bob. 2000. "Zwischen Minenfeldern." *Die Welt,* September 23. https://www. welt.de /print-welt/article534830/Zwischen-Minenfeldern.html.

Constitutional Court. 2009. *Decision of the Constitutional Court on the temporary measure Case KI 11/09, Tomë Krasniqi vs. RTK et al.* Pristina: Republic of Kosovo.

European Broadcasting Union. 2014. "Speech for the Launch of Kosovo's New Channels RTK3 and RTK4." Accessed May 14, 2020. https://www.ebu.ch/news/2014/03/ news-speech-for-launch-of-kosovos-new.

———. 2013. "RTK Pledges to Adopt Core Public Service Values." Accessed May 14, 2020. https://www.ebu.ch/news/2013/03/rtk-pledges-to-adopt-core-public.

European Commission. 2015. *Kosovo 2015 Report.* Accessed May 14, 2020. https:// ec.europa.eu/neighbourhood-enlargement/sites/near/files/pdf/key_documents /2015/20151110_report_kosovo.pdf.

———. 2014. *Kosovo 2014 Progress Report.* Accessed May 14, 2020. https://ec.europa.eu/neigh- bourhood-enlargement/sites/near/files/pdf/key_documents /2014/20141008-koso- vo-progress-report_en.pdf.

———. 2013. *Kosovo 2013 Progress Report.* Accessed May 14, 2020. http://eeas.europa.eu /archives/delegations/kosovo/documents/eu_kosovo/ks_progress_report_2013_ en.pdf.

Government of Kosovo. 2012. *Action Plan on the Negotiations for the Stabilization and Association Agreement (SAA).* Pristina: Government of Kosovo.

Independent Media Commission. 2015. *Annual Report.* Pristina: Independent Media Commission of the Republic of Kosovo.

———. 2013. *Advertising Market Research and Analysis in Kosovo.* Pristina: Independent Media Commission of the Republic of Kosovo.

Indeksonline. 2019. "EBU uron Kastratin për emërimin Drejtor i Përgjithshëm i RTK- së" [EBU congratulates Kastrati on the appointment as Director-General of RTK]. *indeksonline,* May 15. Accessed May 14, 2020. https://indeksonline.net/ebu- uron-kastratin-per-emerimin-drejtor-i-pergjithshem-i-rtk-se/.

Institute for Advanced Studies (GAP). 2011. *RTK's Financial Sustainability: Finding Alternatives to Public Broadcaster Financing.* Pristina: Institute for Advanced Stud- ies. https://www.institutigap.org/documents/78229_RTK-English.pdf.

Jusufi, Nga Sanije. 2019. "Ngadhnjim Kastrati zyrtarisht drejtor i RTK-së, Bordi thotë se votimi për të ishte i drejtë" [Ngadhnjim Kastrati director of RTK, the board says that voting was legitimate]. *Koha,* April 24. Accessed May 14, 2020. https://www. koha.net/arberi/158878/ngadhnjim-kastrati-zyrtarisht-drejtor-i-rtk-se-bordi-tho- te-se-votimi-per-te-ishte-i-drejte/.

Law No. 02/L-47 on Radio Television of Kosovo (Law on RTK 2006). Accessed May 14, 2020. https://gzk.rks-gov.net/ActDocumentDetail.aspx?ActID=2564.

Law No. 04/L-046 on Radio Television of Kosovo (Law on RTK 2012). *Official Gazette of the Republic of Kosovo* 7/12. Accessed May 14, 2020. https://gzk.rks-gov.net / ActDocumentDetail.aspx?ActID=2812.

Law No. 05/L-027 on Digitalization of Terrestrial Broadcasting (Law on Digitalization 2015). *Official Gazette of the Republic of Kosovo* 26/15. Accessed May 14, 2020. https://gzk.rks-gov.net/ActDocumentDetail.aspx?ActID=11021.

Mustafa, Artan. 2006. "Re të zeza mbi RTK-në" [Dark clouds over RTK]. *Gazeta Express*, April 18.

Price, Monroe E. 2000. "Restructuring the Media in Post-Conflict Societies: Four Perspectives: The Experience of Intergovernmental and Non-Governmental Organizations." *Cardozo Online Journal of Conflict Resolution* 2, no 1 (May). https://cardozojcr.com/issues/volume-2-1/article/.

Radio Television of Kosovo. 2016. "Pasqyrat Financiare se bashku me Raportin e Auditorit te Pavarur" [Radio Television of Kosovo financial review and audit report]. Pristina: Radio Television of Kosovo.

——. 2015. "Raport Vjetor i Punes 2015" [RTK annual report 2015]. Pristina: Radio Television of Kosovo.

——. 2008. "Raport Vjetor për vitin 2007" [RTK annual report 2008]. Pristina: Radio Television of Kosovo.

——. 2006. "Raport Vjetor për vitin 2005" [RTK annual report 2005]. Pristina: Radio Television of Kosovo.

Shefkiu, Arbisa. 2019. "Votohet ne parim Projektligji per RTK-ne" [Law on RTK voted in principle]. *Kallxo.com*, May 30. Accessed May 14, 2020. https://kallxo.com/shkurt /votohet-ne-parim-projektligji-per-rtk-ne/.

Statistical Agency. 2017. *Statistical Yearbook of the Republic of Kosovo*. Pristina: Republic of Kosovo.

Thompson, Mark. 2000. *Slovenia, Croatia, Bosnia and Herzegovina, Macedonia (FYROM) and Kosovo. International Assistance to Media*. Vienna: OSCE Representative on Freedom of the Media. https://www.osce.org/fom/25448?download=true.

UNMIK Regulation No. 2001/13 on the Establishment of Radio and Television of Kosovo. Accessed May 14, 2020. http://www.unmikonline.org/regulations/unmikgazette /02english/E2001regs/RE2001_13.pdf.

CHAPTER 6

The Future of Public Service Broadcasting in Montenegro

Nataša Ružić

Introduction

In Montenegro, the former state-controlled broadcaster, Radio-Television of Crna Gora (RTCG) was redefined as a public service broadcaster in 2002. This transformation was purely formal and took place under particular political circumstances. At that time, the Montenegrin authorities needed the support of the EU countries in restoring independence and leaving the state union with Serbia, and therefore they were ready for political compromises.

However, practice indicated that changes in the PSB transformation were rather cosmetic, while the situation did not change even eighteen years after the transformation. Numerous problems of the PSB organization that existed in the past are still an obstacle in the fulfillment of its remit. Political pressures are reflected primarily on the financial stability of the public service broadcaster, but also on its editorial policy. The mentioned factors are correlated because political pressures are also exercised in the form of economic pressures, primarily through the financing of RTCG from the budget, including the financing of the digitization process and taking over the repayment of debts of the public service broadcaster.

On one hand, without the financial support from the government, the public broadcaster could not survive on the media market. But on the other, this situation led to the political pressures which are visible through the process of adoption of legislation and appointment of management bodies, i.e., the "fight" for the dominance in the council that manages the public service broadcaster.

This chapter will deal with several aspects that affected the transformation of the PSB organization in Montenegro and will outline the lessons learned from this process.

Political Background and the Media System in Montenegro

Montenegro is the only country of the former Yugoslav republics in which there has been no change of government since 1989, even though the first multi-party elections were held in 1990 (Vukićević and Vujović 2012, 55). Since 1989 Montenegro has been governed by the same party, first called the League of Communists of Montenegro, which then changed the party's name in 1991 to the Democratic Party of Socialists of Montenegro (DPS). This means that DPS has been in power for 29 years.

The political situation in Montenegro has been reflected in the media system constellation as well. Until 1993 only state-controlled media operated in Montenegro's semi-authoritarian system. That year, the adoption of the Public Information Act resulted in the emergence of the first private media (Tadić Mijović 2009, 30). Thus, in 1994, two new radio stations appeared in the Montenegrin media market: Antena M radio and Elmag radio, followed by the print media company Vijesti three years later. With the next Law on Public Information Service, which was adopted in 1998, Montenegro committed to adhering to international standards on human rights and freedoms outlined in the documents of the United Nations, the OSCE, the Council of Europe and the European Union. Milka Tadić Mijović, a journalist of one of the opposing media outlets, stated in her master's thesis that although the European recommendations have not come to life in practice, there is evident progress in the future of the public service broadcaster by dismissing the editors who were spreading hate speech during the civil war in Yugoslavia. Meanwhile, the minority and opposition parties were given their space on RTCG (Tadić Mijović 2009, 31). Also, the new law resulted in the emergence of new print media, such as the opposition paper *Dan*, which was established in 1998.

Since 2000, Montenegro has been on its way towards European integration and it accepted the Charter of Freedom of the Press. This meant that Montenegro started to plan comprehensive reform of the media system. For this purpose, a working group composed of representatives of the media, media associations, and the government, in cooperation with the international community, was established.[1] Eleven months of work resulted in the Law on Media, the Law on Broadcasting, and the Law on Public Service Broadcasting Media "Radio Montenegro" and "Television of Montenegro" in 2002.

However, despite the optimism surrounding the announcement of expected changes after the adopted legislative framework of media, the situation regarding the level of media freedom has not improved. The media freedom index has been dropping steadily from 2010 to 2015. This is best illustrated by the

---

[1]   Member of the working group in 2002, MNE 01 (interview with the author in March 2015; the interviewee requested to remain anonymous).

fact that according to Reporters Without Borders, Montenegro was ranked 114th in the level of its media freedom in 2015 (Reporters Without Borders, 2015). This result can be explained by physical attacks on journalists, attacks on the opposition media editorial staff, unresolved cases of physical assaults on media workers, and the murder of the editor-in-chief of *Dan*, Duško Jovanović. In 2019, Montenegro climbed up the ranks to the 104th spot in regard to media freedoms, but the position of journalists did not change significantly nonetheless (Reporters Without Borders, 2019).

According to the classification made by Daniel Hallin and Paolo Mancini, the Montenegrin media system can be classified as a Mediterranean system characterized by a low degree of media freedom, a low degree of self-regulation,[2] a high degree of instrumentalization by the government, political parties, and businessmen linked with political centers of power. One of the features of this system is the low level of professionalism of journalists due to political pressures. Journalists are poorly paid, and this profession is perceived exclusively as a springboard for political and social engagement (Hallin and Mancini 2004, 67–68). This is also evidenced by the number of MPs who have turned from the world of journalism to the world of politics or are active members of political parties.

PSB Organization

The Radio-Television of Montenegro (Radio Televizija Crne Gore) started broadcasting its radio program in 1944 and television program in 1964. Until 1991, this media company was named Radio and Television Titograd, but since 1991, Radio-Television of Montenegro have operated as a single broadcasting system known as RTCG. This media was remembered for its war-mongering journalism and the spread of hate speech in the 1990s. RTCG journalist Miomir Maroš explains that open recognition of this fact by the public service broadcaster is, among other things, found in the film titled *Witnesses of a Century* in which Snežana Rakonjac, Sanja Blečić, and Tanja Šuković confirmed "the dishonorable role RTCG played during the war, during the breakup of the SFRY when they had warmongering news programs. The deflection from the editorial policy of the time and a form of apology to their own and the viewers in the region was made by the series program on the RTCG's reporting in that period, with the presence of a critical tone of the journalists, commentators, and narrators" (Maroš 2012, 36–37).

---

[2]   The first self-regulatory body in Montenegro was founded in 2003 with the support of OSCE. This body disbanded a couple of years later, and in 2012 as many as three self-regulatory bodies were established: the Media Self-Regulation Council, the Local Press Council, and a council that comprised three opposition media. The third council never became active, and *Vijesti*, *Dan*, and *Monitor* soon introduced the ombudsman system, not wishing to be part of the Media Self-Regulation Council, composed mostly of pro-government media.

From the very start, RTCG openly promoted the interests of the ruling party. If such an editorial policy was somewhat expected while RTCG had the status of a state-owned media, the situation continued even after the transformation of the former state-owned media into a public service broadcaster. Zvezdan Vukanović claims that the political parties that were represented in the Parliament continued to manage this media company. "The Television of Montenegro was managed mainly by party, and not professional staff, who worked more in the interests of political parties and ruling elites and less in the interests of the profession and the public. And, as it usually happens when you put personal and party interests before the market-economic interests, the overall operating result is discouraging" (Vukanović 2006, 112). The research carried out by Snežana Burzan, based on 23 semi-structured interviews with journalists and people from public life for her master thesis titled "Public service—democratic need of the 21st-century citizens (on the example of RTCG, HRT, RTS, and BHRT)" showed that the majority of interlocutors perceived the Television of Montenegro (TVCG) as "state-owned television and government service, and that "the influence of political subjects on the editorial policy of TVCG is evident as well as the feeling of that media being a state-owned television" (Burzan 2012, 59).

Such a perception of the public broadcaster has not changed to this day. A survey conducted by the Konrad Adenauer Stiftung in 2019, with a sample of 1001 respondents in Montenegro, showed that as much as 71% of those interviewed believed that the public broadcaster was not free from political pressures. When it comes to the citizens' trust in the public broadcaster, the survey established that only 28% of the citizens have high trust in the public broadcaster, 38% of the respondents had a low level of trust, while 14% had no trust in RTCG at all. It is interesting to note that this is the lowest level of the citizens' distrust in the media since as much as 44% of the respondents had little trust in private TV stations (Ružić 2019, 168). This means that Montenegrin society—which generally exhibits a degree of media illiteracy—is aware that the media are manipulating them.

Today the public service broadcaster has two television channels, namely TVCG1 and TVCG2, which broadcast within the territory of Montenegro, and a satellite channel that aims to inform the Montenegrin diaspora. Radio Montenegro broadcasts on two channels, RCG and R98.

The Montenegro market has 22 television channels (3 public service channels, 5 local public service broadcasters and 14 commercial stations) and 51 radio stations (14 local public radio broadcasters, 35 commercial and 2 non-profit radio broadcasters). A large number of media outlets in a small market and low advertising revenues, which according to IREX is EUR 9.5–10 million (Nenezić and Vuković 2017, 7), have led the media into a position of fighting for survival. There is an attempt to resolve this problem through the new draft Law on Media, which provides for the establishment of the Fund for Pluralism and Media Diversity Promotion within the scope of which the state would finance private and non-profit media. Those media outlets that have been active on the market for at least two years would be eligible to apply. To this end, 0.03% of the GDP has been allocated from the budget—one million and 350 thousand euros (Analitika 2019).

Keeping in mind the economic conditions in which the media operate on the market, we are free to say that RTCG is in some way privileged because it is financed by citizens and supported by the state in terms of digitalization funding. However, despite its privileged status, in the last couple of years, RTCG has begun to step into the field of commercial broadcasters by broadcasting commercial content such as the Turkish soap operas in 2013 and 2014 and by acquiring the rights to broadcast exclusive sports events, justifying this by the participation of the Montenegrin national team.

In 2002, RTCG was allowed to start a new chapter through its transformation into a media that will be exclusively in the service of citizens. The transformation process was implemented with the support of the EU and passed through three phases. The preparation phase included an analysis of the European experience with a focus on countries in transition, the preparation of expert analysis, and the establishment of all necessary conditions for the PSB operation. The second phase included defining the structure and program goals of the PSB organization, the structure of the technical base necessary for broadcasting, a functional organizational and staffing scheme, stable sources of funding, and the establishment of an independent company to transmit and distribute radio and television signal in the territory of Montenegro. The third stage included the adoption of new laws, developing their management bodies, a model of funding that would operate on a stable basis, and a functional regulatory framework.[3]

Regulation of PSB in Montenegro

The legal ground for PSB development in Montenegro was set in 2002 by the adoption of several important laws. In 2002, Montenegro legally regulated its media scene and the operation of print and electronic media for the first time by adopting the Media Law, Broadcasting Law, and the Law on Public Broadcasting Services of the "Radio of Montenegro" and the "Television of Montenegro." Amendments to the Law on Public Broadcasting Services of Montenegro were adopted in 2008, 2012 and 2016. The Law on Electronic Media was passed in 2010 and amendments to this Law were adopted in 2011, 2013, and 2016. Since 2018, there have been ongoing activities regarding the draft Law on Media, Law on National Public Broadcasting Radio-Television of Montenegro, and Law on Electronic Media. In other words, the complete legislative framework is being overhauled with the aim of alignment with European regulations and recommendations. The new proposal of the Law on the National Public Broadcaster was adopted by the parliament on October 31, 2019.

The Law on Public Broadcasting Services of Montenegro regulated the functioning, program content, structure, and financing of PSB. While the Law

---

[3]   Member of the working group in 2002, MNE 01 (interview with the author in March 2015; the interviewee requested to remain anonymous).

on Electronic Media, which made differences between public, commercial, and non-profit media, laid down the method of establishing public broadcasters, program content, financing, the work of management bodies, and advertisement and teleshopping airtime. Amendments to the law were made with the support of the EU and the recommendations of international experts, but the public service broadcaster did not abide by certain articles of the media laws, while some legal provisions were not applicable in the Montenegrin market. I will give some examples.

The Law on Public Broadcasting Services of Montenegro laid down that the program content of the public service should meet the needs of citizens. Article 9 of the PSB law and article 74 of the Law on Electronic Media states that RTCG should produce informative, cultural, educational, scientific, sports, entertaining program, as well as the program for all categories of population, i.e., program contents intended for children and youth, members of minority nations, persons with disabilities, and socially vulnerable groups. Through the program contents, the public broadcaster is obliged to respect human rights, deal with topics of public interest, express various religious beliefs, and promote Montenegrin national and cultural identity, as well as the identity of minority nations.

However, according to TVCG's program-production plans, the program obligations of the public service broadcaster were not fulfilled. The amendments to the Law on National Public Service Broadcaster of Radio-Television of Montenegro from 2016, especially Articles 9 and 10 of the proposal of this law, stipulate that RTCG is obliged to draft a proposal for the program plan and organize a public hearing for 45 days where the public would be allowed to react. In such a way, the public would have the opportunity to control the RTCG program content that distanced itself from the public service broadcasting model and to defend its interests. The public debate within which the management of RTCG responded to the suggestions and remarks of the Montenegrin audience was organized in different parts of Montenegro, in Podgorica, Herceg Novi and Bijelo Polje in the period from September 29 to November 13, 2017 (Radio-Television of Montenegro 2017a). Besides, citizens were able to submit their suggestions through radio and television shows: *Mozaic* and *Replika*. Citizens did not fully make use of their rights, which is confirmed by the poor response in all three Montenegrin municipalities, and the public debates turned into a presentation of program contents. Some of the citizens present made remarks about the program contents, asking for more children's programs, educational programs such as foreign language lessons, quizzes, programs dedicated to particular parts of Montenegro, persons with disabilities, and programs on the contribution of the civil sector to the development of the society (Čepić 2017). In the last five years, the public broadcaster's schedule has not undergone any significant changes in terms of the program contents (see Table 6.1). The program schedule of TVCG is dominated by news, movies, and series. Commercial media often accuse the public broadcaster of encroaching upon their field, which is why Article 15a of the Law on the National Public Broadcaster of 2016, as well as Article 22 of the proposal of this law, prescribe that taxpayer money may not be used for financing commercial audiovisual services.

Table 6.1: TVCG Program Content

Type of program	2015	2016	2017	2018	2019
News	50%	53%	49%	49%	48%
Films and series	27%	21%	21%	22%	-
Sport	12%	16%	12%	10%	11%
Documentaries	2%	1%	3%	3%	4%
Science-educational	1%	1%	3%	4%	4%
Children's	0.5%	1%	2%	7%[4]	23%[5]
Program for minorities	2%	2%	2%	2%	2%
Entertainment-commercial	3%	2%	5%	3%	8%

Source: Radio-Television of Montenegro (2015c; 2016b; 2017c; 2018b; 2019b).

As we can see from Table 6.1, there has been a slight rise in documentary and scientific-educational programs on RTCG. However, we cannot precisely determine for 2018 the number of programs dedicated to culture, children, as well as movies and series, which have been presented with a single figure in 2019 as well.

The Montenegrin public service broadcaster has a rather complex organizational structure, as can be seen in Figure 6.1. This structure often results in financial problems due to the surplus of employees. This will be dealt with in more detail in the next section.

When it comes to the structure of the PSB organization, the main administrative authorities are the RTCG Council and the Director-General. The appointment procedures of RTCG, duties of the Council, members' removal from position, termination of office, member suspension, the obligations of the Director-General, and the responsibilities of the TVCG Director are set out from Article 27 to Article 76 of the new proposal of the Law on Public Broadcasting Services of Montenegro.

The Council of RTCG is one of the managing bodies and has 9 members. According to Article 36 of the proposal of the Law on the National Public Service Broadcaster of Radio-Television of Montenegro, membership candidates for the Council are, one each, proposed by the following: Universities in Montenegro, the Montenegrin Academy of Sciences and Arts, *Matica crnogorska*, non-governmental organizations in the field of culture, the Montenegro Chamber of Commerce and Employers' Association, one non-governmental organization in the field of media, NGOs in the field of human rights, national, gender

---

[4]   Program devoted to children, culture and music.
[5]   Program devoted to children, culture, music, films and series.

equality, the right to protection of the environment, consumer protection, the rights of persons with disabilities (2 members), trade unions, and the Montenegrin Olympic and Paralympic Committee. Article 26 of the Law on the National Public Broadcaster of 2016 prescribes that, due to conflict of interest, council members may not be MPs, persons nominated and appointed by the parliament, the President of Montenegro nor the President of the Government, representatives of political parties, RTCG employees, persons engaged in radio and television production, persons who have been pronounced a final judgment for a crime or persons who are relatives of the above. However, the new draft Law on the National Public Broadcaster envisages that representatives of political parties and state officials may not apply for membership in the council for a specific period only, i.e., for at least two years after cessation of the office.

Figure 6.1: Organization of RTCG

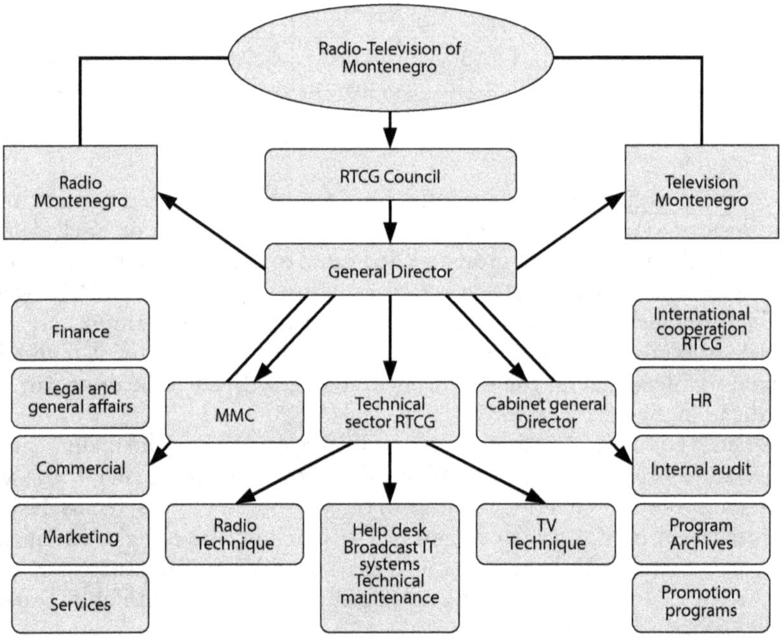

Source: *Radio-Television of Montenegro (2011, 10)*

Article 34 of the Law on the National Public Broadcaster Radio and Television of Montenegro, i.e. Article 41 and Article 42 of the Proposal of this Law, lays down that the procedure for the election of the members of the RTCG Council starts by announcing a public call, published in the *Official Gazette* and one print medium. The authorized proposers must submit their proposals for the candidates for the council members within 40 days, while the working body, the Administrative Board, should establish the proposal for the list for the appointment of the council according to the authorized proposers, within 15 days from the expiration of the deadline for the submission of proposals. According to Article 46 of the proposal of the Law on the National Public Broadcaster, the parliament is to pass a decision on the proposal for the list for the appointment of the council within 60 days. On the legal side, the procedure is precisely and clearly defined, but the parliament can exert political pressure by prolonging the procedure or by choosing the members at its discretion.

For the first time, the open political fight aimed at controlling the public service broadcaster started in 2007 with the parliament itself as a lever of influence. The first Law on Public Service Broadcasting Media Radio Montenegro and Television of Montenegro from 2002 Article 16 prescribes that the Parliament shall confirm the appointment of members of the RTCG Council.[6] This article has been often criticized by oppositional parties, who are in a minority in the Parliament. In 2007, the work of the council was blocked because the parliament did not want to confirm the appointment of five council members. From December 2007 to April 2008, the council could not adopt any decision because the mandate of five (out of 11) members had expired (Tadić Mijović 2009, 39). In April 2008, after the appeal of the OSCE and the European Commission the mandate of one member was confirmed, while the mandates of four representatives of the non-governmental sector were not confirmed. The new Law on Public Broadcasting Services of Radio and Television of Montenegro kept the same practice. Article 27 stipulates that the council shall be appointed and dismissed by the parliament. According to the recommendations of the Council of Europe, state institutions have the right to formally confirm the appointment of the members of the council, which must not be misused, but this recommendation is not applicable in Montenegro. According to the proposal of the new Law on RTCG, the procedure of electing council members leaves room for abuse. Article 35 of the proposal of the Law is titled "Appointment of Council Members," according to which the parliament will deal exclusively with the appointment of council members, but not with their dismissal. However, the description of the procedure itself reveals that this essentially concerns the selection of council members. According to Article 45 of the proposal of the Law, the Administrative Board should compile a list of candidates for council membership based on their biographies, experiences, candidates' interviews with MPs, while also paying attention to the number of civil sector organizations that supported the candidacy.

The Administrative Board has already shown itself to be partial during the selection of council members in 2017, when two opposition-oriented council members, Goran Đurović and Nikola Vukčević, were dismissed due to conflicts of interest and were replaced with members who favor the ruling structure, Goran Sekulović and Ivan Jovetić. After these changes, the ruling party got the majority in the council and dismissed the Director-General of the public service broadcaster, Andrijana Kadija. This shows that the Administrative Board, i.e., the Parliament of Montenegro, should not decide on the members of the council.

If we compare the Law on the PSB from 2002, 2008, and 2016, we find that the first law guaranteed a higher level of freedom with respect to the financing

---

6   The first council was formed in January 2003, as a guarantee of the independence of the public service broadcaster, and the composition of the council was confirmed by the parliament in December 2012.

and structure of the PSB organization. According to the 2002 Law on Public Broadcasting Services, the council had 11 members, and by amending the law in 2008, this number was reduced to 9. According to the 2002 Law, RTCG had three administrative bodies: the Council, the Board of Directors, and the Director-General. The subsequent amendments to the Law in 2008 abolished the Board of Directors. The Centre for Development of NGOs proposed to increase the number of members of the council to 13. The proposal was based on the rationale that a greater number of NGO representatives in the council will ensure the independence of this body. In essence, the non-governmental sector is opposition-oriented, and any changes of this type would result in the takeover of the public service broadcaster by the opposition. Also, the question is raised whether the non-governmental sector wants to increase the number of its representatives because of the high fees paid to the public service council members or they are genuinely fighting for changes. However, this proposal was not adopted, and the council still has 9 members. According to Article 27 of the proposal of the Law on the National Public Broadcaster, a new administrative body has been introduced: the Administrative Financial Board. This body will deal exclusively with financial plans, reports, annual accounts, etc. The proposed administration system is cumbersome and financially unviable, having in mind that, according to Articles 48 and 62, the members of the council and the board are entitled to monthly remuneration in the gross amount of the average gross salary of RTCG employees (Government of Montenegro 2019). According to the financial statement of RTCG for 2018, the average gross salary for employees of the Public Broadcaster amounted to EUR 735 (Radio-Television of Montenegro 2019, 13), which is the best indicator of the additional financial encumbrance of this media outlet. In 2018, only EUR 91,284 was allocated as remuneration for work in the council (Radio-Television of Montenegro 2019, 12). This means that the citizens are going to pay EUR 200,000 for the needs of the administrative bodies—the Council and the Administrative Financial Board—each year.

The Financial Aspects of the PSB in Montenegro

Montenegro's public service broadcaster uses various sources of financing prescribed by the Law on Electronic Media and the Law on Public Broadcasting Services of Montenegro. The Law on the National Public Broadcaster regulates the method of establishment, obligations in terms of program contents, the manner of financing, and management of the public service broadcaster (through the obligations of the administration bodies and the selection procedure). Meanwhile, the Law on Electronic Media defines the obligations for three types of broadcasters: public, commercial, and non-profit. Through Articles 73 to 80, and 92, this law prescribes the method of establishment of national, regional, and local public broadcasters and sets forth the obligations of the public broadcaster in terms of program contents, funding, and advertising times.

Article 76 of the Law on Electronic Media foresees public broadcasters will be funded through the general revenues of the Budget of Montenegro. Article 16 of the Law on Public Broadcasting Services of Montenegro from 2008 obliges the state to allocate 1.2 percent of the annual budget of Montenegro to enable the PSB organization to be operative. This article of the law has been amended and according to the new law, the budget of Montenegro allocates funds "at the annual level of 0.3 percent of GDP (Gross Domestic Product), the estimate of which shall be determined by the Government through the adoption of macro-economic and fiscal policy guidelines" (Law Amending the Law on Public Broadcasting Services of Montenegro). After almost two years this amendment was adopted in the parliament in 2016. According to the new proposal of the Law on the National Public Broadcaster, Article 23 indicates that "the manner and conditions of ensuring funds from the budget must not influence the editorial, financial and institutional independence of RTCG" (Law Amending the Law on Public Broadcasting Services of Montenegro). It becomes clear that the financial independence of the public broadcaster in a country with low levels of media freedoms is out of the question if we observe the structure of revenues from the 2018 financial report of RTCG: budget (90%), marketing (6.1%), commercial (2.6%) and other (1.3%) (Radio-Television of Montenegro 2019, 7).

However, the funds from the state budget are not sufficient for the sustainability of the public service broadcaster. Hence, the public broadcaster has various additional sources of income, which complies with Article 15 of the Law on the National Public Service Broadcaster of Radio and Television of Montenegro:

Table 6.2: Income of PSB in Montenegro (in EUR)

Year	Budget of Montenegro	Budget via the Ministry of Culture	Marketing	Other income[7]	Revenues from equipment donations
2012	7,152,428	200,000	1,516,847	467,420	189,153
2013	7,198,449	200,000	1,416,932	466,580	186,368
2014	7,767,440	290,000	1,534,752	837,369	186,020
2015	12,700,000[8]	150,000	1,141,136	555,051	183,896
2016	14,211,000[9]	/	1,500,000	350,000	180,000
2017	11,511,000[10]	/	1,500,000	470,000[11]	-
2018	12,577,200	/	847,900	182,639	-

Source: Radio-Television of Montenegro (2013; 2014; 2015b; 2016a; 2017b; 2018a; 2019a).

---

[7]   Other income includes income from technical services, donations, income from damages, and the restaurant.
[8]   EUR 100,000 are for the cost of digitalization.
[9]   EUR 3,000,000 are for the cost of digitalization.
[10] EUR 6,350,000 are for the cost of digitalization.
[11] Revenue from EU donations: EUR 120,000.

the production and broadcasting of advertising content, production and sale of audiovisual works, sponsorship of program contents, organization of concerts and from others sources (see Table 6.2 presenting the income of the PSB organization in Montenegro).

As can be seen from Table 6.2, most of the funds for the public service broadcaster are provided from the budget. In 2013, the public service broadcaster received from the general budget revenues of Montenegro EUR 7,198,449.

According to the financial plan in 2016, the state would allocate 11,211,000 euros for the operation of RTCG and EUR 3 million for digitalization costs. In 2017, the PSB organization got EUR 11,511,000 for its operation (Radio-Television of Montenegro 2018, 5). In 2018, the PSB organization got EUR 12,577,200 from the budget.

Another important source of financing the public service broadcaster is through advertising and marketing activities. Article 92 Law on Electronic Media limits the advertising time on PSB to six minutes per hour of broadcast or nine minutes of advertisements per hour and teleshopping. According to Article 93, the commercial broadcasters are allowed to advertise for nine minutes per hour or 12 minutes of advertisements and teleshopping. The new draft Law on the National Public Broadcaster—or more precisely, its Article 25—prescribes that advertisement during the prime-time slot, i.e. from 8 p.m. to 10 p.m., may not be longer than four minutes per hour (Law Amending the Law on Public Service Media Radio-Television of Montenegro). As the non-governmental organization CGO warns in its "Equal chances for all media in Montenegro" reports, the fact that state authorities are exclusively advertising in pro-state (or pro-regime) media (Radio and Television of Montenegro 2015a) puts additional pressure on the media market. On the one hand, in this way, the state makes it difficult for the opposition media to survive, but on the other, it financially supports private media in certain situations.[12] Referring to the request for free access to information, the NGO in question received answers from 67% of public sector authorities. Based on this, it found that state institutions are spending EUR 2.5 million on advertising in the media, and having in mind the fact that 30% of institutions did not deliver the requested information, the Centre for Civic Education concluded that this figure is double the amount indicated (Nenezić and Vuković 2017, 7). Despite the investment boom, large global companies are still not that present in Montenegro, so, logically, they do not represent a significant source of advertising revenue, and politicians use this situation to influence the media.

Many experts warned that the legislation of 2008 did not guarantee the financial stability of the public service broadcaster. Article 9 of the 2002 Law on the Public Broadcasting Services Radio of Montenegro and Television of Montenegro stipulated the financing of the public service from the radio broadcasting fee, part of the fee for radio receivers, advertising, sales of its production, sponsorship of programs, organizing concerts and other events, the budget and

---

[12] Through the Program of State Aid to Broadcasters/Electronic Media (2011–2013), the government assumed the commercial broadcasters' debt of EUR 4,447,639.61 to the Agency for Electronic Communications and the Broadcasting Centre. In addition, it aided commercial print media in the amount of EUR 880,802,32.

other sources. This law established the license fee as the primary source of PSB funding, allowing the public broadcaster to be independent of the state support. The law of 2002 imposed an obligation on every household and the legal person that owns a radio to pay a broadcasting subscription. The Broadcasting Agency Council issued a decision regarding the amount of the broadcasting fee in the Republic of Montenegro, which amounted to EUR 3.5 per month. From 2004 until 2007 the subscription fee was collected through the Telecom operator Montenegro Telekom, with a collection rate of 90.6%.[13] Following the Law, 75% of the funds from the subscription were allocated to RTCG, 5% to the Broadcasting Agency (ARD), 10% to municipal public service broadcasters, and 10%t to commercial public service broadcasters (Tadić Mijović 2009, 54).

Table 6.3: Number of Subscribers

Year	Amount per month (in EUR)	Number of subscribers / Collection rate	Incomes from license fee (in million EUR)
2004	3.5	176,630	5.5
2005	3.5	166,840	7.0
2006	3.5	162,762	6.9
2007	3.5	163,936	5.3

Source: Agency for Electronic Media (personal correspondence with the author)

After the Telekom company was privatized, the public broadcasting service had to find a new way to collect subscription fees. One of the options considered was to collect the public service subscription through the citizens' electricity bills. The new billing model was not in the interest of the public service broadcaster as only 85,000 citizens regularly pay their electricity bills, which is 50% less than those who regularly pay their phone bills (Tadić Mijović, 55; see also Table 6.3). The Agency for Electronic Media collected broadcasting subscription fees for several months, but the public service broadcaster was not pleased with the revenues from subscriptions and proposed to abolish them.

Subsequent amendments to the 2008 Law on Public Broadcasting Services of Montenegro set the public service broadcaster back because both the broadcasting subscription fee and the broadcasting fee were abolished. This meant that the public service broadcaster was funded from and depended on the budget of Montenegro. Instead of abolishing the subscription, a new method of collecting the subscription should have been found. In that way, the public service broadcaster would have had a more stable income and would have achieved a greater degree of financial independence from the state since it would have had more diverse sources of income in addition to the budget and would have built a closer relationship with the audience, as was indicated by numerous international organizations to be the main advantage of subscription. The dependence on state

---

[13] Member of the working group in 2002, MNE 01 (interview with the author in March 2015; the interviewee requested to remain anonymous).

funding is rather problematic for several reasons. One is the potential for state influence through the unpredictability of funding due to the frequent changes of the state budget that negatively influence the availability of funds for RTCG.[14] But it is obvious that without support from the state and good political will, the public service broadcaster is left to the will of the market.

The financial problems of RTCG are also the result of irrational spending of the budget funds. Until 2003, RTCG had 1,014 full-time employees and 200 freelancers (Tadić Mijović 2009, 50). After the recommendations given by international experts, the number of employees was first reduced to 793, and today the public service broadcaster has 717 employees. The irrational spending of funds from the budget is testified by financial statements according to which almost double the amount of money is spent on the disbursement of salaries in comparison with the amount spent on the production of programs or investments in equipment.

Table 6.4: Different Types of Costs of RTCG (in EUR)

Year	Costs of personal earnings	Direct and indirect costs of program production and broadcasting	Costs of current and investment maintenance	Costs of equipment depreciation
2012	7,242,623	4,274,236	135,318	776,811
2013	7,310,128	4,475,152	128,931	799,018
2014	7,609,439	4,354,844	75,011	1,159,687
2015	7,284,899	4,586,457	151,173	814,687
2016	7,372,191	4,150,252	186,176	807,827
2017	7,798,740	4,143,230	184,794	550,479
2018	7,843, 847	4,390,715	162,151	462,701

Source: Radio-Television of Montenegro (2013, 9; 2014, 7; 2015b, 8; 2016a, 9; 2017b, 10; 2018a, 8; 2019a).

As can be seen from Table 6.4 above, the cost of personal earnings was higher than the cost of production and broadcasting of programs, investment maintenance, and depreciation of equipment combined. This data best illustrates the irrational spending of taxpayers' money. It should be noted that the cost of per-

---

[14]   The former vice president of the European Broadcasting Union, Boris Bergant, explained that the funding of the public service broadcaster based on the budget is not a good solution. ."By then it was a crisis, and everyone knew that budgets will be changed several times a year and amended because there is no income. Therefore, out of the calculated EUR 12 million, they should have received on this basis, they received only EUR 7 million (interview with the author on April 20, 2015).

sonal earnings includes salaries, taxes, and contributions on salaries, transport, severance pay, jubilee awards, assistance to socially disadvantaged journalists, and fees for the council. This problem, the excessive number of employees, was discussed even in 2002. RTCG was in financial trouble as it allocated 2/3 of the total income for salaries. Already the experts warned that the public service broadcaster could be financially viable with 680 employees (Tadić Mijović 2009, 50). Regardless of all the recommendations, RTCG continues to go around in circles to overcome the same problems.

New Technologies and Digitalization of Public Service Broadcasting

Montenegrin media belatedly followed the trends with technical innovation and developments in the domain of program distribution and production. Experts, and the media themselves, have warned that a significant number of media will not survive the process of digitalization. The reason for such a pessimistic attitude lies in the fact that the majority of Montenegrin media cannot afford to buy the modern equipment and technology needed to produce digitized content.

The digitalization process has divided the main stakeholders in Montenegro. On the one hand, representatives of the commercial media in Montenegro believed that this process was not necessary because of the era of cable television. The editor of a commercial broadcaster considered it unnecessary to invest large amounts of money to build a digital terrestrial network for transmission, in a situation where cable operators cover 85% of the country.[15] On the other hand, some experts have pointed out the advantages of digitalization, citing the following arguments.

Montenegro officially switched from an analog to a digital signal on June 17, 2015, but work on the digitalization process began in 2009. Montenegro has received significant assistance in this process from the EU, which funded the project "Support to the digitalization of the Montenegrin broadcast system—provision of equipment" (Delegation of the European Union to Montenegro 2009). The project is divided into two phases. The first phase concerns the procurement of most of the equipment while the second phase provides for the purchase of the rest of the equipment, staff training, and implementation of the communication campaign. The budget for the first phase of the project amounted to EUR 1.6 million and the delegation from the EU approved the purchase of additional equipment.

To prepare for the process of digitalization, the state adopted the Law on Digital Broadcasting on July 5, 2011, which specifies the obligations of the state

---

[15] Editor of the commercial broadcaster, MNE 03 (interview with the author in May 2015; the interviewee requested to remain anonymous).

and the media during the transition from analog to digital. The Ministry for Information Society and Technology ensured that citizens were informed about the process of digitization. For the dissemination of information, the Ministry launched a webpage digi-tv.me on the website mid.gov.me.

The digitalization process was officially completed on November 27, 2019, when the public broadcaster started broadcasting in HD only. This date was picked for its symbolic value since it marks the 75th anniversary of the Radio of Montenegro and the 55th anniversary of the Television of Montenegro.

Since 2013, the public service broadcaster has had a web portal where it is possible to follow the content online and on-demand. The audience can use the portal to become informed about events in the country and the world and to follow the TV and radio program live. In 2015, through the design of an iPhone application, the public broadcasting service attempted to attract a younger audience. The RTCG portal plans to improve cooperation with its media and will also offer new multimedia content. Journalists are actively using social networks to advertise their content and attract this audience. The RTCG portal also distributes its news through social networks such as Facebook and Twitter.

Socio-Cultural and Political Aspects

Political problems are the most salient type of problem PSB is facing. From previous chapters, we saw that the political pressures in practice are reflected through determining the normative framework for the operation of the public service broadcaster, allocating funds to public service broadcasting from the budget, and through the process of appointments and dismissal of RTCG Council members.

Struggling for its independence in the period after 2000, Montenegro was committed to undertake substantial democratic reforms, including the transformation of their public service broadcaster. Adapting media laws in line with European principles was the first necessary step towards reform. There is no doubt that the legal provisions adopted in 2002 were close to the best European legal practice, but at the same time, it was obvious that the government did not want to give up control over the public service broadcaster. Consequently, PSB related laws were constantly violated by the government, the parliament, and other power holders. One media expert in Montenegro explains the role and the influence of the government on the public service broadcaster in that period in the following manner:

> In line with the law, the non-governmental civil sector participated in the RTCG Council and, according to the interpretation of the law, the Parliament had no authority to elect the proposed candidates from civil society but only to make sure that the selection procedure was followed and to accept what the

civil sector determined. That never happened. The Parliament continuously violated the law it adopted itself. It was already evident there that there was a problem of the political authorities not wanting to release control over the public service broadcaster and everything else was, in a way, brought into question if you do not have that key factor to free the public service broadcaster from the direct influence of the state government.[16]

Bearing in mind that the same political structure has been in power in Montenegro since 1991, it is clear that there have been no significant changes in the media system regarding media freedom. Since the 1990s, there have been some changes in the media market, such as the establishment of opposition media, the influx of foreign capital on the media market, the adoption of the media legislative framework and the Code of Journalists of Montenegro, the establishment of a self-regulatory body, and the start of formal education of journalists. However, journalists still face pressures not only inside the public service broadcaster but also in the private media. The research of the Trade Union of Montenegrin Media in 2016 based on the analysis of qualitative documents, 12 qualitative interviews with journalists, lawyers and media experts, as well as on a survey with 54 journalists from different media, showed that inside the public service broadcaster "editorial offices are not independent of the administrative bodies and that Government officials influence the public service broadcaster administration" (Camović 2016, 19).

When it comes to the public service broadcaster, which has always been under political pressure, the difference was reflected only in the methods and techniques used to exert pressure on the public service broadcaster. The governing structure has exerted pressure through the deterioration of legislation in terms of public service broadcaster financing and administrative bodies since 2008, as well as through violation of the procedure for adopting laws.

For example, in August 2012, the parliament changed the law three times without any public debate.[17] The situation is significantly different today, and since 2014 the Ministry of Culture has organized public consultations during the drafting of the media-related legislative framework. Today, we are seeing problems of a different nature. At public hearings, comments, and contributions from media professionals and experts highlighting the local trends and context were mostly neglected. Meanwhile, decision-makers almost blindly followed the principles and recommendations from the international community, which also demonstrates the tendency of local actors to uncritically accept external solutions and models and not take into account the local context and the specific circumstances in which these solutions must function.

On the other hand, the opposition was also fighting to take control of the public service broadcaster. They succeeded in their intention for the first time in 2016 but two years later they lost the ability to manage the public service broadcaster. In 2016, the representatives of the opposition parties informed the ruling

---

[16]   Media expert, MNE 08 (interview with the author in January 2015; the interviewee requested to remain anonymous).
[17]   Boris Bergant (interview with the author on April 20, 2015).

Democratic Party of Socialists (DPS) that they would sign the Agreement on Free and Fair Elections only under certain conditions.[18] One of the conditions was to relieve Radojka Rutović, the director of Montenegrin television, of duty. The TVCG Director, news editor, and head of the newsdesk handed in their resignations on April 15, and on April 26 the Agreement on Free and Fair Elections was signed. The opposition took over the management of the public service broadcaster, which led to the emergence of new people in managing positions, reflected in its editorial policy. For example, a long-time editor and journalist of the opposition media, Vladan Mićunović, was elected director of TVCG.

So, on the one hand, the public service broadcaster was under pressure from all sides trying to sustain itself, but it is precisely these pressures that do not allow its real transformation and fulfillment of its obligations towards citizens. On the other hand, political parties are fighting to bring their loyal members to the council because they want to manage the public service broadcaster.

Conclusion

Considering the analyzed trends and ongoing debates in Montenegro, it could be concluded that the PSB transformation has undergone an "imitative transformation." In 2002, the public service broadcaster, Radio-Television of Montenegro (RTCG) was established in Montenegro due to specific political circumstances but it has never been truly transformed from a state media into a public service broadcaster. Political struggles over the public service broadcaster have become apparent and it became clear that political actors are again fighting among themselves for their interests, while the public service broadcaster is merely the object and subject matter of negotiations. Both the governing and oppositional actors use different methods to take control of the RTCG. For example, the ruling structure has dismissed three Directors-General of the public service broadcaster, Branko Vojičić (2011), Rade Vojvodić (2016), and Andrijana Kadija (2018). Also, the ruling party (DPS) controls the election of the members of the council through the parliament, which gives it the possibility to appoint its supporters as council members. Alternatively, the opposition uses pre-election campaigning to condition the ruling party by influencing the election of staff in the RTCG Council to control the public service broadcaster. Also, in the period from 2014 to 2016, the opposition blocked the adoption of amendments to the Law on the Public Service Broadcaster, which should regulate the funding scheme of PSB. The state has supported the public broadcaster and fulfilled the Amsterdam Protocol to ensure stable and transparent revenues for RTCG, but the public broadcaster is still unsustainable without budgetary funding despite the various funding sources. It is clear that, under pressure from

---

[18] Parliamentary elections in Montenegro were held in October 2016.

the international community, a solution is being sought regarding creating conditions for the public broadcaster to work and fulfill its responsibility towards society, which includes the state, its citizens, the public and the civil sector.

As already mentioned from the moment of its transformation from 2002 until 2016, RTCG was under the control of the ruling party. From 2016 to 2018, the opposition had taken over the management of the public service broadcaster, but in 2018, RTCG was brought back under the control of the ruling party. This is especially visible in a situation where there are mass protests in Montenegro by which the citizens express their dissatisfaction with the adopted Law on Religious Freedom. The public broadcaster does not report on these events, holding back information of public interest, thereby violating Article 9 of the Law on National Public Broadcaster, as well as professional and ethical standards.

The following are the recommendations to address the weaknesses of the public service broadcaster that allow its misuse:

1. Political pressure is obvious in the process of appointment of members of managing bodies, and individuals close to the government are nominated to be council members. This is evidenced by the situation in 2007, when the parliament blocked the work of the council for four months because it did not want to confirm the appointment of five members, and the situation in 2017 when, due to conflicts of interest, the parliament dismissed two members of the RTCG Council. These events show that this solution is not good for Montenegro. Therefore, neither the Administrative Board nor the parliament should confirm the mandates of the council members, and it is necessary to transfer this role to the Agency for Electronic Media. If the entire procedure of appointments and dismissals of the council members happens in the parliament, then parliament should have only a formal role. According to the recommendation of the Parliamentary Assembly of the Council of Europe CM/REC 2012 on public service media governance, the state, i.e., public institutions may be involved in the appointment of the highest supervisory authorities under the following conditions: this process must not be misused for political influence on the public service broadcaster; appointing criteria must be observed; appointments are made for a specified term, and care should be paid to the balanced representation of men and women in this authority (Council of Europe 2015, 125). If the independence of the council as an administrative body is ensured, the public service broadcaster will achieve a greater degree of independence.

2. To ensure a stable income and financial independence, the state should exempt RTCG from personal income tax, which amounted to EUR 583,402 in 2018.

3. The members of the council should receive symbolic remuneration since EUR 91,284 was spent in 2018 for this purpose for the council and the council meeting.

It should be noted that the state showed goodwill by amending the Law on the Public Service Broadcaster relating to the financing of the PSB in Montenegro and by financing the digitization process.

Based on all of the above, we can conclude that the only way that RTCG can become media that will care about citizens' needs is if the ruling and the opposition parties show goodwill and a desire for a real transformation of the Montenegrin public service broadcaster and not interfere with the editorial policy of the public service broadcaster. If all the political actors do not show willingness and do not support RTCG by leaving it out of their political games, then the public service broadcaster has no future, and it will continue to be political party service in the hands of one side or the other. Such a public service broadcaster can only be of use to one of the political options, but not to citizens who will be deprived of information that is in line with professional and ethical standards in the era of false news and post-truths.

References

Analitika. 2019. "Formira se Fond za medije, država može finansirati privatne medije" [Media Fund to be formed, the state may finance private media]. *Analitika,* February 22. Accessed May 13, 2020. http://portalanalitika.me/clanak/326840/formira-se-fond-za-medije-drzava-moze-finansirati-privatne-medije.

Burzan, Snežana. 2012. "Javni servis—demokratska potreba građana XXI vijeka (na primjeru RTCG, HRT, RTS i BHRT)" [Public service—the democratic need of 21st-century citizens (on the example of: RTCG, HRT, RTS, and BHRT]. Master's thesis, University of Montenegro.

Camović, Marijana. 2016. *Indikatori nivoa medijskih sloboda i bezbjednosti novinara u Crnoj Gori* [Indicators of the Level of Media Freedoms and Journalist Safety in Montenegro]. Podgorica: Trade Union of Media of Montenegro.

Council of Europe. 2015. *Zbornik odabranih pravnih instrumenata Saveta Evrope u vezi sa medijima 2007–2014* [Collection of selected legal acts of the Council of Europe on media 2007–2014]. Belgrade: Council of Europe.

Čepić, Ljiljana. 2017. "Javna tribina o programskom sadržaju RTCG" [Public discussion on the program contents of RTCG]. *PV portal.me*, May 30. Accessed May 13, 2020. http://pvportal.me/2017/05/javna-tribina-o-programskom-sadrzaju-rtcg/.

Delegation of the European Union to Montenegro. 2009. *Supply of Digital Equipment for the Support to the Transformation of the Radio Television of Montenegro into a Public Service Broadcaster.* Podgorica: Delegation of the European Union to Montenegro. https://www.devex.com/funding/r?report=tender-51161&filter%5Bstatuses%5D %5B%5D=forecast&filter%5Bstatuses%5D%5B%5D=open&sorting%5Border%5D=desc&sorting%5Bfield%5D=updated_at.

Government of Montenegro. 2019. *Proposal of the Law of the National Public Broadcaster Radio and Television of Montenegro.* Accessed May 13, 2020. http://zakoni.skupstina.me/zakoni/web/dokumenta/zakoni-i-drugi-akti/858/2153-12659-10-3-19-1.pdf.

Hallin, Daniel C., and Paolo Mancini. 2004. *Comparing Media Systems: Three Models of Media and Politics*. Cambridge: Cambridge University Press.

Law Amending the Law on Public Broadcasting Services of Montenegro [Zakon o izmjenama i dopunama Zakona o javnim radio-difuznim servisima Crne Gore]. Accessed May 14, 2020. http://www.mku.gov.me/vijesti/142581/Nacrt-zakona-o-izmjenama-i-dopunama-Zakona-o-javnim-radio-difuznim-servisima-u-Crnoj-Gori.html.

Law Amending the Law on Public Service Media Radio and Television of Montenegro [Zakon o izmjenama i dopunama Zakona o nacionalnom javnom emiteru Radio i Televizija Crne Gore]. Accessed May 14, 2020. http://www.mku.gov.me/rubrike/JavneRasprave/195253/J-A-V-N-I-P-O-Z-I-V-za-sprovodenje-javne-rasprave-o-Nacrtu-zakona-o-izmjenama-i-dopunama-Zakona-o-nacionalnom-javnom-emiteru-Rad.html.

Law on Broadcasting [Zakon o radio-difuziji]. *Official Gazette of Montenegro* 51/02.

Law on Electronic Media [Zakon o elektronskim medijima]. *Official Gazette of Montenegro* 46/10 of 6 August 2010, 040/11 of 8 August 2011, 053/11 of 11 November of 2011, 006/13 of 31 January 2013, 055/16 of 17 August 2016, 092/17 of 30 December 2017.

Law on Media [Zakon o medijima]. *Official Gazette of Montenegro* 51/02.

Law on Public Broadcasting Services of Montenegro [Zakon o javnim radio-difuznim servisima Crne Gore]. *Official Gazette of Montenegro* 51/02.

Law on Public Service Broadcasting Media "Radio of Montenegro" and "Television Montenegro" [Zakon o javnim radio-difuznim servisima "Radio Crne Gore" i "Televizija Crne Gore"]. *Official Gazette of Montenegro* 51/02.

Law on the National Public Broadcaster Radio and Television of Montenegro [Zakon o nacionalnom javnom emiteru Radio i Televizija Crne Gore]. *Official Gazette of Montenegro* 079/08 of 23 December 2008, 045/12 of 17 August 2012, 043/16 of 20 July 2016, 054/16 of 15 August 2016.

Maroš, Miomir. 2012. "Brendiranje crnogorskih medija (Na primjerima: RTCG, Pobjede, TV Vijesti i nezavisnog dnevnika Vijesti" [Montenegrin media branding (on the example of RTCG, Pobjeda, TV Vijesti, and independent daily Vijesti)]. Master's thesis, University of Montenegro.

Nenezić, Ana, and Dragoljub Duško Vuković. 2017. *Jednake šanse za sve medije u Crnoj Gori* [Equal chances for all media in Montenegro]. Podgorica: Centar za građansko obrazovanje.

Radio and Television of Montenegro. 2019a. *Finansijski izvještaj RTCG od 01.01. do 31.12.2018* [Financial report from January 1 to December 31, 2018]. Podgorica: RTCG. http://www.rtcg.me/sw4i/download/files/article/FINANSIJSKI%20IZVJESTAJ%20RTCG%202018.pdf?id=2203.

Radio and Television of Montenegro. 2019b. *Program-production Plan for 2019*. Podgorica: RTCG.

Radio and Television of Montenegro. 2018a. *Finansijski izvještaj RTCG od 01.01. do 31.12.2017* [RTCG financial statements for the period from 1 January to 31 December 2017]. Podgorica: RTCG.

——. 2018b. *Program-production Plan for 2018*. Podgorica: RTCG.

——. 2017a. *Izvještaj o sprovođenju javne rasprave o prijedlogu programskih obaveza RTCG* [Report on the public debate on the proposal of programming obligations of RTCG]. Podgorica: RTCG. http://www.rtcg.me/rtcg/javna-rasprava.html.

——. 2017b. *Finansijski izvještaj RTCG od 01.01. do 31.1.2016* [RTCG financial statements for the period from 1 January to 31 December 2016]. Podgorica: RTCG.

——. 2017c. *Program-production Plan for 2017*. Podgorica: RTCG.

——. 2016a. *Finansijski izvještaj RTCG za 2015* [RTCG financial statement for 2015]. Podgorica: RTCG.

——. 2016b. *Program-production Plan for 2016*. Podgorica: RTCG.

——. 2015a. *Prikrivena cenzura urušava slobodu medija* [Covert censorship undermines media freedom]. Podgorica: RTCG.

——. 2015b. *Finansijski izvještaj RTCG za 2014 godinu* [RTCG financial statement for 2014]. Podgorica: RTCG.

——. 2015c. *Program-production Plan for 2015*. Podgorica: RTCG.

——. 2014. *Finansijski izvještaj RTCG za 2013 godinu* [RTCG financial statement for 2013]. Podgorica: RTCG.

——. 2013. *Godišnji izvještaj o finansijskom poslovanju za period od 01.01. do 31.12.2012* [Annual financial statements for the period from January 1 to December 31, 2012]. Podgorica: RTCG.

——. 2011. *Pravilnik o unutrašnjoj organizaciji i sistematizaciji radnih mjesta Javnog preduzeća Radio i Televizija Crne Gore* [Rulebook on internal organization and job descriptions in the public company Radio and Television of Montenegro]. Podgorica: RTCG.

Reporters Without Borders. 2015. *2015 World Press Freedom Index*. Accessed May 13, 2020. https://rsf.org/fr/ranking/2015.

——. 2019. *2019 World Press Freedom Index*. Accessed May 13, 2020. https://rsf.org/en/ranking/2019.

Ružić, Nataša. 2019. "Public Service Media in Montenegro—a Leaf Aflutter in the Wind." In *A Pillar of Democracy on Shaky Ground—Public Service Media in South East Europe*, edited by Darija Fabijanić and Hendrik Sittig, 151–172. Berlin: Konrad-Adenauer-Stiftung. https://www.kas.de/en/web/medien-europa/single-title/-/content/new-book-a-pillar-of-democracy-on-shaky-ground-public-service-media-in-south-east-europe.

Tadić Mijović, Milka. 2009. *Transformacija RTCG u javni servis (zakonski okvir i praksa)* [Transformation of RTCG into a public service broadcaster (legal framework and practice)]. Master's thesis, University of Montenegro.

Vukanović, Zvezdan. 2006. *Strateško pozicioniranje javnog TV servisa: Komparativna analiza iskustava BBC-ja, RTS i RTCG* [Strategic positioning of public service broadcasters: a comparative analysis of BBC, RTS and RTCG]. Podgorica: IAMM.

Vukićević, Boris, and Zlatko Vujović. 2012. "Ustavni i političkopravni okvir parlamenta u Crnoj Gori 1989–2012" [Constitutional and legal-political framework of the parliament in Montenegro, 1989–2012], in *Demokratske performanse parlamenata Srbije, Bosne i Hercegovine i Crne Gore* [Democratic performance of the parliaments of Serbia, Bosnia and Herzegovina and Montenegro], edited by Slaviša Orlović, 55–76. Belgrade/Sarajevo/Podgorica: University of Belgrade/Sarajevo Open Center/University of Montenegro. http://www.fpn.bg.ac.rs/wp-content/uploads /Demokratske-performanse-parlamenata-Srbije-Bosne-i-Hercegovine-i-Crne-Gore-Slavisa-Orlovic.pdf.

CHAPTER 7

Four Normative Principles for Participatory Public Service Model in North Macedonia[1]

Snežana Trpevska and Igor Micevski

Introduction

One of the main reasons for the failure to transform a former state broadcaster into the public service broadcaster in North Macedonia is the political parallelism that has been manifested with the strong and durable links between political parties and media. The all-pervading political pressure on the public broadcaster, has turned from modest, subtle, and concealed (as was the case during the 1990s) to intensive, direct, and open (since 2008). The non-transparent and insufficient funding of PSB, the intensified and direct clientelistic ties between editors, journalists, and political actors, and the open threats and intimidations that resulted in censorship and self-censorship have partaken in the overall "politicization" of the PSB organization's titular mission, namely to operate in the name of the public interest. This chapter explores perspectives for overcoming the obstacles for North Macedonian PSB's transformation along with four principles: citizenship (Thomass 2004), universality, quality (Born and Prosser 2001, 657) and trust (Brevini 2013, 31). These principles are central to the idea of PSB and are revisited in the ongoing debates on PSB in the current technological setting (Lowe and Bardoel 2007; Jakubowicz 2010, 9). While universality and quality are already recognized in the present normative model, citizenship and trust should be elaborated as normative principles with increased value and significance.

These core principles should be considered as a basis for developing the idea of a "Participatory Public Service Model" (PPSM) which would open new channels and protocols for active participation of citizens and civil society in the creation and implementation of public media policies in North Macedonia.

---

[1] The analysis covers the events that took place until the end of 2017, but two years after, the situation in the public service broadcaster has not been substantially changed since the election of the supervisory and managing bodies have been blocked in the parliament.

However, the reification of this idea would require PSB's transformation at all levels including normative, programming, organizational, and technological. It also includes an obligation of the PSB editorial staff to critically monitor and assess the implementation of current policies and to actively encourage and incorporate the opinion of diverse publics in formulating its editorial policy.

Socio-Political Context and PSB's Failed Transformation

The multi-party system in North Macedonia is marked by an ethnically-based divergence where the main political parties are divided into two ethnic blocks representing the country's Macedonian and Albanian ethnic communities. The issue of the power division and balance between the two communities led to a brief armed conflict in 2001, followed by a new agreement on power-sharing at both the central and local levels. Over the last several decades, the Macedonian political system has not evolved into a consolidated democracy. On the contrary, during the rule of the populist VMRO-DPMNE (Internal Macedonian Revolutionary Organization – Democratic Party for Macedonian National Unity) from 2006 until 2017, converse trends of stronger authoritarianism led the state into the group of so-called "hybrid regimes" (Damjanovski 2016). In December 2012, the country entered into the biggest political and social crisis that culminated with the so-called "phone tapping scandal" which indicated large-scale corruption among the ruling party officials, electoral fraud, wiretapping of more than a hundred journalists, direct connections between the highest officials and media owners and many other unlawful activities.[2] The scandal ended with the EU-mediated agreement, known as the "Przino Agreement," which implied serious political reforms including a thorough reform of the media system. The long-term political crisis ended in June 2017 when the opposition political parties managed to establish the parliamentary majority and the new government was formed. The new government committed itself to carry out democratic reforms in several key areas including the media system and accepted the initiative of the non-governmental sector for urgent legal changes which would mark the start of media reforms.

The particularities of the North Macedonian political system affected the country's media system. Though the constitution and the media legislation provide guarantees for freedom of expression and media pluralism, self-regulation mechanisms have been established to ensure professionalism and high ethical standards such as the Code of Ethics of Journalists (Association of Journalists

---

[2]   On February 9, 2015, the main opposition party SDSM began publishing audio-recorded conversations featuring a widespread misuse of authority, election fraud, corruption scandals, the controlled appointment of main judicial office positions, instrumentalization of the police, direct control of the media, etc. The scandal marked the tipping point of a lengthy political crisis in the country.

of Macedonia n.d.), the media in practice are burdened by ethnically-motivated politics. Both the public broadcasting and the commercial media are divided and primarily serve the interests of affiliated ethnic communities and related ethnopolitical elites (Micevski, Trpevska, and Trajkoska 2013, 117). They are also burdened by firm clientelistic ties between media owners, editorial staff, and politicians, which has a negative influence on professional standards and ethics (Trpevska and Micevski 2014, 301). In the last decade, until 2017, the ruling party VMRO-DPMNE dominated the mainstream (commercial and public) media to serve its political and economic interests (Ordanoski 2012).

The public broadcasting in North Macedonia has undergone three major normative transformations since the country became an independent state in 1991.[3] First, the 1997 Broadcasting Law and the 1998 Law on the Founding of the Public Enterprise Macedonian Radio and Television (MRT), set the normative ground for its transformation into a public broadcaster. Second, in 2005, the Law on Broadcasting Activity explicitly defined MRT as a public service with clear provisions for its programming functions, editorial independence and institutional autonomy, including regulation of its governing bodies: the MRT Council, the Managerial Board, and the Executive Director. Finally, while the 2013 Law on Audio and Audiovisual Media Services normatively guarantees the independence of the broadcaster, it decreased the presence of the civil society sector in the MRT Program Council.

There is a general consideration that MRT was only normatively defined as a public service, but that its transformation from a state to a public broadcaster has not occurred (Šopar 2005, 1188). Although international donors have provided significant expert assistance over the years to support the transformation process, MRT has never truly performed the role of a public broadcaster that serves the interests of the citizens instead of those of the ruling parties (Dimitrijevska-Markoski and Daskalovski 2013). Numerous studies have provided evidence that a reverse trend is happening: MRT has always functioned as a state broadcaster and in recent years as a party-colonized broadcaster: it mostly offered one-sided information and critical voices were generally neglected in information programs and it did not provide sufficient space for public debate. Almost all monitoring missions conducted by OSCE/ODIHR during election campaigns demonstrated that MRT continuously gave a prominent place in its prime-time coverage to the representatives of the ruling parties.[4] A range of local monitoring projects of the election coverage came to similar conclusions (Media Development Center 2014, 11).

Our previous studies of the MRTV news broadcasts (Trpevska and Micevski 2013) and of the routines in the newsrooms (Micevski, Trpevska, and Trajkoska 2013), demonstrated that while normatively its functions have been demarcated in the direction of respect for the public interest, practically it failed to produce

---

[3] As it became a member state of the Council of Europe in 1995, Macedonia undertook obligations to incorporate in its legislation the basic tenets of the European media policy, including the concept of PSB.

[4] See more details in the reports from the OSCE Office for Democratic Institutions and Human Rights (n.d.).

high-quality programs that reflect the public interest and restore public trust. In 2015 and 2016 we conducted a comprehensive content analysis of political pluralism in the news programs which demonstrated not only the tremendous party-political grip over the PSB editorial policy but also a synchronization in the daily reporting of both the public television and three pro-governmental TV stations (Sitel, Alfa, and Kanal 5). The selection of topics, sources cited, and the framing of the stories were in favor of the ruling VMRO-DPMNE. Also, the analysis showed that the two public TV channels (MTV1 and MTV2) strongly favored VMRO-DPMNE and DUI (Democratic Union for Integration) respectfully. Thus, they have turned the news into a mouthpiece for the leading parties (Institute for Communication Studies 2015).

MRT has been facing both financial and organizational problems since the late 1990s, which has generated a profound production crisis, a decline of audience shares, and the erosion of its credibility. In the period before and after the adoption of the Broadcasting Law in 2005, the system for the collection of the broadcasting tax collapsed. The Law on Audio and Audiovisual Media Services from 2013 kept the funding model as was the case before, based on the broadcasting tax. This model still contained major deficiencies that prevented MRT from becoming independent. The first deficiency was that MRT had no direct control over the collection of the broadcasting tax but depended on the work of the Public Revenue Office. The second, bigger deficiency of the model was that it was too expensive. So, despite some improvements in the tax collection system, the collected funds could not cover the costs for full operation of MRT which eventually made MRT financially very weak and still dependent on the state budget. In September 2017, the new government abolished the broadcasting tax and adopted amendments to the Law on Audio and Audiovisual Media Services according to which MRT is funded from the state budget. A fixed percentage was determined in the law: 0.5% of the total annual state budget, despite the criticism of the Association of Journalists and experts that this percentage should be doubled to cover MRT's full operational costs.

Formally, MRT is governed by two separate bodies, a Programming Council and a Supervisory Board, the first one entitled to supervise MRT's programming functions and the other to oversee its financial operations. The Programming Council also has a crucial role in setting MRT's governing and editorial structure: it is responsible for the election and dismissal of the Director, Deputy Director, and the members of the Supervisory Board. Also, the Programming Council approves appointments or dismissals of MRT editors. In the last decade, party-political domination over the public broadcaster was exerted primarily through the election of individuals close to the ruling parties in the Programming Council and then, through the influence of the Programming Council, on the election of the highest managing and editorial positions in MRT. This influence was partially a consequence of the appointment model envisaged in the Law on Audio and Audiovisual Media Services which envisages that members of the MRT Programming Council are proposed by state bodies, institutions financed from the state budget and organizations controlled by the political parties. Thus, although certain general safeguards of institutional autonomy and editorial independence do exist in the legislation, in reality, MRT has been indirectly governed by the political parties in power through their daily connections with the management team and key editorial staff (Mitevska 2017, 11).

MRT is a legal entity composed of two main organizational parts: Macedonian Television and Macedonian Radio which broadcast three television and three radio program services. The first television service broadcasts programs in the Macedonian language, the second is reserved for the programs in the languages of several ethnic communities in Macedonia, and the third TV service retransmits the sessions of the parliament and its committees. MRT also broadcasts one television and one radio satellite program in the Macedonian language and special radio programs in foreign languages aimed at the neighboring countries and Europe. On the public radio, the first and the second service are in the Macedonian language, and the third is intended for broadcasting in the languages of the ethnic communities. The total number of employees of the Macedonian Radio and Television in June 2018 was 839 persons.

In addition to the Macedonian language, MRT Broadcasts Programs in several other languages. Macedonian Television Broadcasts Programs in Albanian (14.5 hours daily), Turkish (2.5 hours daily), and Serbian, Roma, Vlach, and Bosnian language (each language: 30 minutes three times weekly, plus one hour monthly). Macedonian radio broadcasts in Albanian (17 hours daily), Turkish (5 hours), and Serbian, Roma, Vlach, and Bosnian language (each language: 30 minutes daily). In addition to that, Macedonian radio broadcasts programs in Bulgarian and Greek language for the listeners in neighboring countries.

The process of digitalization of the terrestrial television (DTT) in North Macedonia ended in May 2013, one year later than the originally planned deadline. The digital transmission of public television services (MTV) was enacted at the beginning of 2012 when two digital networks (MUX4 and MUX5) were legally allocated to the public enterprise Macedonian Broadcasting. Although the usage of digital transmission resources created more space (channels) for public television to fulfill its remit, MRT still broadcasts the same three TV services as in the analog environment. In its strategic document, the regulator emphasized that "the public service, depending on the needs of the audience and the financial capabilities, [has] to conceive, create and develop other specialized services" (Broadcasting Council 2007, 18).

MRT has started using the internet and social media to disseminate news and information produced by its newsroom. There is an official website[5] where the information is published daily, a Facebook page, and a Twitter account[6] where it mostly presents selected information on the activities of the highest officials and most important events in the country. There is also an MRT YouTube channel, but it does not contain any video news or other content produced by MRT.[7] On MRT's website, diverse content is presented: news on the current events in the country and the world, information on MRT programming, program schedule, as well as on-demand service (MRT Play) where news items and

---

5   Available at: http://www.mrt.com.mk/vesti.
6   Available at: https://twitter.com/mrt1web.
7   Available at: https://www.youtube.com/channel/UCurlFwDSxgYvFaX_COFo0mQ

other programs can be watched. In the past years, while VMRO-DPMNE was in power, the news presented on the webpage was selected and framed to favor the ruling political party, but in the last year and a half, there were significant changes in its editorial policy towards more objective and balanced reporting. MRT's webpage does not contain a specific part where the audience is invited to contribute with user-generated content or to make comments on MRT programming, thus giving the audience opportunity to be heard, participate, or to create content.

The main disadvantage of all previous attempts for the normative transformation of MRT was that they neglected the importance of its relationship with its citizens and civil society and left a lot of room for direct political influence. Therefore, our main claim is that the Macedonian PSB has a future only if it moves towards a "participatory model" that would use existing technologies and would create new organizational structures to enable PSB to enact protocols for the inclusion of publics "from below." This model would enable PSB to establish an enduring relationship with the public and civil society as a basic condition for regaining trust and legitimacy in society.

Assessment of the Four Normative Principles

The first step in considering the conditions and prospects for the introduction of PPSM in North Macedonia should be an analysis of the domestic legislation and practice in terms of the aforementioned four normative principles. Some of these principles are to some extent incorporated in the current Law on Audio and Audiovisual Media Services, but it is necessary to discuss their further normative operationalization in the context of transforming the mission of PSB in the new technological environment, strengthening the relationship with citizens and raising the level of trust among the public.

The principle of universality is fundamental for the public service and it should be addressed with two dimensions in mind: the universality of access and universality of content. The universality of access refers to both technical, social, and content aspects (Council of Europe 2007). It means that PSB services should be technically available to all members of society regardless of their geographic or socioeconomic circumstances and should be able to cater to the different interests and tastes of society. As such, universality is defined in the current Law on Audio and Audiovisual Media Services (Art. 110, para. 1 and 2) only as a general obligation: MRT is obliged to develop and broadcast programs available to the overall public, to plan the program scheme in the interest of all societal segments without any discrimination, taking into account the special groups in the society. Available analyses by the regulatory authority and audience research data indicate that MRT services are technically accessible to the audience in the country, but most of the content broadcasted to those services is not viewed at all by the biggest part of the intended audience (Agency for

Audio and Audiovisual Media Services 2011). A clear indicator for that, according to the Nielsen Audience Measurements, is the overall audience share of the two main TV services offered by MRT in 2016 which was 4.1%, the first service having 3.6%, and the second 0.5% of the audience share. In the context of new technologies and the internet, the universality of access is no longer reduced to delivery of terrestrial program services available to all segments of the population, but also that program offers are present on all relevant online platforms. Regarding the use of new technologies to reach larger audiences, it can certainly be said that MRT has not developed any strategy for developing a portfolio of new services, neither generalist nor specialized or tailored for specific audiences.

The second dimension of universality is the requirement for program diversity (universality of content), which is defined in the Law on Audio and Audiovisual Media Services with regard to all its dimensions: the genres of programs offered, the audiences targeted, and the subjects discussed. For example, MRT is obliged to create and broadcast "high-quality programs on all political, economic, social, health-related, cultural, entertaining, educational, scientific, religious, environmental, sporting and other events" (Art. 110, para 3 and 4). However, MRT fails to offer program diversity in its existing program services, neglecting the interests of some important segments of the audience. In the analog environment, Macedonian Television faced serious problems to fulfill its obligation for diversity, primarily since there was a lack of frequencies for terrestrial broadcasting. The same conclusion was made by the regulator in its assessment of MRT's diversity obligation: "the public service needs one more frequency to fulfill its educational function ... because one of the crucial shortcomings of its programming is the lack of a serious approach towards children" (Agency for Audio and Audiovisual Media Services 2011, 19). The problem regarding the lack of frequencies could have been solved with the digitalization process because the DTT allows the distribution of more program services by using the same frequency. However, there is still neither vision nor concrete plans made by MRT managing bodies in that direction.

There are many views and definitions on what represents the principle of quality because this is a concept which varies according to social, cultural, and ethical values of different societal systems. However, in the context of the PSB organization in North Macedonia, we will emphasize the stance which argues that quality is to be conceived as a relation between its programs and set of values that promote citizenship and democracy. In that sense, the first aspect of the principle of quality is the independence of news and current affairs programs which is formally introduced in the law to ensure that MRT is a forum where ideas, opinions, and criticism can be expressed freely and that MRT programs are independent and protected from any kind of influence from the government, political organizations or other centers of economic and political power. But in practice, the main news programs of the PSB organization, both on the first and the second TV channels, do not fulfill the basic requirements for balanced reporting reflecting different political views. A content analysis conducted in 2013 revealed how political bias in MTV newsrooms was constructed during election time (Trpevska and Micevski 2013). MTV 1 allocated most of the time in its prime-time news for the ruling party VMRO/DPMNE's coalition campaign, airing an "enormous number of news items in which the ministers promote the results of the Government's work and announce investments, infrastructural buildings, investments in industrial zones and a series of other projects" (Trpevska and Micevski 2013, 5). On the other side, the main news in the Albanian language on MTV 2 emphasized the campaign of DUI, the ruling party of ethnic Albanians, by directly promoting their achieved results and by using many positive value assessments (Trpevska and Micevski 2013, 12). Recent studies provide evidence on the tremendous political-party grip over PSB editorial policy (Institute for Communication Studies 2015).

A comprehensive qualitative content analysis of the political pluralism in the news programs indicated even synchronization in the daily reporting of the public television and three pro-governmental TV stations Sitel, Alfa and Kanal 5; both the selection of topics, sources cited and the framing of the stories were in favor of the ruling VMRO-DPMNE. Also, the analysis showed that the two public TV channels (MTV1 and MTV2) strongly favor VMRO-DPMNE and DUI, respectively (Institute for Communication Studies 2015).

There are also other aspects of the principle of quality, but here we will also highlight one that is very important for Macedonian society which is divided along ethnic, religious, and ideological lines. The public service has a specific role in this society: to foster social cohesion, to promote tolerance and understanding, respect for differences, the sense of peace, suppression of discrimination and the benefits of the civic society (Law on Audio and Audiovisual Media Services, Art. 110, para 6 to 10). However, the consociational aspects of the Macedonian political system are reflected in the development of the media system, which is described as "a typical segmented plural system in which social cleavages are mapped onto media cleavages" (Bašić Hrvatin and Thompson 2008, 30). This is also reflected in the organizational structure and program output of the Macedonian Radio and Television, which is divided among the two biggest ethnic communities in the country, while the other or "smaller" ethnic groups receive only minor shares in its division. The newsrooms in Macedonian and in the languages of non-majority communities (especially the newsroom in the Albanian language) function as separate, parallel worlds that primarily focus on their ethnic community and frame and observe the events predominantly from the point of view of their own community.

There is no doubt that the quality of programming, especially the issues of impartiality and distance from centers of political power, is directly connected with the principle of trust. So far, trust has not been considered as a normative principle (either at the European or at the national level), but rather as one of the consequences of the achieved quality. We believe that this normative principle has to be taken into consideration in any discussion about the perspectives of PSB in the Western Balkans because it could lead towards the creation of closer connections between the public broadcasters and citizens, but also provide a potential tool of resistance to political and other pressures. For that purpose, it is of crucial importance to oblige PSB, on the one hand, to adopt internal program standards and on the other, to take into consideration the citizens' assessment on the overall program quality and more specifically on the trustworthiness of PSB news programs. In the current Law on Audio and Audiovisual Media Services, there is only one provision that is indirectly related to the principle of trust: the MRT Program Council is obliged to monitor the comments and suggestions of the audience regarding the broadcast program and to ask from the MRT Director "to adjust the scope, structure and overall quality of the program content" (Art. 124). However, it has to be emphasized that to determine the citizens' trust in news and other programs it is not sufficient to monitor comments and suggestions of the audience but to oblige PSB to regularly commission and use reliable data produced by independent research organizations. There is no evidence that the MRT Council has so far systematically taken into consideration audience perceptions about the program quality.

The principle of citizenship is defined as comprising of four dimensions of rights: civil, political, social, and communication rights. This definition is based on a conception of democracy which implies that "citizens are given the opportunity to fully participate in politics and therefore are able to renegotiate the common good" (Brevini 2013, 42). Communication rights are of crucial importance for the accomplishment of other rights and citizens' participation in the overall democratic processes. Therefore, we claim that the requirement for the promotion of citizens' communicative rights should be incorporated as a key normative obligation of the participatory public service media. All the previous normative models of PSB in the Western Balkans failed to take into consideration this requirement and this was probably one of the reasons why the attempts to transform state media into genuine public service broadcasters failed. In the current Law on Audio and Audiovisual Media Services, there is only a general requirement for PSB to "develop and broadcast programs focused on encouraging media literacy" (Art. 110) without elaborating on what media literacy is. Nothing else is mentioned in the legislation in terms of encouraging citizens to create content or to use new online platforms and social networks to promote citizens' participation in the public sphere.

Conclusion

In North Macedonia, as well as in the rest of Southern Europe, the public interest has been disregarded and usually confused with the state interest. In this regard, the concept of PSB has been hijacked by those in power. As a result of the advent of new technologies and multi-platforms that have fragmented audiences and distracted some of the audiences away from PSB content, a new possibility for the future of PSM has arisen. New technologies do not entail blurring of the public interest and loss of audiences. They may entail, on the contrary, strengthening participative democracy, provided that they have a platform to which this participation would be channeled. The online sphere could serve as a gateway to the future of participative citizenship, which will require the conceptualization of a new PSB model that is based on participation as a primary characteristic. In such a participative model, citizens should not be identified with consumers, since their role is not of a consuming nature only, but about bringing societal and political relevance into the public sphere. This concept of citizenship may thus be beneficial for a participative model of PSB.

Consequently, the chapter claims that there is a need for a participatory shift in the functioning of PSB in Macedonia to enable stronger participation. Additionally, this model will enable universality in both access and content terms, but also will bring new quality and trust—referring to the possibility that the future PSB will be able to sustain basic PSB norms on a digital platform. This will entail a greater role for the civil sector and foster active citizenship. The Participatory Public Service Model is not a new concept either at theoretical or at the policy level (Council of Europe 2009), but it represents the most prominent framework to save the public interest idea in the specific societal and political circumstances such as those in North Macedonia. PSB, by definition, is envisaged as space which enables the flourishing of a critical and vibrant public sphere and, therefore, it has a crucial role in enabling citizens' active participation in the process of social change.

Such a participatory model provides citizens with a possibility for stronger participation at various levels—strengthening their involvement not only in supervisory bodies but also in the program assessment and production. The precise modalities of this participatory shift in the organization of PSB are yet to be formulated with respect to the normative ideas of the functioning of its bodies. However, on this occasion as a starting point, we make general suggestions calling upon reform in three basic areas: first, we propose changes in the modes of election, the composition and the functioning of the MRT's Program Council; second, we propose changes in programming and the nomination procedure and the obligations of the editorial staff in the PSB organization; third, we propose changes in the MRT's funding model, as a precondition for PSB transformation; and, fourth, development of media literacy awareness and skills among citizens would serve a long-term strategic goal to promote the value of such a re-conceptualized PSB model.

The first set of changes entail that the majority of the members of the MRT's Council are to be recruited from the relevant segments of the CSO sector, to strengthen its influence on the MRT programming and to safeguard the public interest. This set of changes would include obligations for the members of the MRT's Council to organize regular public hearings within constituencies to discuss all relevant issues related to programming and its editorial independence. Besides, MRT's management should be obliged to commission regular analyses and studies about citizens' perceptions and program appreciations which would be submitted to the council for debate. The interactivity of this sort is an enormous possibility of the digital age and, therefore, this is a rather new opportunity instead of a disadvantage for PSB.

Secondly, the participatory shift in MRT's program departments, especially in the newsrooms, implies their obligation to establish and maintain regular connections with its audiences to foster their active participation in programming. Again, the digital age is an enabling vehicle for this sort of interaction with audiences. We propose changes in the legislation to oblige the PSB organization to promote the democratic participation of the citizens in its programming, as part of its remit. Also, PSB should be legally obliged to develop and adopt specific internal rules on how to encourage interaction with the citizens and how to incorporate citizens' diverse opinions and content in a range of informative, educational, cultural, and other programs. Next, the PSB organization should be obliged to establish a separate department in its internal structure which will regularly contact, collect, and analyze citizens' opinions, proposals, and complaints regarding its programming.

The third set of changes needs to entail transparency in the financing of the PSB organization to enable the break of the clientelistic ties and the party colonization of the MRT. This would require a serious analysis that would precede a legislative change, mainly to address and regulate the state aid. The current proposals for securing stable and independent funding for MRT are focused on finding an appropriate mixed model, i.e., both from the broadcasting tax and from a legally determined percentage of the state budget that will be automatically transferred to MRT. This proposal seems to be a good long-term solution for MRT's institutional autonomy, but additional rules should be incorporated in the Law on Audio and Audiovisual Media Services to foster its financial transparency and accountability. Although the current legal provisions incorporate some rules on financial transparency, it is necessary to elaborate more detailed provisions in order to make MRT's diverse funding sources more transparent.

Finally, the fourth area of intervention should be focused on developing general media literacy skills of citizens, especially their communicative and participative skills. This dimension of the media literacy approach is of special relevance for the participatory PSM model because without such competencies citizens would not be able to use media creatively and to exercise their democratic rights and civil responsibilities. A communicative and participative dimension implies the development of various individual competencies such as (1) social relations, or making and maintaining contacts through media and social media and following trends relayed by the media and peer groups; (2) participation in the public sphere, or maintaining participation with a group that shares common values, using social media to manage strategic contacts with other groups, adopting appropriate presentations of identity and interacting with multiple institutions appropriately; (3) content creation, or sharing commonly created devices, fostering active collaborative work and cooperation, solving problems through active cooperation, collaboration and conceptualizing, and creating and producing new media texts (DTI and EAVI 2011, 24). The development of these competencies would encourage democratic participation, thus transforming the segments of audiences into Media Active Publics (Micevski 2014).

References

Agency for Audio and Audiovisual Media Services. 2011. *Izvestaj od analizata na televiziskite programski servisi na javniot radiodifuzen servis MRT (3–9.10.2011)* [Report from the analysis of the television program services of the public service broadcasting MRT (3–9 October 2011)]. Skopje: Agency for Audio and Audiovisual Media Services. https://avmu.mk/wp-content/uploads/2017/05/Analiza_na_TV_programski_servisi_na_JRS_MRT_2.pdf.

Association of Journalists of Macedonia. n.d. Code of Ethics of Journalists [Кодекс на новинарите на Македонија]. Accessed May 13, 2020. https://znm.org.mk/кодекс-на-новинарите/?lang=en.

Bašić-Hrvatin, Sandra, and Mark Thompson. 2008. "Public Service Broadcasting in Plural and Divided Societies." In *Divided They Fall: Public Service Broadcasting in Multiethnic States*, edited by Sandra Bašić-Hrvatin, Mark Thompson and Tarik Jusić, 7–40. Sarajevo: Mediacentar. https://www.academia.edu/28197065/Divided_They_Fall_Public_Service_Broadcasting_in_Multiethnic_States_ed.

Born, Georgina, and Tony Prosser. 2001. "Culture and Consumerism: Citizenship, Public Service Broadcasting and the BBC's Fair Trading Obligations." *The Modern Law Review* 64, no. 5 (September): 657–687.

Brevini, Benedetta. 2013. *Public Service Broadcasting Online: A Comparative European Policy Study of PSB 2.0.* Basingstoke: Palgrave Macmillan.

Broadcasting Council. 2007. *Strategy for Development of Broadcasting Activity in the Republic of Macedonia: for the period 2007–2012.* Skopje: Broadcasting Council of the Republic of Macedonia. https://www.yumpu.com/en/document/read/54224466/strategy-for-development-of-broadcasting-activity-central-and-.

Council of Europe. 2007. *Recommendation CM/Rec(2007)3 of the Committee of Ministers to the Member States on the Remit of Public Service Media in the Information Society.* Accessed May 13, 2020. https://search.coe.int/cm/Pages/result_details.aspx?ObjectId=09000016805d6bc5.

——. 2009. *Strategies of Public Service Media as Regards Promoting a Wider Democratic Participation of Individuals.* Strasbourg: Council of Europe. https://rm.coe.int/168059bf76.

Damjanovski, Ivan. 2016. *Nations in Transit: Macedonia 2016.* New York: Freedom House.

Dimitrijevska-Markoski, Tamara, and Zhidas Daskalovski. 2013. *Assisting Media Democratization after Low-Intensity Conflict: The Case of Macedonia.* Sarajevo/Skopje: Analitika Center for Social Research/CRPM Center for Research and Policy Making. http://analitika.ba/sites/default/files/publikacije/tamara_and_zhidas_-_rrpp_macedonia_wp05_3dec2013_final_for_publishing.pdf.

DTI (Danish Technological Institute), and EAVI (European Association for Viewers' Interests). 2011. *Testing and Refining Criteria to Assess Media Literacy Levels in Europe: Final Report.* Brussels: European Commission. https://op.europa.eu/en/publication-detail/-/publication/4cbb53b5-689c-4996-b36b-e920df63cd40.

Institute for Communication Studies. 2015. *Report from the Monitoring of the Media Content (November 23 to December 18, 2015).* Skopje: Institute for Communication Studies.

Jakubowicz, Karol. 2010. "PSB 3.0: Reinventing European PSB." In *Reinventing Public Service Communication*, edited by Petros Iosifidis, 9–22. Basingstoke: Palgrave Macmillan.

Law on Audio and Audiovisual Media Services [Zakon za audio i audiovizuelni mediumski uslugi]. *Official Gazette of the Republic of Macedonia* 184/13, 13/14, 44/14, 101/14 and 132/14.

Lowe, Gregory Ferrell, and Jo Bardoel, eds. 2007. *From Public Service Broadcasting to Public Service Media. RIPE@2007*. Göteborg: Nordicom. https://www.nordicom. gu.se/sites/default/files/publikationer-hela-pdf/ripe_2007_from_public_service_ broadcasting_to_public_service_media.pdf.

Media Development Center. 2014. Мониторинг: избори 2014—примената на медиумските одредби од Изборниот законик [Monitoring: elections 2014— implementation of electoral code's provisions on media electoral coverage]. Skopje: Media Development Center.

Micevski, Igor, Snezana Trpevska, and Zaneta Trajkoska. 2013. "Media and the Non-majority Communities in Macedonia: Poor Resources, Low Professional Standards, and Ethno-political Clientelism." In *Information in Minority Languages in the Western Balkans: Freedom, Access, Marginalization*, edited by Davor Marko, 99–122. Sarajevo: Media Plan Institute.

Micevski, Igor. 2014. "Distinctions: Audiences, Lay Publics & Media Active Lay Publics." INFOCORE Working Paper. Accessed May 13, 2020. http://www.infocore. eu/wp-content/uploads/2016/03/INFOCORE-conceptual-paper_media_active_lay_ publics_I.M.pdf.

Mitevska, Liljana. 2017. *Depoliticisation of the Macedonian Radio and Television Programming Council—Precondition for Independence of the Public Broadcaster*. Skopje: Macedonian Institute for Media.

Ordanoski, Saso. 2012. Заробена демократија [Democracy under arrest]. Skopje: Transparency Macedonia.

OSCE Office for Democratic Institutions and Human Rights. n.d. *Elections in North Macedonia*. Accessed May 13, 2020. https://www.osce.org/odihr/elections/ north-macedonia.

Šopar, Vesna, 2005. "Republic of Macedonia." In *Television Across Europe: Regulation, Policy and Independence. Summary*, edited by Open Society Institute, 1165–1230. Budapest: Open Society Institute. https://www.opensocietyfoundations.org/publications/television-across-europe-regulation-policy-and-independence.

Thomass, Barbara. 2004. "Citizenship and Public Broadcasting in Europe." In *Citizenship and Political Education Today*, edited by Jack Demaine, 141–157. London: Palgrave Macmillan.

Trpevska, Snezana, and Igor Micevski. 2014. "Macedonia." In *Media Integrity Matters: Reclaiming Public Service Values in Media and Journalism*, edited by Brankica Petković, 257–326. Ljubljana: Peace Institute. https://www.media.ba/sites/default / files/media_integrity_matters_za_web_final_0.pdf.

——. 2013. *How Does the Media Construct their Political Bias*. Skopje: School of Journalism and Public Relations. http://unescochair-vs.edu.mk/images /attachment/ LOCAL-ELECTIONS-2013_ENG.pdf.

CHAPTER 8

The Future of Public Service Broadcasting in Serbia[1]

Davor Marko

Introduction

This chapter examines the status, role, and main challenges of the Public Service Broadcasting (PSB) in Serbia. The transformation of the former state-controlled Radio-Televizija Srbije (RTS) faced obstacles similar to other countries in the Western Balkans (WB) region—lack of an institutional framework, a small and chaotic media market, an economic situation that was additionally worsened after the global economic crisis, political pressures, and lack of transparency and professionalism. What makes Serbia a special case is the highly negative reputation and image RTS had after the 1990s when the regime of Slobodan Milošević used the public media as a tool for political propaganda (Bujošević 2001; Veljanovski 2005, 217–218). Additionally, its premises and infrastructure were severely damaged in the 1999 NATO bombing. The main RTS building was bombed on April 23, 1999, leading to the death of 16 employees and estimated damages of around EUR 530 million (Andersen 2001).

Thereafter, it was challenging for lawmakers, local experts, and international organizations to create a context conducive to the establishment of PSB, and to foster its development according to European standards (Council of Europe 2008). Additionally, the status and operation of RTS were constantly endangered due to the non-transparent and personalized style of management and unsustainable financial planning, while additional challenges were caused by the inadequate technical and digital developments.

This analysis draws upon the contemporary debates on the status and operation of PSB in a changing media environment. Technological development, commercialization, and the growing role of the market in defining media roles and audience tastes, information abundance, and audience fragmentation significantly define what we know today as "media ecology."[2] In such a context, the

---

[1]   The analysis of public service broadcasters and Serbia was conducted for the period until the end of 2017.

[2]   The term derives from the idea that technology and techniques mediate human affairs, and determine the way media operate and how they are perceived and consumed by people. Initially,

status, funding model, and social role of PSB and its relation with the audience are contested.

This chapter starts with the presentation of the most important background information on PSB in Serbia. The following sections describe Serbian PSB functioning along four main dimensions of analysis: status and regulation, funding, technological and digitalization challenges, and the socio-political aspect of PSB operation. Next, the chapter offers a discussion of the key findings, followed by concluding remarks.

Establishment of PSB in Serbia

The democratization of Serbia took place once the regime of Slobodan Milošević collapsed, following the people's uprising in October 2000 (Spasić and Subotić 2001; Podunavac 2006; Vladisavljević 2008). Successive governments in post-Milošević Serbia established a new media legal framework under the influence and guidance of the European Union (EU), the Council of Europe (CoE), and the Organization for Security and Co-operation in Europe (OSCE). Since 2000, there have been at least three phases of media policy (Matić and Valić Nedeljković 2014) in Serbia: (i) the modernization phase (from 2000–2003) when political actors established a consensus on the EU accession and applied European standards in the media sphere (privatization, self-regulation, establishment of public service, using expertise from civil society and professional associations), (ii) the stagnation phase (2004–2008), which took place during the conservative and EU-skeptic government of the Democratic Party of Serbia led by Vojislav Koštunica (in this phase media policies were restrictive, media privatization frozen, new laws contradicted established principles within media legal framework, and the independence of the RTS was limited), and (iii) the phase of re-emerged Europeanization (2009 to present), when Serbia was granted candidate status, which implies the harmonization of domestic laws with the EU acquis, and the ratification of international acts and adoption of important domestic documents, such as the Strategy for Media Development (Republic of Serbia 2011). Based on the recent trends in Serbia, we can identify the last, and ongoing, phase of (iv) media sector destabilization in which the authoritarian rule of the Serbian Progress Party (SNS), led by President Aleksandar Vučić, imposed harsh control over the media sector, including all significant private broadcasters, public services, telecom operators, as well as public and some advertising sources of revenues. These trends developed in line with the drastic decrease in media freedoms (IREX 2019).

PSB in Serbia was established in 2006, consisting of Radio-Television of Serbia (RTS) and Radio-Television of Vojvodina (RTV). RTV is a rather unique broadcaster in the context of Serbia because it broadcasts in 11 minority

---

the idea was developed by the so-called "Toronto School" and "New York School," to which authors such as Marshall McLuhan and Neil Postman belonged.

languages. At the end of 2017, RTS broadcasted nine TV and four radio stations, while RTV had two TV and four radio channels. It also consists of an extensive network of branch offices, web portals, musical productions with four orchestras and three choirs, and publishing, research, and documentation centers. RTS has been a member of the European Broadcasting Union since 2001 and employs around 3,800 people: 3,200 on a full-time basis and 600 with partial or honoraria status. At the beginning of 2000, when the transformation of RTS into public service began, it employed more than 8,000 people. RTV has two TV (RTV1 and RTV2) and three radio channels, primarily targeting the population of the Autonomous Province of Vojvodina. RTV also owns and governs Studio M, a large concert hall and space used for radio and TV production. According to official data, RTV employed 1,267 people with 83.75% employed on a full-time basis. Analysis of employee structure demonstrated an above-average number of assistants and advisors, and dispersed middle management (editors of programs, heads of departments) (RTV 2013, 20–21).

The transformation of RTS into public service was delayed until the beginning of the 2000s when the Miloševic regime was overthrown. The legal ground for transformation was set up when the Broadcasting Act 2002 was adopted. This law introduced and defined the concept of public service broadcasting and stipulated the establishment of two public broadcasters—RTS, with its base in Belgrade, and RTV, with headquarters in Novi Sad. Only in 2006 did the public broadcasters begin operating formally, when all necessary preconditions were fulfilled (adopting the legislation, establishment of the regulatory body that further elected the public service broadcaster's management, organization of a license fee collection system, etc.). It was a big task for the new RTS management since RTS had lost its reputation during the 1990s, its premises were severely damaged, and it had lost much of its audience. For RTV it was the first time after more than 15 years that it became institutionally, financially, and operationally independent.

Socio-Cultural and Political Patterns

Serbian society inherited a subject political culture from the socialist period and combined it with the influence of authoritarian political culture that was dominant in the 1990s (Golubović, Kuzmanović and Vasović 1995). The regime of Slobodan Milošević misused public media, including the state broadcaster (RTS), to spread fear and propaganda that produced a "hegemonic public sphere in which the ruling party's interpretation of the political situation prevails while oppositional views are marginalized and even delegitimized" (Golubović, Kuzmanović and Vasović 1995, 242). In 1999, when the Kosovo crisis took place, NATO defined the broadcaster's headquarters as a legitimate target. Once Milošević's regime collapsed, the door for the liberation of the broadcaster and its transformation into a public service was opened.

From its inception in 2006, the reformed PSB organization has been perceived as a landmark of democratic development in Serbia, but in practice, it has rarely demonstrated its potential to drive the process of democratization in Serbia. For decision-makers, it was important to establish the structural and institutional contours of the PSB organization, including the adoption of a law and setting the procedures in line with the European standards, but essential change has not been achieved. Local media experts and professional associations continuously criticized how RTS is governed, the lack of universality and plurality of its programming (this relates to both RTS and RTV), and its lack of financial transparency. The way checks and balances of the PSB organization's remit operate in practice has also been criticized. This is mainly related to the "politicized" procedure of electing the members of the regulatory body, and the lack of transparency in the Committee of the Serbian Parliament in charge of media and information. Politicians mainly consider the public media as a "post-election chase" (Čaluković 2011) and use a populist voice when referring to PSB reform, mainly to attract voters before elections.

The structure of the PSB system in Serbia (see Figure 8.1) reflects the territorial organization of the state, with its provincial broadcaster RTV having an emphasized role in representing ethnic diversity with a special focus on national minorities. According to its statute, RTV should produce diverse content of different genres and universal values, use and implementing new program formats and technologies, promote the culture of Vojvodina, and preserve the cultural and national identity of the Serbian people and national minorities (RTV 2014). The Law on Public Media Services 2014 indicates that public broadcasters must respect pluralism, cultural, and ethnic diversity (Article 7). The specific types of programs, including quotas and overall achievement, are not precisely prescribed, but RTV fulfills its role without strict legal provisions.

Figure 8.1: PSB Structure in Serbia

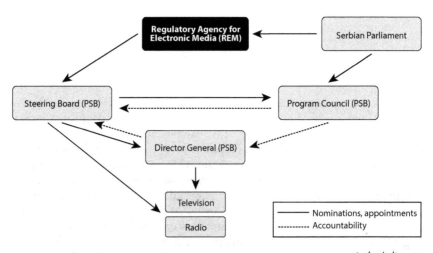

Author's diagram.

Regulation of PSB in Serbia

The Law on Public Media Services 2014 regulates the status and operation and defines the remit of PSB. The law also prescribes that public broadcasters must serve the public interest in the domain of public communication, and also defines the public interest through various obligations (Article 7). The law draws attention to activities PSB organizations have to undertake to ensure public interest including production, purchase, post-production, and broadcasting of radio, television and multimedia content in the domain of information, education, culture and arts, children, entertainment, sports, religion, and other programs that are important for citizens (Article 3).

The public broadcaster, according to the law, is an independent and autonomous legal entity. The Law on Public Media Services provides a sufficient legal basis for its independence by listing the principles of operation of a public service broadcaster that should be followed: independence of editorial policy; independence from any particular funding sources; prohibition of any form of censorship and unlawful influence on the operation of the public service broadcaster, editorial team, and reporters (Article 4). The law also defines the content of the institutional and editorial independence of a PSB organization: determining concepts and selecting programming, scheduling of programming; organizing activities; selecting executive officers, editors-in-chief, and employees; managing financial resources, etc. (Article 5). Finally, this law guarantees PSB independence by stipulating that the method and conditions of securing the means for financing the activity of a PSB organization must not influence its editorial and institutional autonomy (Article 35) (Valić Nedeljković 2015).

As institutional safeguards for PSB organizations, the law defines procedures for the election of their managerial bodies, the Steering Board, and the Director-General. The Steering Board of the public service broadcaster serves as a supervisory body. Board members can be appointed and dismissed by the regulatory authority under conditions prescribed by the law. The law of 2014 broadened the jurisdiction and increased the accountability of the Steering Board. Its new functions include the adoption of the development strategy of PSB, the programming concept, the procurement plan and business plan, control of financial operations, oversight of the legality of activity performance, and making elaborated decisions on the election of the Director-General and other management positions transparent (Valić Nedeljković 2015).

The Director-General of RTS has operational powers. The candidates for this position must have a higher education degree, ten years of experience in senior management positions, and be prominent experts in a relevant field. The candidates for the position additionally have to submit a plan for work and management. The procedure for the election of Director-General involves point-voting by the board members (defined in a special document, adopted by the Management Board). Neither the Steering Board members nor the Director-General can hold a public office or political party positions.

Recent experiences have demonstrated the lack of transparency, credibility, and independence in the work of the Steering Board. During the period from the PSB inception in 2006 until 2013, the Steering Board of RTS was marginalized, dominated by the Director-General and his unilateral decisions and actions. A study of the minutes of the RTS Management Board meetings in 2012 and 2013 concluded that the board did not have a single serious expert debate about any agenda topic (Aksentijević 2015, 15). The former director was serving his third consecutive mandate as Director-General when he suddenly died in 2013. There were many complaints about his management style. Some claimed that his mandate was proof of stability as three different governments did not manage to remove him from this position, while others contended that his success was due to his political affiliations and deals with various politicians. Another weak aspect of the Steering Board relates to its structure. Qualifications for board members are still vague and general, lacking criteria for judging potential candidates as "prominent experts" in the fields of media, culture, management, law, and finance (Article 17). Without such expertise, there remains the question of how the board makes decisions in the crucial domains of the financial and managerial development of PSB (Aksentijević 2015, 23).

The Serbian media regulatory body—the Regulatory Agency for Electronic Media (REM)[3]—is responsible for monitoring the activities and services provided by licensed operators, including public broadcasters. The REM annually publishes reports on the compliance of both RTS and RTV with legal requirements regarding program quotas, advertising, type of production, and use of language. Additionally, the REM Council appoints and dismisses the members of the Steering Board of the PSB organization, by a two-thirds majority support among its members. The REM Council launches a public competition for the appointment of the Steering Board members six months before the board members' tenure expires, under the criteria prescribed by the Law on Public Media Services (Article 17). It also has a significant power with a range of sanctions at its disposal, including reprimands, warnings, the power to impose fines, the publication of decisions in the official journal, and suspension and revocation of licenses.

Programming of the PSB in Serbia

From its inception in 2006, RTS has managed to attract a large portion of the audience. Its RTS 1 program had the largest audience in the country from 2006 to 2012, except for 2010, with a 20–26% audience share. Compared to RTS 1,

---

[3]　It was established in 2003 under the Broadcasting Act 2002 as the Regulatory Broadcasting Agency (RBA), a non-convergent regulator. Following the new Law on Electronic Media (2014), the regulatory body was renamed as REM and has been provided with a broader jurisdiction and mechanisms to perform its duties more efficiently.

the leading commercial station, TV Pink, remained the second most popular station during the same period with an average of about 23% (Surčulija, Pavlović and Jovanović Padejski 2011, 20).

There is no assessment or in-depth evaluation of program quality. Occasionally, the regulator started to evaluate some elements of TV programming but still does not provide enough insight into how public broadcasters are meeting requirements regarding plurality (Matić 2014, 157–158). Aside from the regulator, program councils of the PSB organizations are in charge of assessing program quality. According to the Statute of RTS (RTS 2015, Article 48) and the Statute of RTV (RTV 2014, Article 31), program councils are obliged to organize, at least once a year, a public discussion on the PSB programming, and draft recommendations for the General Manager and the Steering Board (RTV 2014).

Continuous analyses of the PSB content have indicated a high level of content diversity, especially of the second channel of RTV that broadcasts programs entirely for national minorities. Content in the Hungarian language is the most represented with 27.6% in 2013, followed by programs in Romanian (12.2%), Roma (11.72%), Ruthenian (11.66%), and Slovakian (10.23%) (RRA Report 2013). When it comes to quality, recent research detected a shortage of intercultural content (reporting on other minorities, inter-minority relations) and a general focus on majority issues, with dominant topics related to politics and economy (Marko 2013, 76–89).

Serbian PSB organizations rarely use a variety of sources in their informative programming to report professionally and objectively. As Matić observes, the information programs of RTS produces "a thematically universal picture of reality which was dominated by the opinions of authorities that were rarely problematized or opposed" (Matić 2014, 158). Incumbent officials use their political positions (presidential, prime minister, city mayors, etc.) to attract media attention, including PSB, and promote exclusively their party. Other sources indicate that it has become common practice of public officials and politicians "to personally and publicly accuse the media of being against them or maintain that foreign mercenaries are working against the interests of the state" (Zaštitnik građana 2015, 123).

The law regulating public media services in Serbia obliges PSB organizations to operate in the public interest, and the second paragraph of its Article 6 states that "the responsibility of the public service broadcaster to the public and the public's influence on the public service broadcaster's activity shall be exercised particularly through the public's involvement in enhancing radio and television programming." This indicates that PSB has to take an active role towards the audience. But, in practice, this active role of PSB is not being exercised. Additionally, the law foresees that the public service should express plurality in terms of sources and diverse content, and should target a diverse audience, without defining how contact with the audience should be done.

Financial Aspects of PSB in Serbia

The license fee was the main funding model of PSB in Serbia after its inception until its abolishment in 2014. Under the new Law on Public Media Services 2014, the license fee was replaced by a tax. According to its Article 36, main sources of funding are the public service broadcaster tax, the state budget, and net profits from commercial exploitation of the content produced within the main activity of PSB, as well as two additional revenues—commercial and other revenues. Article 37 states that the main activity of PSB shall be financed from a tax that will be uniform within the entire territory of Serbia. The amount was determined, and the system entered into force in 2016.

Regardless of the variety of financial sources prescribed by law, PSB in Serbia has failed to become financially stable. Since its inception, RTS has operated at a loss. The main cause of reduced revenues was a constant decline in the amount collected through the license fee, which was the major reason for its abolishment. The collection rate started dropping after the 2008 economic recession when it was below 50%. The normal functioning of public service broadcasters, by some estimates, requires a collection rate of 75%, or about EUR 100 million annually for normal functioning. In 2011, it collected 75 million, a year later 70, and in 2013 66 million (Fonet 2014).

The lack of transparency in the financial operation and reporting of the RTS is one of the main obstacles to its functioning. The former Director-General refused several times to provide public institutions with information on RTS financial operations. He preferred to pay a fine for violating the Law on Access to Information (Anti-Corruption Council 2011, 36). The non-transparent and illegal operation of RTS under Tijanić's mandate, especially in the domain of financial management, was a highly contentious issue (Aksentijević 2015, 20–21).

It was prescribed by the Law on Public Media Services 2014 that a tax would become the primary source of funding starting from January 1, 2016. With the new system established, PSB managed to collect more than 50% of its incomes from the tax and managed to collect more than EUR 110 million in 2018 (which is one-fourth of the entire value of the Serbian media market) (RTS 2018; RTV 2018).

Digitalization, New Media, and Convergence

Serbia completed the process of switching off the analog signal at the beginning of June 2015, facing along the way many politically-motivated obstacles.[4]

---

[4] As agreed with the International Telecommunication Union (ITU) at a meeting in Geneva in 2006, the Republic of Serbia committed to ending the transition from analog to digital broadcasting by June 17, 2015.

The initial date was set for the first half of 2012 but the end of the process was delayed due to the state's inconsistent decision-making regarding the transition to a digital signal. The Serbian government took the leading role in this process, and the inconsistency in the decision-making could be observed by the pure fact that the jurisdiction over the process was changed five times between 2006 and 2015, depending on the political affinities of the ruling coalitions (Krstić 2014).

The technical precondition of the successful process of digital switchover was the establishment of the public company Broadcasting Equipment and Communications (ETV), which was part of RTS until autumn 2009. The ETV was in charge of establishing primary and secondary networks for transmitting and digital broadcasting. ETV, as a part of the public broadcaster, enabled RTS to control the signal and transmitting process, creating a monopoly on the media market. This monopoly ended once ETV was established as an independent unit.

Between 2010 and 2014, Serbia obtained financial assistance from the EU through the IPA fund to cover a part of the costs regarding the digital network building, and the country managed to expand the digital TV signal to more than 90% by the end of the process in June 2015. According to the plan, the digital signal would be provided on the terrestrial platform through 3 multiplexes. Multiplex 1 includes programs with nationwide coverage, multiplex 2 refers to regional and local programs and multiplex 3 to regional and local programs or Pay-TV (Milivojević, Mišković and Reljin 2015). In both strategies related to the development of broadcasting—the Strategy of Broadcasting Development of the Republic of Serbia (2005) and the Strategy for Switchover from Analogue to Digital Broadcasting of RTV Programs in the Republic of Serbia (2009)—Serbia opted for the DVB-T2 standard with MPEG-4 compression.[5] According to the Strategy for Digital Switchover (2009) public service broadcasters had to play an important role in the public campaign on the digitalization process. A majority of Serbian citizens (87.6%) had heard about the digitalization, but generally were not aware of the technical equipment they needed to receive the digital signal. Most of them expected better quality of the sound and picture (83.8%), more choice of channel offerings (66.9%), non-linear consumption of content (60.9%), etc. (Senić and Josifović 2014, 5).

When it comes to technical aspects, RTS's production capacities were already adapted and upgraded to serve the high standards and demands of digital production. In 2008, RTS Digital was launched as an experimental channel, with 16:9 image, which served as a model of the transition from analog to digital television, providing viewers with 24 hours a day of culture, arts, concerts, documentaries, and film programs including both local and foreign production. Another program (RTS HD) was launched in 2009. It combines the program schema of unconverted RTS 1 with live coverage of various events in high image resolution. Radio-Television of Vojvodina (RTV) adopted its development strategy in 2013, including the introduction of new convergent services. Within

---

[5]   In July 2009, the Government of the Republic of Serbia adopted DVB-T2 as the technical standard for television signal broadcasting, and MPEG-4 Part 10 (ITU-T H.264/AVC) as the technical standard for data compression within multiplexes.

the first phase of convergence in its strategic plans, RTV aimed to create small minority-language newsrooms where journalists from both television and radio would work together. Also, at the level of RTV, a joint newsdesk was created, and this unit coordinated the planning, operation, and distribution of media content produced by all minority newsrooms.

Both RTS and RTV use a wealth of social media to expand their impact and fulfill their PSB role. RTS has a modern web portal, a Facebook page (Internet portal RTS), official YouTube channel and 15 sub-channels (for special TV shows), and a Twitter account. RTV also has a modern web portal, Facebook page (Radio-televizija Vojvodine), official YouTube channel and 10 sub-channels, and a Twitter account. The web portal of RTV was redesigned in 2013, led by the web editor-in-chief, while each online platform has its own editor.

As part of its digital strategy, the RTS prepared and launched its app, RTS Planet, in 2018, the first digital multimedia service to provide linear and on-demand services and programs for its users.

Discussion

Following political changes in 2000, it was unanimously agreed among politicians, media professionals, leading media scholars, and representatives of the international community, that Serbia had to establish a PSB system. The new institution was to bear no or very little resemblance to the regime-controlled institution that RTS was during the 1990s. From a formal point of view, it was indicated that the broadcaster would be newly established. However, initial documents on the necessity for a new PSB in Serbia indicated aspects that RTS needed to transform or improve, among which where the need for new legislation, high quality content, a representative structure, public funding, and channels representing Serbia's territorial and linguistic diversity.

The legacy of socialism combined with the authoritarian rule and harsh control over the media by Milošević's regime during the 1990s played an important role in PSB's transformation. Following the democratic changes in 2000, the PSB reform faced different challenges, the most significant of which was the need to end people's perception of RTS as a tool for political propaganda and as a symbol of the authoritarian regime of Slobodan Milošević.

Due to the adoption of deficient regulation in 2000, the ownership over PSB was unclear (Rhodes 2007, 28), which affected the integrity of this media institution. The initial regulation did not provide a clear definition of the public interest, and only a few articles of the Broadcasting Act 2002 dealt with public service broadcasting (Matić and Valić Nedeljković 2014). As agreed among leading scholars on PSB, media lawyers, and representatives of institutions and authorities in Serbia, the current laws (enacted in 2014), brought certain improvements regarding the regulation of PSB. When it comes to the PSB remit, the debate tackled the scope and breadth of the definition of public interest.

The 2014 regulation recognizes only RTS and RTV as legitimate public service broadcasters, while it also provides an opportunity for other types of media to produce content of the public interest. Some media experts advocate that both public and commercial media should fulfill the function of public service broadcaster, the function of which may be also exercised by providers of media services other than the public ones. In this regard, each media service provider, including commercial media, can fulfill the public interest by providing information relevant to the public.

Since its establishment in 2006, the guarantees of the editorial independence of PSB organizations in Serbia have not been established either by law or in their internal acts (Matić and Valić Nedeljković 2014, 364). Instead of being a guarantee of a stable framework and independent work of the media, the legislation suffers from what scholars call a "floating law" syndrome (Zielonka and Mancini 2011). Since the government acceded to change and amend laws related to the work of RTS and the regulatory body which supervises its work (the RBA, which is also in charge of nominating RTS Board members), the level of autonomy of these two institutions decreased, opening a space for indirect political control.

Although PSB has managed to become a popular media institution, its editorial policy has garnered much criticism. One line of criticism addresses its commercialized and sensationalized content, such as popular TV series (usually re-emitted several times), reality shows, and sports and entertainment programs. It was believed by scholars that it should cover a range of topics, genres, and issues, including those that are deficient on the market (children's programs, documentary programs, programs in minority languages). Instead of being distinct, the program of Serbian PSB (mainly RTS), is similar to that of private media (Matić 2009, 24–69). However, recent research, and interlocutors interviewed during this research, portrayed the case of RTV in a positive light, especially its second channel aired in 11 minority languages.

Funding is the core problem for PSB in Serbia. Since its inception by the Broadcasting Act 2002, the license fee model of funding has been widely discussed and criticized. Some of its critics were politically motivated, some targeted the way this model was implemented (through the electricity bill) and linked that with poor outcomes (the constant decrease in the number of those paying it, especially after 2008), while media experts and scholars were mostly in favor of this model, resisting its abolishment in 2014. There was almost no debate in Serbia regarding other ways of funding, like advertising, budget funding, or donations. Even though tax, as a dominant revenue stream for PSB in Serbia today, is not formally related to budget funding, the practice has demonstrated that this model of funding could be much more easily manipulated by officials than the license fee. Recent practice has shown that financial stability through the established tax system does not necessarily bring editorial independence in the case of the two Serbian broadcasters.

Following the digital switch-off, the crucial questions regarding the role of PSB in a multi-channel environment, and challenges to its legitimacy have not been widely discussed in Serbia. The public debate on digitalization was mainly linked with the digital switchover, while just recently digitalization becomes not only a buzzword but one to be included in an agenda for media service development. So far, strategic documents in the domain of digitalization in Serbia mainly discuss the technical aspect of the process, and the current situation and obstacles using general phrases (such as privatizations, allocation of frequencies, the transformation of RTS), without providing any vision of future development (Milivojević 2009). Debates around public media in "networked society" mainly tackled the technical aspects of digitalization (who will produce, how programs will be distributed, who will provide and control the distribution of programs, how multiplexes will be organized and what they will contain, etc.) while the essential questions on the necessity of PSB in a multichannel environment, its capacities to produce programs with higher production and technical quality, and the relation with its audience, remained poorly discussed.

Conclusion

This chapter discussed the contextually relevant aspects of the PSB transformation in Serbia. In Serbia, the debate is still focused on the survival of PSB either as a public service or a state-funded public broadcaster, while in Europe the debate over PSB legitimacy is even more polarized, between those who advocate for a redefined PSB in a changing environment, and those who follow market logic and use neoliberal arguments to delegitimize PSB.

Key problems with the PSB operation in Serbia are related to the funding model, the lack of transparency in its operation, and the program quality. More than a decade after its establishment, PSB in Serbia still struggles to operate as a financially independent institution. In 2014, due to its low collection rate, the license fee was abolished and replaced with the tax system as a primary source. Following discussions and public debates, a tax was introduced at the beginning of 2016. PSB is still perceived by politicians, and partly by the public, as a "political chase" for those who win elections and control the power in the state. Due to the personalized style of management, many operations linked with PSB— including funding, contact with its audience, internal systematization, criteria for selecting the programming, and measuring its quality—remain unclear and inaccessible to the public. Compared to the PSB organizations in other countries of the region, RTS is a popular channel. Recently, many voices including opposition party leaders, activists, and ordinary citizens consider RTS to be extremely biased in reporting on political, and even daily, issues and this dissatisfaction was demonstrated with protest and open messages to the management and editorial board of the RTS.

For the survival and further development of PSB in Serbia, it is necessary to examine their mission and operation within the changed conditions on the media scene. Further research should tackle the issues of internal restructuration and organization of PSB to make digital production and convergence possible and efficient. It also should seek mechanisms to ensure better visibility of PSB content on the media market, and to re-establish its relationship with its public. Research on the changing habits and information needs of the media public would be valuable to guide PSB management, policymakers, media experts, and professionals, in adapting existing and creating new media policies.

References

Aksentijević, Milan. 2015. *RTS. Naše pravo da znamo sve* [RTS. Our right to know everything]. Prokuplje: Toplički centar za demokratiju i ljudska prava/Užički centar za demokratiju i ljudska prava.

Andersen, Ben. 2001. "Serbia After Milošević: A Progress Report." The United States Helsinki Commission Briefing, March 1. Accessed May 15, 2020. https://www.csce.gov/international-impact/press-and-media/press-releases/serbia-after-milosevic-progress-report? page=17.

Anti-Corruption Council. 2011. *Izveštaj o pritiscima i kontroli medija u Srbiji* [Report on pressures on and control of media in Serbia]. Belgrade: Anti-Corruption Council of the Government of the Republic of Serbia. http://www.antikorupcija-savet.gov.rs/Storage/Global/Documents/izvestaji/izvestaj%20mediji%2026%2002.pdf.

Bujošević, Dragan. 2001. *5 oktobar: 24 časa prevrata* [The Fall of Milošević: The October 5th Revolution]. Belgrade: Mediacentar.

Council of Europe. 2008. *Indicators for Media in a Democracy*. Accessed May 14, 2020. http://www.assembly.coe.int/nw/xml/XRef/X2H-Xref-ViewHTML.asp?FileID=12123&lang=EN.

Čaluković, Nenad. 2011. "Tomislav Nikolić za press: Smeniću Tijanića isto veče" [Tomislav Nikolić: I will ask Tijanić to resign the same evening]. *Pressonline.rs*, July 24. Accessed May 14, 2020. http://www.pressonline.rs/info/politika/169506/tomislav-nikolic-za-press-smenicu-tijanica-isto-vece.html.

Fonet. 2014. "Tijanić: Javni servis preuranjena ideja za Srbiju" [Tijanić: public service is an advanced idea for Serbia]. *Blic*, February 14. Accssed May 14, 2020. http://www.blic.rs/Vesti/Drustvo/367852/Tijanic-Javni-servis-preuranjena-ideja-za-Srbiju.

Golubović, Zagorka, Bora Kuzmanović, and Mirjana Vasović. 1995. *Društveni karakter i društvene promene u svetlu nacionalnih sukoba* [Social character and social changes in the light of national clashes]. Belgrade: Institut za filozofiju i društvenu teoriju i FilipVišnjić.

IREX. 2019. *Media Sustainability Index 2019: Serbia*. Washington, DC: IREX. https://www.irex.org/sites/default/files/pdf/media-sustainability-index-europe-eurasia-2019-serbia.pdf.

Krstić, Aleksandra. 2014. "Digital Switchover in Serbia in a Comparative Perspective." *International Journal of Digital Television* 5, no. 3 (September): 237–253.

Law on Electronic Media 2014 [Zakon o elektronskim medijima]. *Službeni glasnik RS* 83/2014 and 6/2016. Accessed May 15, 2020. https://www.paragraf.rs/propisi / zakon_o_elektronskim_medijima.html.

Law on Public Media Services 2014 [Zakon o javnim medijskim servisima]. *Službeni glasnik RS* 83/2014, 103/2015 and 108/2016. Accessed May 15, 2020. https://www.paragraf.rs/propisi/zakon_o_javnim_medijskim_servisima.html.

Law on Radio-diffusion 2002 [Zakon o radiodifuziji]. *Službeni glasnik RS* 42/02, 97/04, 76/05 and 79/05. Accessed May 15, 2020. http://www.kultura.gov.rs/docs/dokumenti/propisi-iz-oblasti-medija/zakon-o-radiodifuziji.pdf.

Marko, Davor. 2013. "Affirmatively and Uncritically about Self-group, Insufficiently about Others." In *Freedom, Access, Marginalization*, edited by Davor Marko, 76–89. Sarajevo: Media Plan Institute.

Matić, Jovanka, and Dubravka Valić Nedeljković. 2014. "Serbia." In *Media Integrity Matters: Reclaiming Public Service Values in Media and Journalism*, edited by Brankica Petković, 327–390. Ljubljana: Peace Institute. https://www.media.ba /sites/default/files/media_integrity_matters_za_web_final_0.pdf.

Matić, Jovanka. 2014. *Servis građana ili servis vlasti* [Service of citizens or service of government]. Belgrade: Dobar naslov.

———. 2009. "Raznovrsnost TV programa u Srbiji" [Diversity of TV programming in Serbia]. In *Medijski skener* [Media scanner], edited by Dubravka Valić Nedeljković, 24–69. Novi Sad: Novosadska novinarska škola.

Milivojević, Milan, Božimir Mišković, and Irini Reljin. 2015. "DVB-T2: An Outline of HDTV and UHDTV Programmes Broadcasting." *Telfor Journal* 7, no. 2 (January): 86–90.

Milivojević, Snježana. 2009. "Medijska strategija za digitalno doba" [Media strategy for the digital era]. *Peščanik.net*, November 9. Accessed May 14, 2020. http://pescanik.net /medijska-strategija-za-digitalno-doba/.

Podunavac, Milan. 2006. *Revolution, Legitimacy and Order: The Case of Serbia.* Belgrade: Čigoja.

Republic of Serbia. 2011. Finalna verzija Strategije razvoja sistema javnog informisanja u Republici Srbiji do 2016. Godine [Strategy for the Development of the Public Information System in the Republic of Serbia until 2016]. Accessed May 14, 2020. http://www.osce.org/node/88325.

———. 2008. Strategija za prelazak sa analognog na digitalno emitovanje radio i televizijskog programa u Republici Srbiji [Strategy of Digital Switch-off in the Republic of Serbia]. *Službeni glasnik RS* 52/09, 18/12 and 26/2013. Accessed May 15, 2020. https://www.paragraf.rs/propisi/strategija_za_prelazak_sa_analognog_na _digitalno_emitovanje_radio_i_televizijskog_programa.html.

———. 2005. Strategija razvoja radiodifuzije u Republici Srbiji do 2013. godine [Strategy of Development of Radio-diffusion in the Republic of Serbia]. *Službeni glasnik RS* 115/05. Accessed May 15, 2020. http://www.pravno-informacioni-sistem.rs/SlGlasnikPortal/eli/rep/sgrs/drugidrzavniorganiorganizacije/strategija/2005/115/1/reg.

RTS. 2015. Statut Javne medijske ustanove Radio-televizije Srbije [The Statute of the Public Media Institution Radio-Television of Serbia]. Belgrade: Radio Televizija Srbije.

———. 2018. Izveštaj o poslovanju RTS-a za 2018. godinu [RTS Financial Report for 2018]. Accessed May 15, 2020. https://www.rts.rs/upload/storyBoxFileData/2018/07 /03/14784480/IZVESTAJ%20O%20POSLOVANJU%20RTS%20ZA%202018.PDF.

RTV. 2018. Godišnji izveštaj o radu i poslovanju za 2018 [RTV Annual Report for 2018]. Accessed May 15, 2020. http://static.rtv.rs/pdf/2019/07/02/izvestaj-o-radu-i-poslovanju-rtv-2018.pdf.

———. 2014. Statut Javne medijske ustanove Radio-televizija Vojvodine [The Statute of the Public Media Institution Radio-Television of Vojvodina]. Accessed May 14, 2020. http://static.rtv.rs/pdf/2015/01/29/statut-jmu-rtv-pdf.pdf.

——. 2013. Strategija razvoja RUV RTV 2013–2017 [Strategy of Development of the Radio-Television of Vojvodina 2013–2017]. Accessed May 14, 2020. http://static. rtv.rs /pdf/2013/10/29/strategija-razvoja-ruv-rtv-2013-2017-pdf.pdf.

Rhodes, Aaron. 2007. *Ten Years of Media Support to the Balkans: An Assessment*. Amsterdam: Media Task Force of the Stability Pact for South Eastern Europe.

Senić, Nada, and Slavica Josifović. 2014. *Građani Srbije o digitalizaciji televizije* [Citizens of Serbia on digitialisation of TV]. Belgrad: RTS Centar za istraživanje javnog mnjenja, programa i auditorijuma.

Spasić, Ivana, and Milan Subotić. 2001. *Revolution and Order: Serbia after October 2000*. Belgrade: Institute for Philosophy and Social Theory.

Surčulija, Jelena, Biljana Pavlović, and Đurđa Jovanović Padejski. 2011. *Mapping Digital Media: Serbia*. Open Society Foundations: London. https://www.opensociety-foundations.org/sites/default/files/mapping-digital-media-serbia-20111215.pdf.

Valić Nedeljković, Dubravka. 2015. *Public Service Broadcasters are (not) in the Service of Citizens*. Ljubljana: Peace Institute. http://mediaobservatory.net/sites/default/ files/Serbia-Public%20Broadcasters%20are%20%28not%29%20in%20the%20 Service%20of%20Citizens.pdf.

Veljanovski, Rade. 2005. *Javni RTV servis u službi građana* [Public radio-television in the service of citizens]. Belgrade: Clio.

Vladisavljević, Nebojša. 2008. *Serbia's Antibureaucratic Revolution: Milošević, the Fall of Communism and Nationalist Mobilization*. Basingstoke: Palgrave Macmillan.

Zaštitnik građana. 2015. *Redovan godišnji izveštaj Zaštitnika građana za 2014. godinu* [Regular annual report of the ombudsman for 2014]. Republika Srbija: Zaštitnik građana.

Zielonka, Jan, and Paolo Mancini. 2011. *Executive Summary: A Media Map of Central and Eastern Europe*. Oxford: Department of Politics and International Relations. https://de.scribd.com/document/161146265/Zielonka-Jan-and-Paolo-Mancini-2011-A-Media-Map-of-CEE-Summary-Politicisation-of-the-State.

PART II

COMPARATIVE
PERSPECTIVES

CHAPTER 9

The Iron Law of Public Service Television

Péter Bajomi-Lázár

Introduction: The Concept and Practice of Public Service Television

Public service broadcasting is a British invention that has been adopted in the rest of Europe in multiple successive waves. It was introduced in the Northern European countries such as Denmark, Norway, and Sweden in the 1920s and 1930s, in most of Western Europe, including in Germany and Italy, in the 1940s, in the Southern European countries such as Greece, Portugal, and Spain in the 1970s, and Southern and Central Eastern Europe, including Bulgaria, Hungary, Poland, and the countries of former Yugoslavia, in the 1990s and 2000s (Dragomir et al. 2005). While the print book and the press evolved as bottom-up initiatives driven by market forces across most of Europe (Russia being an exception) (Briggs and Burke 2009), the introduction of public service radio and television was a political decision that was managed by the state in all of Europe's countries (Luxembourg, where a purely commercial model had taken roots, being a notable exception to this Europe-wide trend) (Siune and Hultén 1998). While the implementation of public service television is considered a success story in the United Kingdom and Northern Europe (Curran et al. 2009), it is widely seen as a failure in many other European countries, and especially in the third-wave democracies of Southern Europe and Southern and Central Eastern Europe, including the Western Balkans. In most of these countries, public service broadcasters are either politically instrumentalized or commercialized, or both, and fail to provide impartial news bulletins and quality programming (Mungiu-Pippidi 2003; Jakubowicz 2008).

Debates about public service broadcasting are in no way endemic to the third-wave democracies of Europe. Even the British Broadcasting Corporation, the model example of public service broadcasting, has been widely criticized, especially for its alleged paternalism that has turned it into a channel of elite-to-mass communication, ignoring audiences' real needs (Keane 1991, 56). In addition to subscription fees and the state budget, many public service broadcasters rely on commercial revenues, which has been debated on the ground that public outlets are granted competitive privileges vis-à-vis private ones (Siune and Hultén 1998). Also, a permanently changing media landscape with a number of new media outlets and platforms has raised the question of whether the concept and practice of public service broadcasting, originally based on the now obsolete "frequency scarcity" argument, is still warranted. To date, hundreds of private television channels provide in many countries across Europe a variety of content traditionally associated with public service television, including political news and analysis, highbrow culture, as well as educational, scientific, religious, and children's programming (Bajomi-Lázár, Štětka and Sükösd 2012). Based on these observations, critics have repeatedly questioned the legitimacy of the public service broadcasting model, which as a result is now widely seen as an "endangered species" (Bardoel and Vochteloo 2012, 313) going through a "never-ending reform" (Bustamente 2008, 186).

Under these criticisms, media policymakers have, over time, fine-tuned the British public service broadcasting model, originally based on the concepts of universal accessibility, national identity and culture, editorial independence, and political impartiality (Barendt 1995). Since public service television has lost its monopoly position, its remit has been redefined, and now includes a great variety of content (Bašić-Hrvatin and Thompson 2008), which has halted or mitigated a long-term decline in audience figures in both the UK and the Nordic countries (Bajomi-Lázár, Štětka and Sükösd 2012). The public service broadcasting model has been dynamically changing over time. It remains, however, that the public service broadcasting model that Europe's young democracies have attempted to adopt in recent decades has already been challenged in old democracies. As Mungiu-Pippidi observes, "[m]any of the problems encountered by public service television in the [post-communist] region are identical to problems that were experienced by Western countries in the recent past" (Mungiu-Pippidi 2003, 36).

The implementation of the British model may have been successful in Northern Europe, but not so much in Southern Europe and in Southern and Central Eastern Europe. Arguably, the attempt to introduce one element of the media systems of consolidated first- and second-wave democracies in the consolidating third-wave democracies of Europe without regard to the historical legacies and structural conditions of the region is a telling example of "mimetic transplantation" (Jakubowicz and Sükösd 2008, 18); similarities between the media systems of Southern Europe and Southern and Central Eastern Europe are likely owing to similarities between the political systems of the two regions.[1] This chapter looks into the former communist countries of the Western Balkans in an attempt to identify some of the institutional and cultural reasons that make the implementation of genuine public service television a *mission impossible* in the region's countries. Drawing on Michels' "iron law of oligarchy," it introduces the concept of the iron law of public service television, stating that most public

---

[1]   For an overview of some similarities between Southern Europe on the one hand and Southern and Central Eastern Europe on the other, see Bajomi-Lázár (2017).

broadcasters in the former communist countries have been transformed from a means into an end, and serve private interests rather than the public good. Colonized by political parties, these institutions channel public money into the private pockets of party clients, while their nominal objectives have not been achieved. Clientelistic exchanges have a long-standing tradition in the region, and competing political elites seek to consolidate their positions by trading public resources for party support. Finally, this chapter suggests that the closing down of public service television should be given consideration in this region.

A Regional Overview

The transition from a state to public service broadcasting in the former communist countries has been described as "an epic of misunderstandings, mixed intentions, scarce resources, institutional stagnation and shameless delaying tactics" (Bašić-Hrvatin and Thompson 2008, 10), and may, therefore, be regarded as an unfinished and reversible process. Indeed, while the former communist countries of Southern and Central Eastern Europe differ widely in terms of their political and media systems, evincing "divergent paths" thirty years after the fall of communism, the status of public service television displays similar patterns and raises similar issues across the region (Mungiu-Pippidi 2013, 40). According to Jakubowicz, these issues include the poor design and implementation of the regulation, frequent crises of management and personnel, underfunding and financial debts, a lack of programming know-how, and falling audience shares (Jakubowicz 2008). Audience figures are particularly low among the young, who less frequently watch television than the elderly (European Commission 2014, 6). To the list above, Beitika adds corporate influences on public service broadcasters as a result of their heavy reliance on advertising, the unwillingness of some key stakeholders, including the political elites and the staff of public service broadcasters, to enhance the institutional and cultural changes needed for public service television to meet its normatively expected functions, as well as the poor prestige of public service institutions among the general public (Beitika 2011).

What underfunding means, however, may be a matter of debate. Cross-country comparisons are not very informative on the amount of adequate funding, which may depend on the structure of the public service organization and the number of channels (as some multi-ethnic countries have more institutions and channels than mono-ethnic ones, and some public service organizations operate both radio stations and television channels while others do not), the capacities of the state budget and the size of the media market. Besides under-funding, overfunding may be an issue, too. In Hungary for example, the state allocated 80.5 billion forints (EUR 260 million) to the public service media organization, which also includes Hungarian Radio and the Hungarian News Agency, in 2015 (Zsolt 2014). This amount, however, proved insufficient, and in September the same year, the government granted an additional 47.2 billion forints (EUR 152 million) to the organization so that it could pay its debts (Tamás 2015). In that year, the annual budget of the institution amounted to 0.3% of the gross domestic product, which totaled 33,712 billion forints (Deutsch-Ungarische Industrie- und Handelskammer, 2020). The money was spent on seven television channels, seven radio stations, the news production of the national wireless service, and the wages of over 2,000 staff. Top managers were granted high wages as well as extra benefits such as premium cars and mobile telephones (Tamás 2016). By way of comparison, the total estimated advertising spending on the Hungarian radio and television markets was 31 billion forints (EUR 100 million) in the same year (DigitalHungary 2016). Hungary, a success story of media transformation and political democratization until the mid-2000s, compares to date with the Balkan countries, rather than its geographic peers in Central and Eastern Europe such as the Czech Republic and Slovakia.

The flaws of public service television observed in Southern and Central Eastern Europe are also manifest in the Western Balkans, and often in a magnified form. As the studies collected in this volume show, the current status of public service broadcasting in this part of the world evinces—despite repeated regulatory efforts to enhance the British standards—some of the worst practices possible.

Albania is one of the poorest economies in Europe, and struggles with high levels of corruption, writes Blerjana Bino (see Chapter 2 in this volume). A poorly performing economy has exposed the Albanian media to political and corporate pressures, while a polarized pluralist multi-party system, with parties unwilling or unable to seek consensus, has been leading to the rise of a clientelistic media landscape. European organizations and the European Broadcasting Union (EBU) have offered their expertise and know-how when the transformation of the state into public service broadcasters began. However, the fact that the party nominees sitting in the public service broadcaster's steering council have not been able to elect a director-general for two years at the time the contributors' chapter was completed is indicative of the deadlock that conflict politics leads to. State advertising is often allocated in line with political criteria. Journalists are divided along political lines, and the self-regulatory mechanisms enhancing professionalization are largely unknown. Most journalists are politically affiliated, as a result of which news programs display political bias. The prevalence of partisan journalism is further enhanced by low wages and high job insecurity which expose journalists to political and economic pressures. Not surprisingly, then, the public service television channels and the national news agency have long been the mouthpieces of the government. Repeated reforms of media regulation have little improved the situation, if at all, especially because the implementation of the regulation is often flawed, as the media authority has been under the control of political parties. The top managers of the public service broadcasting organization have been accused of mismanagement of resources and, in some cases, downright corruption. At the same time, uniquely in the Albanian media landscape, the public service broadcaster does not struggle with financial difficulties and has doubled its incomes in recent years. It is estimated to have 30% more staff than necessary, many who are members of clientelistic networks. In 2016, its total revenues amounted to EUR 16.4 million, while the total advertising market was estimated at EUR 30 million. No reliable data are available on the audience share of public service television. In Chapter 2 on Albania Bino concludes that public service television "does not fulfill its remit and objectives of quality programming, editorial independence, plurality, diversity and universality," and that "media legislation and policy in Albania have not been driven by the public interest, but have been affected by the specific interests of certain political, economic and media actors."

Bosnia and Herzegovina, a country that has only recently emerged from a state of war, evinces similar issues. The public service broadcasting system was not only imposed from above, but also by external forces, and notably the Office of the High Representative and the European Commission, as a part of the post-war peacemaking process. However, as Nidžara Ahmetašević and Tea Hadžiristić observe in Chapter 3, media reform has been "sabotaged" by domestic political elites, as a result of which public service broadcasting institutions have been "deeply dysfunctional," possibly because the public service broadcasting model imposed had little to do with local needs and conditions. Citizens and media professionals were not consulted during the legislation process. A poor economic situation has fostered the capture of the state and of the media by political parties. The media market is small but overcrowded. As a result, most outlets seek political and corporate patronage, and public service channels are no exception. Political parties are highly divided, including along ethnic cleavages, and have been constantly engaged in bitter policy debates, rather than seeking consensus, which has made cooperation almost impossible. A high level of political parallelism is also reflected in the media landscape, and public service broadcasters are largely believed to be the mouthpieces of the ruling parties of the day, which control it through the appointment of the top management. Public service programming has been widely commercialized. A poorly performing economy has undermined the financial stability of public broadcasters, bringing them to the verge of bankruptcy. The state-level public service broadcaster is severely indebted and can hardly pay its utilities, while it employs surplus labor force. Media analysts question the reliability of official audience ratings. The decision-making body of the media authority has been highly politicized via the appointment mechanism, and key executives are obvious party clients. Parties are believed to have a major impact on the distribution of advertising revenues via their links to the major advertising agencies. Because of the recent war, "patriotic journalism" and hate speech have a tradition in the country; professional journalism in the Anglo-American sense is largely lacking. The implementation of media regulation is often flawed. Problems, especially financial ones, are so acute that, as the authors put it, "the very existence of public service broadcasters in Bosnia has been put into question recently." (see Chapter 3 by Ahmetašević and Hadžiristić in this volume).

Croatia is the only country among those discussed in this volume that has been admitted to the European Union. An externally plural media landscape reflects the pluralism of a multi-party system, but all of the major political actors recognized in the early 2000s the need for media reform, which was also urged during the European accession talks. As Davor Marko observes in Chapter 4, Croatian public service television is an outlier to regional trends in that it has been financially stable and relatively autonomous vis-à-vis political and corporate interests. In recent years, it has rationalized its expenditures, reduced the number of its staff by more than 30%, increased its financial transparency, and produced some profit. Unlike in the other countries discussed in this volume, the Croatian public service broadcaster has made important efforts to engage in a dialogue with both professional organizations and the general public, including via a commissioner for customers. It remains, however, that the top management and editorial personnel are dismissed every now and then after changes in government, while new, politically affiliated staff are appointed, since the vast majority of the members of the main governing bodies of Croatian public service radio and television are directly appointed by parliament. However, the political independence of the organization has improved since the year 2000 in comparison with the 1990s, when the public service broadcaster was unquestionably a mouthpiece of the government. Public service television channels have gradually been losing their viewers in recent years, even though their programming has been increasingly commercialized. The Croatian press market is relatively weak but much stronger than those in the other Western Balkan countries. Despite the heritage of the war, journalism in Croatia has maintained some tradition of independent reporting. All in all, however, the Croatian case shows, in the words of Davor Marko (see Chapter 4 in this volume), that "the process of negotiation and accession to the European Union positively influenced the process of media transformation and development," but "once the accession has been accomplished, the entire climate has been re-shaped and colored mostly from the perspective of politicians and ideological cleavages."

Kosovo is the smallest territorial unit in the region with a low national gross product. As Naser Miftari observes in Chapter 5, Kosovo's media landscape has been transformed under the governance of the United Nations Mission, and a public service broadcaster was introduced from above by international forces. However, the media market is poor in resources, and a multi-party system, divided along political cleavages, is conducive to conflicts rather than consensus in policymaking, including in the area of broadcasting regulation: "In conditions where politics is entrenched in hostile camps, media and journalists tend to replicate political divisions." The public service broadcasting institution, introduced practically from scratch, was based on the BBC model; however, despite formally introduced legal guarantees, it lacks independence, and the implementation of the regulation is often flawed. Political elites exert influence on the public service broadcaster via the selection and appointment of the members of the supervisory board and, consequently, the top management, many of whom are overpaid. The allocation of the institution's revenues from the state budget is another source of political interference. Political pressures are conducive to recurring pro-government bias on the news. In recent years, the annual budget of the public service broadcaster has been twice as high as the combined income of its two private counterparts, while it has been steadily losing audiences. The public service broadcaster is faced with the weak professional performance of journalists, growing debts, a lack of transparency and accountability, and clientelism in the procurement of programming produced outside the broadcaster, also including, according to allegations, nepotism, and corruption. Assessing the trends of the past decade, Miftari concludes that public service broadcasting "was more consolidated and public service oriented ten years ago than it is in 2015," as parties have come to consider the public service broadcaster a political asset, that is, a means of delivering their messages to voters and of channeling resources to their supporters (see Chapter 5 by Miftari in this volume).

Montenegro has a weak media market with a small population, limited advertising revenues, and an extremely high number of outlets. As a result, the state is a key player in the advertising market, allocating public resources in line with political criteria. As Nataša Ružić observes in Chapter 6, this is the only country in the region where, despite a nominally plural party system, the same party—the Democratic Party of Socialists, a successor to the former communist party—has been in office since the demise of communism. The country does not meet the criteria defining a minimal democracy. Clientelism and nepotism are widely practiced, including in the public media. Non-governmental and professional organizations have not been involved in a meaningful way in the drafting of media laws. While media regulation formally meets the accession criteria set by the European Union, the ruling party has permanently kept the public service broadcaster under informal pressures via the nomination of its decision-making body and director-general as well as the control of its budget, directly covered by the state. As a result, the institution is highly politicized and airs biased news and current affairs programs. As Ružić notes, it is widely called a "party broadcaster," rather than a "public broadcaster." Until recently, it had funding difficulties and was largely indebted, while it employed surplus staff. Perhaps surprisingly, it has a relatively high audience share, reaching an estimated 30% on a regular basis, even though the audience data available are unreliable. At the same time, the public service broadcaster's programming has been largely commercialized. Media freedom has been in decline for many years, and journalists have repeatedly been exposed to physical assaults. Professionalism among journalists is low. She concludes that the ruling party in Montenegro does not wish to give up control over the public service broadcaster (see Chapter 6 by Ružić in this volume).

North Macedonia has been facing similar issues. As Snežana Trpevska and Igor Micevski observe in Chapter 7, there is a small and weak press market with a high number of outlets, most of which are financially vulnerable and thus exposed to political pressures. There is a multi-party political system divided along ethnic and religious cleavages. Political conflict occasionally leads to armed conflict, as it did in 2001. The country has taken a neo-authoritarian turn in recent years, after elections compromised by fraud. Parties have captured both the state and the media, including both public service and commercial outlets, and clientelistic practices prevail in many areas, public service broadcasting being no exception. Even though various international organizations have assisted the attempted transformation of the state into public service broadcasting, including the Council of Europe, the Organization for Security and Co-operation (OSCE), and Article 19, political pressures exerted on the public service media have not only persisted but intensified in recent years. Most of the members of the key decision-making bodies of the institution are nominated by non-governmental organizations and elected by parliament. However, given the politicization of civil society, this construction only disguises the political pressures that are exerted through the appointment of party clients. News bulletins on the public service broadcaster have persistently displayed a marked pro-government bias. The organization has been struggling with financial difficulties that make it vulnerable to political pressures, and has been steadily losing audiences over the years. In Chapter 7 on North Macedonia, Trpevska and Micevski conclude that "the transformation from a state into a public broadcaster has not occurred," and that Macedonian Radio and Television "has never truly performed the role of a public service broadcaster that serves the interest of the citizens instead of those of the ruling parties." They also observe that "journalists [of the public service media] do not perceive themselves as neutral observers of the government, but rather as its constructive partners." They add that the public service broadcaster has been acting as a means of disintegration rather than one of social cohesion.

Serbia, writes Davor Marko in Chapter 8, has an overcrowded media market for a relatively small population. As a result, audiences are fragmented, and most outlets are financially unsustainable. In fact, the presence of too many outlets on the market appears to be a sign that most owners consider media a financially non-lucrative investment that serves political and other business interests. Serbia is a multi-party democracy that emerged after the collapse of the Milošević regime in 2000, which was marked by totalitarian control over the media, including censorship, state propaganda, as well as a legacy of hate speech and incitement for war. Public service broadcasting was established in close cooperation with international bodies, and especially the Media Department of the Organization for Security and Cooperation in Europe (OSCE). There are two public service institutions with a total of seven television channels and seven radio stations and a total of more than 5,000 staff. Until recently, the parliamentary majority had exerted pressures on both institutions via the appointment of the members of the media authority, who in turn appointed the members of the steering boards of the two public service institutions, and had, therefore, a key impact on the selection and appointment of the directors-general—the highly transparent election of a new director-general in 2015 being a notable change in comparison to former practices and may possibly be explained by the country's efforts to meet European accession criteria. Public service news and current affairs programs are moderately biased in favor of the ruling parties. Both public service institutions are lacking stable financial bases. Their financial affairs are non-transparent, non-accountable, and possibly mismanaged. Professional journalism is lacking, which is probably explained by a long history of media instrumentalization by political actors, lasting until the year 2000 and beyond. Public service television channels have a relatively high audience share, which, however, may be attributed to their commercialized programming. Marko (see Chapter 8 in this volume) concludes that "media policy and legislation in Serbia, [while] reflecting European principles and practices, was instrumentalized by political parties," which has been leading to indirect political control over the public service broadcasters.

The studies collected in this volume confirm former research findings (Dragomir et al. 2005; Dragomir and Thompson 2008), but the picture drawn is darker than before, as it shows that the status of public service broadcasting in Southern and Central Eastern Europe has not improved, and has in some cases worsened, despite repeated legislative efforts to ensure that its operation complies with European standards. The chapters of this volume, briefly overviewed above, attest to some recurring patterns across the Western Balkans, including:

1. The politicization of public service television through the appointment of their supervisory boards and via the allocation of their financial sources, partly or mostly covered by the state budget.
2. A lack of political will to transform the state into genuine public service broadcasters.
3. The instrumentalization of public service broadcasters as a means of transferring public resources—such as well-paid positions and funds dedicated to program production and advertising—to party clients (Croatia being an exception in terms of the number of people employed by public television).
4. Pro-government bias and, in some cases, overt propaganda on public service news bulletins and current affairs programs.
5. A lack of professional know-how among public service media staff.
6. The commercialization of programs aired by public service broadcasters and the lack of high-quality programming output.
7. The underfunding of public service broadcasters (with the exception of Albania and Croatia).
8. The exposure of public service broadcasters to corporate pressures, given their heavy reliance on advertising.
9. The non-transparent, non-accountable, and occasionally illicit financial management of public service broadcasting institutions.
10. Low audience ratings (with the exception of Montenegro and Serbia) and the resulting inability of public service media to enhance social integration and cohesion.

In short, state television in the Western Balkans has only formally been transformed into public service television. The omnipresence of political parties, explained by the weakness of trade unions, professional bodies, and civil society organizations has undermined the professional autonomy of public service television. By playing a key part in legislation and in its implementation, parties have colonized and politically instrumentalized the media. While political elites appear to be devoted to the ideal of public service broadcasting on the rhetorical level, in real terms they consider the media a resource to capture and to exploit.

Public Service and Private Interests

Why has the implementation of a genuine public service model failed in the countries discussed in this volume? What conditions are missing for public service television to meet its mission in the Western Balkans? Why does public service television currently display largely similar flaws across the region? The reasons for these similarities are arguably rooted in the specific historical trajectories and current structural conditions of these post-communist, and in some cases post-war, countries.

Some of these reasons are likely related to the economic conditions of the former communist countries. The United Kingdom, where public service broadcasting is based on subscription fees and carries no advertisements (BBC World and Channel 4 being exceptions), has a population of nearly 65 million and is among the world's leading countries in terms of gross domestic product. The Nordic countries also distinguish themselves with high domestic income figures. By contrast, the transition economies of Southern and Central Eastern Europe are relatively poor and have small populations (World Bank 2019). This is especially true for the Western Balkan countries, most of which have just recently been devastated by war. Even though public service television in these countries carries commercial advertisements, underfunding, a natural outcome of the region's economic conditions, is difficult to overcome. Financial difficulties undermine the political independence of public service broadcasters and enhance the commercialization of their programming.

Other reasons may lie in the political cultures of the region's countries. Public service broadcasting is not only normatively expected to enhance social integration and cohesion but is also historically rooted in widely shared consensus; the concepts of universal accessibility and impartial reporting are reflections of this dual role. The political systems of both the United Kingdom and the Nordic countries have traditionally been based on an agreement shared by many groups constituting and representing society, including parties, churches, trade unions, and non-governmental organizations. There, the major political actors observe the rules of democracy as "the only game in town," while anti-system parties have rarely, if ever, earned much support among voters. The United Kingdom has traditionally been a two-party or a two-and-a-half-party system with the dominance of center-left and center-right parties, even though the British party system has in recent years been transformed and increasingly polarized over the Brexit debate; the Nordic countries have been multi-party systems evincing more marked ideological cleavages, but parties have often formed grand coalitions since the 1930s (Hallin and Mancini 2004). By contrast, the transition societies of Southern and Central Eastern Europe have long been politically polarized, and in some cases fragmented, and political cleavages are often coupled with ethnic, linguistic, cultural, and religious cleavages—especially in the Western Balkans (Balčytienė, Lauk and Głowacki 2014). The interruption of democratic consolidation, and in some countries, the de-consolidation of democracy

(Dobek-Ostrowska 2015; Głowacki 2015) is a sign that these transition societies have no consensual visions about their future development. Anti-system proto-hegemonic parties have in recent years taken office in Hungary and in Poland, where neo-authoritarian regimes are now on the rise (Sükösd 2014). Serbia was subject to authoritarian rule under Milošević, and Montenegro has had the same party in office for 27 years. Some political parties overtly question, while other ones covertly undermine media pluralism in an effort to promote their ideologies and to marginalize those of their rivals. Consequently, the media often become a battlefield of conflicting views and ideologies rather than a forum for meaningful debate, and public service television finds itself in the midst of political conflicts. Ideally conceived to be a means of conflict management among different social and political groups via dialogue (Bašić-Hrvatin and Thompson 2008), public service television has come to reflect, and possibly to enhance conflicts. It not only mirrors, but may also deepen, the existing social, political, and ideological cleavages.

In technical terms, unbiased reporting is more easily attained in the context of political cultures evincing moderate pluralism, while in polarized pluralist countries most issues are politicized, which makes rational discussion and factual analysis difficult. The roots of polarized pluralism can be traced back to the weakness of the middle classes. This, in turn, is related to a belated industrial revolution (Hallin and Mancini 2004) and, in the case of Southern and Central Eastern Europe, to the subjugation of many countries to foreign powers that have widely extracted economic resources, blocking the development of the domestic bourgeoisie. The rise of the middle classes was also hindered by the massive extermination of Jewish communities in many of the region's countries during World War II (Bulgaria being a notable exception). Regulation, even if well-designed, cannot eliminate the effects of these historical legacies overnight, and the divided nature of these societies may remain a reality for a long time to come, undermining the development of a viable and widely shared concept and practice of public service television.

Other reasons may have to do with the journalism cultures of the region's countries. Partisan or cause-promoting journalism—as opposed to neutrally objective journalism (Kunczik 2001)—has long-established traditions in the Southern and Central Eastern European countries, including in the Western Balkans (Lauk 2009). The concept and practice of neutrally objective journalism, developed in the United Kingdom and the United States (Chalaby 1996), and often associated with the social responsibility model of the press (Siebert, Peterson and Schramm 1956), lies at the very heart of the British public service broadcasting model's focus on editorial independence and political impartiality. However, in Southern and Central Eastern Europe, foreign rule over many countries, including Ottoman, German, and Russian/Soviet occupation, has been conducive to the rise of cause-promoting journalism, as many journalists considered themselves public intellectuals with a duty to protect and to enhance national culture and identity, rather than independent and politically neutral observers. Hence, the literary tradition of journalism, including partisan and cause-promoting reporting, has deep roots in the region (Lauk 2008). In the countries of former Yugoslavia, this legacy is coupled with a memory of war propaganda, or "patriotic journalism," as sadly observed in the 1990s. Also, a lack of robust press markets in Southern and Central Eastern Europe (with the exception of Poland), coupled with a long tradition of direct political control over editors and journalists by party-states during the decades of communism, was unfavorable for the non-partisan model of journalism to emerge and to consolidate. The impact of efforts by Western multinational companies to enhance non-partisan journalism after the fall of communism was also limited, as, after the 2008 financial and economic crisis, many investors decided to withdraw from the press and media markets of the Southern and Central Eastern European countries, which has yet again exposed journalists to pressures by domestic business and political elites, and hence obstructed the professionalization of journalism (Štětka 2012). Controversial journalism practices, including advertorial, black PR, and even blackmail continue to exist across Southern and Central Eastern Europe as well as in the post-Soviet countries (Örnebring 2012; Pasti 2015). Because cultural change unfolds at a slower pace than institutional change (Balčytienė 2015), the tradition of partisan journalism lives on, including on public service television.

Yet other reasons may have to do with political institutions, and perhaps most importantly with parties and party systems. As noted elsewhere (Bajomi-Lázár 2014), political parties in the consolidating democracies of Europe have fewer members and a lower level of public trust than those in the consolidated ones. Electoral volatility is higher, party splits and mergers are more frequent, and parties switch ideologies more often. Many of the parties created during and after the fall of communism struggle with high levels of intra-party instability, low levels of party loyalty and discipline, and a lack of party institutionalization. New parties are created on a regular basis, while old ones are dissolved. Parties in young democracies are necessarily younger and have fewer resources for party building and organization. As a result, many of them act as cartel parties and colonize the state and the media in an effort to cement their positions by exploring the resources of these. Public service television is no exception to this rule: parties delegate clients into well-paid positions, thus enabling them to influence strategic and managerial decisions, including the distribution of resources. Parties select their cadres on the basis of political rather than professional criteria, and as a result, public media managers do not consider themselves "public servants" but "party servants." As managers have a great influence on the nomination of the senior editorial personnel, they tend to appoint staff loyal to their party's line. The institutional guarantees designed to protect the editorial independence and political impartiality of public service television do not work properly, as political parties have a key role in the implementation of the regulation. Informal rules overwrite formal ones. Public resources such as programming and advertising funds are channeled via public service television to party clients in exchange for various services rendered to the same parties. Clientelism has a long tradition in Southern and Central Eastern Europe. Once again, the public service ideal is compromised.

Thus, the conditions for the successful implementation of public service television have largely been missing in Southern and Central Eastern Europe, including in the Western Balkans. None of the structural reasons that may explain the failed implementation of the public service ideal can be changed overnight—nor in a few decades, as the examples of public service broadcasting organizations in the slightly older democracies of Southern Europe suggest. Four decades have passed since the demise of authoritarian regimes in Greece, Portugal, and Spain, and yet the party politicization of public service institutions continues to be a reality in all of these countries, albeit with varying intensity (Papathanassopoulos 2017; Costa e Silva and Sousa 2017; Bergés 2017).

Institutional reform does not transform culture in the short or medium run. The funding and supervisory mechanisms of public service television can be fine-tuned via legislation, yet it remains that public service television in the Western Balkans continues to serve private interests, including, most notably, political parties and their clients. More often than not, public service television is only nominally "public."

Conclusion: The Iron Law of Public Service Television

The findings of this volume attest to the enduring and potentially never-ending crisis of public service broadcasting in the Western Balkans and allow for two diametrically opposed conclusions to be made. One is that more legislative effort, more money, and more time is needed for the status of public service television to be improved. The other is that it is time to stop spending taxpayer money on public service television. The author of this chapter subscribes to the second one.

Michels' landmark book (2009 [1911]) has introduced the concept of "the iron law of oligarchy," suggesting that political parties (and, within parties, political leaders) have a vested interest in maximizing their powers and stabilizing their positions. He writes this: "The party is created as a means to secure an end" (Michels 2009, 353) but, over time, "from a means, organization becomes an end. To the institutions and qualities which at the outset were destined simply to ensure the good working of the party machine ... a greater importance comes ultimately to be attached than to the productivity of the machine" (Michels 2009, 338). This inevitably leads to the rise of oligarchic leadership within the party and, in some cases, in the country. Michels (2009, 50, emphasis added) also notes that there are "immanent oligarchical tendencies *in every kind of human organization* which strives for the attainment of definite ends."

Public service television organizations in Southern and Central Eastern Europe are no exception. These have been created as a means to a public end, including the information, education, and integration of the public, but have over time been transformed into a means primarily serving private interests. Public service television channels have been colonized, via regulation and funding, by political parties, and are widely used to channel public money into the pockets of party clients, while their nominal objectives have not been achieved. The context in which the establishment of public service television has been attempted, including the specific historical trajectories and current structural conditions of this region, as well as the long list of problems related to public service television—including a poor regulatory design and implementation, political and corporate pressures, funding difficulties, commercialization, and poor audience ratings—make it highly unlikely that the original objectives of public service broadcasting will be reached in the foreseeable future. Yet, despite thirty years of quasi-permanent failure, public service television has been maintained to date. Its privileges, including broadcasting frequencies and other public resources, have been secured and repeatedly renewed via legislation by political actors. Public service organizations seem to be more important than the objectives they were originally created for.

Drawing on Michels' concept, the iron law of public service television suggests that this institution in Southern and Central Eastern Europe, including the Western Balkans, is a bottomless well into which public resources are endlessly poured, while it brings little benefit to the public. More often than not, public service television is a means of money laundering and illicit party funding. The high costs, low audience ratings, and lack of legitimacy suggest that closing down this institution should be considered.

Who is the main agent behind the iron law of public service television? In other words, who are the major beneficiaries of a dysfunctional public service television? A long list can be compiled. Direct beneficiaries include political parties and their clients, top managers, senior editors, and journalists, as well as advertisers and program producers. Indirect beneficiaries include international actors such as the European Parliament, the European Commission, the Parliamentary Assembly of the Council of Europe, UNESCO, the Media Department of OSCE, Article 19, the EBU, and a number of other expert bodies that keep producing green papers and white papers, recommendations, resolutions, guidelines, and directives addressing the crisis and never-ending reform of public service television. Indirect beneficiaries may also include academics like us, the authors of this volume, who receive grants to study public service television. In short, various lobby groups benefit from public service television, while the general public rarely does so in Southern and Central Eastern Europe.

One may ask the question of whether there is an alternative to reach the objectives originally included in the public service remit. To date, digital and mobile communication technologies ease public access to a variety of new platforms of information, education, and integration. The resources now devoted to public service television could arguably be much more efficiently used if spent on the creation of public service social media platforms that differ from established private ones such as Facebook and Instagram. A public service social media platform should neither be driven by algorithms designed to maximize commercial gain nor should it encourage the politically motivated distribution of fake news. In contrast, a public service social media platform may be capable of attracting audiences, especially the young ones, that legacy television has lost in recent years. It may also allow for the more active participation in content production of the audiences and hence re-establish the missing link between public service media producers and consumers. And it may make a meaningful contribution to a rational and critical debate on public matters if adequately moderated and if based on elaborate fact-checking methods. Last but not least, it would not require the infrastructure and staff currently associated with public service media that are largely abused by the political elites of Southern and Central Eastern Europe for their own benefits. Short of media resources of a similar scale, such a public service social media platform could be less attractive for the political class to capture and to exploit than legacy public service television.

References

Bajomi-Lázár, Péter, Václav Štětka, and Miklós Sükösd. 2012. "Public Service Television in the European Union Countries: Old Issues, New Challenges in the 'East' and 'West'." In *Trends in Communication Policy Research. New Theories, Methods and Subjects* edited by Natascha Just and Manuel Puppis, 355–380. Bristol/Chicago: Intellect.

Bajomi-Lázár, Péter. 2014. *Party Colonisation of the Media in Central and Eastern Europe.* Budapest: CEU Press.

——. 2017. "Introduction: The Media Systems of Third-Wave Democracies in Southern and in Central/Eastern Europe." In *Media in Third-Wave Democracies: Southern and Central/Eastern Europe in a Comparative Perspective*, edited by Péter Bajomi-Lázár, 13–18. Paris/Budapest: L'Harmattan.

Balčytienė, Aukse, Epp Lauk, and Michal Głowacki. 2014. "Roller Coasters of Social Change, Democracy and Journalism in Central and Eastern Europe." In *Journalism that Matters: Views from Central and Eastern Europe*, edited by Michał Głowacki, Epp Lauk and Auksė Balčytienė, 9–19. Frankfurt am Main: Peter Lang.

Balčytienė, Aukse. 2015. "Institutions and Cultures: An Analytical Framework for the Study of Democratization and Media Transformations in Central and Eastern Europe." In *Democracy and Media in Central and Eastern Europe 25 Years On*, edited by Bogusława Dobek-Ostrowska and Michal Głowacki, 47–62. Frankfurt am Main: Peter Lang.

Bardoel, Jo and Marit Vochteloo. 2012. "Conditional Access for Public Service Broadcasting to New Media Platforms: EU State-Aid Policy vis-à-vis Public Service Broadcasting: the Dutch Case." In *Trends in Communication Policy Research: New Theories, Methods and Subjects* edited by Natascha Just and Manuel Puppis, 301–315. Bristol/Chicago: Intellect.

Barendt, Eric. 1994. *Broadcasting Law: A Comparative Study.* Oxford: Clarendon Press.

Bašić-Hrvatin, Sandra, and Mark Thompson. 2008. "Public Service Broadcasting in Plural and Divided Societies." In *Divided They Fall: Public Service Broadcasting in Multiethnic States*, edited by Sandra Bašić-Hrvatin, Mark Thompson and Tarik Jusić, 7–40. Sarajevo: Mediacentar. https://www.academia.edu/28197065/Divided_They_Fall_Public_Service_Broadcasting_in_Multiethnic_States_ed.

Beitika, Ieva. 2011. "Development of Public Service Broadcasting: Local and Global Challenges and the Public Value." *Media Transformations* 5 (February): 44–65.

Bergés, Laura. 2017. "Spain: Traces of the Authoritarian Past or Signals of a Western Neo-Authoritarian Future?" In *Media in Third-Wave Democracies: Southern and*

Central/Eastern Europe in a Comparative Perspective, edited by Péter Bajomi-Lázár, 109–135. Paris/Budapest: L'Harmattan.

Briggs, Asa and Peter Burke. 2009. *A Social History of the Media: From Gutenberg to the Internet.* Cambridge: Polity Press.

Bustamante, Enrique. 2008. "Public Service in the Digital Age: Opportunities and Threats in a Diverse Europe." In *Communications and Cultural Policies in Europe*, edited by Isabel Fernández Alonso and Miquel de Moragas, 185–216. Barcelona: Government of Catalonia.

Chalaby, Jean K. 1996. "Journalism as an Anglo-American Invention: A Comparison of the Development of French and Anglo-American Journalism, 1830s–1920s." *European Journal of Communication* 11, no. 3 (September): 303–326.

Costa e Silva, Elsa, and Helena Sousa. 2017. "Portugal: The Challenges of Democratisation." In *Media in Third-Wave Democracies: Southern and Central/Eastern Europe in a Comparative Perspective*, edited by Péter Bajomi-Lázár, 90–108. Paris/Budapest: L'Harmattan.

Curran, James, Shanto Iyengar, Anker Brink Lund, and Inka Salovaara-Moring. 2009. "Media System, Public Knowledge and Democracy: A Comparative Study." *European Journal of Communication* 24, no. 1 (March): 5–26.

Deutsch-Ungarische Industrie- und Handelskammer. 2020. Ungarns Wirtschaft auf einen Blick. Accessed May 5, 2020. https://www.ahkungarn.hu/fileadmin/AHK_Ungarn /Dokumente/Wirtschaft/Statistik/Konjunkturdaten_de.pdf.

DigitalHungary. 2016. "Evolution 2016: növekedett a reklámköltés, élénkül a piac." Accessed May 5, 2020. http://www.digitalhungary.hu/marketing/Evolution-2016-novekedett-a-reklamkoltes-elenkul-a-piac/2596/.

Dobek-Ostrowska, Bogusława. 2015. "25 Years after Communism: Four Models of Media and Politics in Central and Eastern Europe." In *Democracy and Media in Central and Eastern Europe 25 Years On*, edited by Bogusława Dobek-Ostrowska and Michal Głowacki, 11–45. Frankfurt am Main: Peter Lang.

Dragomir, Marius, and Mark Thompson. 2008. "Overview." In *Television Across Europe: More Channels, Less Independence. Follow-Up Reports*, edited by Open Society Institute, 13–66. Budapest: Open Society Institute. https://www.opensocietyfoundations.org/publications/television-across-europe-more-channels-less-independence.

Dragomir, Marius, Dušan Reljić, Mark Thompson, and Andreas Grünwald. 2005. "Overview." In *Television Across Europe: Regulation, Policy and Independence. Summary*, edited by Open Society Institute, 13–184. Budapest: Open Society Institute. https://www.opensocietyfoundations.org/publications/television-across-europe-regulation-policy-and-independence.

European Commission. 2014. *Standard Eurobarometer 82. Media Use in the European Union.* Accessed May 5, 2020. http://ec.europa.eu/public_opinion/archives/eb / eb82/eb82_media_en.pdf.

Głowacki, Michal. 2015. "Conclusions: Mapping the Outcomes of Media Transformation in Central and Eastern Europe." In *Democracy and Media in Central and Eastern Europe 25 Years On*, edited by Bogusława Dobek-Ostrowska and Michal Głowacki, 255–270. Frankfurt am Main: Peter Lang.

Hallin, Daniel C., and Paolo Mancini. 2004. *Comparing Media Systems: Three Models of Media and Politics.* Cambridge/New York: Cambridge University Press.

Jakubowicz, Karol, and Miklós Sükösd. 2008. "Twelve Concepts Regarding Media System Evolution and Democratization in Post-Communist Societies." In *Finding the*

Right Place on the Map: Central and Eastern European Media Change in a Global Perspective, edited by Karol Jakubowicz and Miklós Sükösd, 9–40. Bristol/Chicago: Intellect.

Jakubowicz, Karol. 2008. "Finding the Right Place on the Map: Prospects for Public Service Broadcasting in Post-Communist Countries." In *Finding the Right Place on the Map: Central and Eastern European Media Change in a Global Perspective*, edited by Karol Jakubowicz and Miklós Sükösd, 101–124. Bristol/Chicago: Intellect.

Keane, John. 1991. *The Media and Democracy*. Cambridge: Polity Press.

Kunczik, Michael. 2001. "Media and Democracy: Are Western Concepts of Press Freedom Applicable in New Democracies?" In *Media and Politics,* edited by Péter Bajomi-Lázár and István Hegedűs, 59–99. Budapest: New Mandate Publishing House.

Lauk, Epp. 2008. "How Will It All Unfold? Media Systems and Journalism Cultures in Post-Communist Countries." In *Finding the Right Place on the Map: Central and Eastern European Media Change in a Global Perspective*, edited by Karol Jakubowicz and Miklós Sükösd, 193–212. Bristol/Chicago: Intellect.

——. 2009. "Reflection on Changing Patterns of Journalism in the New EU countries." *Journalism Studies* 10, no. 1 (February): 69–84.

Michels, Robert. 2009 [1911]. *Political Parties: A Sociological Study of the Oligarchical Tendencies of Modern Democracy*. New Brunswick, NJ/London: Transaction Publishers.

Mungiu-Pippidi, Alina. 2003. "From State to Public Service: The Failed Reform of State TV in Central Eastern Europe." In *Reinventing Media. Media Policy Reform in East-Central Europe*, edited by Miklós Sükösd and Péter Bajomi-Lázár, 31–84. Budapest: CEU Press.

——. 2013. "Freedom without Impartiality: The Vicious Circle of Media Capture." In *Media Transformations in the Post-Communist World. Eastern Europe's Tortured Path to Change,* edited by Peter Gross and Karol Jakubowicz, 33–47. Lanham: Lexington Books.

Örnebring, Henrik. "Clientelism, Elites, and the Media in Central and Eastern Europe." *The International Journal of Press/Politics* 17, no. 4 (July): 497–515.

Papathanassopoulos, Stylianos. 2017. "Greece: A Continuous Interplay between Media and Politicians." In *Media in Third-Wave Democracies: Southern and Central/Eastern Europe in a Comparative Perspective*, edited by Péter Bajomi-Lázár, 75–89. Paris/Budapest: L'Harmattan.

Pasti, Svetlana. 2015. "A Passion for Robin Hood: A Case Study of Journalistic (In)dependence in Russia." In *Democracy and Media in Central and Eastern Europe 25 Years On*, edited by Bogusława Dobek-Ostrowska and Michal Głowacki, 117–136. Frankfurt am Main: Peter Lang.

Siebert, Fred S., Theodore Peterson, and Wilbur Schramm. 1956. *Four Theories of the Press: The Authoritarian, Libertarian, Social Responsibility and Soviet Communist Concept of What the Press Should Be and Do*. Urbana/Chicago/London: University of Illinois Press.

Siune, Karen, and Olof Hultén. 1998. "Does Public Broadcasting have a Future?" In *Media Policy: Convergence, Concentration and Commerce,* edited by Denis McQuail and Karen Siune, 23–37. London/Thousand Oaks/New Delhi: Sage.

Štětka, Václav. 2012. "From Multinationals to Business Tycoons: Media Ownership and Journalistic Autonomy in Central and Eastern Europe." *The International Journal of Press/Politics* 17, no. 4 (July): 433–456.

Sükösd, Miklós. 2014. "'East' of 'West'—Media in Central and Eastern Europe, Eurasia and China: Multiple Post-communisms and Shifting Geopolitical Realities." In *Journalism that Matters: Views from Central and Eastern Europe*, edited by Michał Głowacki, Epp Lauk and Auksė Balčytienė, 21–33. Frankfurt am Main: Peter Lang.

Tamás, Botos. 2015. "Az MTVA 47,2 milliárdos adósságát átvenné a kormány!" *444.hu*. Accessed May 5, 2020. http://444.hu/2015/09/21/az-mtva-472-milliardos-adossagat-atvenne-a-kormany4/.

——. 2016. "Jó dolgozni a közmédiánál: négyszázezer körül az átlagfizetés." *444.hu*. Accessed May 5, 2020. http://444.hu/2016/05/10/jo-dolgozni-a-kozmedianal-negyszazezer-korul-az-atlagfizetes.

World Bank. 2019. *Gross Domestic Product 2018*. Accessed May 5, 2020. http://databank .worldbank.org/data/download/GDP.pdf.

Zsolt, Papp. 2014. "Még több pénzt kap a közmédia." *Napi.hu*. Accessed May 5, 2020. http://www.napi.hu/magyar_vallalatok/meg_tobb_penzt_kap_a_kozmedia.588091 .html.

CHAPTER 10

Overcoming Path Dependencies in Public Service Broadcasting Developments in Southeast Europe

Zrinjka Peruško

Introduction

The normative media reform perspective has not proved very useful in understanding the failures of the post-socialist transformations of state broadcasters into public service broadcasters in Central and Eastern Europe. In this chapter, the media systems approach is reinforced with the historical institutionalist (HI) approach in the study of PSB transformation, allowing for a more profitable analysis of the media policy dimension in historical context.[1] This analysis extends the results of the historical institutionalist comparative study of institutional circumstances influencing six successor states of socialist Yugoslavia to the issue of public service broadcasting development. These six states—Slovenia, Croatia, Bosnia and Herzegovina, Montenegro, North Macedonia and Serbia (Kosovo is not included as data for the socialist period was not available) are chosen in the most similar case design where the transformation changes start from the same socialist state framework but develop in different policy and contextual configurations after democratization within separate independent states.

Peruško (2016) focuses on three distinct historical periods following formative critical junctures, namely, the 19th-century modernization period, the post-World War Two socialist period, and the period of post-1989 democratic transformation (Peruško 2016). The cluster analysis was employed and shows that the institutional conditions of political and economic development, including the type of communism, were, despite the shared state in part of the first and the second time frame, different, and consequently produced different conditions for the media system development. Two clusters of countries with similar/dissimilar historical contextual conditions were shown—Slovenia and Croatia in one cluster, and the remaining four countries in the other. The socialist period

---

[1]   The final version of this chapter was submitted to the editors in April 2017. The HI analysis of media system developments in Southeast Europe was extended meanwhile in Peruško, Vozab, and Čuvalo (2020).

was the only one with some integrative influence on the political and economic conditions for media development, and periods of first modernization and post-socialist democratization influenced divergent contextual conditions.

In this chapter, transformations of PSB policies and practices in these Southeast European countries are examined from the standpoint of the influence of earlier institutional conditions in later historical periods of PSB development.

Let me review the main points of the argument for preferring the media systems approach over the normative media reform perspective (Peruško 2014). First of all, it is the descriptive character of the media reform perspective, as opposed to the analytical character of the media systems approach. The focus on legislative content and its implementation is another feature of the normative approach, which does not usually afford an understanding of why certain legislative solutions are present or not. Comparative studies of legal structures do map the trends in regulation within and between regions, but the understanding of social consequences and foundations of media regulation is better accomplished by media system analysis in which media policy is considered as only one of, and in conjunction with, the other dimensions and variables which can help in understanding the reasons behind different policy solutions, and their consequences.

Another drawback of the media reform approach is its ahistorical nature, where the *longue durée* of institutional development preceding the present set of circumstances and choices is out of the picture. This is where the media system analysis fortified with the historical institutionalist approach is preferable and helps us to investigate and understand the repercussions of historical conditions that can be seen in contemporary media systems (Hallin and Mancini 2012; Humphreys 2012; Peruško 2013, Peruško 2016).

In addition to the categorization of similar cases according to variation in the observed patterns, the purpose of classifications in comparative research also points to common trends within the cluster of similar cases that can alert us to common causes of phenomena or institutional setups. In this chapter, the focus is on public service broadcasting in Southeast Europe, in six states which used to be republics in the SFRY. The EU pragmatic "Western Balkans" categorization (used to describe those countries in SEE who are not yet members of EU) is not followed here, as the theoretical framework of historical institutionalism is employed to look for similarities and differences among a group of countries with a long-term common history.

Before we explore these historical circumstances of media development, how do these six countries compare in the present day to other central and Eastern European media systems?

Southeast Europe in a European Comparative Perspective

European post-socialist media systems do not group only into one common media system (as it is often erroneously expected), but in two of the three empirical models constructed with cluster analysis (Peruško, Vozab and Čuvalo 2013) based on the operationalization of the Hallin and Mancini (2012) original model of media systems together with Western European countries. The three empirical models resemble only partially the distribution of countries and the main features of the three Hallin and Mancini models. The empirical models which describe Central, Eastern, and Southeastern European countries are the South and East European Model, the Nordic Model, and European Mainstream Model (Peruško 2016; see also the analysis of CEE countries which confirms multiple models, in Castro Herrero et al. 2017).

The South and East European empirical cluster resembles most closely the Mediterranean Model from the Hallin and Mancini typology. The majority of CEE countries are found in this cluster alongside Italy, Greece, and Spain from the Mediterranean Model. In addition to Croatia, Lithuania, Hungary, Romania and Bulgaria, North Macedonia, Serbia, Lithuania, Ukraine, and Russia also cluster in the South/East European Model (Peruško 2016). These countries all have in common newspaper circulation that is lower than average for the analyzed group of countries, political parallelism is higher, and professionalization of journalism is lower than average. This cluster shows a lower to medium quality of public service television, the indicator for the role of the state.

The empirical Nordic Model resembles the Democratic Corporatist Model except that it shows lower than average values in political parallelism (Hallin and Mancini 2012). This feature of the Liberal Model in the Hallin and Mancini typology could be seen as support of the convergence thesis by Hallin and Mancini.

The third empirical European Mainstream Model exhibits intermediate values of political parallelism and journalistic professionalism. It includes countries from all three Models in the Hallin and Mancini typology: UK and Ireland from the European Liberal Model countries; France and Portugal from the Mediterranean Model; and Germany, Austria, and Belgium from the Democratic Corporatist Model (see Table 10.1). This cluster also includes several of the CEE countries: the Czech Republic, Slovenia, Slovakia, Poland, and Estonia.

While the features of the media system—the quality of public service broadcasting (indicating the role of the state in media systems), newspaper circulation (indicating the character of the media market—mass circulation in some countries vs. smaller readership figures in others), party and owner influence in the media (indicating the Hallin and Mancini dimension of political and economic parallelism), and journalistic culture as the indicator of professionalization of journalism—are such that differentiate them from the other European countries included in the analysis and sufficiently similar to group them in one cluster (based on the cluster analysis used), at one glance we know something is wrong with this classification and that the relationship between media and politics in these countries cannot be in the same category. The most striking problem is with Russia which is classified as an authoritarian regime by the EIU Democracy Index 2015. Whatever the shape of the media system dimensions this political category influences the autonomy and position of the news and other media in ways that surpass the differences between different types of democratic political systems. Media systems that fall at the edge of, or out of, the democracy zone need further descriptive dimension.

Table 10.1: Three empirical models of media systems in West, Central, and East Europe

	The South/East European model	The European mainstream model	The Nordic model
Countries	Greece, Spain, Lithuania, Croatia, Hungary, Italy, Romania, Bulgaria, Serbia, North Macedonia, Russia	Austria, Poland, Belgium, Estonia, Czech Republic, Germany, France, Slovenia, Ireland, Great Britain, Portugal, Slovakia	Finland, Sweden, Denmark, Netherlands
Role of the state	Lower to medium quality of public television	*Not a distinguishing factor*	Higher quality of public television
Media market	Lower newspaper circulation	*Not a distinguishing factor*	Higher newspaper circulation
Political and economic parallelism	Higher party influence	Middle values of party influence	Lower party influence
Professionalization of journalism	Lower professionalism and independence	Middle values of professionalism and independence	Higher professionalism and independence

Source: Peruško 2016

Peruško et al.'s (2013) analysis is useful in showing that CEE countries group in different media system clusters in Europe and in this way show differences also between the Eastern European media systems. While disproving those who expect CEE countries to form one media system (Curran and Park 2000; Puppis et al. 2009; Terzis 2007; Voltmer 2008) based only on the fact that they all had a socialist regime in place after World War Two, the countries need to be further analyzed to show nuances in their media system development concerning their political, economic and social settings as well as in a comparative perspective.

Based on the data from the 2010 survey of media systems (Popescu et al. 2011), among the countries we focus on in this chapter, only Slovenia clusters in the European Mainstream Model and Croatia, Serbia, and North Macedonia in the South/East Model (data for Montenegro and Bosnia and Herzegovina were not collected). The historical institutionalist approach in comparative media systems analysis showed that during the three significant time frames analyzed these media systems clustered differently—Slovenia and Croatia clustered in one group, and other countries in the other (Peruško 2016). In the following, I summarize these findings before proceeding to build on this explanatory analysis of the state of development of public service broadcasting in these countries.

The Historical Institutionalist Approach to Media Systems Analysis

The HI approach extends the causal arena to the past and is a comparative method which thus also includes the longitudinal view. Two key concepts define HI approach: the concept of critical juncture and the concept of path dependency (Mahoney 2000). While most authors stress the critical junctures as the point of analysis (Ekiert and Ziblatt 2013), which are those points in history when the change in institutional character is possible after (usually) momentous change, in this chapter we will focus more on institutional inertia linked to path dependency. Path dependency is associated with the continuation of institutional development along the same path, barring changes at the point of a critical juncture which is a contingent, unexpected event, sometimes a revolution and sometimes a culmination point of a set of evolutionary developments. In the case studied here, the post-Yugoslav case of six states in Southeast Europe, three critical junctures were identified with respect to media system change. All were regime changes (for detailed information on sources for the HI analysis see Peruško 2016).

The analyzed countries had membership in the same state for 70 years, between 1919 and 1990. The common state was first formed at the end of World War One, in which the Habsburg Monarchy as the state context for Slovenia and Croatia was dissolved, and when the Ottoman Empire relinquished its hold on North Macedonia, Montenegro, Bosnia and Herzegovina, and a few decades earlier, over Serbia, and dissolved in 1991 after the first democratic elections were held in the republics in 1990.

The first juncture marks the beginning of modernization processes in the nineteenth century (later than the rest of Europe). The second juncture marks the beginning of socialism in 1945, at the end of World War Two. The third juncture marks the beginning of the democratic transition in 1989. These time frames apply specifically to the chosen countries, and they are similar for most of CEE, though not for Russia, or the Baltic states. In each of these periods, certain contextual circumstances prevailed, and certain media and politics relationships existed. Unless the institutional character was changed at one of the critical junctures, they influence these media systems in all the following time frames to this date.

The first period is the nineteenth century, showing uneven developments in modernization among the studied countries. Croatia had most of the capital ownership and the first newspapers were published there, while Slovenia had the largest industrial production (followed by Croatia) and literacy rates: Slovenia had only 8.8% of illiterate population, Croatia had 32%, Serbia 64%, Montenegro 67%, Bosnia and Herzegovina 80% and North Macedonia 83.8% (comparative data based on Bilandžić 1999). At the beginning of the nineteenth century, Slovenia and Croatia were part of an absolutistic monarchy of the Habsburg Empire, the other countries were part of the sultanate of the Ottoman Empire. Neither were very supportive of the development of press: the monarchy at that time censored newspapers but the institution of the press did develop even if with limitations, and the sultanate forbade them completely (for historical information on the six countries, see Banac 1984).

In the socialist period, Yugoslavia, as a non-aligned country and with its version of self-management socialism, was more open and pluralistic than the other CEE countries, and especially Albania which was under Enver Hodža the most isolated European regime with the highest repression (Romania was similar in this respect while being part of the Soviet Bloc). Even during socialism, the conditions for media development were not the same in all the republics. Disparities continued, with the greatest GDP per capita created in Slovenia in 1989 (197 index points to the 100 average of Yugoslavia), followed by Croatia (126), Serbia about average (103), while others produced between 64 and 73%. Croatia and Slovenia had a larger percentage of the urban population, while newspaper circulation was largest in Croatia—169 copies per 1000, Serbia had 158, and Slovenia 145. In the other three republics, press circulation was around 30 copies per 1000 inhabitants (Peruško 2016). Slovenia and Croatia also had a different type of socialism (communism)—Kitschelt (1995) finds that among the three types found in the European socialist states after World War Two, the open to reform national-accommodative type where the ruling communist elites accommodated the opposing political or social forces to enable degrees of pluralism was present in Poland, Croatia, and Slovenia. In a later book, Kitschelt et al. (1999) reassign Serbia from the predominating group of fully patrimonial communist countries (where all the other republics are situated and in which the clientelistic type of communist regime follows the logic of the earlier sultanate and is averse to any reform) of Eastern Europe halfway to the accommodative type. The third type, bureaucratic-authoritarian communism which developed in those countries with earlier modernization (like the Czech), was not present in any of the Yugoslavian republics.

The cluster analysis shows that the institutional conditions of political and economic development, including the type of communism, were, despite belonging to the same federal state in part of the first and in the second time frame, different, and consequently produced different conditions for media system development.

The socialist period was the only one with some integrative influence on the political and economic conditions for media development in some of the republics in former Yugoslavia, namely Serbia which moved to the more developed cluster, and the periods of first modernization and post-socialist democratization influenced divergent developments. Despite this, disparities continued in development conditions between the two more developed republics and the rest. More analysis is needed to understand the conditions of socialist media in these and other European socialist countries. At present, the invalid stereotype of one and the same media "theory" in all socialist states (following the Siebert, Peterson, and Schramm "description" of Soviet media theory) persists despite mounting evidence to the contrary (Robinson 1977; Sparks 1998; Siebert, Peterson, and Schramm 1956). Clearly, this direction of research is important for the future.

After the third juncture in 1989 which begins the period of democratic transition, selected data show that the disparities are continued. The institutions of this period should be shaped to support democracy, but it seems that some still exhibit path dependencies and instead of showing breaks with the past, show continuities.

Quality of democracy is highest in Slovenia (the only country of the SFRY which mostly escaped the 1990s war), followed by Croatia, and the lowest scores are in Bosnia and Herzegovina and Montenegro, followed by North Macedonia and Serbia. The inclusiveness of institutions, which is partly evaluated with the quality of democracy index, is also evaluated with the social and economic inclusiveness, measured with the UNDP Human Development Index (HDI) comprising education, wealth, and life expectancy/health. Slovenia and Croatia are again separate in a different, more developed cluster. Freedom of the press shows a similar story, Slovenia in the lead, and Croatia, while having better scores than the rest, is evaluated somewhat more closely to some of the other countries in the region (North Macedonia and Montenegro are placed last). The length of EU integration and the length of independence from the SFRY also play a role. While these indicators need to be complemented with case studies to explain institutional developments, cluster analysis again separates Slovenia and Croatia into one group.

In the following section, transformations of PSB policies and practices in these Southeast European countries in the post-socialist era are examined in view of path dependencies in institutional development. Has the process of European integration in the post-socialist period acted as a factor of convergence to Western European ideals for PSB, or have other contextual influences contributed to further divergence? Is the convergence to the Western European PSB ideal type even possible, in the political, economic, and social context of some of these societies?

The analysis proceeds from the expectation that path dependencies, which cluster the media systems of states in Southeast Europe into two groups, will be continued in the state of progress of their PSB.

Public service broadcasting developed (in Western Europe in the 1950s) in a political culture of the welfare state imbued with the idea of the common good, in which the content provided by radio and television broadcasters had to equally inform, entertain and educate the citizens. Mancini lists four requirements in political culture that support the development of public service broadcasting: 1) the more consolidated the democracy, the better for public service broadcasting; 2) the more consensus about the "rules of the game" for PSB the better—if there is a contest about its mission, it is more difficult to establish; 3) strong political and social organizations ensure that the rules will be fulfilled, and guarantee stability, and also have the interest in an independent channel to distribute their news (even when they are not in power); 4) PSB developed better in those political cultures closer to the practice of the rational legal author, and further away from clientelistic and particularistic practices (Mancini 2014). The last feature is important both in consensus and majoritarian democracies, as both types of power-sharing have a "higher" and a "lower" manifestation. In the first, well established democratic procedures and strong social and political institutions ensure that PSB equally serves all groups, while with weakened rules some groups may attempt to control programming in their interest. In majoritarian democracies, in the presence of ingrained rules, the government would seek to ensure independent programming (expecting it to continue when they are in opposition), while in the circumstance of weak rule of law the influence over PSB would be exercised to further its particular over general interests (Mancini 2014, 16–17).

In the next section, the HI approach to media systems will be extended to public service broadcasters' development in SEE, combining the contextual variables and time frames from the portrayed historical institutionalist analysis of media systems and the four political field variables developed by Mancini.

From State Broadcasting to Public Service Broadcasting in Southeast Europe: Institutional Inertia?

The normative approach to media transformation is particularly active regarding public service broadcasting. Mostly imitative policies (Harcourt 2003; Jakubowicz and Sükösd 2008; Splichal 2000) translated laws from the Western European countries into local languages and implemented them in completely different policies and social contexts. The reforms of public service broadcasting (PSB) systems in Eastern Europe are probably the most disappointing outcome of these imitative policies. Only decades later are media researchers pointing to the fact that normative solutions from one type of media system will not work in another without "domestication," i.e., before being adapted to the shape of the media market, the relationship between politics and the media, the political culture and structures of power in the implementing country. This failure to understand that the context of the whole media and political system influences the possibility of imported models to be successfully applied is the reason for the perception of failed reforms. The primary problem is, however, the absence of consensus about the aims and status of PSB.

The idea of public service broadcasting rests on the philosophy of the welfare state and common good, which, in addition to other services (education, health, solidarity care) include information and communication (Mancini 2014). While this philosophy is linked to the Western European democracies in the post-World War Two period, an argument could be made that socialist countries also subscribed to some of these ideals. In the present case relating to the post-socialist space of post-Yugoslavian countries, we might argue that while broadcasting and press were used during socialism for authoritarian aims of the government (i.e., promotion of the ruling elite and its programs and ideas, but not in a monolithic way), the idea of universal service concerning education, information and entertainment of the people through radio and television broadcasting was present as well.

The introduction of radio in Croatia and Slovenia happened in the first period of media modernization, and the influence of the institutional structures from that period needs to be further studied. The second historical institutionalist period of self-management socialism significantly influenced the development of broadcasting in Yugoslavia, with possible path dependencies in today's public service broadcasting policies or organization. The space of this chapter only allows a brief sketch of the much broader field in need of further research.

Broadcasting in Self-Management Socialism (the Second HI Time Period)

In conceptualizing the transformation of state broadcasters into public service broadcasters in the countries that were part of the federation of socialist Yugoslavia (1945–1991), we focus first on the character of the state broadcasters and the influence of this on the possibility of PSB development in the new democracies.

The status of public service broadcasters in socialist Yugoslavia was different than in other countries of CEE, which belonged to the Warsaw Pact and the Soviet sphere of influence and control, or were, like Albania, largely isolated. The self-management type of economy, in which the role of the state was reduced and the autonomy of decision making of business organizations increased (it was greater in comparison to the state-managed economy of the Soviet type, but smaller in comparison to a market economy) extended also to institutions like the media. And while the radio and television broadcasters were certainly not outside of the sphere of influence of politics—either in terms of employment policies where the prominent editorial positions were reserved for those with communist party approval, or editorial policies where it was quite clear that one of the roles of the broadcaster was the promotion of the positive view of the socialist project—there was no prior censorship after the mid-1950s (it existed in many CEE countries until the fall of the regimes in 1989/90), and independence in terms of programming policies was also much greater.

The central federal government influenced nevertheless many media-related developments, especially in the first decades.

It is also important to point to institutional continuity at the state/territorial level in these countries. Broadcasting was organized in the republics, and each capital of the republics—which are now independent states—had its broadcaster (Peruško and Čuvalo 2014). Far from having to build the institutions from scratch, the broadcasters existed in all the countries in the Southeastern European region, together with technological infrastructures that were, in some cases, on a par with their western neighbors. At the beginning of the 1990s Television Zagreb in Croatia, which was the EBU exchange center for Yugoslavia and also the organizer of the 1990 Eurovision song contest, was technically the most developed and was comparable in this respect to Austrian radio and television. Also inherited from the period of self-management socialism was the license fee which was the main source of funding for television broadcasters from early 1960, and for radio even earlier—the first radio program was broadcast in 1926, and Radio Zagreb became the member in the International Radio-diffusion Union (the precursor of EBU) in 1928. At that time, none of the other countries in the region had started broadcasting (Virtualni radio-museum n.d.).

As most prominent research and analysis on the post-socialist development of PSB is from the Polish point of view (Karol Jakubowicz) or about Romania (Peter Gross), different consequences of self-management socialism for the media have not been seriously reviewed.

The idea that the "media system and political system had to be created from scratch" (Mungiu-Pippidi 2008) is challenged and overturned by the historical institutionalist approach, which shows how the institutional continuity influences present-day media developments (see also Sparks 1998). Mungiu-Pippidi also claims that the pre-communist tradition does not influence the success of the post-transition development of media freedom in European post-socialist states. The characterizations of the communist/socialist times are also often inaccurate in their generalizations; since the 1950s, most CEE countries did not live in totalitarian but in authoritarian regimes, with perhaps the exception of Romania and Albania. Among differences which cannot be detailed here, Splichal describes the development of the institution of the "letter to the editor" in the mid-1980s as a result of the constitutional right to publish their opinions in the media for the citizens of socialist Yugoslavia, and the protection of this right by the courts in Slovenia (Splichal 1995).

Unlike in some other socialist European states, state broadcasting had some institutional traits in socialist Yugoslavia that could have transferred positive institutional benefits to the development of public service broadcasting in the new multi-party states (if not for the negative influence of the war in the 1990s).

The first was the organization of broadcasting in the republics, with an umbrella organization (JRT) whose role was only in organizing the sharing of programs. The programming, production, staffing, and funding was at the level of the republics. This meant that the technology and technical and production expertise existed already for the creation of PSB, especially in some future states. Perhaps the most important positive legacy of broadcasting in the SFRY was the license fee model of financing, which was introduced first for radio broadcasting, and then with the advent of television, also for television. Commercials were also allowed and present from the beginning. This ensured that stable independent financing, which is one of the most difficult things to ensure in PSB, was already well entrenched at the time of democratic transition. Why is it that in some countries this model was successfully continued (Croatia and Slovenia), while others are still struggling with establishing secure and stable funding for the public service broadcaster?

Public Service Broadcasting Policies in Post-Socialist Democracies

How was this last critical juncture used in relation to public service media? Can we identify a significant change in institutional direction in the democratic transition period which would support the development of a different institutional framework to replace state television from the socialist era? Here we review the four conditions from the political field necessary for successful PSB establishment (Mancini 2014).

Consolidation of democracy and nation-building/state-building

Consolidation of democracy is related to better chances for public service broadcasting (Mancini 2014), and the quality of democracy is one of the indicators of the degree of inclusiveness of media systems. In the most inclusive media systems with highest democracy scores, in the Nordic countries, public service broadcasters have the most prominent place among the first three audience choices of television (Peruško 2017).

In the latest Democracy Index (EIU Democracy Index 2017), Slovenia, Croatia and Serbia score as flawed democracies, while Montenegro, North Macedonia, Bosnia and Herzegovina, Albania score as hybrid regimes (Kosovo is not included), with the lowest scores in the functioning of the government and political culture (for Slovenia and Croatia the lowest scores are political culture and political participation). Data shows that the worst performers in this regard, Bosnia and Herzegovina, and North Macedonia, also have the most trouble with the establishment of public service broadcasting. Bosnia and Herzegovina and Albania are characterized as countries with "fleckless pluralism," i.e., ineffective pluralism, which despite showing some expected democratic moves does not produce the expected results (Carothers 2002). Ahmetašević and Hadžiristić (see Chapter 3 in this volume) show the dire situation of public service broadcasting in Bosnia and Herzegovina. Trpevska and Micevski (see Chapter 7 in this volume) show how the pressures of political authoritarianism coupled with technological and commercial challenges make the future of PSB in North Macedonia uncertain in what they name a hegemonic polarized media system. Unlike in Bosnia and Herzegovina where the ethnic and language cleavages are largely ignored or dismissed as inconsequential, in North Macedonia, the "social cleavages are mapped onto media cleavages" (Bašić-Hrvatin and Thompson 2008, 30).

Clientelism is present in the media, and the government colonized both commercial and public media. Structural relationships exist between privately-owned media outlets and the ruling political party. Despite the early consensus and enthusiasm for the pluralism and diversity of a democratic media system, the financial framework for public broadcasting was not successfully put in place. At 9% share for the three channels, Macedonian public television probably has the lowest audience figures from all included countries. Although viewership figures seem to be disputed, information available on the RTVBIH webpage puts Federalna TV at some 11% and BH1 at 4.3 average in 2016. HRT in Croatia had a 29% average audience share of its four channels in 2015, which fell to 26.7% in January 2017 after concerted policies of the devastation of the independent and critical voice of the public service broadcaster. In Macedonia, studies find "discrepancy between the normative and actual transformation of the MRT into a PSB organization, lack of its editorial independence and institutional autonomy, and its long-lasting financial, production, and technological crisis." (see Chapter 7 by Trpevska and Micevski in this volume).

In Serbia, the state broadcaster was established as a public service broadcaster only in 2006 (6 years after the fall of Slobodan Milošević and the start of the democratic transition). It is not quite clear what prompted the breakdown of license fee collection after 2007, and it is contrary to democratic standards that yearly reports on the financial and programming matters were not submitted to parliament or a regulatory body.

Development of PSB in the Southeast European region of post-Yugoslav states needs to acknowledge also the state-building that was taking place. This process is not finished in some countries, including Bosnia and Herzegovina, Kosovo, or North Macedonia where the basic consensus of the citizens is either precarious or non-existent. Despite many state-like prerogatives of the republics in the federal structure (belated, like modernization) nation-building and state-building took place alongside democratization, market economy development, and media transformation, and for some, war. Hence, the stage of public service development in these countries has some similarities to earlier post-war state-building stages of PSB development in Western Europe, in which the contribution of PSB is expected in national identity building.

Consensus about the public service broadcasting mission and purpose

The existence of consensus about the "rules of the game" for PSB improves the chance of its successful establishment, and contest about its mission detracts from the chances of success (Mancini 2014). This is one of the key problems for PSB in Southeast Europe, as even in the more successful countries (Slovenia, Croatia) the challenges to the (sometimes precarious) consensus are multiple and constant.

We can identify three main phases in the post-socialist media policy in CEE: 1) de-linking the media from the state, 2) media market development—including privatization of media companies, creation of new ones, and foreign investments in the media, and 3) EU harmonization. The same phases apply also in Southeast Europe, but here with a shift in timing. In some countries of SEE, the first and second phase overlap after 2000 with market developments leading even in cases of unfinished phase one. The third phase engaged only the EU candidate countries, and in the 2000s involved the transposition of the Television Without Frontiers Directive, and later the Audiovisual Media Services Directive (AVMSD). The length of EU harmonization was an influential dimension shaping the context for media development in participating countries.

The first phase of media policy in the 1990s dealt with freedom of expression issues and de-linking the media from the state. The three main topics were the introduction of public service broadcasting, the passing of press laws enabling the free establishment of media institutions, including codification of the rights of journalists and freedom of expression, and the third was the regulation of broadcasting frequency distribution (for an overview of the earlier developments in different countries, see Dragomir et al. 2005). Public service broadcasting was the most difficult task to tackle, although it was on the media policy agenda of all the countries without exception.

The often-mentioned imitative media policy proves particularly troubling and produces adverse results in those countries and media systems that exhibit completely different political and social structures from the policy "role model." Two sources were primary as role models: the BBC, a broadcaster from a majoritarian democracy with a long public-service tradition, rule of law, and a high degree of journalism autonomy, as well as low political parallelism (Hallin and Mancini 2012). The BBC model was used as the template in Bosnia and Herzegovina, a deeply nationally divided state. A model taking account of these divisions, and the national social segments present, would probably have worked better. The Swiss model accommodates this kind of divisions and serves all the national segments equally, public service television policy promotes, unsuccessfully, a single national/federal broadcaster (Jusić and Džihana 2008). In the Swiss model, regional corporations are affiliated to specific language channels (German, French, Italian, and Romansh) and jointly form a broadcasting association (Cola and Prario 2012).

The idea that the fractured society and polity can be put together by one common broadcaster proved naïve because it denied the new reality of the country, and the insistence on the unitary model delayed the development of public service broadcasting in the country. The recognition of the state-building and nation-building character of the past 25 years in Bosnia and Herzegovina may clarify the troubles of the positioning of public service broadcasting; the tensions from these parallel and contentious processes necessarily spill over into what public media means for different national groups in the country. At issue is thus not only how to create autonomy, independence and sustainability of a professional public service broadcaster (or, more likely to be politically and socially viable, broadcasters) so that it should participate in democracy, but what role does (and should) public service broadcasting have in the (belated but still undeniable) nation-building and state-building process.

The second role model were PSB systems from democratic corporatist countries, primarily Germany. In these countries, the representatives of civil society play a key role in ensuring social pluralism in the governance of public service broadcasting, as in the case of Germany and the Netherlands. Also, these countries employ a consensual type of government, not present in many of the CEE countries. The second model was the template in Croatia, which has no historical social segments that should be represented in the civil society filled governing boards (i.e. historically strong unions, churches, or other social groups) and no significant social cleavages. The membership in the Program Council of the PSB organization (HRT) of the representatives of civil society are drawn from different NGOs, including the Actors guild, churches, the Association for the Protection of Consumers, (any one of the numerous) associations of war veterans, etc. These organizations, while members of the developing civil society, have no relationship to the original *reason* for the social representation in media governing bodies in the countries of the Democratic Corporatist Model. As in Croatia, in other similar countries where the civil society is not rooted in the actual social segment with durable interests, the influence of informal political powers on the civil society representatives in the media governing bodies is easier (also see Peruško 2014).

Regarding consensus about the "rules of the game" for PSB, in the 1990s Croatian public service broadcasting struggled between three competing concepts: state control for broadcasting "in the state interest" (i.e., the "state-building paradigm"), Italian style *lottizzazione* (division of three channels of television and radio under the political control of different parties), and the minority voices speaking for the editorially independent public service broadcaster in service of the citizens. The latter prevailed in 2000, after which this ideal became part of the media policy consensus in the "pluralist paradigm." With time this consensus came under attack from two main opponents: the media promoting free market and competition in an attempt to abolish commercials on the public service (with every change in the law, they succeed in limiting the market presence of HRT, now to the point that its share in the advertising market is almost insignificant), and the side of the "reformers" of PSB who want to abolish or decrease the license fee, ostensibly to force HRT to become more efficient, but actually in order to decrease its editorial independence. The wish for PSB to contribute to "national" goals in culture and politics is always present in some political quarters, both in CEE (most aggressively in Poland and Hungary) and in SEE. Slovenia is the most recent case in point, where the new legal framework increases domestic music quotas even in commercial radio stations, making them worried about their sustained possibility to attract audiences who prefer the international music fair. Public service television is seen as the most important cultural producer in the media field in Slovenia (Milosavljevič 2008). In Croatia, editorial changes in HRT after recent parliamentary elections and change in government have retarded again some positive developments in program autonomy from the earlier period.

Strong political and social organizations

Strong political and social organizations ensure that rules will be fulfilled, and guarantee stability, and have the interest to have an independent channel to distribute their news (even when they are not in power). The stability of the political sector, measured with the World Bank Political Stability Index for 2015 (-2.5 is weak, 2.5 strong) shows again a similar distribution as in Peruško (2016): Slovenia 0.92, Croatia 0.58 (the UK scores 0.56), Serbia 0.23, Montenegro 0.13, North Macedonia -.20, and Bosnia and Herzegovina -.45.

Davor Marko (see Chapter 8 in this volume) in his account of the PSB development in Serbia mentions the "lack of institutional framework necessary for its functionality, small and chaotic media market, economic situation, ... political pressures, and lack of transparency and professionalism as a general problem when it comes to public institutions." Not only in North Macedonia (see Chapter 7 by Trpevska and Micevski in this volume), but also in Bosnia and Herzegovina, the "political system requires (1) ethnic power-sharing (consociational state), but ... (2) creates a tendency of majoritarianism in both 'ethnic political blocks." Clearly this dimension is also related to the overall democratic consolidation.

The rule of law

PSB in general works better in those countries with better rule of law which supports a democratic universalistic political culture (Mancini 2014, 16) and are further away from clientelistic and particularistic practices.

Regarding the rule of law in the region, the World Bank places Slovenia first in the region with .95 points, Croatia .20 (Italy .25), Serbia -0.09, North Macedonia -0.17, Bosnia and Herzegovina -0.29 (Montenegro is not included).

This dimension relates also to the type of socialism/communism practiced in SEE. Kitschelt (1995) shows that in SEE none of the countries practiced bureaucratic-authoritarian communism, and most countries practiced the patrimonial type, with only Slovenia and Croatia (and partly Serbia) as exceptions belonging to the national accommodative type which is further away from the clientelistic practices of the patrimonial regime. Rule of law is also a category observed by the EU in the accession process, so those countries with longer EU integration experiences would have been positively influenced in this regard.

Conclusion

It is a common conclusion that the state broadcasters in the Western Balkan countries (Bosnia and Herzegovina, Serbia, Montenegro, North Macedonia, Kosovo, Albania) have not successfully transformed into public service broadcasters.

We can observe the stubbornness of institutional patterns of the dependence of PSB, coupled with the low development of journalistic professionalization. The critical juncture of the fall of the communist regime was not successfully employed to change the policy direction.

Main faults are found with political/government interference in editorial issues and its inability (or unwillingness) to organize financial independence for the broadcaster, which is seen to produce low-quality programs and biased political news and information. Comparative study of institutional circumstances influencing six successor states of socialist Yugoslavia found two clusters of countries with similar/dissimilar historical-contextual conditions in the three distinct historical periods following formative critical junctures, namely, the nineteenth-century modernization period, the post-World War Two socialist period, and the period of post-1989 democratic transformation (Peruško 2016). The findings from that analysis in which Slovenia and Croatia share contextual conditions for media development, and Bosnia and Herzegovina, Serbia, Montenegro, and North Macedonia group in the other cluster, also seem relevant in relation to PSB development in the democratic transformation period. The second and third historical period were considered in this regard, with four new dimensions explored in the democratic transformation period. The countries continued to exhibit similar mutual relationships regarding the consolidation of democracy, the rule of law, and the strength of political institutions. Lack of political consensus about the role and position of public service broadcasting is one of the main obstacles in its development.

A question which needs a clearer answer is: What exactly would we accept as evidence of public service, both in terms of the program content and organization of production and distribution? This issue brings us back to one of the starting questions: What should public service broadcasting be in the time of media abundance? After 25 years, the concept of imitative media policies, which may have been useful for the first years of transition, is no longer working. If there is no clear policy or consensus of what to do with public service broadcasting, this can no longer be explained by the surprise at the changes of the regime.

References

Banac, Ivo. 1984. *The National Question in Yugoslavia*. Ithaca: Cornel University Press.
Bašić-Hrvatin, Sandra, and Mark Thompson. 2008. "Public Service Broadcasting in Plural and Divided Societies." In *Divided They Fall: Public Service Broadcasting in Multiethnic States*, edited by Sandra Bašić-Hrvatin, Mark Thompson and Tarik Jusić, 7–40. Sarajevo: Mediacentar. https://www.academia.edu/28197065/Divided_They_Fall_Public_Service_Broadcasting_in_Multiethnic_States_ed.
Bilandžić, Dušan. 1999. *Hrvatska Moderna Povijest*. Zagreb: Golden Marketing.
Castro Herrero, Leia, Edda Humprecht, Sven Engesser, Michael Brüggemann, and Florin Büchel. 2017. "Rethinking Hallin and Mancini Beyond the West: an Analysis

of Media Systems in Central and Eastern Europe." *International Journal of Communication* 11 (January): 4797–4823.

Carothers, Thomas. 2002. "The End of the Transition Paradigm." *Journal of Democracy* 13, no. 1 (January): 5–21.

Cola, Marta and Benedetta Prario. 2012. "New Ways of Consumption: the Audiences of Public Service Media in Italy and Switzerland." *Media, Culture & Society* 34, no. 2 (April): 181–194.

Curran, James and Myung-Jin Park, eds. 2000. *De-Westernizing Media Studies.* London/ New York: Routledge.

Dragomir, Marius, Dušan Reljić, Mark Thompson, and Andreas Grünwald. 2005. "Overview." In *Television Across Europe: Regulation, Policy and Independence. Summary*, edited by Open Society Institute, 13–184. Budapest: Open Society Institute. https://www.opensocietyfoundations.org/publications/television-across-europe-regulation-policy-and-independence.

Ekiert, Grzegorz and Daniel Ziblatt. 2013. "Democracy in Central and Eastern Europe One Hundred Years On." *East European Politics and Societies* 27, no. 1 (February): 90–107.

Hallin, Daniel C. and Paolo Mancini, eds. 2012. *Comparing Media Systems Beyond the Western World.* Cambridge: Cambridge University Press.

Harcourt, Alison. 2003. "The Regulation of Media Markets in selected EU Accession States in Central and Eastern Europe." *European Law Journal* 9, no. 3 (June): 316–340.

Humphreys, Peter. 2012. "A Political Scientist's Contribution to the Comparative Study of Media Systems in Europe: A Response to Hallin and Mancini." In *Trends in Communication Policy Research,* edited by Natascha Just and Manuel Puppis, 157–179. Bristol/Chicago: Intellect.

Jakubowicz, Karol, and Miklós Sükösd, eds. 2008. *Finding the Right Place on the Map: Central and Eastern European Media Change in Global Perspective.* Bristol/Chicago: Intellect.

Jusić, Tarik and Amer Džihana. 2008. "Bosnia and Herzegovina." In *Divided They Fall: Public Service Broadcasting in Multiethnic States,* edited by Sandra Bašić-Hrvatin, Mark Thompson and Tarik Jusić, 81–118. Sarajevo: Mediacentar. https://www.academia.edu/28197065/Divided_They_Fall_Public_Service_Broadcasting_in_ Multiethnic_States_ed.

Kitschelt, Herbert. 1995. "Formation of Party Cleavages in Post-Communist Democracies: Theoretical Propositions." *Party Politics* 1, no. 4 (October): 447–472.

Kitschelt, Herbert, Zdenka Mansfeldova, Radoslaw Markowski and Gabor Toka. 1999. *Post-Communist Party Systems: Competition, Representation, And Inter-Party Cooperation.* Cambridge: Cambridge University Press.

Mahoney, James. 2000. "Path Dependence in Historical Sociology." *Theory and Society* 29, no. 4 (August): 507–548.

Mancini, Paolo. 2014. "Public Service Media and the Political System." *Mediji i komunikacije* 1, no. 2 (November): 9–19.

Milosavljevič, Marko. 2008. "Can Technical Needs Dictate Cultural and Public Interests? Public Service Programming and the Digital Age in Slovenia." *In Public Service Television in the Digital Age. Strategies and Opportunities in Five South-East European Countries,* edited by Miklós Sükösd and Adla Isanović, 39–97. Sarajevo: Mediacentar. https://www.media.ba/sites/default/files/digital_age_final_with _cover.pdf.

Mungiu-Pippidi, Alina. 2008. "How Media and Politics Shape Each Other in the New Europe." In *Finding the Right Place on the Map: Central and Eastern European Media*

Change in a Global Perspective, edited by Karol Jakubowicz and Miklós Sükösd, 87–100. Bristol/Chicago: Intellect.

Peruško, Zrinjka. 2017. "Mediatization: From Structure to Agency (and Back Again)." In *Dynamics of Mediatization: Institutional Change and Everyday Transformations in a Digital Age,* edited by Olivier Driessens, Göran Bolin, Andreas Hepp, and Stig Hjarvard, 57–83. Basingstoke: Palgrave Macmillan.

——. 2016. "Historical Institutionalist Approach in Comparative Media Systems Research: The Case of Post-Yugoslavia." *Javnost—The Public* 23, no. 3 (September): 255–272.

——. 2014. "Great expectations: On experiences with media reform in post-socialist Europe (and some Unexpected Outcomes)." *Central European Journal of Communication* 7, no. 2 (Fall): 241–252.

——. 2013. "Rediscovering the Mediterranean Characteristics of the Croatian Media System." *East European Politics and Societies* 27, no. 4 (November): 709–726.

Peruško, Zrinjka and Antonija Čuvalo. 2014. "Comparing Socialist and Post-Socialist Television Culture: Fifty Years of Television in Croatia." *View—Journal of European Television, History And Culture* 3, no. 5 (June): 131–150.

Peruško, Zrinjka, Dina Vozab and Antonija Čuvalo. 2013. "Audiences as a Source of Agency in Media Systems: Post-socialist Europe in Comparative Perspective." *Medialni studia* 14, no. 2 (November): 137–154.

——. 2020. *Comparing Post-socialist Media Systems: The Case of Southeast Europe.* London: Routledge.

Puppis, Manuel, Leen d'Haenens, Thomas Steinmaurer, and Matthias Kunzler. 2009. "The European and Global Dimension: Taking Small Media Systems Research to the Next Level." *International Communication Gazette* 71, no. 1–2 (February): 105–112.

Popescu, Marina, Gabor Toka, Tania Gosselin, and Jose Santana Pereira. 2011. *European Media Systems Survey 2010: Results and Documentation.* Colchester: University of Essex. http://www.mediasystemsineurope.org/results.htm.

Robinson, Gertrude J. 1977. "Tito's Maverick Media: The Politics of Mass Communications in Yugoslavia (Epilogue)." *Canadian Journal of Communication* 4, no. 3: 12–19.

Sparks, Colin. 1998. *Communism, Capitalism and the Mass Media.* London: Sage.

Siebert, Fred S., Theodore Peterson, and Wilbur Schramm. 1956. *Four Theories of the Press: The Authoritarian, Libertarian, Social Responsibility and Soviet Communist Concept of What the Press should Be and Do.* Urbana/Chicago/London: University of Illinois Press.

Splichal, Slavko. 2000. "Reproducing Political Capitalism in the Media of East-Central Europe." *Medijska istraživanja* 6, no. 1: 5–17.

Splichal, Slavko. 1995. "Slovenia: The Period of 'Capitalist Enlightenment.'" *Javnost—The Public* 2, no. 3: 97–114.

Terzis, Georgios, eds. 2007. *European Media Governance: National and Regional Dimensions.* Bristol/Chicago: Intellect.

Virtualni radio-museum. n.d. "Povijest radija u Hrvatskoj." Accessed May 12, 2020. http://free-sk.htnet.hr/radio_museum/Povijest%20radija%20u%20Hrvatskoj.htm.

Voltmer, Katrin. 2008. "Comparing Media Systems in New Democracies: East meets South meets West." *Central European Journal of Communication* 1 (January): 23–40.

CHAPTER 11

Public Service Broadcasting in Central and Eastern Europe and the Western Balkans: Mission, Values and Challenges

Gregory Ferrell Lowe

The successful introduction of public service broadcasting (PSB) is so extraordinarily difficult to achieve that it could be regarded as a true test of post-Communist transformation in general—specifically in terms of the consolidation of democracy. ... In general terms, the introduction of PSB in post-Communist countries has amounted to an attempt to introduce a media institution born in a completely different historical time and altogether different social, political, cultural and technological circumstances—and now beleaguered everywhere and in urgent need of a redefinition of its rationale and purpose.

(Jakubowicz 2004, 53, 67)

Introduction

In autumn 2015, I was invited to present a paper on the values of public service media (PSM) at the start of an EBU project to develop social impact indicators (Lowe 2016). I employed a heuristic earlier developed by Picard (2006) to assess challenges in the US newspaper industry that hinges on three types of value (intrinsic, use, and exchange). It proved useful for developing insight and understanding of contemporary challenges facing PSM in Western Europe. This chapter applies the same heuristic in the analysis of public service broadcasting (PSB) in Central and Eastern Europe (CEE) and then considers specific implications related to PSB in the Western Balkan (WB) region.

PSB was developed in Western Europe, particularly Britain, in the first half of the twentieth century. Readers are likely familiar with the historic roots. With modifications, the BBC model was adapted across northern Europe and imposed on post-war Germany. Intrinsic values that legitimate the classical model were nurtured by a socio-historic experience that is not fully shared in Eastern European societies. There is a European heritage, certainly, but for most of the twentieth century these societies were Soviet states. They are young democracies today. Issues related to social order and security are important, and economic development is a priority. Political parties in the region are typically weak and not widely or consistently supported.

The intrinsic value of PSB is complicated in this region due to the immaturity of contextual political and cultural features. For example, the value of independence from political control is arguably at odds with the value of social cohesion, which is often a serious problem in many societies. Social cohesion refers to bridging signal differences between groups within a population to achieve a shared sense of belonging, which is essential for internal peace and prosperity. That is why, for example, the Finnish PSM provider, Yle, provides equitable services for the Swedish-speaking minority (about 5.5% of the population). The bilingual nature of Finnish society is recognized in their Constitution and Yle has a historically important role in service provision. Achieving that costs the organization about 15% of its annual budget.

Moreover, the use value of public sector media in the East is more tangled with political power than in Western Europe. The primary value is not for audiences but for political parties who use state-owned broadcasting organizations for self-serving interests. Further, exchange value is not about value for public money, but rather the financial value politicians and parties derive from media colonization. This is achieved by awarding plum managerial posts and exclusive advertising and other contracts as political favors in the practice of crony capitalism.

As a result, transplanting the classical model has most often been a mission impossible because the context is not conducive for rooting and fruiting something that is idealized even in the West. This suggests that developing an appropriate media system for delivering public value and satisfying public interest values must be "native" to each societal context where PSB is operational, and properly aligned with an evolving institutional infrastructure at each stage of ongoing development.

In this chapter, I begin with an overview of Western ideals about PSB that demonstrates the complication in trying to transplant Western PSB in this region (and arguably beyond). I then examine the three types of value to situate discussion about the implausibility of transplanting Western(ized) PSB in the region. This is evident in a general failure to transform state broadcasting institutions and the dispiriting lack of success in international media assistance efforts. Afterward, I discuss implications for the WB region based on analysis undertaken by Davor Marko in the book that I co-edited (Lowe, Van Den Bulck and Donders 2018).

The Classical (Western) Model of PSB

In 2012, the European Broadcasting Union published a declaration on the core values of public service media (PSM) that emphasize key features of the classical Western PSB model (European Broadcasting Union 2012):

- PSM organizations belong to citizens and seek to create a public sphere where they can form and express public opinion.
- PSM organizations want to play a defining role in guaranteeing freedom of expression and pluralism of views.
- PSM strives to be impartial and independent from political and commercial influences.
- Trust is the heart of PSM relations with audiences, which is the central premise for all decisions taken.
- PSM is free to challenge the powerful, test prevailing assumptions, and should contribute to an informed citizenry.
- PSM organizations' values can only be realized through appropriate actions and behaviors.

Each of these proposed intrinsic values is problematic in Eastern Europe. In many countries in this region, even calling the organization 'PSB' is an inaccurate gloss on state broadcasting. Many of the organizations do not serve citizens first and foremost, cannot guarantee freedom of expression, and are not independent from political influence. They are not free to challenge the powerful and they are not trusted by most citizens. The last page of the declaration lists the signatory EBU member organizations, which include many Eastern and Southern European (ESE) countries where PSB is dysfunctional or in trouble: Belarus, Croatia, Greece, Hungary, Poland, Romania, the Russian Federation, and Serbia.

The Public Media Alliance (PMA) proposed eight attributes (Abbot 2016, 12) for PSB. When applied to Eastern and Southern Europe (ESE), at least six are absent or complicated (italicized text by the author):

1. A clear and legal mandate (*often missing, outdated or only on paper*);
2. Nationwide access with maximum interactivity (*access perhaps, but not interactivity*);
3. An independently appointed strategic board of directors with guaranteed protection from government and commercial interests (*not characteristic in either appointment or protection*);
4. Editorial impartiality on political issues (*in many cases, these are partisan tools*);
5. Substantial funding, ideally on a three-year basis, with regular inflation reviews (*as a complete package, nowhere characteristic*);
6. A range of accountability and transparency mechanisms (*both are lacking*).

In the 2012 recommendation on PSM governance from the Council of Europe, the Committee of Ministers agreed that the right to seek and receive information is fundamental for citizens in EU member states and that PSM is a vital facilitator for enacting that right. They also agreed PSM requires a sustainable governance framework to ensure editorial independence and public accountability. Political appointments to management positions should, therefore, be resisted to avoid state interference. These intrinsic values resonate with the classical model, but the ministers lamented two general failures in practical application in the ESE region: "The transition from State to public service, and from broadcasting to public service media, has yet to be successfully completed in many Council of Europe member States" (Council of Europe 2012).

This overview of normative values is important for a fair sense of what are presumed to be intrinsic features of the public service ethos, and equally, for indicating the real possibility they are not actually intrinsic but constructed. Typical practice outside the narrow and relatively privileged context of Western Europe indicates this, and it is noticeably problematic even there. This has been empirically verified by sharpening declines in media independence and freedom of the press in Western Europe and other OECD countries (Dunham 2016): In 2015, Freedom House concluded that only 13% of the world population has a free press. Most people live in countries where state interference is routine, where the press is subjected to legal and economic pressures that prevent independence, and where the safety of journalists is neither guaranteed nor rigorously protected. And the general situation has been worsening globally (Dunham 2016).

For example, France suffered steep declines in freedom of the press in 2015 in the aftermath of extremist attacks on Charlie Hebdo. An intelligence bill adopted that year gave the French government sweeping surveillance powers without much oversight. In Spain, a new public security law was adopted in March 2015 that imposes heavy fines for distributing "unauthorized images" of law enforcement personnel. The Freedom House report observed that "security-minded governments and populist politicians" are exerting increasing pressure on media everywhere (Dunham 2016). Although laws have not (yet) constrained American news media, the Trump administration's persistent rhetorical attacks on legitimate news providers as "fake news media" and characterizing journalists as "enemies of the American people" are alarming. In recent months, Al-Jazeera has been targeted for closure by a coalition led by Saudi Arabia as one requirement for lifting a blockade imposed on Qatar. Even Finland has lost its vaunted first-place position on the Press Freedom Index due to friction between Yle news and Prime Minister Juha Sipilä that resulted in the resignation of the former Yle Director of News and Current Affairs (Koivunen 2017).

The situation is worrisome in many countries, and especially alarming in the Western Balkans. In Serbia and Bosnia and Herzegovina, journalists suffered physical assaults in 2015, which fueled self-censorship. In North Macedonia (and elsewhere) governments have engaged in large-scale, illegal wiretapping of journalists' phones. In Croatia, HRT was subjected to a "radical reshuffling" of managers and a sharp decline in editorial independence after a new conservative government took office in 2015. Greece has suffered steep declines in press freedom and growing government interference. Since 2014, freedom of the press has markedly deteriorated in Albania, Bosnia and Herzegovina, Bulgaria, Croatia, Greece, Hungary, Italy, Kosovo, North Macedonia, Montenegro, Poland, Romania, Russia, and Serbia. In the ESE region, it has remained stable only in the Baltic states and Slovenia. Thus, the 2016 Freedom House report concluded: "Over the past 10 years, Europe as a whole has suffered the largest drop in press freedom of any region" (Dunham 2016).

Three Types of Value

The viability of PSB in the ESE region, and much of the world beyond, is uncertain so long as development depends on transplanting the classical Western model. Even in the West, this model is in trouble as an institutional form, as the series of RIPE Readers published by Nordicom since 2003 documents. The future viability of PSB depends on the degrees to which publics find its services of greater value than the expense required for their provision, on the degree to which political systems exert a will to guarantee editorial independence, whether sufficient funding is provided or can be earned without strings attached, whether populations come to see former state broadcasting institutions as independently serving the public's interests, and how rapidly and competently these organizations adapt operations to the online media environment favored by young people everywhere. That is a complicated construct, to put the matter mildly.

Social legitimacy in the West is based on the prioritization of certain values that are presumed to be intrinsic to PSB and typically described as an ethos (Hendy 2013). In fact, values are not universal and are variously interpreted across time and even within host cultures. Values are contingent on the socio-cultural context (Herrnstein Smith 1988), which differs in cultures, periods, political systems, and institutional structures, as well as degrees of stability and cohesion. Moreover, intrinsic values are only part of the puzzle because exchange value and use value are equally important. What, then, distinguishes these three types of value?

Intrinsic value is steeped in moral philosophy (Zimmerman 2001). In Kantian terms, something with intrinsic value does not depend for its value on external relationships. Truth and beauty presumably have value in their own right. I say "presumably" because, as commonly acknowledged, "beauty is in the eye of the beholder" and truth is difficult to establish beyond question. In the classical Western model of PSB, intrinsic values of historic importance include universality, enlightenment, and independence—in other words, Western values (Jakubowicz 2006). ESE societies share these to varying degrees but have not for as long or as deeply as in the West due to Soviet dominion in the twentieth century. Intrinsic values are presumed to naturally pertain to the public service roles and functions of media. This is presumed because each of these values was constructed in various struggles in diverse societies. The earlier discussion about freedom of the press demonstrates the need for continued effort to maintain such values. They only seem natural because over time they become naturalized. This is not to suggest there is nothing intrinsic in or about certain values, but rather that much is presumed and the result of long and often conflicting processes of social negotiation.

Exchange value is about the result of an economic transaction—what a consumer gets in exchange for what she spends. The exchange of one kind of value for another is premised on buying "utility," understood as a tool or capacity for accomplishing something the buyer considers essential. Exchange value fluctuates based on scarcity and necessity (Picard 2006, 48). Thus, things that are comparatively rare cost more (such as diamonds), and things that enhance life quality can be pricey (e.g., a home or automobile). Exchange value does not presume a deep or abiding relationship between seller and buyer and often deteriorates as a result of use, which is called "depreciation." The widespread focus on PSM "value for money" is a core issue for exchange value today (Lowe and Martin 2014).

Use value is about the practical benefit an individual derives from what she has acquired. If the good enables fulfilling a need with satisfaction, the thing has a higher use value than otherwise. If she paid a lot but can only use it a little or not as needed, it has low use value. Use value is personal, whereas intrinsic value is not (Bowman and Ambrosini 2000). Use value is correlated with exchange value but might have nothing to do with intrinsic value. For example, PSB might provide good value for the money but fail to provide universal service or facilitate enlightenment. Exchange value is only apparent at the point of purchase, whereas the use value can be cumulative over time. For PSB, trust must be earned and that does not happen merely as a result of good marketing. It requires persistent, consistent quality of services that demonstrate trustworthiness in practice over time. Even if intrinsic value is important, it might have little to do with use or exchange value. Thus, PSB might not be economically efficient in serving minority populations but it might provide considerable social value by guaranteeing an adequate provision of merit goods.[1]

PSB scholars and managers usually base legitimacy claims on intrinsic values and focus on prescriptive principles (Nicholas 2014). This suggests PS in B is understood primarily as an ethos comprised of core values that are manifest in the assumptions, attitudes, and aspirations of an individual or organization that advocates them. Discourse about PSB is rich with moral assertions that presume a high degree of generalizability in values that are considered to be intrinsic, as illustrated earlier. In fact, this premise has always been shaky due to cultural and linguistic differences in definitions, meanings, and norms, and because of institutional self-interests that can conflict with orientation principles (Lowe 2010). Moreover, very often intrinsic values cannot be empirically proven. For example, how would one empirically prove the accomplishment of enlightenment, especially as something solely due to PSB content, or the relative difference in the overall quality of life in a society that has had PSB for decades if that society had not had PSB?

The classical model is a construct that has a moral center of gravity. This is evident in advocating a public mission that prioritizes enlightenment, universalism, pluralism, and democratization. The orientation privileges a collective public interest, which is not to be confused with whatever the public is interested in from time to time. PSB is intended to provide use value for the general public as such, which might require considerable patience from particular individuals from time to time. In the West, the public service mission often conveys a quasi-religious connotation in alluding to social obligations and implying a need

---

[1]   In *The Theory of Public Finance*, Richard Musgrave (1959) proposed the term to define goods that are worth more to society than their economic value. This would apply to vital public services such as education, health care, and media for democratic practice, as examples.

to make sacrifices. The sacred tone is not surprising given that Sir John Reith, the primary architect of the classical model at the BBC in the early twentieth century, had Scottish Presbyterian convictions as the son of a minister. Reith's philosophy of broadcasting was notably evangelistic.

Thus, Picard (2006, 48) suggests that any discussion about value must go beyond the presumed intrinsic qualities to address "value for what?" and "value for whom?" The answers to both will vary across stakeholders. Moreover, something with a high value of any type in one period or context can have low or even no value in another period or context, or a different kind of value over time and across populations. In short, value is complex, contextual, and unstable. Therein lies much of the problem with attempts to transplant a model and system that is not indigenous.

Transplanting the Classical Model?

In 1994, the Council of Europe convened the 4th European Ministerial Conference on Mass Media in Prague to consider how media systems should operate in the newly independent Central and Eastern European (CEE) countries as requirements for ascending to EU membership. The ministers encouraged importing the classical model of PSB from Western Europe on the belief that it has been an effective tool for democratization (Jakubowicz 1996). This model is based on the principle of social responsibility in media. Two problems rooted in the nature of an organization immediately arise.

One is the tendency for employees, particularly managers, to prioritize internal interests for which they are primarily responsible. Regarding PSB, this has been represented in a duality between public service as an organization and as an orientation (Lowe 2010). When threats are existential, the imperative for organizational survival can trump the institutional orientation. A second problem is the tendency of power centers to grasp at media for their use value in exerting social influence. Public organizations are particularly vulnerable because they are inescapably political, even if mainly indirectly, as in northwest Europe (Nissen 2016). Complications that arise from the intersection of internal organizational interests and external political interests represent a continual tension between serving the public interest versus private interests. Difficulty resolving this tension explains a growing contemporary interest in non-institutional(ized) forms of public service provision in media, especially activist in nature. In many countries, this might be the only viable means of ensuring the arm's length condition due to the problem of "media capture" (Schriffrin 2017).

The public service mission prioritizes communication as a civic and innate human right (Horowitz and Nieminen 2016), as an intrinsic value. The belief that the press has an adversarial role vis-à-vis government is part of this package and based on the principle of checks and balances for constraining an autocratic exercise of power. This aspirational ideal legitimates the importance of PSB as a non-partisan provider of quality news and information for citizens in a democracy. How this is organized and operationalized varies. It is typically handled either via requirements for news provision in every media organization, private as well as public, or by mandating primary responsibility to a public institution. Public service is the mission, but the means for accomplishing that mission are diverse and always culturally embedded.

This ethos clearly grounded the perspective of Western agencies that sought to help ESE countries transition from autocracies to democracies. As the late Karol Jakubowicz observed in 1996, there were two key goals for building PSB in post-communist societies. One goal was to cultivate civil societies in countries without a democratic heritage. The second was to transition state broadcasting institutions into PSB organizations. Considerable aid was invested. But accomplishment was confounded by their socio-cultural experiences with state media over decades of communist state rule, and because capital interests from the West and within ESE countries were keen on developing the private commercial sector, which was an easier sell. He wrote, only a few years after the start of these efforts, "talk of extensive public intervention into the media, or any other field of social life, sends shivers down the spine of most Central and Eastern Europeans, convinced on the basis of long and painful experience, that such interventionism would not serve the public interest but narrow, sectoral political interests" (Jakubowicz 1996, 55). The twin tracks of regional media development (public service and private commercial) were intended to secure media independence by cultivating the Western European dual broadcasting system. But efforts were confused as to how to accomplish both and which was primary. Thus, returning to Picard, value for what and for whom featured confounding contradictions. Complications and contradictions in the applicability and the relative priorities of intrinsic, exchange, and use values explain much of the schizophrenic character of media policy and practice in the ESE region.

Since independence in the early 1990s, political parties have been plentiful but also weak in this region. That is not surprising because a relatively high degree of stability and maturity is necessary for institutional infrastructure to enable a genuine public service orientation and operation in media. Lacking this, the parts of the media system under direct government control are highly dependent on the state and therefore always susceptible to capture. Jakubowicz suggested four aspects of decision-making that he considered fundamental to the viability of a genuine public service system:

1. The system's placement between power centers and the state.
2. The system's placement in relation to the three primary branches of government.
3. The geographic structure of the system.
4. The system's status in relation to the state and the market (Jakubowicz 1996).

All four aspects point to values that are important in the classical Western model of PSB. Numbers one, two, and four are premised on the value of independence. The third aspect has to do with degrees of centralization versus decentralization, which is more about use value. A reasonable degree of centralization is necessary to ensure universalism in service provision and encourage social cohesion, but an overly centralized system neglects the pluralistic needs of diverse populations and cultures within a country. In former Yugoslavia (1945–1990) the broadcasting system was highly decentralized within each of the republics that were members, which are independent countries today. Each had its own broadcasting organization. Decentralization was territorial and political, following mainly on ethno-territorial divisions established in the Yugoslav Constitution from 1974. At the broader level, an umbrella organization (Yugoslav Radio-Television) existed, but only to co-ordinate program exchange and secure stricter control by state authorities and the Communist Party.

Although laws in every EU member state guarantee freedom of expression and freedom of the press, in practice such freedoms are often squelched either by direct censorship (less common) or informal pressures (quite common). Regarding the latter, governments reserve the right to appoint senior managers and members to oversight bodies and regulatory agencies, and funding structures are rife with opportunities to interfere. One would be mistaken in thinking this only applies to ESE societies. As Nissen (2016) documented, informal political influences are influential in Western European PSM organizations—a point underscored by Hallin and Mancini's (2004) analysis of broadcasting and the press in Southern Europe, which they characterized as a "polarized pluralist model" where clientelism is a defining feature. As Karol Jakubowicz observed, during the Soviet era national broadcasting was controlled by the communist party and governments, so at the time of independence, many politicians saw these organizations as "a direct extension of the power structure, designed to perform the old function of its 'transmission belt' to the masses" (Jakubowicz 1996).

These complications indicate the tangled complexion of intrinsic and use values for 'public' broadcasting in the region. The intrinsic value of communication as a civil right and the use value of broadcasting for social control are conflicted. The Soviet heritage encourages prioritizing the latter when conditions are unstable, especially. Post-communist societies are familiar with a state monopoly in broadcasting, a large proportion of older employees worked for state broadcasting organizations, and many of the senior managers were schooled in the communist system. The general public is accustomed to all of this, which accounts for considerable skepticism about "public" media. Consequently, a majority in each country believes only private media can actually be independent (Mijatović 2016). The true value of PSB is based on lived experience rather than idealistic potential, and a shared social experience works against public broadcasting as anything very different from the state broadcasting heritage.

As for governments, the use value of state media was proven by statist practices in the Soviet era. In the USSR leaders positioned media as tools for conditioning thought and perceptions, and thus as the primary ideological weapon in a comprehensive struggle to build communist societies. This perspective equally pertained to former Yugoslavia. From the start of the Bolshevik government in 1917, nothing could be printed without permission from the communist party. In the USSR, libraries had closed sections that could only be used with special permission. Subscriptions to newspapers and magazines were strictly regulated.

There was a strong faith in the power of the press, and fear of that power as well. As historian Arkady Ostrovsky (2015, 15) documented, in 1957 Krushchev encouraged Soviet writers to understand that, "Just like a soldier cannot fight without ammunition, the party cannot conduct war without print. Print is our main ideological weapon and we cannot pass it into unreliable hands. It must be kept in the most reliable, most trustworthy hands." Newspaper editors were supposed to shape and block information to support the state. Mikhail Gorbachev worried that Glasnost was getting out of hand and urged the KGB to clamp down because "it is clear that the weakening of ideological work as a means of defending socialist ideals cannot be replaced by any other political force." (Ostrovsky 2015, 109). Yeltsin recognized the importance of controlling media and wrote in his memoirs that taking over the central TV tower in Moscow to resist the attempted coup was vital because "it is almost like a nuclear button." (Ostrovsky 2015, 148).

The mission and functions of state broadcasting conditioned perspectives in post-communist societies that might change in time but remain influential for now. Outside the Baltic region and Slovenia, there is not a generally shared understanding of public media having a non-partisan public service mission. Journalists are poorly paid, and funding is tightly controlled to keep a rein on supposedly public broadcasters. Media partisanship is high, many media managers and owners are cronies of political elites, and there is still no consolidated professional ethic of independence (Jakubowicz 1996). With all of that in mind, it requires a great leap of faith to believe the classical Western model of PSB could be transplanted in most ESE countries.

The Failure to Transform State Broadcasting Institutions

Efforts to transform state broadcasting institutions have met with mostly disappointing results. Changing an organization is always an enormous challenge, and doubly difficult in societies where accomplishing that is but one part of a broad and complex transformation process required to build a societal infrastructure that is essential for nourishing and defending democracy. While one could hope PSB would be a key facilitator, in most ESE cases it has not been due to political meddling, lack of resources, and legacy path dependencies.

The Soviet collapse was highly disruptive throughout ESE. Prescriptions for change promoted imitative or mimetic development, or copying models from Western Europe and North America (Jakubowicz 2004). Although well-intentioned, national cultural and structural properties cannot be replicated quickly, easily, or ever all that precisely. The USA was supposed to be the model for private commercial broadcasting and the UK for public service broadcasting. Arguably, however, both countries are aberrations, not models. The size and wealth of the USA, and its zest for individualism and economic capitalism, is comparatively unique. The BBC is a large, wealthy, and storied organization with about EUR 5 billion in annual revenue. A regrettable lack of realism was evident among American and European development advisors for whom imitation "was conceived as a way of achieving approximation to 'the West'; including full liberalization of the print media and creation of a balanced dual system in broadcasting" (Jakubowicz 2014, 57). This is more astonishing because, as Jakubowicz (2014, 52) observed:

> It was understood that social, political, and cultural prerequisites for the proper operation of independent and impartial PSB organizations did not really exist. From the start, the assumption was that transplantation of the legal and institutional frameworks of PSB would have to be followed by a long period of development of the kind of political and journalistic culture required for PSB to be able to flourish.

Herein lies the familiar chicken-and-egg problem. The lack of the necessary societal infrastructure to facilitate PSB was known, but experts assumed that what was needed to start with could be imported and then (somehow) evolve (eventually) into a rooted local configuration. This smacks of a "faith-based initiative." Neither was there much nuance in international assistance efforts. Development agencies chose to ignore the fact that ESE countries are as diverse in cultures, values, and systems as countries in Western Europe, as evident in significant differences between the Baltics and the Balkans in CEE as in the West between Scandinavian and Mediterranean countries. Nuances and differing levels of economic and political development were minimized to get on with the job.

Jakubowicz (2014) argued that achieving this unrealistic mimetic goal was further confounded by a simultaneous "atavistic orientation" that has succeeded all too well. This orientation has encouraged media colonization by political parties. Media policies in these countries feature an unstable blend of the two orientations. Oddly, it does not seem that West European advisors engaged with these efforts were cognizant of the fact that the dual broadcasting system back home is itself a compromise only agreed upon after decades of PSB monopoly and achieved mainly in the framework of building the European Union—a project with no small share of problems in itself.

Most so-called PSB organizations in the region have remained in a persistent state of crisis, which Jakubowicz (2014) ascribed to a range of factors that suggest the complexity involved here: haphazard media legislation; hybridization by adaptive borrowing from abroad; political efforts to control the media; weak civil societies; ponderous bureaucratic structures and poor management; lack of funding; lack of new technology and expertise; small commercial markets; low public support and uncertain political commitment to the intrinsic values of the classical Western PSB model. Experience has proven the lack of realism about what could be achieved, how it could be achieved, and how long mimetic achievement would take. And, equally, how the atavistic orientation is carrying the day.

Media Assistance and Media Colonization

International media assistance efforts have been well-intentioned, but not very successful. I do not want to lambast agents of goodwill for working and investing so much over recent decades. But we need to understand why and how the project has gone wrong, so such mistakes are not repeated in the wider world today. Monroe Price (2009) provided an insightful critical retrospective on media assistance results in CEE "transition societies" and pondered whether all of the effort and expense made much practical difference. He concluded that it has not, and precisely because institutions evolve in alignment with the context rather than in opposition to it. Lived experience and decisions taken earlier in time create path dependencies that can only be changed after different, persistent, cumulative experiences that a majority of any population considers to be an improvement.

Failure to achieve anticipated benefits quickly, or widely distributed enough, encouraged political parties in many ESE countries to pursue what amounts to a restoration of familiar institutions, values, and patterns—essentially revamped aspects of an increasingly romanticized Soviet-era heritage. This inclination was fomented by the economic turmoil that populations experienced as a crisis after complications in global markets since the 2008 recession and, associated with that, growing disarray within the EU. The 2015 influx of refugees from the Middle East has been alarming for people in the region more recently. In contemporary Poland, it has been observed that people are "afraid of losing their families [to emigration] ... and worry about their national identity and religion in a time of general insecurity and immigration" (Whyatt 2016, 18). Such worries account for the PiS conservative party's landslide victory despite the liberal government's influence over public broadcasting and newspapers during the most recent Polish elections.

Good intentions have run afoul of poor conditions. As Jakubowicz observed in 2004, the premise for media assistance from the West was flawed in three contextually dependent aspects:

1. The conviction that transplanted media institutions can operate properly without requisite political, social, and cultural institutions to support, defend, and develop them.
2. The assumption that PSB can be detached from politics rather easily and then operate by Western standards.
3. The belief that state broadcasters can be transformed into public broadcasters and, as such, compete effectively with private broadcasters.

None of this has proven true in most of the ESE region, where governments have displayed only half-hearted support for PSB at best and public opinion has been too weak, uncertain, and disorganized to force governments to do better.

In Price's (2009) view, Western aid was flawed in mainly encouraging Americanization, modernization, and commercialization, which have apparently had the only significant impact more or less everywhere. This was driven by economic pressure from the EU, the World Bank, the International Monetary Fund, and global markets. As he noted, "it would be hard to capture all the contradictions of expectation and reality that accompanied the effort to import or create 'public service' models in the transition societies," (Price 2009, 490) which depended on severing the tether between state broadcasting and the State. That has not happened in most cases. The reason hinges on the usefulness of state media properties for "media colonization," as formulated by Péter Bajomi-Lázár (2013). His analysis of Hungary since 2010 suggests the Orbán government provided an unsavory but far more successful model for governments in the region—a model for state capture of public media.

Far from embracing the Western PSB model, the Hungarian Media Authority visited the People's Republic of China in April 2010 to "study" their approach to media policy (Bajomi-Lázár 2013). Later that month a Fidesz-dominated parliament approved a new National Media and Telecommunications Authority and created a Public Service Foundation to manage Magyar Rádió és Magyar Televízió. The new regulations condoned a government takeover of public media, more accurately a restoration of state broadcasting. Hungary's score on the Freedom House index subsequently dropped six points in one year, from 36 in 2010 to 30 in 2011. By 2015 Hungary's global ranking for media independence and press freedom had declined to 78 (Dunham 2016), worse than Egypt (#77) and Myanmar (#73).

Governments and politicians value media for its political use value in propaganda, censorship, and colonization, which is defined as "a strategy where state resources are traded for political support in order to enable parties to compensate their feeble positions in society by a strong grip over the public sector ... that aims at enhancing party patronage" (Bajomi-Lázár 2013, 75). Further, in many ESE countries, the use value of state media is linked with exchange value because state media can be big business, as documented in reports about collusion between the state and collusive enterprises in Hungary (MMM 2016). Thus, use value and exchange value are integrated into the practice of crony capitalism. The governing political party appoints managers to state-owned companies, oversight boards, and committees who are owners or investors in media production companies, or who have a vested interest in the buying and trading of international content. The government also spends public money for advertising on state channels, which are at least partly commercial, enhancing the private gain of their clients. Price (2009, 493) suggests this can be understood as "...a market for loyalties" [in which] "large-scale competitors for power, in a shuffle for allegiances, use the regulation of communications to organize a cartel of imagery and identity among themselves. State entities, governments, interest groups, businesses, and other institutions are the sellers ... [and] the buyers are the citizens, subjects, nationals and consumers."

Parties with weak connections to the public want to colonize broadcasting to have a direct pipeline for transmitting to the public. Control also denies access to political rivals. All of this is ultimately about the struggle for power and money—ironically, perhaps, the two historic concerns that legitimate the "arm's length" principle in PSB (state and market). As observed by Abbot (2016), assistance efforts to promote independent media have been aggravated by collusion between commercial media and governments that are only semi-democratic, at best (i.e., illiberal).

Thus, the persistent challenge lies in figuring out how to enable an indigenous development of public service provision that is both free from government interference and financially viable but at arm's length from commercial interests. Political will matters, but media independence can only be guaranteed when there is sufficient support from the public. A characteristic problem is that the public in developing democracies, not only in ESE countries but far more broadly, often associates PSB with state broadcasting and do not trust these organizations to be independent—with good reason. Accomplishing a sustainable media transformation is also complicated by competing visions about what independent or free media means, the uncertainty of financial support, general instability, and competition with the private commercial sector.

As discussed earlier, the models that media assistance efforts have touted are not viable because it is not possible to transfer value systems or transplant structures, institutions, and conditions. As Susan Abbot concluded: "It would be worthwhile for the media development sector as a whole to think about ... what types of media interventions actually yield the most impact and lead to overarching goals of nation-building, democratization, and stability" (Abbot 2016, 8).

The Western Balkans

Rather than redoing a body of work already well accomplished by a colleague researching PSB failures in the Western Balkan (WB) region, I will summarize relevant insights from Davor Marko (2018) in the light of our discussion. As he observes, in deliberations leading up to and surrounding the 2003 EU Thessaloniki Declaration that specifies the principled groundwork for WB countries to ascend to the Union, each and all are expected to transform state broadcasting institutions as a requirement and the classical Western model is the basis. Construed as a case of "competitive authoritarianism," Marko observes that although democratic institutions exist in all the WB countries on paper, in very many cases the rules are not enforced and can be violated without penalty. Political parties take elections seriously and manipulation of media is expected as the way things work. As elsewhere in the ESE region, political parties are comparatively weak, and the institutional framework is subordinate to the interests of a ruling elite with atavistic tendencies. Thus, media capture is a typical pursuit.

The WB region is comprised of seven countries that, except Albania, were part of Yugoslavia until 1991. Unlike most of the USSR, Yugoslavia was comparatively more independent as a member of the non-aligned movement. Here socialism encouraged worker participation in routine activities, although not in political issues. So, although power was somewhat decentralized, it was nonetheless generally constrained. The media systems in each country were more localized than the highly centralized approach in Moscow, but there was a general belief in their importance as levers of ideological power and the interests of the state trumped individual concerns. In the post-communist period, the region was embroiled in a series of devastating wars, the worst in Europe since World War Two, and state media were continued as instruments for war-related propaganda. As Marko observes, "this severely damaged trust in the institutions and is an important obstacle to their transformation in PSM" (Marko 2018, 128).

In addition to the application of public media for propaganda, these countries suffered considerable damage to their infrastructures as a consequence of war which put them even further behind the development curve afterward. Thus, technological development is taking place, but is uneven across the WB countries and lags conditions in Western Europe. As with transforming the state broadcasting organizations, the impetus for general technological development in media is driven by external interests—in this case, the International Telecommunication Union (ITU) and the EU. But as Marko concludes, the most persistent problem for WB countries is a severe economic disadvantage with all of them ranking at the EU bottom on every economic indicator. This, he says, encourages clientelism in a handicapped democratization process "wounded by wars that took a heavy toll on infrastructure and human life" (Marko 2018, 130) and resulting in conceptualizing state agencies as resources in competition between political parties and oligarchs, which facilitates media capture and crony capitalism. Political and financial pressures have thoroughly undone the potential for transformation to PSB, and the economic situation combined with immature infrastructure inhibit the possibility of development of PSM. The situation, in general, is very similar, he notes, to what has been happening in Hungary and Poland in recent years. Marko summarizes the situation thusly:

> PSB institutions are in the vanguard of the trend to colonize public resources. The omnipresence of political parties, explained by the weakness of trade unions, professional bodies, and civil society organizations, has undermined independence in public service television especially. Parties select managers based on political rather than professional criteria. As a result, public media managers do not consider themselves 'independent professionals' but 'party servants.' Institutional guarantees on paper that are supposed to safeguard editorial independence and political impartiality do not work. Political parties play the leading role in formulating regulations, too, and informal rules override formal laws. Public resources, especially programming and advertising funds, are channeled to party clients via public service television money in exchange for various services rendered to the parties (Marko 2018, 132).

In essence, the values that are presumed to be intrinsic to the classical Western model of PSB are laudable but not necessarily imitable, which raises the question as to whether these ideals really are intrinsic to the public service enterprise in media? Contextual conditions and historic legacies greatly constrain the potential for a genuine PSB system to develop here, as elsewhere in the ESE region—and, indeed, in much of the rest of the world in which conditions and historic experiences are much the same. The use value of media is largely political and tangled with their exchange value in political-economic terms. The idea of public media does not resonate with most citizens, who rightly perceive these organizations as political organs administered by states, in some ways directly and in others indirectly—but fundamentally in signal respects. That is not to imply that everyone working within or in relation to these broadcasting organizations goes along quietly or lacks idealized ambitions to change the situation. But it is to observe that the system as such is the essential problem when properly understood as comprised of integral dimensions that include political dynamics, economic conditions, technological capabilities, historic experiences, international influences, and domestic instabilities.

Discussion

Sad to say, it is difficult to assess much difference that more than twenty years of international aid and investment have thus far made for media development in the ESE region as a whole. There are countries where it has gone better (e.g., Slovenia and the Baltic region, and Taiwan), but several cases that were earlier lauded now raise deep concern (e.g., Hong Kong, Hungary, and Poland). The Open Society Foundation has been a crucial source of financial support for PSB development in the Eastern European societies but has apparently become dissatisfied with results and has pulled back to invest more instead in supporting entrepreneurial journalism rather than institution-building. In fact, the overall results call into question the best approach for external as well as internal investment to build an independent media sector within a comprehensive system. It is abundantly clear that the classical Western model is not actually that in most cases; it is not a model in the sense that it can be imported, transplanted, or imitated. It can be an inspiration but is not often a realistic aspiration.

Despite best intentions, there are persistent problems with external donor involvement. One is that donor country representatives have sensibilities, ideals, and intentions that are the product of very different socio-political and cultural histories, which combine to create a problem with what I call "perceptual nativism." That, in turn, foments a second problem, which is unrealistic expectations for changing the attitudes and perceptions of media workers and managers in countries that lack the institutional infrastructure to facilitate the sustainability of any change that might be accomplished. A third problem is related to the project-based nature of external donor involvement because every project must eventually end—otherwise, it is an operation, not a project. When financial support ends and well-meaning experts move on, the system typically reverts to path-dependent patterns because the familiar system is engrained, and media are embedded in society with an institutional structure that determines what is and is not sustainable. That is even more likely when economic, political, and/or social conditions are unstable.

I agree with Marius Dragomir in his suggestion that "the future of PSB as we know it is going to be fundamentally different from the present and the past" (Abbot 2016, 22). I further support the idea forwarded by James Deane, Director of Policy and Learning for BBC Media Action, who suggested four essential questions that should be addressed by those seeking to develop PSB in any country:

1. Why are we interested in PSB now?
2. What do we expect PSB to deliver that others would not?
3. What is PSB's role in society?
4. For what purposes are we doing this? (Abbot 2016).

The answers to numbers 1 and 3 hinge on intrinsic value as the basis for legitimating the effort and investment needed to develop public service in media. What I think is defensible as inherently intrinsic is the notion of social responsibility and arm's length independence from the state. In broader terms, the emphasis will typically be supporting the development of civil society as an essential basis for democracy. Numbers 2 and 4 are about a combination of use value and exchange value as an intertwined dynamic. If PSB does not do anything differently from state broadcasting, it is not PSB. Unfortunately, in many ESE countries, the primary purposes so far have mainly to do with the state's interests rather than any genuine public or civic interest.

In the end, the clincher is the lack of clarity about how much or how many citizens in ESE countries care about public service in broadcasting or even distinguish that from state broadcasting. It seems fair to say that most do not care much, and many journalists are accepting if not actively encouraging the return to government control in hopes of securing jobs with higher stability and better benefits. Thus, so-called public broadcasting in many ESE countries merits Arkady Ostrovsky's (2015, 163) critique of media in the Russian Federation where the media "bore a large share of responsibility" for the problems that developed in the failure to achieve a Russian democracy because they "did not try to educate, explain and engage the majority of the country in politics. Despite (or because of) being owned by the state, they performed no public duty." With noted exceptions, that is what we are seeing in the restoration of state broadcasting in much of Southern and Central Europe, including most states in the Western Balkans.

References

Abbot, Susan. 2016. *Rethinking Public Service Broadcasting's Place in International Media Development*. Washington, DC: Center for International Media Assistance (CIMA). http://www.cima.ned.org/wp-content/uploads/2016/02/CIMA_2016_Public_Service_Broadcasting.pdf.

Aslama Horowitz, Minna, and Hannu Nieminen. 2016. "European Public Service Media and Communication Rights." In *Crossing Borders and Boundaries in Public Service*

Media, edited by Gregory Ferrell Lowe and Nobuto Yamamoto, 95–106. Göteborg: Nordicom.

Bajomi Lázár, Péter. 2013. "The Party Colonisation of the Media: The Case of Hungary." *East European Politics and Societies and Cultures* 27, no. 1 (November): 69–89.

Bowman, Cliff, and Veronique Ambrosini. 2000. "Value Creation Versus Value Capture." *British Journal of Management* 11, no. 1 (December): 1–15.

Council of Europe. 2012. *Recommendation CM/Rec(2012)1 of the Committee of Ministers to Member States on Public Service Media Governance.* Accessed May 11, 2020. https://search.coe.int/cm/Pages/result_details.aspx?ObjectID=09000016805cb4b4.

Dunham, Jennifer. 2016. *Freedom of the Press 2016: The Battle for the Dominant Message. Key Findings.* Washington, DC: Freedom House. https://freedomhouse.org/report/freedom-press/2016/battle-dominant-message.

European Broadcasting Union. 2012. *Empowering Society: A Declaration on the Core Values of Public Service Media.* Geneva: European Broadcasting Union.

Hallin, Daniel C., and Paolo Mancini. 2004. *Comparing Media Systems: Three Models of Media and Politics.* Cambridge/New York: Cambridge University Press.

Hendy, David. 2013. *Public Service Broadcasting.* Basingstoke: Palgrave Macmillan.

Herrnstein Smith, Barbara. 1988. *Contingencies of Value.* Cambridge: Harvard University Press.

Jakubowicz, Karol. 2004. "Ideas in our Heads: Introduction of PSB as Part of Media System Change in Central and Eastern Europe." *European Journal of Communication* 19, no. 1 (March): 53–74.

——. 2006. "If Not Us, Then Who? Public Service Broadcasting and Culture in the 21st Century." In *Making a Difference: Public Service Broadcasting in the European Media Landscape,* edited by Christina S. Nissen, 35–50. Eastleigh: John Libbey.

——. 1996. "Civil Society and Public Service Broadcasting in Central and Eastern Europe." *Javnost—The Public* 3, no. 2 (Month): 51–69.

Koivunen, Anu. 2017. "#Sipiägate and the Break-up of the Political Bromance: Crisis in the Relationship between Finnish Media and Politicians." *Nordicom Information* 39, no. 1 (May): 44–51.

Lowe, Gregory Ferrell. 2016. *The Value and Values of Public Service Media.* Geneva: EBU.

——. 2010. "Beyond Altruism: Why Public Participation in Public Service Media Matters." In *The Public in Public Service Media,* edited by Gregory Ferrell Lowe, 9–35. Göteborg: Nordicom.

——, Hilde Van den Bulck, and Karen Donders. 2018. *Public Service Media in the Networked Society.* Göteborg: Nordicom.

——, and Fiona Martin. 2014. *The Value of Public Service Media.* Göteborg: Nordicom.

Marko, Davor. 2018. "The Feasibility of Public Service Orientation in Western Balkan States: Complications for a 'Networked Society' in an Illiberal Context." In *Public Service Media in the Networked Society,* edited by Gregory Ferrell Lowe, Hilde Van den Bulck and Karen Donders, 125–141. Göteborg: Nordicom.

McQuail, Dennis. 2010. *McQuail's Mass Communication Theory.* 6th ed. London: Sage.

Mijatović, Dunja. 2016. "Why Quality Public Service Media Has Not Caught on in Transition Societies." *Xindex: The Voice of Free Expression,* June 6. Accessed May 12, 2020. https://www.indexoncensorship.org/2016/06/dunja-mijatovic/?utm_content=bufferaed42&utm_medium=social&utm_source=twitter.com&utm_campaign=buffer.

Musgrave, Richard. 1959. *The Theory of Public Finance.* New York: McGraw-Hill.

Nicholas, Sian. 2014. "The Reithian Legacy and Contemporary Public Service Ethos."

In *The Routledge Companion on British Media History*, edited by Martin Conboy and John Steele, 323–333. London: Routledge.

Nissen, Christian S. 2016. "Obeying his Masters' Voices: Managing Independence and Accountability in Public Service Media Between Civil Society and State." In *Managing Media Firms and Industries: What's so Special About Media Management?* edited by Gregory Ferrell Lowe and Charles Brown, 121–141. Heidelberg: Springer.

Ostrovsky, Arkady. 2015. *The Invention of Russia: The Journey from Gorbachev's Freedom to Putin's War*. London: Atlantic Books.

Picard, Robert G. 2006. *Journalism, Value Creation and the Future of News Organizations*. Cambridge, MA: Joan Shorenstein Center on the Press, Politics and Public Policy. https://shorensteincenter.org/wp-content/uploads/2012/03/r27_picard.pdf.

Price, Monroe E. 2009. "Media Transitions in the Rear-view Mirror: Some Reflections." *International Journal of Politics, Culture and Society* 22: 485–496.

Schriffrin, Anya, ed. 2017. *In the Service of Power: Media Capture and the Threat to Democracy*. Washington, DC: Center for International Media Assistance. https://www.cima.ned.org/resource/service-power-media-capture-threat-democracy/.

Whyatt, Jane. 2016. "Poles Apart: New Media Laws Split the Nation and Challenge the EU." *ORF Texte* 17: 14–18. https://zukunft.orf.at/rte/upload/isabelle/16i1110.pdf.

Zimmerman, Michael. 2001. *The Nature of Intrinsic Value*. Lanham: Rowman & Littlefield.

CHAPTER 12

Public Service Media in the Context of Adaptation and Change: A Call for Organizational Culture Analysis

Michał Głowacki

Introduction

Changes in the organizational structures of public service media (PSM) are likely to be necessary for the age of the "Fourth Industrial Revolution," typified by increased use of digital and data-driven media, machine-mediated communications and users' engagement across a wider range of platforms (see Floridi 2014; Schwab 2016). For example, firms in creative and high technology industries are now composed of high concentrations of freelancers and SMEs (small to medium-sized firms) with observable clustering of symbiotic businesses in certain locations (Karlsson and Picard 2011). They are highly entrepreneurial and operate on a basis of continuous change and adaptation; decision-making is swift, increasing the ability to pivot in response to external technological, cultural, and societal change. Their structures have fewer rules and hierarchies preferring the development of trust relationships through higher levels of sociability (Ries 2017). On the other hand, departmentalization, a pyramid of power, and a related hierarchy of management inherited from the past might limit the inter-operability between management systems in PSM. Rigid PSM structures and their respective departments are at different stages of evolution and change; there is an identifiable need for PSM to be able to pivot more quickly in response to agile organizational models. Without this, PSM loses visibility, and this is particularly the case amongst young people, the next generation of audiences.

In line with this, several policy documents and studies by the Council of Europe (2012), the European Broadcasting Union (2015; 2019), Ted Krichels and Stephen Holmes (2013) and Päivi Maijanen (2017) looked at the importance of managing change and organizational shifts necessary to fit the digital and data-driven era. In addition to this, Christian S. Nissen (2014), a former Director-General of the Danish PSM, acknowledged the existence of two separate cultures in public service media, firstly that of content-makers and secondly that of managers. The author underlined the shifting power balance from the monopoly over the market competition, and further called for the development of a new organizational culture. More recently, Michał Głowacki and Lizzie Jackson (2019) conducted a four-year international study on organizational cultures in 10 high technology clusters. The researchers evidenced that only a few PSM organizations in Europe and North America are experimenting with their institutional fabric, due to top-down management structures, resistance to change, and the lack of agility. In several cases, organizational restructuring, for example, the creation of multimedia newsrooms and partnership relations with companies from the high technology clusters, reveals a high level of protectionism rather than a willingness to evolve to meet external media market conditions. The goal is to find a balance between novelty and tradition and to further address organizational-cultural approaches.

This chapter aims at investigating public service media in the context of adaptation and change. Through the mapping of several features of PSM organizational structures in the Western Balkans, this contribution evidences key organizational path-dependencies inherited from the pre-internet era. Based on data related to a legal entity, working conditions, awareness of technology trends (multimedia projects, newsrooms integration), the practice of R and D, and a related hierarchy of management the goal is also to encourage further research via the lenses of organizational culture. The hypothesis is that organizational structures of public service media in the Western Balkans share several characteristics of the old broadcasting (industrial) models. Institutional adaptation and change to the network (post-industrial) age, it is argued here, requires an understanding of people, values, and processes alongside more advanced methodological approaches.

Theories on PSM Adaptation: From Structures to Cultures

Key features of organizational structures, such as the size of a media company, hierarchy of management and the level of multimedia integration are critical to assess the level of PSM adaptation alongside PSM growth and innovation capacity (see for instance Mintzberg 1983 and Daft 1989). Organizational structures affect people—their values and skills—as well as internal processes related to team composition, recruitment systems, styles of decision-making, and building communities via formal and informal relations. Des Freedman (2014, 92) noted that in the age of new media and technologies "power has shifted from palaces to pipes and from armies to algorithms" and therefore legacy media, including the PSM, need new power facilities for more engaged relations with their publics and surroundings. According to Arie De Geus (2002), each company is a living organic entity, which is sensitive to its environment and therefore needs to constantly learn and adapt.

The institutional fabric of public service media originates from the pre-internet and data-driven era. Both public service radio and public service television created in the twentieth century were organized as top-down organizations with separated innovation departments for content and technology and separate units responsible for their budgets. Typical for mechanistic organizational structures, traditional PSM outlets have often been regarded as top-down, silo-based, hierarchical (Burns and Stalker 2001) as well as over-sized and poorly governed (Suárez Candel 2017). Although there is a willingness to embrace change and agility—demonstrated by strategic reorganizations, prototyping, and collaborations with independent producers—the concept of PSM is still rooted between two models: the broadcast (industrial) and the network (post-industrial). There is some success at blending them, but often the adjustment to such potential hybridity is problematic (Głowacki and Jackson 2014). As noted by Maijanen (2017, 194), public service media "are in a situation where the old and new world co-exist or/and collide. Managers have to simultaneously deal with the old and new paradigm. In this challenging situation the managers are confronted by path-dependent organizational rigidities typical to incumbent organizations with long traditions."

In 2015–2019 Głowacki and Jackson investigated the internal organizational cultures of the ten successful high technology clusters and public service media in North America and Europe to identify factors for successful change and adaptation. To answer the question of what people, values, and processes should PSM embody going forward the researchers found an urgent need for adaptation. 500+ photographs and 150 semi-structured interviews with company managers, City Hall strategists, entrepreneurs, cultural activists and leaders of the co-working spaces in ten cities (four in North America: Austin, Boston/Cambridge, Detroit and Toronto and six in Europe: Brussels, Copenhagen, London, Tallinn, Vienna, and Warsaw) identified highly linked and interwoven organizational-cultural characteristics for PSM and firms in high technology clusters (see Table 12.1).

Table 12.1: Organizational Culture of Public Service Media and High Technology Clusters

Public Service Media	High Technology Clusters
Isolation	Aggregation
Islands of innovation	Entrepreneurialism
Rigidity	Agility
Emerging pro-working spaces	Advanced pro-working spaces
Contractual frameworks	Communities of practice
Corporate headquarters	Technology-oriented neighborhoods

Source: Michał Głowacki and Lizzie Jackson, Organizational Culture of Public Service Media: People, Values, Processes. Project Report. Warsaw and London, 2019. Retrieved February 10, 2020, from https://www.creativemediaclusters.com/findings.

For instance, the study evidenced that firms in high technology clusters are often located in co-working spaces that may also offer aggregation, acceleration, and incubation facilities. They promote intense knowledge-sharing in contrast to public service media which are largely internally focused. The more advanced firms in high technology clusters employ community managers who deal with networking evenings, "beers on a Friday," or after-work parties. In contrast, relationship managers in PSM often represent a more traditional approach, based on commissioning and contractual frameworks with universities and culture/arts institutions. The more successful co-working and creative hubs have carefully designed their workspaces to support specific activities whether it be a café or bar, reconfigurable desk and project spaces, communication booths, or rooftop gardens. The majority of PSM examined in the study are located in corporate headquarters either outside of the city center or close to cultural or civic districts. Both location and infrastructure of PSM (including architecture and workspace design) are seen as critical for establishing informal partnership relations with high technology clusters and contributing to local communities via social entrepreneurship and urban regeneration (Głowacki and Jackson 2019).

Public service media across a wide range of countries have gone through strategic reorganizations. For instance, many PSMs have successfully merged traditionally separated TV and radio means and extended traditional broadcasting via thematic channels, online platforms, mobile applications, and so on (see Brevini 2013 and Lowe, Van den Bulck and Donders 2018). Another response has been to invest in PSM facilities and to position public service media in the center of hubs, media cities, or creative corridors in the city neighborhoods.[1] In addition to this, PSM firms in several countries, including Estonia, Flanders, the United Kingdom, France, and the Netherlands have supported collaboration between established media companies with entrepreneurs, start-ups, and high-tech SMEs via "Sandbox" initiatives (MediaRoad n.d.). However, the study by Głowacki and Jackson also found the blend of the old and the new, since entrepreneurial people in PSM working in small R and D departments felt they were working in islands of innovation. Small experiments towards cross-media production were often not taken forward due to the risk-averse approach, high level of protectionism, and the existence of different PSM subcultures even down to specific departments. Finally, the study evidenced that the formal structure of a PSM corporation, based on the traditional hierarchy of management and associated "referral upwards" strategies, was counter to agile working (Głowacki and Jackson 2019).

---

[1]   See the examples of Media City Bergen (Bergen, Norway), Media Quarter Marx (Vienna, Austria), DR Byen (Copenhagen, Denmark) or Media Park Brussels (Brussels, Belgium).

Case Studies from the Western Balkans: Mapping Pre-Conditions for Organizational Culture Analysis

The case studies of public service media organizations in Albania, Bosnia and Herzegovina, Croatia, Kosovo, North Macedonia, Montenegro, and Serbia are used here to map pre-conditions for organizational culture analysis in the Western Balkans. The data collected as a part of the international research project "The Prospect and Development of Public Service Media: Comparative Study of PSB Development in the Western Balkans in Light of EU Integration," indicate key organizational characteristics concerning path-dependencies from the broadcasting era as well as examples of institutional adaptation to the post-industrial approach. The data on legal entity, working conditions, awareness of technology trends (multimedia projects, newsrooms integration), the practice of R and D, and a related hierarchy of management collected in 2017 is now being used to call for a more in-depth examination of institutional fabric of PSM. Mapping pre-conditions of organizational culture analysis includes discussion on the potential of PSM infrastructure and location in the context of adaptation and change.

The Concept of PSM

As in many other countries, the concept of public service media in the Western Balkans was understood and organized in several ways. For instance, the system of PSM in Bosnia and Herzegovina comprised of three different institutions. The reason for multiple PSM in the country is explained by cultural factors alongside territorial divisions of the post-war Bosnia and Herzegovina. In Serbia, PSM tasks were carried out by Radio-Televizija Srbije (RTS) and a PSM outlet RTV in Autonomous Province of Vojvodina. PSM in the Western Balkans were created as single companies with different layers of management for radio, TV, and online respectively.

Size of the PSM and Working Conditions

Bearing in mind differences in the number of inhabitants and the country size, PSM in the Western Balkans differed with respect to the size of PSM firms. The data gathered from country experts evidenced that the biggest PSM enterprise was RTS in Serbia with 3800 employees and the smallest PSM was represented by RTGC in Montenegro (720 employees), RTK in Kosovo (701) and RTRS in

Bosnia and Herzegovina (550 employees).[2] The data which combined the number of PSM employees with the number of country citizens further identified the biggest PSMs in Croatia and Montenegro. The "smallest" PSM firm in this respect was recognized in Kosovo (approximately 1 PSM employee for 2659 citizens).[3] In its annual report, PSM in Kosovo RTK estimated the number of staff worked for TV1 and Radio Kosova at the level of 315 and 170 staff members accordingly.[4] While the number of employees of PSM in North Macedonia increased, a decrease from 725 to 720 was found in Montenegro.[5] Similarly, Croatian PSM experienced a reduction of staff members as a response to a strategy to reorganize HRT's organizational structure. One of the biggest decreases in the number of employees was evidenced in Serbian RTS. In all the public service media studied, permanent and full-time positions were among the most popular forms of employment. For instance, in December 2015 only 5 out of 720 PSM employees in North Macedonia were regarded as having fixed-term employment conditions.[6] At the time of the research, approximately 88% of staff at Serbian RTV were employed on a full-time basis.[7]

Extension of Traditional PSM Channels

PSM in the Western Balkans are present at different platforms (Table 12.2). As in many other European countries, the models of PSM have been extended into specialized thematic channels, including those available in HD. For instance, in addition to two main TV stations—TVSH and TVSH 1—public service media enterprise in Albania offered dedicated channels to culture and arts, music, and sports. The model of Croatian HRT included channels on culture and arts (HRT3), 24-hours news channel (HRT4), and TV channel via satellite.[8] In addition to this, HRT offers 2 international radio channels. A satellite channel to inform the diaspora was also found in Montenegro. The second TV channel of PSM—RTK TV2—broadcasted in the Serbian language. Language diversity was also one of the reasons for multiple PSM offerings in North Macedonia; MRT1 broadcasted in the Macedonian language, while MRT2 provided broadcasting services in Albanian, Turkish, Roma, Serbian, Vlach, and Bosnian.

Online PSM Platforms

All PSMs in the region have launched online platforms dedicated to information and extending the offer of radio and TV (see Table 12.2). For instance, news

---

[2]   Data gathered from the country experts: Nataša Ružić (Montenegro), Naser Miftari (Kosovo) and Borislav Vukojević (Bosnia and Herzegovina).
[3]   Data delivered by the country expert: Naser Miftari (Kosovo).
[4]   RTK Annual Report delivered by the country expert: Naser Miftari (Kosovo).
[5]   Data delivered by the country expert: Nataša Ružić (Montenegro).
[6]   Data delivered by the country expert: Snežana Trpevska (North Macedonia).
[7]   Data delivered by the country expert: Davor Marko (Serbia).
[8]   Data delivered by the country expert: Blerjana Bino (Albania).

organized under different thematic sections was published on the PSM online services in Bosnia and Herzegovina, Croatia, Kosovo, Montenegro, and Serbia. In Albania, online services of RTSH offered a section on videos and news stories based on text, photos, video, and audio. At the time of data collection, PSM firms in Albania and Kosovo did not allow watching video-on-demand news. Finally, the PSM online offerings in Croatia, Serbia, and Bosnia and Herzegovina (RTRS) included an opportunity to share the video and comment on the news by the users. More advanced services to engage with users via blogs, e-mail subscriptions, and WAP were launched by RTV in Serbia.[9] In all the cases in the region, online platforms were mostly used to redistribute content produced for traditional PSM channels. There was also a low amount of broadcast and new media integration, illustrated by separation of departments dealing with broadcasting and online/digital media.

Table 12.2: PSM in the Western Balkans: Channels and Platforms

	Albania	Bosnia and Herzegovina		Croatia	Kosovo	Monte-negro	North Mace-donia	Serbia	
PSM	RTSH	FBiH	BHRT	HRT	RTK	RTCG	MRT	RTS	RTV
TV	TVSH TVSH1 RTHS Arts RTHS Music RTSH Sports	FTV	BHT	HRT1 HRT2 HRT3 HRT4	RTK TV1 RTK TV2	TVCG1 TVCG2	MRT1 MRT2	RTS1 RTS2 RTS3	RTV1 RTV2
Radio	Radio Tirana Radio Tirana 2 Radio Tirana 3	Radio FbiH Radio 202	BH Radio 1	HR1 HR2 HR3 8 regional radio channels 2 inter-national channels	Radio Kosovo 1 Radio Kosovo 2	RCG R98	MR1 MR2 MR3	Radio Belgrade 1 Radio Belgrade 2 Radio Belgrade 3 Belgrade 202	Radio 1 Radio 2 Radio 3
Online	www.rtsh.al	www.rtrs.tv	www.bhrt.ba	www.hrt.hr	www.rtklive.com	www.rtcg.me	www.mrt.com.mk	www.rts.rs	www.rtv.rs

Source: Author; Data gathered in 2017.

---

9   Data delivered by the country expert: Davor Marko (Serbia).

Newsroom Integration

In Albania news was produced and disseminated in radio and TV departments. In Serbian RTV the editor-in-chief was in charge of the PSM news website.[10] RTS employed 3 staff members to deal with news online. In 2015, one person in the structure of RTK Kosovo was responsible for the online news platform.[11] Following its internal strategy adopted in 2013, HRT in Croatia started to re-organize newsrooms via the Integrated Media Service (IMS). Although changes in the organizational structures opened up a room for multimedia projects, they were criticized by members of the HRT Program Council, who considered the work at IMS as inefficient, with unclear structure, and overlapping duties and re-sponsibilities, with no significant contribution to the quality of the news offer.[12] Similarly to this, RTRS in Bosnia and Herzegovina had the Multimedia De-partment for news published online; the unit was located in the RTRS premises and was fully integrated with the TV newsroom. A modernization plan with multimedia training for journalists was announced in 2016 in Montenegro.

Departmentalization and R and D

RTRS in Bosnia and Herzegovina operated via five organizational units, namely: Directorate, TV Department, Radio Division, Unit for Economic and Financial Affairs, and the Multimedia Department. Similarly, PSM in Montenegro had separate units for finance, legal and general affairs, commercial, marketing, ar-chives, and so on. Among the units evidenced in the case of Croatian PSM pro-duction, business and technology were located in separate departments. As part of the HRT structure, there was also a separate unit for communication, which was tasked to deal with the R and D understood as market research. In RTRS in Bosnia and Herzegovina R and D activities were among tasks for staff working in the Multimedia Department. Other PSM in the region did not manage to develop a holistic strategy for R and D.

Hierarchy of Management

Public service media in Montenegro was governed by the RTCG Council and the Director-General with additional levels of management for TV and radio. Governance structures of PSM in Kosovo included RTK Board and the CEO. In Croatia, the list of bodies active in the processes of HRT governance included Director-General, Directorate, Programming Council, and Supervisory Board. In RTS in Serbia, the power was shared between the Steering Board, Program Council, and Director-General. In all these cases, examination of selected or-ganizational charts further evidenced that PSM structures represented vertical approaches to governance.

---

[10] Data delivered by the country expert: Blerjana Bino (Albania).
[11] Data gathered from the country experts: Naser Miftari (Kosovo) and Davor Marko (Serbia).
[12] Data delivered by the country expert: Davor Marko (Croatia).

Location and Infrastructure

PSM headquarters in the Western Balkan countries were mostly located in the capital cities. RTSH in Albania had two buildings, one for radio and one for television, that were located next to each other. Croatian PSM had its central premises in Zagreb; the headquarters of HRT included a center with three main buildings. MRT in Skopje shared a building with state agencies including offices of the Ministry of Interior Affairs responsible for issuing ID cards for Macedonian citizens. In Serbia, RTS' main corporate headquarters and four studios were located in the center of Belgrade. The second studio in the capital city of Serbia dealt with documentary, film, and culture/arts production. In Vojvodina they rented a building in Novi Sad to host the news department. RTV owned Studio M, a large concert hall and space used for radio and TV production. Except for PSM headquarters in Croatia and Bosnia and Herzegovina, only a few PSM in the region made attempts to adjust their physical workspace towards multimedia. Overall, PSM in the Western Balkans operate in the premises originated from the broadcasting era, often with a Soviet-style architecture and planning.

Discussion and Conclusion: A Call for Organizational Culture Analysis

The data gathered in the Western Balkans shows that public service media organizations face several institutional challenges when approaching adaptation and change in the post-industrial era. Mapping pre-conditions for organizational culture analysis has proven that PSM across the region share both organizational path-dependencies inherited from the broadcasting age with the examples of successful developments.

Like in many other countries, PSM enterprises in the region were created in line with the idea of mass production, formalization, separation of budgets, and rigid systems of management. With the rise of digital media and technologies, several PSMs have extended their operations beyond radio and TV channels, and in line with the overall global trends, introduced thematic broadcasting channels on culture and arts, sports, news, and so on. On the other hand, online and mobile services found in the Western Balkans have so far been used mostly as a 'bolt-on' to traditional broadcast means with a rather low level of responsiveness, regular updates and limited room for users' interaction. The "broadcast-first" approach has also been evidenced when examining the news production and a lack of clear strategy for publishing news online. Only in several countries, including Bosnia and Herzegovina, Croatia, Montenegro, and Serbia, has PSM attempted to integrate newsrooms, support multimedia projects, and open up a room for transmedia forms. In addition to this, the organizational separation into radio, television, and online followed the high level of departmentalization and a related hierarchy of management. PSM structures across the region are typified by mechanistic power structures and low effectiveness of R and D-minded units. Mapping key characteristics of the Western Balkans PSM enterprises also evidenced potential barriers for evolution connected with old infrastructure and the lack of modernization strategies. Discussions on potential reorganization and restructuring of current corporate structures have only been evidenced in Montenegro and Croatia. The organizational structures and systems of management shall be further analyzed together with the overall PSM system development, its regulatory restraints, funding, leadership, and a mindset that would support the evolution of PSM fabric beyond radio and TV.

The theory and methodology developed in 2019 as a result of the international study "Organizational culture of Public Service Media: People, Values, and Processes," offers room for a more in-depth examination of the institutional fabric of public service media. In the context of the Western Balkans, further research is needed to examine people, values, and processes in the context of adaptation and change. In line with this, critical analysis of adaptation and change alongside mapping potential ways to move forward requires qualitative research on decision-making processes, internal communications (events included), and PSM leaders' attitudes towards entrepreneurialism and innovation. It has also been argued here that to fully understand the current stage of the PSM evolution one needs to consider examination of partnership systems and organizational-cultural characteristics of high technology clusters, which can also be found in the Western Balkans. For instance, one of the questions would be to what extent the inner-city location of corporate headquarters in the countries across the region supports urban regeneration processes and city revitalization? Another task would be to critically examine partnership systems between PSM and other firms in high technology clusters (cultural institutions, universities, co-working spaces, cultural hubs, and so on) to evidence the PSM structures support aggregation over isolation and develop a community of practice in addition to traditional commissioning. Examination of PSM infrastructure could also highlight the role of architecture and workplace design inherited from the socialist era as one of the potential factors for not being change-ready.

Overall, it is expected that the proposed organizational and cultural models found within either the high technology clusters or in-proximity PSM locations will be tested and evaluated in future research. Responses to some of the challenges highlighted here might be found in other chapters in this collection.

Acknowledgements

This chapter draws on findings from two research projects. Data on organizational structures in the Western Balkans was collected in 2017 to support an international project titled "The Prospect and Development of Public Service Media: Comparative Study of PSB Development in Western Balkans in Light of EU Integration."[13] Results of that project are presented in the first part of this volume. An opportunity to update and rewrite the chapter in early 2020 offered more advanced theoretical approaches through the integration of findings from "Organizational Culture of Public Service Media: People, Values, Processes," an international research project funded by the National Science Center (Narodowe Centrum Nauki—NCN) and completed in late 2019 by the author and professor Lizzie Jackson (London South Bank University).[14]

References

Brevini, Benedetta. 2013. *Public Service Broadcasting Online: A Comparative European Policy Study of PSB 2.0.* Basingstoke: Palgrave Macmillan.

Burns, Tom, and G. M. Stalker. 2001 [1961]. *The Management of Innovation.* Oxford, Oxford University Press.

Council of Europe. 2012. *Recommendation CM/Rec(2012)1 of the Committee of Ministers to Member States on Public Service Media Governance.* Accessed February 10, 2020. https://wcd.coe.int/ViewDoc.jsp?id=1908265.

Daft, Richard L. 1989. *Organization Theory and Design.* 3rd ed. St. Paul/New York: West Publishing Company.

De Geus, Arie. 2002. *The Living Company: Habits for Survival in a Turbulent Business Environment.* Boston, Mass: Harvard Business Review Press.

European Broadcasting Union. 2015. *Vision 2020: Connect, Grow and Influence.* Geneva: EBU. https://www.ebu.ch/files/live/sites/ebu/files/Publications/EBU-Vision2020-Connect_EN.pdf.

——. 2019. *Moving Fast or Moving Forward? The Shift from a Partnership Agenda to Collaboration as the True Fabric of Public Service Media.* Geneva: EBU.

Floridi, Luciano. 2014. *The 4th Revolution: How the Infosphere is Reshaping Human Reality.* Oxford: Oxford University Press.

Freedman, Des. 2014. *The Contradictions of Media Power.* London: Bloomsbury.

Głowacki, Michał, and Lizzie Jackson, eds. 2014. *Public Media Management for the Twenty-first Century: Creativity, Innovation and Interaction.* New York/London: Routledge.

——. 2019. *Organizational Culture of Public Service Media: People, Values, Processes. Project Report.* Warsaw/London, 2019. Accessed February 10, 2020. https://www.creativemediaclusters.com/findings.

Karlsson, Charlie, and Robert G. Picard, eds. 2011. *Media Clusters: Spatial Agglomeration and Content Capabilities.* Cheltenham: Edward Elgar.

Krichels, Ted, and Stephen Holmes. 2013. *Public Media Models of the Future.* Accessed May 5, 2020. https://current.org/wp-content/uploads/2014/01/Models-of-the-Future-report.pdf.

---

[13] The study builds on selected findings related to management structures and supervision. Detailed analyses of public service media governance and related policies have been included in other chapters in this volume.

[14] See the project website: www.creativemediaclusters.com.

Lowe, Gregory Ferrell, Hilde Van den Bulck, and Karen Donders, eds. 2018. *Public Service Media in the Networked Society.* Gothenburg: Nordicom.

Maijanen, Päivi. 2017. "The Blessing and Curse of Being Public: Managing Change in Public Service Media in Finland." In *Public Service Media Renewal: Adaptation to Digital Network Challenges,* edited by Michał Głowacki and Alicja Jaskiernia, 193–212. Frankfurt am Main: Peter Lang.

MediaRoad. n.d. *About Sandbox Hub.* Accessed January 21, 2020. https://www.media-road .eu/about-sandbox-hub.

Mintzberg, Henry. 1983. *Structure in Fives: Designing Effective Organizations.* Englewood Cliffs, NJ: Prentice-Hall.

Nissen, Christian S. 2014. "Organizational Cultures and Structures in Public Media Management: In Search of a Model for the Digital Era?" In *Public Media Management for the Twenty-first Century: Creativity, Innovation and Interaction*, edited by Michał Głowacki and Lizzie Jackson, 81–102. New York/London: Routledge.

Ries, Eric. 2017. *The Startup Way: How Modern Companies Use Entrepreneurial Management to Transform Culture & Drive Long-Term Growth.* New York: Currency.

Schwab, Klaus. 2016. *The Fourth Industrial Revolution.* New York: Crown Business.

Suárez Candel, Roberto. 2017. "Preface. Facing Criticism and a New Reality: The Need for a New PSM Mindset." In *Public Service Media Renewal: Adaptation to Digital Network Challenges,* edited by Michał Głowacki and Alicja Jaskiernia, 7–12. Frankfurt am Main: Peter Lang.

CHAPTER 13

Between the Hammer and the Anvil: Public Service Broadcasters in the Western Balkans Squeezed Between Commercialization and Politicization[1]

Marko Milosavljević and Melita Poler Kovačič

Introduction

The role and the position of public service media (PSM or, historically, PSB; for historical reasons we opted to use "public service broadcasters" and PSB) has been a topic of numerous research studies as well as many policy documents and recommendations, both by national governments and international institutions like the European Parliament, the Council of Europe, and the European Broadcasting Union. Most of these studies and documents emphasize the unclear position of PSB within the contemporary media environment, facing issues regarding "philosophical" aspects (raison d'être within the transformations, digitalization of society, the definition of the public role and public interest), financial aspects (the model of financing, the relationship between commercial and public aspects and content, the role of commercials) and political aspects (the independence and the relationship between PSB and the politics, government, and civil society).

The issues that PSB in the Western Balkans is facing today are the same as those in other European countries: they reflect dilemmas and problems on a philosophical, financial, and political level. This chapter focuses on seven countries in the Western Balkans, based on country reports from this edited volume, but also on other available research, and finds that the lack of autonomy was recognized as one of the main problems of public service broadcasters in the Western Balkans. However, even though most of the research emphasized public service broadcasters' political ties and dependence, their economic instability, which is caused by the lack of financial resources and inefficient system of collecting license, has

---

[1] The paper was written in summer 2017. It is an edited and adapted version of the paper that was published in *Medijska istraživanja/Media Research* journal in 2018 (Milosavljević and Poler Kovačič 2018).

been among the key reasons affecting the quality of their programs. To survive on the media market filled with competition, they began to imitate commercial broadcasters and thus commercialized their programs. The research revealed two trends taking place simultaneously: on the one hand, there has been an increase in broadcasting different entertainment formats, such as reality shows, TV-series and sports, while on the other hand, neglecting certain types of content in the public interest, such as education, culture, and minority contents, has been noticed.

Before we analyze the characteristics of these trends in detail, we must emphasize that there are idiosyncratic, specific characteristics of each country in Central and Eastern Europe, including countries within the Western Balkans, and thus it is important to avoid over-generalization. The development of PSB in Eastern Europe has been affected to a great degree by the political culture of each society (Rupnik and Zielonka 2013). This culture "defines attitudes toward political systems and their components, as well as toward orientations vis-à-vis different social objects or processes," with different experiences with political culture leading to different interpretations and implementations of overall European PSB traditions (Brikse 2010, 9).

In addition to these warnings about the specifics of different countries and their public service broadcasters, Sükösd (2014) uses the concept of "multiple post-communisms" to describe the current status of political and media systems in the former communist countries. Some of these countries continue to compare with Western Europe, but others, especially Hungary and Poland since a neo-authoritarian turn taken in recent years, have begun to bear more similarities with non-European countries such as Russia and Turkey (Bajomi-Lázár 2017).

Even within the Western Balkans, these countries had different histories, including recent history after the fall of socialism/communism:

- Only Albania existed before the fall of communism. All countries were part of Yugoslavia and thus lacked independence and long-term nation-state traditions;
- some became nation-states in the first phase of transition at the beginning of 1990s, with a relatively peaceful transformation (Slovenia as another former Yugoslavian republic that was included in definitions of Western Balkans until the 2000s);
- some were involved in lengthy wars (Croatia, Bosnia and Herzegovina) and armed conflicts (Kosovo);
- some became an independent state very recently (Montenegro in 2006).

History is also important in terms of developments and levels of freedom at different periods:

- Some of these countries had hard-lined communistic regimes until the fall of communism in the late 1980s (Albania);
- some were ruled by communistic autocratic rulers even in the 1990s, although they were officially multi-party states (Serbia);

- some have had the same politician as the head of the country ever since 1991 (Montenegro with Milo Đukanović who had ruled as prime minister or president for the last 25 years);
- and some have regimes that are highly controversial in terms of human rights and media freedom still in 2016 (North Macedonia).

Within the context of PSB, there are some countries where the transition from state-controlled broadcaster toward a public system has been described as more successful and with softer forms of media capture in this area (Slovenia), and others that had different levels of success with the transition, stepping back and forth regarding, for example, political capture of its PSB organization (such as Croatia).

This is to be expected considering the developments, including armed conflicts, ethnic and religious tensions, and so forth in the region within the last 25 years. These circumstances, including highly discontinuous social change (rapid change, broad in scale), according to Eckstein (1996), generally have pathological consequences. It is difficult to imagine a more discontinuous and conflict-generating process of social change than the all-embracing transition of post-communist countries. Also, certain highly consequential political issues generate especially intense conflicts.

The Western Balkans as a region thus continues to differ in multiple ways from Western Europe as a region. Key differences include, among other things, smaller national states, weaker industrialization, belated digitalization and internet penetration, a fragile economy, and unconsolidated political systems with frequent political turbulences and/or violence (see Milosavljević 2013; 2014). However, countries of the Western Balkans also share a number of similarities with some of the Western European countries, and particularly those in the southern part of Europe, including the weakness of press markets and the predominance of television over newspapers, the weakness of public service broadcasters and the dominance of commercial ones, and low levels of journalistic professionalization (Bajomi-Lázár 2017) leading to many criticisms of the state of the media in these countries, including the (failure of) PSB (Mungiu-Pippidi 2003; Jakubowicz 2007).

Additionally, the analyzed countries share several other issues regarding PSB, such as its position and role in society, and its programming. Based on seven country reports within this project, we have identified two key characteristics of (and consequences for) PSB in these countries: the commercialization of programs on one hand and disregard for the public interest on the other.

Competing with Commercial Broadcasters by Advancing Entertainment

Commercialization of public service broadcasters in the Western Balkans has been particularly evident when observing their program schedules, which offer various entertainment formats that are similar to the commercial competition. The trend of commercialization has been visible in all the countries included in our analysis, even though there has been more available data and research studies in some countries than the others.

In Albania, the public service broadcaster Radio-Television of Albania (RTSH) has been "increasingly turning to program formats that are characteristic of commercial TV stations" (Londo 2013, 45). RTSH's public mission and its independence from any political and corporate influence have been a serious cause of concern and a constant source of debate over the last two decades, according to Londo (2012).

One of the major problems of PSB in Bosnia and Herzegovina has been "excessive commercialization of content" (Hodžić 2014, 158). Public service broadcasters have been challenged by the emerging competition from commercial media (Isanović 2008). Even though public service broadcasters still have the leading role in the provision of news, "growing competition has resulted in overt commercialization of their output" (Džihana, Ćendić and Tahmaz 2012, 7). Even though PSB has a legal obligation to balance between information and entertainment programs, entertainment programs have taken a prominent role particularly on Radio-Television of the Federation of Bosnia and Herzegovina (RTVFBiH), according to the IREX Media Sustainability Index 2016 (IREX 2016). Private broadcasters are increasingly becoming competitors of PSB in terms of prime-time news as well as in other segments (see Chapter 3 by Ahmetašević and Hadžiristić in this volume). The analysis of the program profiles reveals a growing presence in entertainment, while some other genres remain underrepresented and marginalized if compared to commercial programming (Isanović 2008). Federation TV broadcasts the best program of all other public broadcasting services, but "it has practically become a commercial television station" (Tešanović 2014, 39).

PSB in Bosnia and Herzegovina is complicated and non-sustainable, which is due to a low collection of RTV tax, particularly in the Federation of BiH, where Bosnian-Herzegovinian Croats, dissatisfied with the editorial policy, refuse to fulfill this legal obligation. Due to the absence of legislation which would impose the collection of this tax as mandatory, some public service broadcasters have become greatly commercialized (Tešanović 2014). Actually, PSB in Bosnia and Herzegovina has never become economically sustainable and truly independent, as revenues collected through subscription were always insufficient, which made PSB "an easy target for the control and influence by various interest groups" (Tadić Mijović and Šajkaš 2016, 5).

In Croatia, the main areas of criticism of the public service broadcaster, Croatian Radio and Television (HRT), "relate to the commercialization, popularization and even tabloidization" of the content of public television HTV (Car and Andrijašević 2012, 33). According to Car and Andrijašević (2012), HTV was not prepared for commercial competition when Nova TV was launched in 1999, but continued to broadcast output which reflected its monopolistic environment from the past. The newly launched competitor was financially and technically weak and thus initially unable to compete with HTV. In 2004, RTL was launched and Nova TV got a new owner (CME) and finally started to compete for viewers. At that time, HTV reacted to the new environment, but instead of fulfilling its public service mission, it tried to adapt to new market conditions: "Not wanting to lose its share of the advertising pie, it began to commercialize its programming, allowing advertisers to involve themselves in the process of selecting content" (Car and Andrijašević 2012, 29). It began to popularize its content. After Nova TV launched a reality talent competition, *Story Super Nova*, HTV responded with *Coca-Cola Music Star*, and by putting the sponsor into the show's name, it commercialized its program beyond reasonable acceptability. In the same year, RTL launched the reality show *Big Brother*, and HTV responded by importing the British format quiz show *Who Wants to be a Millionaire?* Soon, HTV's editors launched the reality show *Survivor: Odisejev otok* (Car and Andrijašević 2012). The annual report submitted by the Program Council of HRT for the period between 2012 and 2013 emphasized that a trend of commercialization is visible especially in the frequent appearance of formats such as sitcoms and soap operas. Special concerns were expressed regarding the television channel HTV2 and radio channel HR 2, which did not have a clear public service agenda (Popović 2014).

The public service broadcaster in Kosovo, Radio-Television of Kosovo (RTK), established in 1999 through a comprehensive international assistance program, was at first successful in meeting important socio-cultural and political objectives faced by Kosovo in its fragile post-conflict democratization process (Miftari 2016). But after the handover from international management to local ownership, and particularly after 2009, its financial situation grew increasingly vulnerable: the license fee paid by all TV households was suspended and RTK became fully dependent on state funding. In terms of ratings, RTK and commercial broadcasters KTV and RTV 21 have experienced a decline over the years. RTK still holds primacy regarding news bulletins and its prime-time news attract high ratings. However, its overall viewership rates are declining, especially during primetime. There is strong competition from commercial television channels with Latin American and Turkish soap operas and other entertainment programs, according to Miftari (see Chapter 5 in this volume).

The public service broadcaster in North Macedonia, Macedonian Radio and Television (MRT), has also been experiencing a funding crisis (Belicanec and Ricliev 2012). Pressures from commercial media have been a great challenge; despite being financed through the broadcasting tax and restricted in advertising during primetime, MRT has been subject to market pressures and has gradually lost its audience shares (see Chapter 7 by Trpevska and Micevski in this volume). Entertainment occupies more than half of the program structure of TV channels

MTV1 and MTV2, while education and information are merely minority genres; the first channel of the public radio (MR1) broadcasts predominantly information, but the second radio channel (MR2) is mostly entertainment (Belicanec and Ricliev 2012). PSB in North Macedonia has faced financial and organizational problems for many years, and they "generated a profound production-technological crisis resulting in the decline of the audience and erosion of its media identity" (Trpevska and Micevski 2014, 294).

Radio-Television of Montenegro (RTCG) was established as a public service broadcaster in 2002 but has not gone through significant changes until today. According to Ružić (see Chapter 6 in this volume), despite legislative and regulatory changes and media reforms, the persistent problems of RTCG are related to financial losses, state funding, state influence on editorial policy, a surplus of employees, outdated equipment, and delays in the process of digitalization. RTCG has been criticized for broadcasting content inappropriate for public television (Perović-Korać 2014; see also Chapter 6 by Ružić in this volume). As interviews conducted by Ružić show, popular programs, such as *Women from Dedinje*, *Suleiman the Magnificent*, and *My Kitchen*, have nothing to do with the goals of PSB. Various types of reality show represent a shift towards the commercial broadcaster market and an effort to raise ratings. RTCG is "commercialized to a worrying extent." The financial reports of the PSB organization show that RTCG allocates large funds to purchase films and rights to broadcast sports programs. Its popularity is a result of these types of programs, and not because of the quality of the program in its production, according to Ružić (see Chapter 6 in this volume).

The editorial policy of the PSB organizations in Serbia, that is, Radio-Television of Serbia (RTS) and Radio-Television of Vojvodina (RTV), has also attracted much criticism, according to Marko (see Chapter 7 in this volume). Some of the criticism refers to its commercialized and sensationalized content, such as popular TV series, reality shows, sports, and entertainment. There are serious concerns that RTS "has commercialized its output in order to enhance its ratings—for example, by introducing reality and quiz show formats—meaning that public opinion feels that these ways of increasing income are not suitable for the public service broadcaster" (Surčulija, Pavlović and Jovanović Padejski 2011, 29). RTS began to follow the trend of other commercial broadcasters by broadcasting reality shows such as *48-Hour Wedding* and other entertainment formats like the lottery, quizzes, and so forth. The broadcaster has even intensified its commercial activities, for example, commercial sponsors are featured during the national news in the sports segment (Surčulija, Pavlović and Jovanović Padejski 2011). The former management defended this editorial policy, arguing that it helped to build the most popular TV station in Serbia, while some media experts, researchers, and professionals from media associations insisted that PSB should not compete with commercial stations, but rather cover a range of topics, genres, and issues, including children's programs, documentary programs, and programs in minority languages (see Chapter 8 by Marko in this volume).

Disregarding the Public Interest

In recent years, the Albanian RTSH increased significantly its programming more in terms of covering topics related to education, entertainment, sports, culture and socio-economic and international rather than political and current affairs, and is the only mainstream media that produces programs for ethnic-national and linguistic minorities in Albania (see Chapter 2 by Bino in this volume). Thus we could conclude that RTSH has shown some progress in its efforts to offer newscasts for people with disabilities and to broadcast part of its programs in Greek and Macedonian for the ethnic minorities (Londo 2012). It has attempted to fulfill part of its legal requirements and the general obligation to produce programs that are of interest to all social groups, ages, religions, and ethnic backgrounds, including programs for children, programs on education, agriculture, on social topics, etc. (Londo 2013). However, despite these achievements, RTSH has been constantly criticized for the poor quality of its programs (Sulce 2016). According to Londo (2013), the offer of richer content is counteracted by competition with commercial TV stations, financial struggle, and the legacy of culture and programs produced by RTSH before the 1990s; even though there have been attempts to offer richer content, the quality is debatable. RTSH is legally dependent on Albania's parliament and is financed by the state budget and advertising revenue, so it has never managed to become a truly public television station (IREX 2016), and continues to have serious shortcomings in addressing social or cultural problems neglected by commercial media. Albania has no experience of a real public broadcaster and it has failed to turn into a public institution despite several efforts by foreign and national actors, according to Sulce (2016).

In Bosnia and Herzegovina, one of the major problems of PSB is its poor performance which neglects the public interest (Hodžić 2014). Part of its responsibility has been taken over by their commercial competition; referring to the media watchdog portal Analiziraj.ba, which performs weekly assessments of programs of major TV stations in the country. Ahmetašević and Hadžiristić (see Chapter 3 in this volume) cited data indicating that currently commercial TV stations are leading in the production of children's and cultural programs, and they are also catching up with the public broadcasters at informational services; for example, in 2015 only 3% of BHRT programming was children's broadcasting and 6% cultural, and in 2014, RTRS had 4% of children's programming and 6% of cultural shows. According to Isanović (2008), private stations are leading with educational programming; however, these programs are mostly imported. This is not in line with expectations that PSB should have the leading role in this kind of programming. Data on programming show that culture and education programs are not the priority of PSB (Isanović 2008). There are no programs offering information about minorities concerning the way they can achieve their rights, and no programs in the languages of minorities, according to Tešanović: "Diversities are often trivialised also in religious programmes that promote commercial interests for example in the promotion of certain foods or dietary customs" (Tešanović 2014, 33). However, despite criticism that PSB in Croatia mimics commercial television, it is also true that it takes the lead in fulfilling the media's public role, as among television channels with the national reach it offers the highest percentage of news programs; its coverage of issues concerning "civil society activities, children and youth, disabled people, retired citizens, ethnic or religious minorities, nongovernmental organizations, asylum seekers, gender rights, sexual minorities rights—again confirms the distinctiveness of PSB" (Popović 2015, 32).

In Croatia, the Law on HRT points out the importance of satisfying the public interest on the national, regional and local level, and ensuring that all types of programs (informative, arts, cultural, educational, children's, entertainment, sports, and others) are represented. To discuss the program quality, HRT Program Council organizes thematic sessions about certain topics that PSB should report on. During one of the sessions, which was dedicated to national minorities, the council supported views expressed by the representatives of the national minorities that national minorities have to be more present in the regular program of PSB. Another thematic session, which was dedicated to culture, confirmed the higher presence of cultural contents in the program of PSB but concluded that there is a need for more information on culture and arts from the world as well as contents focused on literature (see Chapter 4 by Marko in this volume).

In North Macedonia, a series of research studies conducted by the School of Journalism and Public Relations between 2011 and 2013 revealed that the programming "completely disregards the public interest"; the journalists and editors are under immense pressure from political and business elites or they willingly serve their patrons (see Chapter 7 by Trpevska and Micevski in this volume). The general public has continuously criticized the performance of PSB. A report by the Broadcasting Council in 2010, for example, confirmed that public criticism is grounded in the fact that "entertainment is predominant on the first and second channel of MRT ... open debates are lacking ... important topics remain insufficiently covered due to inconsistent editorial policy and the program is not a reference point for the public" (Belicanec and Ricliev 2012, 30). These faults are linked to the poor financial situation of PSB, which is at least partly the consequence of the inability to collect the license fee, as the public does not value PSB and believes that its poor quality does not warrant paying the tax. The funds collected from the broadcasting tax are not sufficient to enable independent operation of MRT: "The financial dependence of MRT from the state budget has increased over the past decade, which resulted in its diverging from the fundamental role of a public service broadcaster—protection of the public interest" (Nikodinoska and Ljubica Grozdanovska-Dimiškovska 2015, 12).

The program schedule of the Montenegrin RTCG shows that it has a variety of programs, which does not fully meet the principles of PSB; representatives of minority communities are dissatisfied with their representation, there are few educational programs, while large space is given to entertainment and sports (see Chapter 6 by Ružić in this volume).

In Serbia, the concept of PSB was defined in 2002 by the Broadcasting Law, which stipulated the transformation of the state-run broadcaster into two equal public broadcasters—a national one (Radio-Television of Serbia, or RTS) and a provincial one (Radio-Television of Vojvodina, or RTV). In 2013 it became obvious that the institution of PSB in Serbia is in crisis. Both broadcasters were on a verge of a financial collapse, and there have been other difficulties, such as political pressures on the programming, a too large staff, non-transparent decision-making, a privileged position of RTS over RTV, a better position of television compared to radio, low programming diversity, inadequate personnel policy, and others (Matić and Valić Nedeljković 2014). According to Marko (see Chapter 8 in this volume), funding is the core problem for PSB in Serbia. RTS is a highly rated TV station and its programming is dominated by entertainment, while the influence of its informative program is in decline, political shows are rare, and programs in minority languages are only available at RTV. The transformation of the state's national broadcasters into PSB organizations was completed in 2006, yet difficulties with both broadcasters (RTS and RTV) persist; one of the major problems is financial sustainability, especially after 2008 when the percentage of collection of payment decreased. In 2011, the Anti-Corruption Council of Serbia found that clientelistic relations existed between the management of RTS and the political and business ruling elite. Such relations were especially noticeable in arbitrary decisions on purchases of independent production programming (Mihajlov Prokopović and Vulić 2015). In 2014, due to the low collection rate, the license fee was replaced with budget funding, but the tax was then reintroduced at the beginning of 2016, but with no proper legal basis or mechanism to make its collection more successful (see Chapter 8 by Marko in this volume).

Conclusion

In general, the analysis of PSB in the Western Balkans in terms of its commercialization and functioning shows a number of shared characteristics within the region. These key characteristics represent a wider network of problems that PSB in the region faces today and that influence the position of PSB in each of these countries when facing the issues of commercialization, financial situation, and the role of public interest in defining the programs of these PSB organizations.

These key characteristics are:

Small advertising markets and potential: Within the Western Balkans, all countries face significant limitations regarding the size of the population and thus the potential amount of collected license fees or advertising income. According to the advertisers, the market is so small that the economy of scope does not function. Investments in specific channels are simply too big compared to the results. Slovenian advertiser Gal Erbežnik wrote:

In the time of mass media, for example television, this was still possible. It is true that the reach was small, but the media buying and production were cheap as well. With everything that is brought by modern communication this is sadly not the case. And it does not matter if it is about the mobile app or guerrilla in outdoor advertising. The costs of app development or the creation of a giant puppet are in Slovenia very similar to those in much bigger countries, except that here they are seen by much smaller number of people (Erbežnik 2013, 8).

The countries in the Western Balkans face the same and similar issues, including their PSB, and the potential and the strength of these markets (or populations) is the most important impediment that limits the economic strength of these public service broadcasters.

Lack of tradition in terms of independent countries and democracies: The fundamental difference between the systems in the "West" and the "East" is in the fact that East-Central European societies, including the Western Balkans, have never experienced political democracy in any full sense.

With a partial exception of Poland which has been often split between Austria, Russia and Prussia, they represented for centuries stateless nations, although with different degrees of autonomy: Bulgarians, Romanians, Serbs, and Montenegrins until the fall of the Ottoman Empire, following the war between Russia and Turkey; Czechs, Slovaks, Slovenians and Croatians until the end of the First World War and the fall of Austro-Hungarian Monarchy (Splichal 1993, 27).

Some of the countries are even mentioned as typical examples of "Vanished Kingdoms," countries in Europe that existed for a certain period within the previous centuries and then vanished. Such is the case of Montenegro (Davies 2012).

Positive perceptions of market capture compared to the political aspects: The first period after the democratic changes in the Western Balkans after decades of the non-market economy and state-controlled media was determined by a strong belief that freedom of ownership and, particularly, private ownership was the guarantor of democracy and free press. Privatization was seen as the only instrument to reduce and, possibly, abolish state intervention in the media (Splichal 1993, 32). Commercial motives of the media were thus often regarded as mainly limiting state penetration, without having any unfavorable consequences (Splichal 1993, 18). It is only in the last period, within the last decade, that this perception of market capture as having only positive consequences is changing. After twenty years of press freedom and construction of civil society on the one hand, and the growing pressures of the capitalist market, on the other hand, it has become obvious that free market journalism is not providing the conditions also for the free journalism. The professional choices and decisions of journalists depend increasingly on the interests of their employers. This "is reflected in the growing degree of self-censorship" (Lauk 2009, 406), showing important threats by commercial, market influence, and pressure on the media. This includes public service broadcasters in the Western Balkans, where commercial interests can influence editorial decisions and, in many ways, lead to self-censorship (for example regarding key advertisers or sponsors).

In the early 1990s it was true that "the effects of media commercialization and privatization are still limited due to severe economic problems all East-Central European countries have, and because of paternalistic actions performed by governments" (Splichal 1993, 32). Twenty-five years later, due to relentless political interferences, the effects of the commercialization of PSB in the Western Balkans are still in the shadows of paternalistic actions or pressure performed by governments and political groups. This is reflected also in the seven country reports published in this edited volume; however, the commercial issues and their effects on the programs contribute to the level of public support, as well as to the philosophical issue of identity and the purpose. It, therefore, needs to be addressed with more research and vigor in the future, if the complex position of PSB in the Western Balkans is to be adequately defined or even solved.

References

Bajomi-Lázár, Péter. 2017. "Introduction: The Media Systems of Third-Wave Democracies in Southern and in Central/Eastern Europe." In *Media in Third-Wave Democracies: Southern and Central/Eastern Europe in a Comparative Perspective*, edited by Péter Bajomi-Lázár, 13–18. Paris/Budapest: L'Harmattan.

Belicanec, Roberto, and Zoran Ricliev. 2012. *Mapping Digital Media: Macedonia.* Open Society Foundations: London. https://www.opensocietyfoundations.org/sites /default/files/mapping-digital-media-macedonia-20120625.pdf.

Brikse, Inta. 2010. "An Understanding of the Public Media and the Context of Political Culture." Accessed May 5, 2020. http://iamcr.org/sites/default/files/European %20Public%20Broadcasting%20Pol.%20WG.pdf.

Car, Viktorija, and Ivana Andrijašević. 2012. *Mapping Digital Media: Croatia.* Open Society Foundations: London. https://www.opensocietyfoundations.org/sites/default /files/mapping-digital-media-croatia-20120906.pdf.

Davies, Norman. 2012. *Vanished Kingdoms—The History of Half-Forgotten Europe.* London: Penguin.

Džihana, Amer, Kristina Ćendić, and Meliha Tahmaz. 2012. *Mapping Digital Media: Bosnia and Herzegovina.* Open Society Foundations: London. https://www.opensocietyfoundations.org/sites/default/files/mapping-digital-media-bosnia-20120706. pdf.

Eckstein, Harry. 1996. "Lessons for the 'Third Wave' from the First: An Essay on Democratization." Accessed May 5, 2020. https://escholarship.org/uc/item/6c9087q7.

Erbežnik, Gal. 2013, "Tri, dve, ena ... Gremo!" *Marketing Magazin,* February 2013, 8.

Hodžić, Sanela. 2014. "Bosnia and Herzegovina." In *Media Integrity Matters: Reclaiming Public Service Values in Media and Journalism,* edited by Brankica Petković, 119–191. Ljubljana: Peace Institute. https://www.media.ba/sites/default/files / media_integrity_matters_za_web_final_0.pdf.

IREX. 2016. *Media Sustainability Index 2016: Albania*. Accessed May 5, 2020. https://www.irex.org/sites/default/files/pdf/media-sustainability-index-europe-eurasia-2016-albania.pdf.pdf.

———. 2016. *Media Sustainability Index 2016: Bosnia and Herzegovina*. Accessed May 5, 2020. https://www.irex.org/sites/default/files/pdf/media-sustainability-index-europe-eurasia-2016-bosnia.pdf.pdf.

Isanović, Adla. 2008. "Will the Digital Revolution Be Televised? Concerns about the Future of Public Service Programming in Bosnia and Herzegovina." In *Public Service Television in the Digital Age: Strategies and Opportunities in Five South-East European Countries*, edited by Miklós Sükösd and Adla Isanović, 239–315. Sarajevo: Mediacentar. https://www.media.ba/sites/default/files/digital_age_final_with_cover.pdf.

Jakubowicz, Karol. 2007. *Rude Awakening: Social and Media Change in Central and Eastern Europe*. Cresskill, NJ: Hampton Press.

Lauk, Epp. 2009. "The Estonian Journalism Education Landscape." In *European Journalism Education*, edited by Georgios Terzis, 393–407. Bristol: Intellect.

Londo, Ilda. 2012. *Mapping Digital Media: Albania*. Open Society Foundations: London. https://www.opensocietyfoundations.org/sites/default/files/mapping-digital-media-albania-20120217.pdf.

———. 2013. *Balkan Media Barometer: Albania 2013*. Tirana: Friedrich-Ebert-Stiftung. http://library.fes.de/pdf-files/bueros/albanien/10892.pdf.

Matić, Jovanka, and Dubravka Valić Nedeljković. 2014. "Serbia." In *Media Integrity Matters: Reclaiming Public Service Values in Media and Journalism*, edited by Brankica Petković, 327–390. Ljubljana: Peace Institute. https://www.media.ba /sites/default/files/media_integrity_matters_za_web_final_0.pdf.

Miftari, Naser. 2016. "How Kosovo's Public Television Lost Its Luster." *Media Power Monitor*. http://mediapowermonitor.com/content/how-kosovos-public-television-lost-its-luster.

Mihajlov Prokopović, Anka, and Tatjana Vulić. 2015. "Clientelistic Relations and the Media in Transitional Serbia." *Časopis za društvene nauke* 39, no. 4: 1563–1582.

Milosavljević Marko, and Melita Poler Kovačič. 2018. "Between Scylla and Charybdis: Public Service Broadcasters in the Western Balkans between Commercialization and Politicization." *Medijska istraživanja/Media Research* 24, no. 2: 5–29.

Milosavljević, Marko. 2013. *Economic Survey on Implementation of New Services*. Accessed May 5, 2020. http://www.southeast-europe.net/document.cmt?id=593.

———. 2014. "Financing of the Media in South East Europe." Accessed May 5, 2020. https://blogs.lse.ac.uk/eurocrisispress/2014/12/23/financing-of-the-media-in-south-east-europe/.

Mungiu-Pippidi, Alina. 2003. "From State to Public Service: The Failed Reform of State TV in Central Eastern Europe." In *Reinventing Media: Media Policy Reform in East-Central Europe*, edited by Miklós Sükösd and Péter Bajomi-Lázár, 31–84. Budapest: CEU Press.

Nikodinoska, Vesna, and Ljubica Grozdanovska-Dimiškovska. 2015. *State-Media Financial Relations in Macedonia: Media Freedom Curbed with Public Money*. Ljubljana: Peace Institute. https://mediaobservatory.net/sites/default/files/State-Media %20Financial%20Relations%20in%20Macedonia.pdf.

Perović-Korać, Milena. 2014. "Komercijalizacija i privatizacija RTCG: Naše, a njihovo." *Monitor*. https://www.monitor.co.me/komercijalizacija-i-privatizacija-rtcg-nae-a-njihovo/.

Popović, Helena. 2014. "Croatia." In *Media Integrity Matters: Reclaiming Public Service*

Values in Media and Journalism, edited by Brankica Petković, 193–256. Ljubljana: Peace Institute. https://www.media.ba/sites/default/files/media_integrity_matters_za_web_final_0.pdf.

——. 2015. "Commercialization and Privatization of Media in Southeast Europe: A Wolf in Sheep's Clothing?" *The Political Economy of Communication* 3, no. 1: 25–38.

Rupnik, Jacques, and Jan Zielonka. 2013. "The State of Democracy 20 Years on: Domestic and External Factors." *East European Politics & Societies* 27, no. 1 (December): 3–25.

Spichal, Slavko. 1993. "Post-socialism and the Media: What Kind of Transition?" In *Media in Transition: An East-West Dialogue*, edited by Slavko Splichal and Ildiko Kovats, 5–34. Budapest/Ljuljana: Hungarian Academy of Sciences/Eotvos Lorand University.

Sükösd, Miklós. 2014. "'East' of 'West'—Media in Central and Eastern Europe, Eurasia and China: Multiple Post-communisms and Shifting Geopolitical Realities." In *Journalism that Matters: Views from Central and Eastern Europe*, edited by Michał Głowacki, Epp Lauk and Auksė Balčytienė, 21–33. Frankfurt am Main: Peter Lang.

Sulce, Valbona. 2016. "Albania: Partners, Rather than Friends or Foes." In *Media and Civil Society in the Western Balkans*, edited by Remzi Lani, 15–31. Tirana: Albanian Media Institute. https://seenpm.org/wp-content/uploads/2016/11/Media-and-Civil-Society-in-the-Western-Balkans-Final.pdf.

Surčulija, Jelena, Biljana Pavlović, and Đurđa Jovanović Padejski. 2011. *Mapping Digital Media: Serbia*. Open Society Foundations: London. https://www.opensocietyfoundations.org/sites/default/files/mapping-digital-media-serbia-20111215.pdf.

Tadić Mijović, Milka, and Marija Šajkaš. 2016. "Captured News Media: Bosnia and Herzegovina, Serbia, and Montenegro." Washington, DC: CIMA/NED. http://www.cima.ned.org/resource/captured-news-media-bosnia-herzegovina-serbia-montenegro/.

Tešanović, Nataša, ed. 2014. *Balkan Media Barometer: Bosnia and Herzegovina 2014*. Sarajevo: Friedrich-Ebert-Stiftung. http://library.fes.de/pdf-files/bueros /sarajevo/11101.pdf.

Trpevska, Snežana, and Igor Micevski. 2014. "Macedonia." In *Media Integrity Matters: Reclaiming Public Service Values in Media and Journalism*, edited by Brankica Petković, 257–326. Ljubljana: Peace Institute. https://www.media.ba/sites /default/ files/media_integrity_matters_za_web_final_0.pdf.

CHAPTER 14

Digital Switchover and Public Service Media in the Western Balkans

Sally Broughton Micova

Introduction

The switchover of television broadcasting from analog to digital terrestrial transmission has been one of the most important developments in broadcasting in the Western Balkans since the radical market liberalization that took place after the dissolution of Yugoslavia and end of single-party rule. For some states in the region it was not an easy process, and two of them, Bosnia and Herzegovina (BiH) and Kosovo, had yet to complete the process at the time of writing. The exact role that public service media (PSM), and in particular each state's public service broadcaster, has played differs across the cases with varying implications, but it has been a key player across the board.

This chapter will cover the brief history of the lead up to and execution of digital switchover in the former Yugoslav states of the Western Balkans, focusing on the position and role of PSM in those processes. First, it will give the background and context of digital switchover in the region. Then, discussing each state in turn, it will identify the characteristics of the leaders and the laggards in achieving switchover. It will compare the starting positions of each PSB organization at the outset of the process and the use of state intervention across the states. It will argue that, although the PSB organizations made varying contributions to the consumer take-up of digital broadcasting, PSM defined more broadly to include the publicly owned network operators, has been privileged and often a crucial vehicle for implementing the steps necessary to achieve switchover. The story of digital switchover in this region also raises some important questions about the elements of PSM and the role of the state in ensuring its provision.

Why Digital Switchover?

Within the countries that led the move from analog to digital broadcasting, there were a variety of important industrial interests providing the incentive to make the switch. The US's transition was encouraged by the technology industry's race to beat the Japanese in setting the standard for High Definition TV (García Leiva and Starks 2007), and switchovers in China and Brazil were motivated by similar desires to set technological standards both internally and among their neighbors so as to provide markets for their own companies (Albornoz and García Leiva 2012). European drivers were more centered on the use of spectrum and what might be done if more were freed up for other uses (García Leiva and Starks 2007). In the UK, for example, the major terrestrial broadcasters were eager to expand their terrestrial offering as a response to competition from then BSkyB's satellite services (Starks 2013). In many Western European countries there was also pressure from mobile operators for a more and better spectrum and providing it to them had the potential of bringing in revenues to the public purse as well as boosting the domestic mobile industry.

In the Western Balkans, none of those incentives were at play. Most of the broadcasters had little capacity to expand their offerings, there were no domestic technology companies poised to benefit from standard-setting, and there was little demand for spectrum from mobile telephone providers. In this region, the main drivers were the external deadlines set by the International Telecommunication Union (ITU) and the European Union, and the threat of interference from neighboring countries if those were not met. Thanks in part to pressure from the European Commission and the EU member states during its 2006 Regional Radiocommunication Conference (RRC06), ITU set a deadline of June 17, 2015, for the completion of digital switchover. From that point, those analog frequencies still in use would no longer be protected, meaning interference from neighboring states would be highly likely. The EU's deadline for member states was 2012 (Milosavljević and Broughton Micova 2013).

When this decision was made, it only applied to Slovenia, which entered the EU in 2004, but as the region was surrounded by EU member states and included some hopeful candidate countries, the EU's internal deadline was still a source of pressure. The EU's internal deadline was also relevant to the Western Balkans because the struggles of some of the member states to meet the deadline eventually led to a change in EU policy regarding the use of 'state aid' in helping the process along. The use of state funding or resources, "state aid," to interfere in the market is generally not allowed under EU competition rules, to which the candidate and pre-accession countries of the Western Balkans were trying to adhere as part of the conditionality of the accession process.[1] In the early years of the analog to digital transition, the use of state aid to assist with the process had been ruled unacceptable by the Competition Directorate, yet the attitude gradually changed as spectrum featured heavily in the EU's development strategies for 2020, and it became increasingly clear that some of the newer member states would not meet the deadline without it (Wheeler 2012). As will be seen

---

[1]   State aid rules fall under the EU's competition policy, which is Chapter 8 of the Acquis Communautaire containing all of the common rights and obligations with which states attempting to join the EU must comply by integrating them into their domestic legislation and policy. The EU's rules on state aid make specific allowances for state aid to be used to support public broadcasting under tight criteria (European Commission 2009a).

in the narratives that follow, not only has the use of state aid been important to the completion of digital switchover in the Western Balkans, it has even been supplemented by EU funds.

How Switchover Happened ... or Not

The process of digital switchover in the Western Balkans has been a mixed bag. Croatia and Slovenia both finished quickly and well ahead of even the EU's deadline, while BiH and Kosovo still had not switched off analog signals by the end of 2019. Of course, these countries started from very different positions in terms of their overall political and economic situations and the state of their broadcasting markets. Slovenia and Croatia were arguably ahead of the group. Slovenia was relatively removed from the conflicts in the rest of the former Yugoslavia, and Croatia's government had invested heavily in broadcasting since the war, with the PSB organizations in both countries facing limited national level competition in the markets. Serbia and Montenegro, fellow constituent republics of the rump Yugoslavia until 2006, suffered years of isolation until the overthrow of Slobodan Milošević, which had significant consequences for the technological preparedness of their public service broadcasters. As Marko describes in Chapter 8 on Serbia, Serbia's PSB organization had lost a great deal of credibility from years of being used for propaganda, in addition to suffering significant material damage during the NATO bombing in 1999. BiH and Kosovo were ravaged by conflict much more than the others and had internationally lead governance systems in place for several years before they were completely self-governing. Chapter 3 on Bosnia and Herzegovina and Chapter 5 on Kosovo highlight the significant role that international community actors played in the shaping of the media systems and PSB structures in each of these countries. The various starting conditions have influenced the digital switchover processes that have taken place or are underway in the former Yugoslav states as will be evident in the accounts that follow. Nevertheless, commonalities emerge in the strategies and implementation in terms of the privileged roles of PSB organizations, the use of state aid and even international aid, and the prominent role of publicly owned network operators.

Croatia

Already in 2007, Croatia adopted its Analogue to Digital Television Broadcasting Switchover Strategy, and it became the first country in the region to complete switchover on October 5, 2010. Croatia's success can be attributed to the high level of concentration in the broadcasting market, which included a very strong public service broadcaster, and extensive consumer subsidies for set-top boxes ahead of switchover. Hrvatska radiotelevizija (HRT), the country's PSB organization, maintained the highest audience shares in the 20 consecutive years before switchover. At the time HRT had two terrestrial channels, HTV1 and HTV2, and one satellite channel, HTVPlus. It got its first national commercial competition only in 1999 when Nova TV was granted a license, and its second in mid-2004, after what had been HTV3 was sold to the German company RTL. The 21 local stations in operation at the time were little competition to the three strong national brands and HRT was the leader among them. Exact figures for the take-up of the various transmission systems ahead of switchover were not available, but as late as 2013 nearly 60% of the population depended on terrestrial broadcasting (SEE Digi.TV 2013), meaning that the popularity of HRT and people's desire to continue receiving it would have been an important factor contributing to the take-up of digital terrestrial television (DTT).

Broadcasting in Croatia used five multiplexes (MUXs), two of which were dedicated to the transmission of PSB channels and the national commercial broadcasters. The operation of these two main MUXs was granted to the state-owned Transmitters and Communications Ltd. (Odašiljači i veze) that resulted from the separation of what had been HRT's links and transmitters department into a new and distinct public company in 2009. The following year it also was given the third MUX to further the local stations and additional services of the national commercial broadcasters. By 2012, the company also assumed the operation of the remaining two MUXs, which are used for pay-tv services.

Although no financial support from the state was provided for the infrastructure for DTT or the digitalization of HRT, the operation of MUXs was done by a state-owned company, and HRT was given automatic access to the new distribution system without the lengthy tender procedures commercial channels went through. With the heavy reliance on terrestrial broadcasting, the incentives for both broadcasters and the public were relatively high. Nevertheless, the Croatian government also provided a subsidy to all citizens paying the license fee for the purchase of set-top boxes of HRK 75 (approx. EUR 11), which covered between 20–50% of the cost depending on the model of set-top box chosen (Milosavljević and Broughton Micova 2013).

Following the switchover, a series of new specialist channels were launched along with catch-up and specialized channels of the existing national commercial broadcasters. HRT also launched its thematic channel HTV3, a 24-hour news channel, and heavily expanded its online offering to include apps and catch-up services. As Marko describes in Chapter 4 on Croatia, HRT has struggled to meet the demands of its expanded services through internal reorganizations. Due to the small size of the market and overall declines in television advertising, not all the new commercial channels survived, but the increased competition and fragmentation of the audience enabled by digital switchover meant that HRT lost the dominant position it had held for two decades.

Slovenia

Slovenia was the next country to make the switchover in the region, and it also started with a strong public service broadcaster and concentrated market.

Similarly, the country set 2010 as its target for switchover back in 2007, but its path was otherwise very different from Croatia's. Slovenia was the only state in the region that did not move the links and transmissions department of its former state broadcaster into a new, separate public company. Its PSB organization, Radio-Television Slovenia (RTVSLO), which already owned the vast network of locations and towers, was given EUR 1.2 million in state support for the technical equipment needed for the rollout of DTT, and it was quickly able to take advantage of operating the DTT network with the best coverage in the country (Milosavljević and Kerševan Smokvina 2012). RTVSLO received one MUX granted to it by law, while another was granted to the Norwegian company Norkring, following a tender, and the other was dedicated to regional broadcasters and allocated through the regulator. The government facilitated switchover at the consumer level through a subsidy program for set-top boxes for those in need and even free ones for the particularly vulnerable groups. The process was also eased by the very low dependence on terrestrial broadcasting in general as penetration of cable and IPTV services in the country around the time of switchover were already above 80% (Milosavljevic and Broughton Micova 2013). It all went smoothly and analog switch-off was achieved in December 2010 as planned.

This arrangement did not last long because of a provision in the law that gave RTVSLO free reign to use its extra MUX capacity, which was quickly made available to its commercial competitors, driving Norkring out of business (Broughton Micova 2013). Though the Digital Broadcasting Act in 2012 subsequently banned RTVSLO from using its MUX for commercial purposes, when the commercial MUX was re-tendered, it won as the only applicant. RTVSLO, therefore, carries its 3 main channels and 2 regional channels on its MUX and operates the other MUX for a handful of commercial channels including PopTV, the dominant national commercial broadcaster.

North Macedonia

North Macedonia was the next country to achieve switchover and the only other one to manage well ahead of the ITU deadline. Its process was quite different from the others, inasmuch as the country first tendered three MUXs for com- mercial use for subscription services. This 2012 tender was won by the sole bidder, the company One, a subsidiary of Slovenia Telekom. An obligation of the deal was that the company would provide free set-top boxes to its customers, as a way to encourage take-up (Milosavljević and Broughton Micova 2013). Another two MUXs were granted by law to the public company Macedonian Radio Diffusion (MRD), which was formed from the former links and transmissions department of the public service broadcaster, solely to broadcast the channels of Macedonian Radio and Television (MRT). MRD received money from the state budget for the necessary infrastructure, so essentially MRT's transition to DTT was covered by state funds.

According to the regulator, by 2012 penetration of subscription services had reached 80.5% so a relatively low percentage of the population was reliant on free to air transmission (AVMU 2015). Nevertheless, there was little awareness of the process among the population ahead of switchover, which was likely due to the fact that the period for simulcast and information campaigns, in the end, was drastically shorter than those foreseen in The Strategy for the Development of Broadcasting Activity in Macedonia 2007–2012 that had originally set out a plan for achieving switchover closer to the ITU deadline (Nikodinoska 2016). Approximately 40,000 set-top boxes were distributed to people from vulnerable groups and on social assistance, but the analog switch-off on March 31, 2013, seemed to catch many people unprepared, and crowds were noted at the stores of One, which had in the meantime also won an uncontested tender for the running of the remaining MUXs that had been designated for free to air broadcast (Nikodinoska 2016).

The Macedonian PSB organization, MRT, seems to have been given a rather privileged position through the process leading to switchover. It was given more than ample MUX capacity and the MRD received government funds to build the network to carry its signals. However, it was also not central to the process in any way. The low dependency on terrestrial transmission and the incredibly low popularity of MRT at the time meant that it was not a driver of take-up among the population. Its free to air transmission on the MRD's network by 2014 was only serving 6.2% of the population, while 16.4% used One's subscription DTT services, and others used cable, IPTV, or personal satellite (AVMU 2015). North Macedonia's switchover was a large commercial project with the publicly owned network and the public service broadcaster playing a minor role.

Serbia

Serbia had to overcome significant challenges to manage switchover just days before the ITU's deadline. Although it had a public company for transmission that had been set up from its public service broadcaster's links and transmissions department, that company inherited a severely damaged network of locations and towers. The company was created in 2009 following the plan set up in the Strategy for Switchover from Analogue to Digital Broadcasting of Radio and Television Programs in the Republic of Serbia (Government of the Republic of Serbia 2009) that came out that year with the determination that a single company would operate the MUXs and make transmission available at non-discriminatory, cost-based prices. Though the strategy had set out a deadline of April 2012, it was quickly clear that this was not achievable.

The country received EUR 10.5 million for infrastructure and for a public information campaign aimed at encouraging take up through the EU's Instrument for Pre-Accession Assistance (IPA) (European Commission 2009b). This was a significant contribution to the overall estimated cost of EUR 37 million and helped lead to what was by most accounts a smooth switchover (Velojic 2016). The PSB organization, Radio-Televizija Srbije (RTS) played a leading role. Still highly popular at the time of switchover, RTS contributed significantly to the extensive public information campaign aimed at preparing the public and was a likely driver of take-up due to its relative popularity despite competition from five national commercial stations. In the year before switchover, 2013, the penetration of subscription services had been just over 60% and was on the rise (Dziadul 2014), but still, more than 30% of the population was probably dependent on terrestrial broadcasting by the time of switchover. The Serbian government provided nearly 160,000 free set-top boxes to the most socially and economically vulnerable households (Velojic 2016), which likely helped with the transition.

RTS was automatically granted MUX capacity and broadcasts three channels free to air. The national stations also migrated seamlessly, but there were indications that local and regional stations struggled afterward to pay the costs of broadcasting on the DTT platforms, particularly the new license fees (Velojic 2016). RTS was generally technologically prepared for digital switchover partly due to its long-running experimental digital channels, but as of the end of 2016, it still lacked a strategy to make use of the resources granted to it on the MUX or the reduction in competition as the multitude of commercial broadcasters in Serbia slowly consolidated.

Montenegro

Montenegro only just made the June 17, 2015 deadline, officially declaring switchover completed on that day. However, this was achieved with considerable assistance from EU funds and was reported as having been somewhat incomplete still on that date as a number of stations were still not present on the DTT platform (Žugić 2016). The public company Broadcasting Centre (Radio Difuzni Centar), which, as in most of the neighboring countries, had been formed from the public service broadcaster's former links and transmissions department, played a key role in the process. The Broadcasting Centre received two rounds of funding through the EU's IPA. The first EUR 1.6 million was for the equipment and some training (Delegation of the European Union to Montenegro 2009). Despite another round of EUR 1.5 million through IPA for the equipment needed for the network, the technical implementation of the DTT rollout was plagued by delays and poor performance (Žugić 2016). The Broadcasting Centre only had to provide for the one MUX it had been granted and the process was finished in time. Another regional MUX was granted to a private company, Mir & Teuta, for on-demand services in the area of Ulcinj, and access to local MUXs in some municipalities was also granted but was not essential to enabling switch-off.

Montenegro's PSB organization, Radio-Television of Crna Gore (RTCG) was privileged in the process in that the Broadcasting Centre was obliged to carry its two channels on the DTT platform automatically and without compensation. The very high penetration rate of subscription services also meant it was not a likely driver of take-up. Over 80% of the households in the country were using other platforms to receive subscription-based television services in the months leading up to analog switch-off, though this figure was much lower in the mountainous northern region (Montenegro Agency for Electronic Media 2015). The Montenegrin government provided EUR 410,000 for the purchase of set-top boxes to be distributed free of charge to those in socially and economically vulnerable categories (Žugić 2016), which at least would have allowed those in poor rural communities in the north and other areas access to the programs of RTCG and the three national commercial broadcasters on the MUX operated by the Broadcasting Centre. As Ružić explains in Chapter 6 on Montenegro, RTCG struggled to be technologically prepared for digital broadcasting as was relying on very old analog equipment until shortly before switchover, and some local channels were not able to bear the financial burden of making the transition to DTT, opting for cable only transmission to cover their area.

Bosnia and Herzegovina

The process of moving towards digital switchover in BiH has been one of the starts and stops and resulted in the country missing the 2015 deadline for analog switch-off. The first burst of energy was displayed in 2009 when the Strategy on the Digital Switchover within the Frequency Bands of 174–230 MHz and 470–862 MHz was adopted by the Council of Ministers that represent the three constituent regions. This strategy relied significantly on co-operation among the public service broadcasters and involvement of commercial stations, for which there was little interest or capacity (Milosavljević and Broughton Micova 2013). There was no real movement until an action plan was finally adopted in 2012, and in 2013 a decision was made by the Council of Ministers that finally resulted in a tender for the necessary equipment and infrastructure installation was launched.

The process was again stalled, as not only the first tender failed, but a series of them won by private companies were overturned until finally a successful contract was made in March 2014 with the Croatian public company that operates that country's DTT network (Hodžić 2016). Equipment was purchased and implementation has begun but was again halted because of a lack of co-operation among the PSB organizations and refusals by one of them to take charge of and use the equipment (Hodžić 2016). These obstructions were eventually overcome and the installation of BiH's MUX A dedicated to PSB channels was completed in 2016, finishing the first phase of the process (Odašiljači i veze 2016). The second phase for the private broadcasters must be completed before analog switch-off though arguably became less pressing as the penetration of subscription television on cable and IPTV grew drastically, reaching 74% of households by the end of 2017 (Fry 2018). The success of the Croatian public network operator with the first phase was not an indication of future progress, however. Though the second phase was less reliant on cooperation among the public service broadcasters, which had been one of the main obstacles in the first phase, it also did not go smoothly. The tender for the second phase was launched in March 2017 with completion intended for early 2018, however, by the end of 2018 delays persisted (Biznis.ba 2018). The regulator granted the license for the third multiplex, MUX C, to a consortium of commercial television broadcasters at the end of October 2019 (Regulatorna Agencija za Komunikacije 2019) and was still tendering for licenses for commercial broadcasters to use MUX C in early 2020.

Kosovo

Digitalization in Kosovo was hindered from the start by the fact that the republic was not yet recognized in 2006 when the ITU conference allocating frequencies for DTT was held. The frequency plan that had been negotiated by the Serbian delegation did not match the eventual border of Kosovo. Essentially the country was given two broadcasting points, but these were at a lower power than needed to cover the whole area and not compatible with creating a single frequency network (SFN) (Independent Media Commission Kosovo 2009). After a series of meetings, and with the international support being given to Kosovo's Independent Media Commission at the time, a draft strategy for digitalization was produced in 2012. A revised one was published in March 2015 and was largely reflected in the Law on Digitalization of Terrestrial Broadcasting passed finally in August 2015.

The 2015 strategy (Independent Media Commission Kosovo 2015) set out a detailed plan for changes to the frequency allocation set at WRC06 and comprehensive frequency plan that would give Kosovo 3 MUXs, two of which would be used initially and the third that would be made available after channels were moved onto the first two. According to the 2015 plan, Kosovo's PSB organization Radio Televizionit të Kosovës (RTK) would receive its own MUX, but only after the other two were in operation. MUX1 and MUX2 would be granted to an operator through a tendering procedure with "must carry" obligations placed on that operator to carry the channels of RTK and the two national commercial television stations until RTK's MUX3 was operational. In December 2017, a final strategy was adopted, and the basic plan remained the same as in the 2015 draft (Independent Media Commission Kosovo 2017). In addition to the three national multiplexes, five regional "sub-allotments" were planned for regional and local broadcasting, and eventually two more national MUXs granted via a "beauty contest."

The Role of PSB

There was great variance in the starting positions of the PSB organizations at the beginning of the switchover process, and those that were stronger played a great role in making switchover happen. Croatian and Slovenian public service broadcasters were both highly popular and very strong compared to the commercial broadcasters. Both had only a small number of real competitors. RTS in Serbia was also relatively popular and well-positioned in the market. In all three of these cases, the PSB organization was one of the drivers of the process. These public service broadcasters functioned as drivers by informing citizens and participating in campaigns to encourage people to get set-top boxes, and by serving as an incentive to those dependent on terrestrial broadcasting. If people wanted to keep watching them, they would need to get the set-top box or use another platform, which was particularly important in Croatia and Serbia where there were still large portions of the population dependent on terrestrial broadcasting. As described in the accounts above, in all three of these cases the greater number of channels available on DTT after switchover diminished their positions in the market. Following a switchover, they faced greater competition, particularly from national commercial channels, and more pressure to produce content and fill channels.

In North Macedonia and Montenegro, the public service broadcasters played less of a role in driving the switchover process. They may have participated in the information campaigns, but these would have reached far smaller percentages of the population than in some of the neighboring states where PSB had much larger audiences. This was especially true in North Macedonia where, as mentioned above, the campaign was very brief. At the same time, the high penetration of alternative subscription services meant that the incentive of continued access to them for households was not an important driver of the process, and this was not counted on in the national strategies for achieving switchover. There was some evidence of complaints from those suddenly cut off from terrestrial signal following analog switch-off in North Macedonia and a rush to other platforms, but these were still from a relatively small portion of the population and did not stop the government from declaring switchover a success. In both cases, the domestic commercial stations were likely just as much, if not more, of an incentive than the PSB organizations for those reliant on terrestrial broadcasting to get their set-top boxes.

In all five of the states that completed switchover on time, public service broadcasters were privileged in some way. The most privileged was RTVSLO in Slovenia, which received not only a dedicated MUX but also the operation of it, because unlike the others, it still had a links and transmissions department that served as an operator. It also received extensive funding for the infrastructure needed. North Macedonia's MRT also benefited from a dedicated MUX, the infrastructure for which was paid for by the state, but the funds for this infrastructure and operation of the MUX went to the public network operator MRD. PSB organizations in Serbia and Montenegro each received automatic dedicated space on a MUX operated by the public network company, which received aid for the completion of the infrastructure. In Croatia, where HRT was highly popular and there was the highest proportion of people dependent on terrestrial broadcasting, the public service broadcaster was the least privileged. It was granted capacity on the main national MUXs without a tender, but this was only a slight administrative advantage over the national commercial broadcasters.

Only in BiH, does the evidence suggest that the public service broadcasters have been a hindrance to digital switchover. Nevertheless, they have still been privileged with a dedicated MUX and support for the necessary infrastructure via the Croatian public network operator that won the bid for operating the Bosnian DTT network. The Kosovar plan would also grant PSB special access to the network by giving it first a dedicated space on a MUX together with commercial broadcasters and then its own MUX once frequencies had been freed up. Regardless of how unpopular or even problematic their public service broadcasters were, as Table 14.1 below shows, the countries in the Western Balkans that made the ITU deadline largely privileged them in their digital switchover process.

Table 14.1: Overview of Switchover Process in Those Completing Before the ITU Deadline

	Aid to PSB	Aid for infrastructure	Campaign	Consumer subsidy
Slovenia	1 MUX	EUR 1.2 mill (to PSB)	Yes	Yes for vulnerable
Croatia	Tender waived for MUX access	None	Yes	20-50% cost of STB
Serbia	Dedicated space on MUX1	Yes, inc. EU IPA funds	Yes, inc. with EU IPA funds	Yes for vulnerable
North Macedonia	1 MUX dedicated	Yes, state budget covered PSB MUX	Yes	Yes for vulnerable and obligations on private MUX
Montenegro	Dedicated space on MUX1	Yes, inc. EU IPA funds	Yes	Yes for vulnerable

Source: The author.

Public Network Operators as Public Service Media?

Another thing the comparison in Table 14.1 shows is that the successful switchover in these countries relied on state or other aid for the necessary infrastructure in all cases except that of Croatia. In Serbia, North Macedonia, and Montenegro the recipient of that aid was a public network operator, a publicly owned company set up by the divestiture of the former links and transmissions department of their public service broadcasters. In Slovenia, the recipient was the PSB organization directly as it never divested and continues to serve as both broadcaster and DTT network operator. Though in Croatia no direct subsidies for infrastructure were identified, the DTT network operator was also a public company established in the same manner as in the other public network operators.

These public network operators played a crucial role in enabling switchover and continue to be the main or only DTT operator in all but North Macedonia, where a commercial operator also has national coverage (though less complete than that of the public company that carries PSB channels). They were certainly fundamental to the distribution of PSB channels. They allow them to fulfill their coverage obligations, even if in some of the cases this is only about 15% of the population, mainly in rural mountainous areas. In the face of ever-expanding subscription service take-up, these public DTT networks also provide a secure alternative in case of any difficulties or disagreements with the companies providing those services. They keep PSB organizations from being completely dependent on commercial gatekeepers for accessing their audiences.

The role played by these public network operators in digital switchover and their continued importance in the functioning of DTT networks in the Western Balkans would seem to indicate that they are serving the public interest in providing media. The commercial value of operating DTT networks in the region is questionable. In Slovenia, Serbia, and North Macedonia there is clear evidence that for many local and regional broadcasters it is not worth it for them to pay fees to a DTT network operator to access the DTT network, and instead they give up on free-to-air transmission (See Milosavljević and Broughton Micova 2013; Nikodinoska 2016; Velojic 2016). With low dependence on terrestrial television and generally weak media markets, there may be less and less interest from commercial players to pay for DTT distribution. Nevertheless, the public interest in maintaining the publicly owned DTT network, for the security it provides and for those isolated communities that depend on it, might warrant continued operation as a form of public service media.

Conclusion

Public service broadcasting was at the heart of the story of digital switchover in the Western Balkans. In some cases, public service broadcasters were important drivers of the process, and in all cases, they were treated differently from the commercial broadcasters, with most receiving highly preferential treatment. Among those countries that met the deadline set within the ITU, four dedicated spaces on the DTT network to PSB without charge, and Croatia offered it without a tender. These PSB organizations were all in a different situation from those in BiH and Kosovo. They had not suffered as much from the destructive conflicts or the challenging context of fragile state-building processes and mostly new institutions of governance.[2] BiH and Kosovo seemed to have learned lessons from their neighbors, however, and followed similar paths as they tried to catch up.

The privileged and prominent role of PSB in the switchover processes of the region does not, however, mean they have universally benefited greatly from the process. On the contrary, some of those that were particularly strong, such as Croatia's HRT, have suffered somewhat from the increased competition that digitalization has brought about. The digital switchover was something that

---

[2]　The RTS building in Serbia was bombed directly during NATO's intervention in the conflict in Kosovo and parts of its transmission network were damaged, but the institution was largely intact, and the infrastructure was quickly repaired after 1999.

these countries had to do, yet there was little incentive other than the impending deadline for them to do it. In most cases, it seems, the public service broadcasters were helped in various ways to make the process as painless as possible for them.

One thing the experience in the Western Balkans has highlighted is that network operation, or distribution can also be a vital part of what makes up public service media. In all the completed processes except for Croatia, state aid to the public network operator was crucial to completing switchover. Even though Croatia's strategy did not involve direct support for infrastructure, the public network operator was still given the main task of operating the MUX without a tender procedure. Croatia's public network operator has since been playing the leading role in moving BiH towards switchover, having won the contracts via tenders in a region in which there has been a little incentive and little chance of future profit.

References

Albornoz, Luis A. and María Trinidad García Leiva. 2012. "The Political Economy of DTT: An International Overview." *International Journal of Digital Television* 3, no. 3 (October): 301–319.

AVMU. 2015. *Анализа На Пазарот На Аудио И Аудиовизуелни Медиумски Услуги За 2014 Година* [Analysis of the market for audio and audiovisual media services in 2014]. Skopje: AVMU.

Biznis.ba. 2018. "BH IT: Digitalizacija u Bosni i Hercegovini." [BH IT: Digitalization in Bosnia and Herzegovina] *Bisnis.ba,* December 27. Accessed February 17, 2020. http://biznis.ba/bh-it-digitalizacija-u-bosni-i-hercegovini/.

Broughton Micova, Sally. 2013. *Small and Resistant: Europeanization in Media Governance in Slovenia and Macedonia.* London: London School of Economics and Political Science.

Delegation of the European Union to Montenegro. 2009. *Support to the Digitalisation of the Montenegrin Public Broadcasting.* Podgorica: Delegation of the European Union to Montenegro.

Dziadul, Chirs. 2014. "Serbian Pay-TV: The Stats." *Broadband TV News*, September 29. Accessed June 20, 2017. http://www.broadbandtvnews.com/2014/09/29/serbian-pay-tv-the-stats/.

European Commission. 2009a. "Communication from the Commission on the Application of State Aid Rules to Public Service Broadcasting." *Official Journal of the European Communities* C257, 1–14.

——. 2009b. *Standard Summary Project Fiche—IPA Centralised Programmes Project Number 16: Assistance to the Digital Broadcasting Switchover in Serbia (CRIS Number: 2009/021-765).* Brussels: European Commission.

Fry, Andy. 2018. "Bosnian Pay TV Market on the Up, Says Kagan S&P." *DigitalTV Europe*, June 14. Accessed February 17, 2020. https://www.digitaltveurope.com/2018/06/14/bosnian-pay-tv-market-on-the-up-says-kagan-sp/.

García Leiva, María T. and Michael Starks. 2009. "Digital Switchover across the Globe:

The Emergence of Complex Regional Patterns." *Media, Culture & Society* 31, no. 5 (September): 787–806.

Government of the Republic of Serbia. 2009. *Strategy for Switchover from Analogue to Digital Broadcasting of Radio and Television Programs in the Republic of Serbia.* Belgrade: Government of the Republic of Serbia.

Hodžić, Sanela. 2016. "Bosnia and Herzegovina: The Story of Political Obstructions." In *Time Zero of the Digital Switchover in SEE,* edited by Center for Independent Journalism, 19–21. Bucharest: Center for Independent Journalism. http://www.mc.rs/upload/documents/projekti/regionalna%20saradnja/Time-%20Zero.pdf.

Independent Media Commission Kosovo. 2017. *Strategy for the Transition to Digital Terrestrial Broadcasting in the Republic of Kosovo.* Prishtina: Independent Media Commission Kosovo.

——. 2015. *Draft Strategy: Transition from Analogue to Digital Broadcasting in Republic of Kosova.* Prishtina: Independent Media Commission Kosovo.

——. 2009. "Introduction of Digital Broadcasting in Kosovo and the Region. Strategies." Paper presented at the International Conference on Strategies and Experiences on the Process of Switchover to Digital Broadcasting in Kosovo and the Region, Prishtina, December 3–5.

Milosavljević, Marko and Sally Broughton Micova. 2013. "Because We Have To: Digitalization of Terrestrial Television in South East Europe." *International Journal of Digital Television* 4, no 3 (September): 261–277.

Milosavljević, Marko and Tanja Kerševan Smokvina. 2012. *Mapping Digital Media: Slovenia.* London: Open Society Foundations. https://www.opensocietyfoundations.org/uploads/18f8a811-6061-41ed-97cd-53a80abdda3e/mapping-digital-media-slovenia-20130605.pdf.

Montenegro Agency for Electronic Media. 2015. *Market Report on Radio and TV Programme Distribution to End Users, September 2015.* Podgorica: Montenegro Agency for Electronic Media.

Nikodinoska, Vesna. 2016. "Macedonia: Local Broadcasters. Lost in Digitization." In *Time Zero of the Digital Switchover in SEE,* edited by Center for Independent Journalism, 21–26. Bucharest: Center for Independent Journalism. http://www.mc.rs/upload /documents/projekti/regionalna%20saradnja/Time-%20Zero.pdf.

Odašiljači i veze. 2016. "Odašiljači i Veze D.O.O. Uspješno Završili Prvu Fazu Digitalizacije Televizije U Bosni I Hercegovini [OIV successfully completes the first phase of the digitalisation of television in Bosnia and Herzegovina]." *OIV news release,* October 14. Accessed May 8, 2020. https://oiv.hr/hr/vijesti/objave-za-javnost/odasiljaci-i-veze-doo-uspjesno-zavrsili-prvu-fazu-digitalizacije-televizije-u-bosni-i-hercegovini/.

Regulatorna Agencija za Kommunikacija. 2019. *RAK Dodijelio Dozvolu za Korištenje Multipleksa C.* Sarajevo: Regulatorna Agencija za Komunikacije RAK, October 29. Accessed February 17, 2020. https://www.rak.ba/hr/news/1630.

SEE Digi.TV. 2013. *Switching on the SEE Region: Cooperation for the Digital Era.* Ljubljana: Digi.TV.

Starks, Michael. 2013. *The Digital Television Revolution: Origins to Outcomes.* Basingstoke: Palgrave Macmillan.

——. 2007. *Switching to Digital Television: UK Public Policy and the Market.* Bristol/ Chicago: Intellect.

Velojic, Mladen. 2016. "Serbia: The Digital Switchover. Prosperity or Collapse." In *Time Zero of the Digital Switchover in SEE,* edited by Center for Independent Journalism,

33–36. Bucharest: Center for Independent Journalism. http://www.mc.rs/upload /documents/projekti/regionalna%20saradnja/Time-%20Zero.pdf.

Wheeler, Mark. 2012. "European Union State Aid, Public Subsidies and Analogue Switch-Off/Digital Switchover." *International Journal of Digital Television* 3, no. 2 (Feburary): 7–22.

Žugić, Ljiljana. 2016. "Montenegro: Challenges yet to Come." In *Time Zero of the Digital Switchover in SEE*, edited by Center for Independent Journalism, 26–29. Bucharest: Center for Independent Journalism. http://www.mc.rs/upload/documents/pro-jekti /regionalna%20saradnja/Time-%20Zero.pdf.

CHAPTER 15

Prospects for Post-Switchover Media Policy in the Western Balkan Countries

Kenneth Murphy

Introduction

Public service broadcasters are facing many challenges, amongst which are the processes of digitalization and convergence. The gradual adaptation of broadcasting organizations to digital broadcast distribution and medium convergence within digital media ecologies generates both opportunities and challenges. Digitalization, convergence, and the development of the internet enables new sets of communicative practices and the remediation of older ones, partially shaped by new dynamic relationships between media, technology, and telecommunications sectors and content. Broadcasting is now intertwined in networks and receivers made up of differential digital media content existing in and between logics of broadcast and networked communication. The artifacts, practices, and social arrangements that make up this dynamic media environment can be referred to as the digital media ecology (Mansell 2016). Competitive economic development, public policy, the strategies of various public and market actors, and user behavior within defined economic conditions drive the digitalization of broadcasting. Successful digitalization has, in Europe, for the most part, incorporated public broadcasters and the retention of free-to-air platforms. Public broadcasters' engagements with medium convergence (understood as how older mediums are redetermined as interactive and digital, even as digitalization and interactivity are shaped by the social sphere) are significantly shaped by economics, public policy, technology, organizational strategy, and adaptation to consumer behavior. Traditional broadcast organizations are managing the transition from traditional media systems to complex global digital media ecologies (Media-IT-Telecom) through an evolving transformation of traditional value chains to complex value chains (Simon 2016). Whereas nothing is guaranteed, continued support for public service media in the digitalization of broadcasting transmission and appropriation of medium convergence by public service organizations may offer a route to continued relevance for public service media (Glowacki and Jaskiernia 2018).

In Europe the ability of public media organizations to adapt to complex media/communication ecologies and medium convergence, and define those in the interests of the public, is shaped by the overall interaction of coalitions of transnational actors and institutions, state structure and political field, market size and value, market structures and strategies, social structure and the legacy of pre-existing media systems/infrastructure. Three key variables for these adjustments are thus technology, economics, and policy. The technological environment enables and constrains what is possible in digital development (broadband diffusion, multichannel competition, etc.). The economic environment within which media organizations operate will determine the resources available for digital transitions, and policy can either enable or constrain the extension, replacement, and reproduction of public purposes in communication as well as its character (public or commercial). Alongside user behavior, these variables thus interact to institutionalize the emerging complex media ecology and how public media are positioned within it. The development of competing distribution systems within a context of liberalized convergence is one aspect of the digital transition and the restructuring of public service broadcasting, and digital media organizations is another. Requisite funding for adjustment as well as enabling policy that supports the transition to networked digital public broadcasting will help determine its extent and character.

The evolving relationship and interconnections between digitalization of distribution (switchover) and medium convergence needs to be in the foreground. The content that public service media organizations (PSM) remediate is for the most part broadcast content (Beutler 2016). The revenues that mixed funding PSM generate continue to be overwhelmingly from linear digital broadcasting. The mission of PSM can still be expressed in terms of the importance of the socio-communicative form of broadcasting in a complex media-technology-telecoms ecology. A successful digital transition that retains the centrality of PSM as universal, independent, free-to-air public services with the capacity to produce quality, diverse, linear broadcast content is a prerequisite for the remediation of that broadcast content across various platforms. It also serves as an indicator of the political will to legalize the institutional norms of public service "free at the point of access" content in a digital environment. External and internal conditions will either enable or constrain 1) the continued strategic repositioning of public service in the complex ecology, 2) the shift of PSM from value chains to value network models of operation and 3) the expansion and extension of public purposes (citizenship, quality, universality) in media. The argument presented here is that all three of these aspects of transition are necessary conditions for each other.

Broadcasting and Digitalization

The digitalization of media systems is shaped by techno-economic logic, sociocultural change, politics, and regulation. Digitalization creates the potential for convergence, but convergence is not a linear, totalizing, or inevitable process.

The EU is facilitating network and industrial convergence, but service or medium convergence is regarded as an evolutionary process (Dal 2013). Broadcast technologies and forms are undergoing a process of remediation. Paul Chadwick points to the reality of hybrid media systems wherein mass media and network media logics exist in dialectical relationships with each other (Chadwick 2013). Within such a system, digitalization and interactivity do not necessarily entail the disappearance of broadcast architectures of communications but new relationships between it and the broader communicative environment. Broadcast content can be distributed across multiple platforms, and new and emerging platforms provide the basis for interactivity and evolution of broadcast forms. Digital broadcasting is thus characterized by medium perseverance and renewal (Pierson and Bauwens 2015).

The digital switchover, as developed in the EU, has been succeeded by a wider process of trans-European market development of network competition and service development i.e. the Digital Single Market. The digital transition in broadcasting is thus a critical juncture for neo-statist intervention if public policy related to normative values of broadcast media is to have future relevance (Ala-Fossi, forthcoming) in these contexts. If intervention is not timely and effective, the development of the post-analog media ecology will likely be largely market-driven, commercial, and de-emphasize the social importance of broadcasting as a socio-cultural form. Neo-statist intervention which helps to reposition PS organizations' in the digital television and radio environment, affords them the opportunity to use their media advantages in a new context to develop their core commitments to universality, trust and citizenship (Born and Prosser 2003) and to continue to innovate as digital media organizations. Arguably, timeliness is crucial for small states as there are fewer resources available and further fragmentation of attention and revenues will undermine attempts to forge a cultural space and project policy influence in the global digital media ecology.

It is in these contexts that PSM must realize new public purposes, extend existing ones, and replace redundant ones. Externally, politics, technological development, economics, and regulation determine the position and potentials for PSM (Sehl, Cornia and Nielsen 2016). Internally, PS organizations must be able to adapt and develop compelling visions for networked public purposes that justify their existence. This would entail new relationships with public institutions, public media creative collaborators, and most importantly, directly with the public (Glowacki and Jaskiernia 2018). This careful re-articulation of how value is created and distributed requires internal restructuring that is technological, structural, managerial, cultural, and strategic. It is the transition from an organization based on the logic of value chains to one based on public value networks (Pierson and Bauwens 2015). PSM and their representative bodies can influence the external conditions of their evolution but must lead with the internal ones. The current chapter compares and contrasts the processes of digitalization and convergence across the Western Balkan states based on the chapters in this volume. Working from the contextual field outlined in the chapters of this book it first evaluates how PSB is repositioned in the digital switchover in the Western Balkans, and in the second section, how public service providers are restructuring to adapt. Connecting both of these dynamics is the context created for, and the actions taken in, the transition to a value network model of organization. Lastly, the challenges facing public policy and media system governance and the need to adapt to the changing contexts for broadcasting and the challenges of institutionalizing its public purposes as part of the wider digital media ecology will be addressed.

International Frameworks: Evolving Hybrid Media Ecologies

The digitalization of broadcasting as an object of EU policy developed within a wider policy framework towards media convergence. The guiding aim was to stimulate the potential of the market, industrial and service convergence in media, communications, and ICT. In the current study, Croatia is a full member of the EU and the remaining countries are either full candidate countries (Serbia, North Macedonia, Albania, and Montenegro) or potential candidate countries (Bosnia and Herzegovina, BiH, and Kosovo) and have been encouraged to adhere to the market and regulatory structure of liberalized convergence that has been institutionalized in EU member states since the early 1990s. In general terms, this is a structure based on horizontal regulation of networks (cable, terrestrial, mobile, satellite, fixed wire) through the 2009 Electronic Communications Regulatory Framework and vertical regulation of industry segments (television, radio, print media, online) e.g. the 2018 Audiovisual Media Services Directive. The horizontal regulation of networks adheres to the basic principles of competition, technological neutrality, and harmonized basic regulations.

The vertical regulation of content/production/services indicates the degree to which medium convergence is being approached as an evolutionary process. The hybrid linear/non-linear nature of broadcast television is recognized within the Audiovisual Media Services Directive (Directive 2010/13/EU). The extension of regulation to non-linear audiovisual services also indicates a continued distinction between on-demand audiovisual ("television like") services and the myriad audiovisual content sharing services that have developed across digital networks. The place of public service media in this evolving context is supported by myriad interventions at the European level. The directives and guidelines thus create the space for public service media to be re-institutionalized at a national level. The EU has not been prescriptive in terms of the strength and/or centrality of public service media in the digital transition but has generated tension between market development of new services, re-regulation (with evolving public service media as a market-friendly feature), and its conditional support for plural media systems (Brevini 2013).

Digital Switchover in the Western Balkans

In the short term, for public media organizations, digitalization infers competition in multichannel television markets and the integration of television into bundled service built around digital cable, satellite, terrestrial, and fixed wire service provision. In Western Europe, DTT has been pursued as a central platform of public policy to achieve multiple policy goals such as:

- Enabling analog switch-off and the release of the spectrum,
- Ensuring plurality in multichannel television markets,
- Maintaining provision of universal, independent and free-to-air television services,
- Support for indigenous audiovisual industries and
- Maintenance of public service broadcasting's universality and accessibility.

Public broadcasters have contributed to the digital switchover through support for the development of DTT infrastructure (allowing analog switch-off), spearheading multiplex development, generating new channels and content to make the platform attractive, and informing the public about the purposes and processes of the digital transition. In short, the political choices made within the developed market structure of converged communications have made PSM's future survival dependent on wider support for digitalization (through analog switch-off). Conversely, public broadcasters have supported DTT as a means of retaining legitimacy in digital broadcasting as it is repositioned within digital network and service markets.

For PSM, broadcasting is at the core of wider strategies to adjust to the complex media ecosystem. In the short term, it legitimizes its continuation, potentially shores up its continued relevance in multichannel markets and provides a politically accepted justification for investing in content that benefits its content service provision across multiple distribution systems (cable, satellite, terrestrial, broadband) and multiple platforms (on-demand players, mobile, apps, web, etc.). Evolving networked public purposes, the requisite organizational structure to fulfill them and sound funding models are key to PSM's adjustment to the digital transition and its techno-economic, socio-cultural, regulatory, and political drivers (Pierson and Bauwens 2015).

Policy choices about the role of DTT in the digital transition (bandwidth for development, funding for infrastructure, timely plan for the switchover, information for the public, subsidies for content and or adjustment, updated regulation for digital services) and the place of PSM within that transition (development of channels, multiplex capacity, expansion of remit, funding for new content), have significant implications for the future of broadcasting within digital ecosystems and the role of PSM therein. Transitions deemed to be successful and supportive of the ethos and legitimacy of public service within an evolving media ecology give broadcast organizations the funding and legitimacy to adapt to the evolving ecology, albeit within constraints, and develop their public purposes. For PSM, digital switchover also entails generating more content with relatively fewer resources and rationalizing its internal productions systems in structural, technological and cultural terms to be able to develop and realize the core content of its channels as both media-specific cultural forms and the source of "digital objects" that can be flexibly distributed, repurposed or remediated across the complex media ecology.

Of the Western Balkan states, Albania, Croatia, Serbia, North Macedonia, and Montenegro have all achieved digital switchover, Bosnia and Herzegovina is suspended between switchover and switch-off and Kosovo has yet to achieve switchover as of early 2020. It is not unusual that each of the countries has experienced difficulties, as the digital transition has been problematic for many nation-states entailing trial and error approaches as technological, economic, and legislative dynamics are negotiated. However, many of the Balkan states face the additional challenge of media sustainability, fragmented television and radio markets, and politically and economically compromised public broadcasters. In Western Europe, public service broadcasters that are firmly embedded in their respective media systems have supported the overall objective of digital switchover. Many of the Western Balkan public broadcasters are relatively recently restructured and as such are not yet well integrated into either the media system or the fragile institutional spheres of civil society and politics. In many of the states, the policy is driven by the switchover agenda rather than a vision of digital broadcasting within a converged media infrastructure and the place of public service media therein (Milosavljević and Broughton Micova 2013). This is compounded by economic contexts of relatively low GDP by European standards, and the lower demand and investment in cultural industries. In technological terms, the infrastructure for competitive service development is advancing, mainly through foreign investment, but DTT is underdeveloped. In short, the European model of market-driven competitive platform development and regulatory neutrality for converged digital services, of which DTT is an element, is one additional element of policy/institutional transfer that risks overloading the existing institutional capacity of Western Balkan states to adapt (Marko 2019). Milosavljević and Broughton Micova illustrate how the initial stages of the digital transition in the Western Balkans have, for the most part, been dependent on public service broadcasters, government subsidies, and newly formed public network operators. However, a vision and political will to support culturally specific public purposes in digital broadcasting, beyond switchover, is absent.

The chapters in this volume all document how political, economic, and regulatory contexts have impacted the success, or otherwise, of the digital transition. All of these factors create myriad challenges for public broadcasters: how to establish and retain their political and economic autonomy, how to meet myriad policy demands surrounding the digital transition (DTT management and channel expansion), and how to manage their internal digital transition (value networks). The fate of DTT is uncertain in these circumstances, as attractive content and technological evolution are central to its continued relevance. Without the drivers of diffusion available in larger, wealthier states, there are significant grounds for intervention to sustain the public policy dimensions of DTT, either from the EU or other trans-national sources. Both the European Commission and the European Broadcasting Union (EBU) have redoubled their input in this regard with multiple initiatives to sustain institutional and technological development (see below). Terrestrial broadcasting remains important due to its relative autonomy, universality, capacity, and accessibility, and as such, if it is to be an enabling component of wider infrastructure development and digital services, then public support is necessary. The policy goals behind the EU's model of convergence may not be germane to the Western Balkan states just now, but eventually they will be. Broadband diffusion, competition, and new service development are ultimately central platforms of the EU's digital agenda, digital single market, and overall agenda for economic growth and integration.

Croatia

Croatia started its digitalization process early (2002) and switched off the analog transmission in 2010. The Croatian process was characterized by strong political coordination of the transition along with collaboration from public and private media interests and state support for technological infrastructure (public ownership of the terrestrial transmission company). Figures for 2017 demonstrate that DTT is the dominant distribution system with 53.4% of households relying on it. IPTV makes up 25.8% of the market with cable at 10% and satellite at 7% (European Audiovisual Observatory. n.d.-c). The DTT platform is state-owned and has a hybrid free-to-air/pay-TV structure with expansive free and niche channels. The government supported DTT diffusion through the subsidization of set-top boxes (Milosavljević and Broughton Micova 2013). The public broadcaster HRT was allocated a national multiplex for its 2 channels and was authorized to develop two new specialist channels and HD offerings in 2012, a news channel and culture and arts channel). HRT had to fund its new channels through its existing resources. Crucially, it adapted to the logic of internal digitalization and the necessity of digital infrastructure to enable more efficient workflow as well as a system that enables content to be re-used and repurposed across different platforms (Create Once, Publish Everywhere). This has been accompanied by internal restructuring to enable more coordination across media production (television, radio, online). The overall transition is accompanied by the adaptation of managerial ethos to digital logics of the media system whilst retaining the link between digital broadcasting and digital content service provision. Political stability, a relatively unified media structure capable of developing new content and channels, a larger market, higher GDP, and advanced European integration, together with a more rooted public service media system, are what distinguish Croatia from some of its neighboring states.

Serbia

Before switchover, half of Serbian households subscribed to multichannel services with the majority of those being cable. An EU candidate country, Serbia achieved digital switchover in 2015 and the public broadcasters (RTS/RTV) were once again central to the process. Political leadership and coordination were important but in contrast to Croatia, political instability and inconsistency in decision-making delayed the process. A subsidiary company was established by RTS to manage the upgrade of the terrestrial broadcast infrastructure and this was eventually separated as a public company. The European Commission contributed funding that was partially used by this company to upgrade the infrastructure (Milosavljević and Broughton Micova 2013). RTS was legally obliged to upgrade its production infrastructure to be capable and ready for the changes. RTS launched additional channels and developed HD in 2008 and 2009 and upgraded its audio description capabilities. A key issue in Serbia relates to political interference in PSB and problems with the funding model. Depoliticized programming and commercial fare demonstrate how a successful digital switchover and repositioning of the nominal public broadcaster does not necessarily entail expanded public purposes. In the case of Serbia, technological digitization has been achieved but the socio-political and socio-cultural questions surrounding public broadcasting in a digital environment have not been addressed. Likewise, the benefits of utilizing digital production technology to expand on networked content provision appear absent in the Serbian context.

Montenegro and North Macedonia

Montenegro is a small state with a fragmented media structure and problematic institutionalization of PSB. It achieved the launch of DTT in 2015 with significant aid from the EU and despite internal divisions amongst media stakeholders. Delays in the development of DTT have allowed for the expansion of cable (21%), satellite (27%) and IPTV services (33.6%) (European Audiovisual Observatory. n.d.-d). A public company, Broadcasting Centre of Montenegro (BCM), manages the free-to-air multiplex for both national commercial and PSB channels. RTCG in Montenegro has not been realized as a functioning public institution and has significant financial difficulties. The digital switchover has been technologically achieved but the input of RTCG was not pivotal. There has been no extension of activities in a multichannel environment and no significant organizational adjustment to prepare for digital media ecology. The public broadcaster has not engaged in any significant internal restructuring or technological upgrading and despite some financing from the EU, its internal production system is outdated.

North Macedonia is a small market with a highly fragmented media structure and a "near sustainable" mixed media system (IREX 2019). It completed its digital switchover in 2013. Delays occurred in the process due to lack of cohesion between state departments, but the government directly subsidized the upgrade of the terrestrial infrastructure. Unusually, DTT began in 2009 as a privately run subscription-based service, carrying public and private services but this was reversed in 2012 when the PSB channels (MRT) were given their own free-to-air multiplexes. DTT was thus developed a hybrid free-to-air/commercial service with the commercial service provider (Telecom Austria) managing the multiplexes of subscriber services and Makedonska Radiodifuzia (JPMRD) managing the free-to-air multiplexes (European Audiovisual Observatory. n.d.-e). DTT is currently the most extensive means of television distribution followed by cable, IPTV, and satellite. The public broadcaster MRT is once again not fully developed as a public institution and accounts for just 6.7% of television viewing. There has been little attempt to expand its channel provision and a lack of public debate on public purposes for PSB in a multichannel environment.

Albania and Kosovo

Albania and Kosovo are two small states with near sustainable mixed media systems (IREX 2019). Albania has a small and highly fragmented media market. Digital satellite is taken up by 50% of households, cable has 5% penetration, and the main telecom company ALB Telecom now offers IPTV (European Audiovisual Observatory. n.d.-a). A sizeable proportion of the population thus relies on terrestrial services (no specific figures are attainable). The digital transition has been marked by political disagreement and a lack of institutional coordination as well as legal wrangles, but a switchover strategy was developed in 2012–2013. A new government organization, ART, was formed in 2015 to oversee the switchover process, including management of multiplexes, and a German company won the contract to upgrade the infrastructure. Multiplex launches were planned for 2016 and switchover was eventually achieved in 2019. The public broadcaster was once again, via legislation, given a role in transition with RTSH developing four additional channels (including high definition) with a legislative requirement to expand this to twelve. RTSH has been steadily upgrading its production capacity but by any standards, the production and distribution of twelve channels will stretch capacity even as its funding mechanism appears stable.

Kosovo is also a very small state with a fragmented media system, and its PSB organization (RTK) has not been fully realized as a public institution (it has been politically and financially captured). Kosovo has faced unique difficulties in the digital transition because it was absent from the WRC06 and therefore was not included in the frequency plan. The regulator IMC was given the responsibility to implement the strategy for digital switchover following a legislative framework developed in 2015 by the Ministry of Economic Development. Due to institutional overlap and a lack of clarity in terms of sequence and responsibility, there have been delays in the implementation of the combined strategy. The national terrestrial broadcast system, KTTN, was rebuilt in 2000, and according to a South European Media Observatory report has lost considerable ground to 35 cable operators, licensed by the IMC (UBO Consulting 2015). RTK has been given a central role in managing a multiplex. However, the switchover has not been appropriately planned for and the costs, responsibilities, and timing for the different elements have not been developed. At a political and state level, the digital transition is marred by a lack of cohesion and clarity. RTK has engaged in internal digitalization but given the lack of a DTT platform, they lack a plan for multichannel. They are attempting to integrate the production structure but overall there is significant concern that market development of platforms will overtake and negate DTT, calling into question a terrestrial component of the digital broadcasting future.

Bosnia and Herzegovina (BiH)

BiH is a larger state, and a potential candidate country of the EU, which is caught between digital switchover and analog switch-off. Bosnia's broadcast system is highly fragmented and the public broadcasters (BHRT/RTVFBiH/RTRS) once again cannot, due to political control and problematic funding, be considered fully operating according to the public interest. In relation to broadcasting, terrestrial is the dominant form of distribution with 40% of households still relying on it, with cable (31%), satellite (10%), and IPTV (18.8%) becoming increasingly well diffused (European Audiovisual Observatory. n.d.-b). A forum was created in 2006 to establish a route map for the introduction of DTT and the regulator adopted a strategy in 2009. The process of launching DTT was held up due to complications surrounding the bidding procedures for the proposed transmission and multiplex company and the fragmented nature of the public service system. DTT was eventually launched and operational in Mostar, Sarajevo, and Banja Luka from 2016 but has yet to be expanded to the rest of the country. Some commercial broadcasters utilize the digital terrestrial transmission system, but some continue to broadcast in analog. A further complication is the lack of functioning of the institution (the corporation) planned to create consonance between the three public broadcasters in terms of technological planning and upgrading. The fragmented nature of public broadcast organizations has negatively impacted the digital transition. There is no evidence of channel development of the public broadcasters and internal infrastructure development is also conspicuous by its absence. Issues concerning politicization overshadow public consideration of the expansion of PSB in terms of the public purposes of additional channels and related services, and organizational separation along ethnic-nationalist lines entails little evidence of possible integration of the public service broadcasters over time. In 2018 the EBU contacted the government of Bosnia and Herzegovina to express its concerns on the financial and institutional deterioration of public service media in general and the imminent closure of BHRT in particular.

Analysis & Comparison

The transition to DTT in the Western Balkan states has thus far had mixed results. For the most part, public service broadcasters and subsidies have had a positive influence as has the formation of public companies to operate the DTT network infrastructure (see Chapter 14 by Broughton Micova in this volume).

Concurrently, terrestrial transmission remains important and in many cases is a dominant means of distribution. The states that have negotiated these challenges (Serbia, Croatia, Montenegro, North Macedonia) to affect switchover all, share features of coordinated governance, effective institutions, and regulation in the media and communications sector. In essence, the state can act, despite the challenging circumstances. Albania has achieved switchover through significant intervention from transnational agencies. In BiH and Kosovo, state capacity and political will have been problematic. Both BiH and Kosovo are just potential EU candidate countries and therefore lack the institutional and infrastructural context and motivation to ensure digital switchover. Both, however, have experienced difficulties concerning political conflict, institutional incoherence, and lack of capacity at the regulatory level. Legal issues with licensing and management have also delayed switchover. Beyond technological transitions, state capacity and political will is a prerequisite for the re-institutionalization of PSB as PSM and has bearing on the transition to the value network model of operation.

The digital transition is the occasion to reposition broadcasting within a digital media infrastructure and DTT is a means of re-institutionalizing PSB in this framework. As markets and technologies evolve, this repositioning is crucial to allow the PSB organizations to undertake internal restructuring in conditions of relative stability. State commitment to European media structures may exist in the Western Balkan states but without political will and state capacity, public organizations will not be able to adapt to the new environment that is created. In turn, organizations find themselves facing significant transmission, upgrade, and production costs in circumstances of further revenue diminution. PSB has been centrally important for enabling the digital transition in these states and PS broadcasters should benefit from these developments. However, continued support is needed as PSB organizations develop public purposes in a multichannel digital environment and DTT needs to evolve in changing technological contexts (e.g., incorporation of on-demand functionality). In all of the cases above there remains a need and potential for DTT to develop in technological terms as a key distribution platform safeguarding the legitimacy of PSM and for PSB to develop its public purposes in digital broadcasting.

In 2018, in recognition of the challenging contexts for the institutionalization of public service media institutions, the EU initiated and funded the 'Technical Assistance to Public Service Media in the Western Balkans' project, which, excepting Croatia, includes all of the countries in the above analysis. With EUR 1.5 million of funding, it is overseen by the EBU and a consortium of media and journalism related bodies. The project aims are to strengthen interregional cooperation between Western Balkan public service broadcasters through focusing on the enhancement of their institutional autonomy and financial sustainability. It also targets cooperation around journalistic protection and the extension of journalistic freedom. Arising out of this, in 2020, a memorandum of understanding on common principles for public service media governance was signed. Also, in 2018, the EU launched the Digital Agenda for the Western Balkans to invest EUR 30 million in broadband development and develop regulatory and economic conditions for increased digitalization of the economy and society as part of a wider reform process to drive forward integration.

Medium Convergence and the Digital Ecosystem

Concurrent to the digitalization of broadcasting, PSM are reacting to successive waves of techno-economic change centered on the internet/broadband through the development of web offerings, streamed media, on-demand players, over the top applications, mobile-ready services, social media presence, and other evolving forms. Technology, economics, and policy (external conditions) together with an evolving vision for PSM have helped determine how different broadcasters in different states have been able to react to these developments. A recent study of media organizations by Reuters suggests that internally, successfully adapted media organizations display a commitment to a pro-digital culture and permanent adaptation to an evolving technological context characterized by change (Sehl, Cornia and Nielsen 2016). Internally, at the level of production, this entails the development of a production culture attuned to the complex media system and built around the existing media advantages of a given organization (broadcast content aggregation and packaging, production of broadcast appropriate cultural forms, maintenance of broadcast distribution platforms) and the extension of those advantages into content service provision in digitally networked contexts (Picard 2010). The broad paradigm is summarized as Create Once, Publish Everywhere (COPE). Additionally, public service media must extend existing public purposes (citizenship, quality, universality) and develop new ones appropriate for new political, economic, and techno-economic contexts.

Whereas the digital transition entails significant external costs, its occasion is also the justification for PSB's internal upgrading in terms of resources and political support. Internally, adaptation to a complex value network entails a new framework for the public service production culture. Organizational restructuring, digital infrastructure development, the development of new roles relationships and practices, upskilling and reskilling, and a managerial ethos attuned to the range of possibilities presented through content service provision and co-creation, content service and technology consumption. All of these adaptations are further costs for public service organizations and represent adjustments that entail a significant investment of time and resources. Table 15.1 below gives a brief overview of the detail of internal adjustment along these lines. Consequently, these adjustments must be met by a governance and policy approach that privileges PSM within a multi-platform media system (see final section).

Table 15.1: Aspects of Digital Transformation

Internal Restructuring: New Departments Department Merging	e.g. creation of focused digital departments, centralization of distribution strategies, merging of radio, television and online to create awareness and synergies across different areas of service delivery
Digital Infrastructure Development: Digitization of production	e.g. the development and adaptation of internal end-to-end workflow systems that enable increased control and coordination of content across services, platforms, and distribution channels
New Roles, Relationships and Practices	e.g. appointment of digital managers, development of content management roles and relationships Digital Analyst/Web Analyst Digital-ready production staff (Digital producers) Creation of relationships between content, design, and technology staff
Upskilling/Reskilling	Opportunities for existing staff to adapt to digital production tools Continuous instruction around technology/ market/user/public developments
Managerial/Production Culture	Content production attuned to the COPE dynamic and potential 360-degree production Attention to interactivity (producer-public, public to public, public-content) Adaptation of digital storytelling dynamics (trans-media storytelling) Digitally generated content (data journalism, CGI, and graphical content, etc.) Focus on medium advantages and evolving AV eco-system surrounding it.

Source: The author.

Whereas the digitalization of broadcast distribution is the occasion for the repositioning of broadcasting within wider digital infrastructures, the internal adaptation involves organizational adjustments that will enable PSM to adapt to unpredictable digital evolutions according to public purposes. In this regard, the digital transition predicates or helps sustain success in linear television and radio broadcasting but also is the occasion for capital investment in organizational readjustment that retains medium-specific advantages with new networked interactive opportunities.

In 2016, internet penetration rates in the Western Balkans were closer to access rates in Western Europe in 2007. Since 2016, there has been a significant increase in internet penetration, but it is still behind the European average. The roll-out and diffusion of broadband have also accelerated in the period from 2016–2020 but there are still key access issues to be addressed concerning cost and the urban/rural divide. This partially explains the slow adjustment and development in the online strategies of public broadcasters. Liberalized convergence underpins digitalization and internet diffusion in Western Europe (of which DTT is an element). The liberalization of telecommunication markets and the creation of proto markets based on competitive dynamics and re-regulation are partially driven by commercial investment and state coordination/re-regulation. These dynamics create infrastructures and sources of demand for new networked audiovisual services. This is why DTT (above) also serves as an indicator of the likely development of competition in telecommunications that will drive internet roll out and drive up broadband speeds. DTT acts as both an incentive for digitalization and frees up bandwidth that in the EU has been auctioned primarily to diffuse 4G and next-generation mobile broadband (LTTC/5G). It is this wider context that suggests the technological capacity for Serbia, North Macedonia, and Montenegro may develop more quickly based on their governance capabilities. However, the internal organizational preparation for increased internet diffusion and increased broadband speed, and the multiple services and platforms that it will enable, is a priority for PSM. Wider state adaptation to regulation and policy that encourages public purposes in networked settings is also necessary.

Croatia has a functionally institutionalized PSB organization and the early digital transition has also made significant advances in adjusting to the complex media ecology. As of 2019 82.2% of the population has access to the internet (IREX 2019, 40). Recent legislation (2010) enables the extension of HRT into multimedia and online content services. HRT has developed its web presence since 1995 and has digitized its internal production (file-based production system) from 2004. HRT has also undertaken internal restructuring creating generic production, program, technology, and business divisions, creating more synergies across media divisions. HRT has also rationalized its web and social media presence, employing generic policies and centralizing web activities. It also offers an online on-demand service. HRT's financial stability and continued relevance in the digital broadcasting environment has positioned it to internally fund these adjustments. An issue for Croatian adaptation is the pull towards commercial development of its new services based on its dependence on advertising revenue. Technological and platform adjustments need to be complemented with public value networks.

In Serbia, 72.9% of the population has access to the internet (IREX 2019, 104). The digital public purposes of RTS/RTV are also legislatively recognized but having recently navigated the digital transition it is not yet focused on the challenges of medium, industrial and device convergence. RTS has however digitalized its internal production systems as required to do so under legislation from 2002 and set up a digital division. RTV has begun to centralize its newsroom to utilize regionally produced content across its networks. Both have well-developed web sites. RTS.rs (domestic rank of 46 in Alexa) has a regularly updated web presence that includes multimedia, live and streamed services but suffers from design shortcomings. RTS and RTV have also made apps available for various platforms but a fully functional on-demand, over the top player, is not yet available for either service. RTV and RTS have also responded to Web 2.0 by creating platform managers and distributing content and operating across various social networks, specifically YouTube and Facebook. Media producers are upskilling in digital production techniques. In the case of RTS, its lean towards commercial populism also calls into question its potential negotiation of public network opportunities.

North Macedonia and Montenegro both exhibit challenging economic circumstances and a fragmented media landscape as well as social and political contexts that undermine public institutions. In North Macedonia, 50% of the population has access to the internet (IREX 2016, 80). North Macedonia's MRT struggles with funding and has relatively low viewing figures. The regulator has, however, encouraged its expansion into digital media services. MRT's website (MRT.com.mk) provides a breaking news service and on-demand services but lacks the application of multimedia and is not comprehensive in its news updates. MRT also has a presence across social media including Twitter, Facebook, and YouTube, and offers a selection of on-demand programs online. It has yet to develop platform ready on-demand/streaming applications. Otherwise, MRT exhibits little attempts at restructuring, infrastructure upgrade, new internal roles, or a shift in the culture of production. Political control and underfunding block developing digital strategies that would enable the institution to become more interactive with its many publics. In Montenegro, 71.27% of the population has access to the internet (IREX 2019, 64). Montenegro's RTCG also operates in challenging political and economic circumstances. RTCG's internal digitalization process is much needed, as the broadcaster's infrastructure is antiquated. With support from the European Commission, upgrading began in 2014 and is happening in several phases whereas upskilling and reskilling with international agencies are taking place in 2016. RTCG manages a live web site (rtcg.me) that is also a portal for accessing streamed live radio and television. The website does little to incorporate multimedia and has no on-demand function for radio and television programs, but its domestic ranking on Alexa has moved from 104 in 2017 to 28 in 2020. It has also moved into the development of apps to reach younger demographics accessing content via smartphones. Without internal restructuring the interface with multiple content services provision is absent.

Albania and Kosovo are two small states, the former achieving switchover in 2019 and the latter yet to achieve digital switchover. In Albania, figures for 2016 show that 59.42% of the population has access to the internet (IREX 2016, 4). Albania's RTSH was chiefly preoccupied with the digitalization of the distribution process and has until recently had few resources for internal restructuring and digitalization. It was enabled by legislation in 2013 to upgrade its production infrastructure but this depends on central funds from the state to do so. From 2017, renewed efforts and investments have been made to upgrade production facilities and to expand into networked content services. The once rudimentary website (rtsh.al) has been upgraded to offer multiple radio and television streaming services. In 2017, the RTSH Tani app was also launched, enabling access to all of RTSH's digital television channels (live and catch-up) via both iOS and Android platforms. It has also developed an app to access its main radio station. It is active across Facebook and YouTube. The extension across platforms offers possibilities for greater civic partnerships and public participation.

In Kosovo, 88% of the population has access to the internet (IREX 2019, 64). RTK is involved in the digital transition and is legislatively required to explore multiple distribution and content service options. It digitalized its internal production structure and has drawn on international assistance (Japanese International Development Agency) to adjust to a digital culture of production, developing its newsroom as an integrated media service. Its online presence (rtklive.com) has little reach and impact but this may change as it enhances its multimedia elements. It has recently added the online live streaming of all of its digital television channels. It has also developed iOS and Android mobile access to its channels but no independent on-demand player. It is active across social media networks. There is a lack of adjustment internally to its expanded role but also a lack of political will and public funding to develop as a public service media organization.

In BiH, 86.77% of the population has access to the internet (IREX 2019, 14). RTRS has begun upgrading its production structure and moving towards integrated internal structures (radio, television, and online). All three broadcasters (RTRS/rtrs.tv BHRT/bhrt.ba and RTVFBiH/federalna.ba) do have web operations and have developed various means of accessing broadcast content. The websites, however, offer limited interactivity and are producing little that is innovative in terms of narrative/multimedia/interactive forms and functions. They lack on-demand services. They are all active across social networks but only RTRS has developed stand-alone applications. These websites do not have extensive reach which helps to legitimize the newer concepts of universality as developed by the EBU (the most developed, RTRS, ranks just 109 in Alexa's domestic rankings). There is a limited internal adaptation to the digital challenge. As noted in the former section, the Joint Corporation for PSB was intended to coordinate a development strategy as well as a technical and organizational upgrade but has yet to be developed. At a regulatory level, the CRA has done little to update or adapt regulation for the complex media system. Combined with funding crises (see above), a lack of political will, and public interest, the necessary conditions for organizational adaptation on the part of public service broadcasters are all but missing. These external conditions are matched by an organizational culture that lacks the capacity and motivation to exact change in the production culture.

Lack of political will and popular support, funding crises, and underdeveloped regulatory adjustment to debate and develop networked and non-linear public service media are notable in many cases (BiH, Montenegro, North Macedonia, Serbia). Requisite funding to invest in an internal upgrade, retrain, reskill, and restructure is absent also in many cases (BiH, Kosovo, Albania, North Macedonia). Twinned with an internal managerial and production culture that is unwilling and unable to change (BiH, North Macedonia, Montenegro), the prospects for transition to public value networks could be limited to incremental adjustments to software, platform, and device contexts. However, given the late diffusion of the internet and broadband and some of the policy problems associated with it (as discussed below), internal adaptation and restructuring may be best served by more modest platform strategies combined with a value network orientation. Given the rapid diffusion of mobile broadband and smartphone take-up across the region, mobile distribution and on-demand strategies that create focal points for public participation and co-creation may be a key strategic orientation. Changing consumption patterns of PSM in Western Europe show a widening socio-demographic gap. Younger, more pluralistic audiences that consume material online, across platforms, and via mobile devices are deserting public service broadcast media. An internal restructuring that strives for quality production and co-production with the public, and the repurposing of that content for networked and mobile contexts, presents a logical strategy. Multiform audiovisual content, distribution strategies, and co-creation/co-production based around broadcast forms may offer a midterm strategy that ensures continued reach in both broadcast and networked, linear and non-linear contexts.

Policy and the Evolving Digital Ecology

Renewed public purposes, internal restructuring for adaptation to the value network model of operation, a re-oriented production culture, and continued political, economic, and social support are necessarily entangled aspects of the transition to public service media. The complexity of the evolving media ecology entails adaptation to continuous change and varied combinations of media technologies, practices, intermediaries, and artifacts. However, as the phrase suggests, evolution is a slow process and does not entail the wholesale replacement or transplantation of media forms and media institutions. Change and adaptation can be facilitated through attention to the legislation, practices, infrastructure, and values that support public media in changed techno-economic circumstances. In complex social systems, technology is integrated with politics, economics, and culture and for this reason, the contours of the digital transition and PSM within it will be different for each state. The peculiar contexts that pertain to the Balkan states suggest this institutional development exists in precarious circumstances. Adaptation is piecemeal and is led by technological emphases (adjustment to the newest and latest platforms) and the structural adjustment to the complex media ecology is, in many cases, absent. As noted, there is also the absence of an extended vision of public purposes in networked media that is not simply led by, and deferential to the logic of, developments in platform capitalism and/or Western European models of PSM. However, there has been significant investment in the transition to digital television and terrestrial free-to-air broadcasting remains an important aspect of the various media systems.

The power struggles to define the future of audiovisual media is one important aspect of the evolving media system and the varied economic, political, and social institutions, interests, and ideas that constitute the digital media ecology. Broadcasting is no longer a discrete activity and the blurring of boundaries concerning its technologies, media forms, and audiences' consumption habits is an articulation of digitalization. At present, there are two powerful imaginaries: a vision of a future hybrid digital media system with the remediation of broadcasting within a patchwork of mixed delivery platforms or a post-broadcast media system characterized by broadband-based distribution to IP based technologies converging towards total online media consumption. The current research presents strong evidence to suggest that the hybrid media system persists and digital broadcasting, if politically and economically supported, can continue to be a socially, politically, and culturally important aspect of the media system as well as offering technological affordances that are inimitable to democratic cultures (Ala-Fossi, forthcoming). Political will and policy can address the question, not just of the place of PSM in the digital ecology, but the place of broadcasting as a historically contingent medium within that system.

The concept of a post-broadcast future for PSM has been strengthened by the recent commitments of Finland's YLE and the UK's BBC to gradually move towards a fully IP-based broadband-enabled distribution model (Ala-Fossi and Lax 2016). This is a vision of the future that has been sold also by mobile phone and various IP-based industries keen to strategically define future developments within their interests whilst wrapping it up in a bow of technological inevitability. It is also politically popular with governments who will eye up the release of the valuable spectrum from terrestrial broadcast systems and the larger strategies of moving as many public services online to support the digital roll-out, take up and development. However, this vision was called into question in recent debates over the future of spectrum allocations within the ITU 2012 and 2015 meetings with the European Commission accepting projections that linear broadcast distribution systems will continue to be an important part of the mixed distribution system until at least 2025 and will be reviewed again thereafter. This suggests a mid-term future for broadcasting that is a hybrid mix of distribution systems, platforms, program and service forms, and consumption habits with a longer future that may entail the incorporation of broadcasting into fully broadband/ IP-based systems of production, distribution, and consumption. Negotiating the mid-term future is key to positioning well for the long haul.

Policy developments at the national and transnational levels indicate the evolutionary development of regulation that is sensitive to both convergence and internationalization. The concept of governance alerts us to the multi-level, multi-sphere contexts within which national policies operate. Increasingly, converging technologies, markets, and platforms are blurring the boundaries between media, and regulation needs to also move across those boundaries. At a structural level, this means increased coherence of telecommunications, online and media-specific regulation to take into account the dynamics of digitally mediated communication. It also points to the development of different regulatory styles including top-down regulation, co-regulation, and self-regulation. At the core of governance and policy, principles offer guidance for coherent actions at multiple sites and levels.

In the report "The Future of Television," a Goldsmiths based research team points to the general conditions necessary for institutionalizing PSM in the hybrid media system (Freedman et al. 2016). PSM, which supports trust, diversity, universal provision, and quality in the media system, must be addressed through organizational development, governance, and sustainable funding mechanisms. First, governance structures should guarantee the independence of regulation as well as adhering to principles that constitute public service development as not just a function of market failure. Public services institutions and their missions should be statutorily recognized, independently governed, and involve representation/input of diverse communities. Funding should be proportionate and recognize the variety of content forms and distribution systems that PSM travels through moving to stable subsidies through general taxation and/or household taxes.

The economic and social sustainability of national broadcasting ecologies is another central policy issue. The development of competition from global audiovisual services and the migration of advertising online are just two of the effects of waves of technological change centered on digitalization and market- centric governance. The traditional policy tools of public service, license fees, subsidies, quotas, ownership and control regulation, license commitments and tax breaks can all be reconfigured to support indigenous and culturally relevant audiovisual services and industries attentive to the new dynamics of the value network system of production. As Park et al. (2015) suggest, broadcasting policy can be reformed in a context where markets and national boundaries are blurring. Policy and regulation can continue to support the economic sustainability and cultural value of audiovisual industries in national, regional, and local contexts. A systemic approach to public service media that goes beyond individual institutions is an important element of sustaining public service logic and values that are mutually reinforcing. Vibrant public service content on commercial or community channels and a healthy independent sector with a commitment to public service values are all parts of the public service production ecology. One example of this is the targeted investment and tax incentives in genre-specific co-productions that created enough critical mass to enable high quality content for local audiences to also compete in international markets or on non-linear on-demand services such as Netflix (e.g., children's animation in Ireland, Scotland, Wales and England, and crime drama in the Nordic countries).

Recognizing and enabling the development of myriad public service content across different media forms, infrastructures and platforms has been one reaction to the hybrid media system at the national level in Western Europe as has the development of regulatory systems to take into account public purposes in linear and non-linear audiovisual services at the European level (e.g., the AVMSD). Regulatory mechanisms also need to continue to support the prominence, findability, and accessibility of public service content across distribution systems, platforms, and consumption devices. This involves incentive regulation and "must be found" provisions (Hege 2013). Examples of this include the guaranteed position of channels on electronic program guides, app presence on smart TVs, and the interfaces of on-demand devices, prominence of content, or at least content neutrality within search results/browsers, and presence across content platforms. The gate-keeping function of new intermediaries such as social media, technology companies, and ISPs thus becomes an area of concern, and regulation needs to span both content and network regulation (Foster 2015). A related regulatory issue is the so-called value gap that has emerged within the hybrid media system wherein the value of content does not accrue to its creators as it is distributed across platforms. Ensuring, for example, that satellite distribution companies pay a fair price for public service channels is one way of closing the value gap, as are possible levies on technology companies who have centralized due to network effects, and internet service providers, both of which benefit from high-quality content production (Freedman et al. 2016).

Regulating across distribution systems, platforms and consumer devices requires multi-agency and multi-level policy coordination. In the hybrid media system, the focus remains on the continued strength of linear broadcast services across multiple distribution infrastructures and the possibility of leveraging attention and visibility in the online multimedia domain. Several analyses, however, point to the pitfalls of assuming that the institutional features of public service media, and indeed the basic principles of democratic media policy, can be easily transposed into a post-broadcast environment of near-total broadband and IP-based production, distribution, and consumption. Conjoining content, platform, and distribution regulation comes up against contradictory structural, economic, and institutional logic in a purely online environment. Dealing with these issues poses significant challenges for media policy makers (Ala-Fossi 2014). Accessibility to the open internet is predicated on the availability of broadband even as it in itself is not subject to universal service obligation. The degree and extent of access are based on the ability to pay distinctions (network, service, and device issues) that exacerbate information inequality and are inherently biased against high-level data consumption associated with broadcast content. These factors undermine universality principles. Vulnerability to the operating models of network/intermediary/platform operators also undermines the independence and autonomy of public service institutions. All intermediaries and gatekeepers have the potential to influence content creation. IP-based distribution also calls into question citizenship principles as citizens who access content via IP-based devices are open to both state and commercial surveillance to an unprecedented degree.

Conclusion

As the EU turns its attention from the digital switchover to the digital single market, attention to member states', and potential member states', democratic digital media policy becomes increasingly important. Broadcasters are in the process of managing the digitalization of distribution and production, and, reorientation to the wider dynamics of digitalization as a society-wide process. Policymakers are concurrently negotiating digital switchover, digitalization of society, and the re-institutionalization of public media principles and purposes within the media ecosystem. It is proposed here that the transition and maintenance of free-to-air broadcasting into the digital future create the bedrock for public broadcasters to transition to PSM and that remediated forms of broadcasting paired with public network development offer a potential re-articulation of mediated public space within the evolving media ecology. To get there requires consonance and coordination on the part of public media organizations, policymakers, governments, and the public. This, rather than technological development, would appear to be the core challenge for the Western Balkan states.

The remediation of free-to-air broadcasting and its institutionalization as a public service is important because it makes possible media that have public value and continue to be popular, universal, accessible, and, ideally, democratically controlled. The remediation and renewal of PSB as PSM offers a potential route to some form of media autonomy in the face of the new intermediaries and gatekeepers that increasingly dominate the global digital media ecology (Moore and Tambini 2016). Remediated broadcast forms, technologies, and institutional frameworks can continue to be important resources in sustaining democracy, civility, and intersubjective reasoning. These would appear to be priority goals in the Western Balkans where institutions of democracy are, at varying levels, threatened by public indifference, state capture, political hostility, and the under-realization of civil society. At a time of extremes and where various agencies are attempting to shape the media system, governance and policy ought to continue to prioritize the place of broadcasting and its democratic institutional features within the actually existing hybrid media system and the evolving digital media ecology. Concurrently, traditional broadcasters in the Balkans, as elsewhere, can innovate to extend and renew broadcast distribution, forms, and content in a digital ecology by moving to the public value network production paradigm. A multi-level policy that privileges public service content in a convergence oriented multi-platform environment is the quid pro quo for such innovation.

References

Ala-Fossi, Marko. 2014. "PSM dilemmas with Net Neutrality." Paper presented at the RIPE@2014 Conference, Tokyo, August 27–29.

—. Forthcoming. *Switchover or Switch Off?* Nordicom.

—, and Stephen Lax. 2016. "The Short Future of Public Broadcasting: Replacing Digital Terrestrial Television with Internet Protocol?" *The International Communication Gazette* 78, no. 4 (February): 365–382.

Beutler, Roland. 2016. *Evolution of Broadcast Content Distribution.* Cham: Springer.

Born, Georgina, and Tony Prosser. 2003. "Culture and Consumerism: Citizenship, Public Service Broadcasting and the BBC's Fair Trading Obligations." *The Modern Law Review* 64, no. 5 (February): 657–687.

Brevini, Benedetta. 2013. *Public Service Broadcasting Online: A Comparative European Policy Study of PSB 2.0.* Basingstoke: Palgrave Macmillan.

Chadwick, Paul. 2013. *The Hybrid Media System: Politics and Power.* Oxford: Oxford University Press.

Dal, Yong Jin. 2013. *Deconvergence of Global Media Industries.* London: Routledge.

Directive 2010/13/EU of the European Parliament and Council on the coordination of certain provisions laid down by law, regulation and administrative action in member states concerning the provision of audiovisual media services (Audiovisual Media Services Directive). *Official Journal of the European Communities* L95: 1–24.

European Audiovisual Observatory. n.d.-a. *MAVISE Database: Albania.* Accessed May 11, 2020. http://mavise.obs.coe.int/f/ondemand/advanced?countryofestablishment=4.

European Audiovisual Observatory. n.d.-b. *MAVISE Database: Bosnia and Herzegovina.* Accessed May 11, 2020. http://mavise.obs.coe.int/f/ondemand/advanced?countryofestablishment=15.

European Audiovisual Observatory. n.d.-c. *MAVISE Database: Croatia.* Accessed May 11, 2020. http://mavise.obs.coe.int/f/ondemand/advanced?countryofestablishment=88.

European Audiovisual Observatory. n.d.-d. *MAVISE Database: Montenegro.* Accessed May 11, 2020. http://mavise.obs.coe.int/f/ondemand/advanced?countryofestablishment=123.

European Audiovisual Observatory. n.d.-e. *MAVISE Database: North Macedonia.* Accessed May 11, 2020. http://mavise.obs.coe.int/f/ondemand/advanced?countryofestablishment=125.

Foster, Robin. 2015. "Access to Platforms and Findability of Content." Paper presented at EBU expert workshop on platform regulation, November.

Freedman, Des, Chris Tryhorn, Vana Goblot, Georgina Born, Pat Loughrey, Andrew Chitty, Andrew Griffee, Neil Watson, Sue Clayton, Sir David Normington, Omega Douglas, and Baroness Onora O'Neill. 2016. *A Future for Public Service Television: Content and Platforms in a Digital World.* London: Goldsmiths University of London. http://futureoftv.org.uk/wp-content/uploads/2016/06/FOTV-Report-Online-SP.pdf.

Głowacki, Michał, and Alicja Jaskiernia. 2018. *Public Service Media Renewal: Adaptation to Digital Network Challenges.* Frankfurt am Main: Peter Lang.

Hege, Hans. 2013. "Neutrality versus Priority in the Net—Facing the Challenges of Convergence." In *Digitisation 2013: Broadcasting and the Internet—Thesis, Antithesis, Synthesis?* edited by Andreas Hamann and Kristian Kunow, 9–15. Berlin: Die Medienanstalten. https://www.die-medienanstalten.de/fileadmin/user_upload /die_medienanstalten/Publikationen/Digibericht_Video_19/Digitalisierungsbericht_Video_2018/Digitalisierungsbericht_Archiv/DigiBericht_2013_englisch.pdf.

IREX. 2019. *Media Sustainability Index: The Development of Sustainable Independent Media in Europe and Eurasia 2019.* Washington, DC: IREX. Accessed January 15, 2020. https://www.irex.org/sites/default/files/pdf/media-sustainability-index-europe-eurasia-2019-full.pdf.

——. 2016. *Media Sustainability Index: The Development of Sustainable Independent Media in Europe and Eurasia 2016.* Washington, DC: IREX. Accessed May 8, 2002. https://www.irex.org/sites/default/files/pdf/media-sustainability-index-europe-eurasia-2016-full.pdf.pdf.

Mansell, Robin. 2016. "Media Convergence Policy Issues." *Oxford Research Encyclopedia of Communication.* Accessed May 11, 2020. https://oxfordre.com/communication / view/10.1093/acrefore/9780190228613.001.0001/acrefore-9780190228613-e-62.

Marko, Davor. 2019. "PSM Transformation in Western Balkan Countries." In *Public Service Broadcasting and Media Systems in Troubled Democracies,* edited by Eva Potonska and Charlie Beckett, 177–191. Basingstoke: Palgrave Macmillan.

Milosavljević, Marko, and Sally Broughton Micova. 2013. "Because We Have To: Digitalization of Terrestrial Television in South Eastern Europe." *International Journal of Digital Television Volume* 4, no. 3 (September): 261–277.

Moore, Martin, and Damian Tambini. 2016. *Digital Dominance: The Power of Google, Amazon, Facebook and Apple.* Oxford: Oxford University Press.

Park, Sora, Charles H. Davis, Franco Papandrea and Robert G. Picard. 2015. *Domestic Content Policies in the Broadband Age: A Four-country Analysis.* Canberra: University of Canberra. https://www.canberra.edu.au/research/faculty-research-centres/nmrc/publications/documents/Domestic-Content-Policy-Report.pdf.

Picard, Robert G. 2010. *Value Creation and the Future of News Organizations: Why and How Journalism Must Change to Remain Relevant in the Twenty-First Century.* Lisbon: Media XXI.

Pierson, Jo, and Joke Bauwens. 2015. *Digital Broadcasting: An Introduction to New Media.* London: Bloomsbury.

Sehl, Annika, Alessio Cornia and Rasmus Kleis Nielsen. 2016. *Public Service News and Digital Media.* Oxford: Reuters Institute for the Study of Journalism. https://reutersinstitute.politics.ox.ac.uk/sites/default/files/research/files/Public%2520Service%2520News%2520and%2520Digital%2520Media.pdf.

Simon, Jean Paul. 2016. "Moving to Digital Media Worlds: Three Successive Transformational Waves." In *Digital Media Worlds: The New Economy of Media,* edited by Giuditta De Prato, Esteve Sanz and Jean Paul Simon, 27–41. Basingstoke: Palgrave Macmillan.

UBO Consulting. 2015. *Media Indicators 2015: A Thorough Study from a Journalists' Point of View on Kosovo's Media Freedom and Conditions.* Prishtina: Kosovo Glocal— Kosovo 2.0, COHU and Kosovo Press Council. http://mediaobservatory.net/library/kosovo-media-indicators-2015.

CHAPTER 16

State of the Art and the Future of Public Service Media in the Western Balkans

Barbara Thomass

Introduction

Since the end of communist rule, the dissolution of the former Yugoslav state, the wars which accompanied these overthrows, and the end of communism in Albania, many of the societal structures had been changed, with the perspectives to build modern nations with strong institutions. These changes happened in the former Yugoslav states in a post-conflict situation, with all the implications a weak and unstable statehood creates. The international community, mainly the Council of Europe and the European Commission, were important drivers of these changes, which were brought to a variety of social institutions. One crucial element of this nation-building and social change was broadcasting. As the media had played a rather destructive role during the Yugoslav wars, and independent media were an object of permanent oppression and discrimination, it seemed to be a consequent endeavor to focus on the mediascape in order to support a democratic transition. The reconstruction of the former state-owned electronic media was affected following the pattern of the public service broadcasting/public service media (PSM) institutions that were since long established in Western Europe and which were in the phase of their emergence an expression of the welfare state.

The previous chapters show the state of development and the role of PSM, as well as the prospects for further development, in seven countries of the Western Balkans—Albania, Croatia, Bosnia and Herzegovina (BiH), Kosovo, Montenegro, North Macedonia, and Serbia. The overall picture is not encouraging. Even if one admits that PSM can take on many forms, the analysis reveals that PSM in the Western Balkans is far from being a success story. The reasons are manifold. As PSM is a public institution that is highly embedded in the historical, cultural, and political conditions of a given society, any comparison, which wants to answer these questions, and any explanations for the current state must account for those contextual specifics. Moreover, an evaluation of the state of PSM also needs common criteria for such a comparison. The following concept provides this ground.

PSM, at its core, is an institution for public communication which needs solid funding as protection against market forces. It is orientated to cultural, social, and democratic obligations, which are laid down in the remit, and these privileges and obligations must be secured by public control, which ensures its independence. This public control is not valuable if there are no strong links to society. The remit, the public control, and the links PSM maintain towards society can be regarded as the legal and political factors that have been analyzed in this study. In addition, given the importance of adaptation of PSM to the changes of the digital mediascape, innovation is a further core element of its viability which refers to the challenges of digitization. These three elements—funding, the remit in connection with the independence of the organization, and its capacity for, and a real implementation of innovation—are the factors that influence the future of PSM. They are the factors according to which the state and the prospects of PSM in the Western Balkans are evaluated in this chapter. Special attention will be paid to the interdependence of these factors, i.e., if a certain degree of the solidity of funding promotes innovation, or if links to society augment the independence of PSM or vice versa.

The introduction of PSM in post-communist countries is so "extraordinarily difficult to achieve ... that it could be regarded as a true test of post-communist transformation overall, specifically in terms of the consolidation of democracy" (Jakubowicz 2004, 54). If this test can be regarded as successful or not, and what are the reasons for this outcome is the question for this concluding chapter, which concentrates on the present and tries an outlook for the future. A common observation for the countries under study is that the communist period from 1950 to 1990, as well the years of the 1990s, can be described for most of the countries as the period of state television, which is understood as an opposite to PSM. Only in the early 2000s did the governments loosen the grip on the state-owned broadcasters, and they began to achieve a certain amount of independence. Since then, the international community had, and in some countries still has, a strong influence on the shape of the mediascapes in the Western Balkans. This common starting point allows for some comparative considerations, although the comparison cannot be drawn in all aspects. Lacking adequate and up to date data is a common problem for all the countries under study so that we cannot draw a reliable comparison on funding schemes, market share, and similar aspects of their operations. Especially data that would allow comparison of the financial situation of the PSMs to the overall economic situation are not available. But we can look, as stated before, to the situation in legal and technological dimensions, as well as the general funding situation of the broadcasting institutions.

The Legal Dimension, Remit, and the Independence of the Organization

Looking at the legal dimension is the first and most important aspect to understand the situation of a public broadcaster in a given country. The legal foundation determines the character of the remit which has itself a decisive impact on the performance of a public broadcaster with respect to the programs. The given broadcasting law and its implementation have an impact on the independence of the organization, which is a prerequisite for a true public service orientated program. Moreover, the way a public service broadcaster communicates with its audience is to a great extent dependent on the level of its independence. Therefore, the legal framework and its implementation, the formulation of the remit, the state of independence, and the connection to and with the audiences are the factors that are considered first in a comparative perspective.

The change of the legal grounds of the former state broadcasters was a main endeavor after the political changes. Either the governments themselves were willing to give the hitherto state broadcasters a new organizational form, or they were entering the path of independent broadcasting as a consequence of the consultation with EU representatives in the hope for accession to the EU.

In Albania, the transformation of the Albanian Radio and Television RTSH was started by Law No. 8410 on Public and Private Radio and Television in 1998 that was prepared with a great deal of support by several European institutions, such as the OSCE, the Council of Europe, the British Embassy and the British Council, as well as the US Embassy (see Chapter 2 by Bino in this volume). The remit is oriented to a public mission and stipulates the classical PSM remit. But the implementation of the law saw many inconsistencies. The fact that the ruling majority nearly constantly achieved control of the majority of seats in the regulatory authority, the National Council of Radio and Television (KKRT), led to the situation where clientelism ruled the governance and independence of the Albanian PSM was not achieved. Biased programming favoring the government and ignoring oppositional voices was the consequence. Bino did not find that RTSH was well connected to its audiences, which would be a sign of a real independent broadcaster and a chance for a greater variety of opinion in current affairs programs. With only 5-6% of the audience share at present RTSH is far from being a crucial media player in Albania (Reporters Without Borders and BIRN Albania, n.d.).

Bino shows that the media legislation and policy in Albania have not been driven by the public interest but have been affected by specific interests of certain political, economic, and media actors. They claim that a clear vision and strategy for the future development of media in line with the increasing demands of the public is missing. While media legislation only had been introduced after media realities such as commercial media, digital broadcasting, and online media were already in place, the media policy processes have been influenced by powerful media actors who pursue their own economic and political interest, rather than

the public interest. Given a weak civil society, there are no strong voices to advocate for the public interest in media policy and legislation.

In Bosnia and Herzegovina (BiH) the situation seems to be even worse
as described by Ahmetašević and Hadžiristić (see Chapter 3 in this volume):
it is an example of what was identified as a weak and selective rule of law while
ethnopolitics rule broadcasting policies, which is a permanent threat for an ethnically divided country like BiH. Although media reform was considered a key
in peacebuilding and democratization processes in BiH, the legal provisions for
one state-wide broadcaster and two entity broadcasters, which were imposed by the
Office of the High Representative (OHR)[1] in 2002, did not result in independent
broadcasters serving the whole country, but ended in failure. Not only were local
media experts and representatives of the entities hardly consulted, but the legal
framework was never fully implemented. The laws introduced by OHR in 2002
were updated between 2005 and 2008, giving BiH politicians enough room to
maneuver and to underperform in the PSM arena. The result was a far-reaching
political dependence of the PSMs and the politicization that is prevalent in the
influence of ruling political parties on the appointment of managerial positions
at entity PSMs. As consultation with BiH representatives was not sought, the
term of the PSM remit acting in the public interest was not defined precisely,
nor were the ideas of what it could mean debated. Independence of the PSM
in BiH has no chance because of the dominance of political parties in the PSM
system. Furthermore, the representation of minorities like Roma, Jews, and the
undeclared others, which could contribute to some differentiation of voices, are
excluded from PSM employment quotas. Thus, the political elite of the three
official constituents of BiH[2] maintain a damaging influence on the structure and
the staff, and the needed reconciliation of the different ethnic groups of the population cannot be supported by an unbiased information program. Connection
to, and communication with, civil society is an anathema, both in the regulatory
structures of PSB and in consultative processes.

The country failed with respect to all of the core elements of a public service media system: independence, remit, and, as we will see, the funding and
adoption of new technologies as well. It is now closer than ever to collapse and
faces key challenges: the lack of incentive for local elites to foster independent
public media, PSMs' lack of collective legitimacy, and institutional inertia within public broadcasting institutions. The unfinished transformation of Bosnia's
state broadcaster to public service broadcasting reflects the stagnation and "unfinished transition" plagued by state capture and crony capitalism. As the EU,
which started the process to implement PSM in BiH is no longer active in the
field and leaves the problem to the local politicians, two requirements seem pertinent: on the one hand is the necessity of incentive to transform PSM and underscore its legitimacy, while on the other is their bare survival in financial terms.

Croatia seems to be, despite some weaknesses and compared to PSM in the
rest of Western Balkans, an endangered success story (see Chapter 4 by Marko

---

[1]   The Office of the High Representative controls since 1995 the implementation of the Dayton
      Peace Accord of 1995. It was established by Resolution 1031 of the UN Security Council.
[2]   Bosniaks, Serbs, and Croats are referred to in the constitution as constituent nations, meaning
      that none of them can be considered a minority or immigrant.

in this volume). It shows financial stability and legal independence in combination with a lack of institutional independence and editorial autonomy. New broadcasting legislation was already introduced in 1990 after the first multi-party elections, but the Croatian Radio-Television (HRT) persisted as a state broadcaster until 2000 when the autonomy and independence of HRT and the role of PSM for the Croatian society became a hot topic of debate. The transformation of HRT from a state broadcaster into public service has taken place and it has been significantly influenced by a broad arrangement of stakeholders like local actors, media professionals, scholars, and policymakers. This was possible because authorities in the Republic of Croatia, despite their ideological orientation, acknowledged the need for media reforms. But more important, however, was the fact that the entire process was accelerated by the EU accession process which obliged Croatia to apply European standards and principles and to adopt its media-related legislation in line with the *acquis*. Accordingly, the external support of CoE, OSCE, and the EU to draft laws in line with established standards in the audiovisual domain helped to develop viable institutions.

The broadcasting law of 2010 prescribes the services of HRT as a public institution, and important for the implementation of true independence, precisely defines the process of nomination and election of the supervising program council members. The introduction of a Commissioner for Consumers in 2011 allowed PSM to relate better to audiences and improved programs. A new broadcasting law of 2012, which brought a new management structure, is criticized by the political opposition and other local actors as having reintroduced political influence over HRT. Especially since 2015, when a right-wing party came into government, misuse of public funds to promote their exclusive political interests can be observed, as Marko states. This indicates that PSB in Croatia is still highly vulnerable to political influence.

PSM in Kosovo was similar to the situation in BiH—established by external pressure after the end of the conflict there, which can be dated with the UN Security Council Resolution 1244 of June 1999 (see Chapter 5 by Miftari in this volume). The UN mission in Kosovo agreed in a Memorandum of Understanding with the European Broadcasting Union on the creation of a public service broadcaster which created the unique situation on the Western Balkans, that Radio-Television of Kosovo (RTK) could start without the heritage of having been a state broadcaster. In 2001, RTK was established as an independent public service broadcaster with a board of directors made up of local staff and a local Director-General. However, as a consequence of riots in Kosovo in 2004, international consultants and monitors from OSCE were imposed back at RTK until 2006. This international interference in editorial issues meant as well that locally based professionalization in leading the broadcaster could not truly be developed.

Only with the declaration of Kosovo's independence in 2008 was RTK handed over to local ownership. Since then RTK has been the political football of the several competing political groups, and the Kosovo case can serve as a telling example of how low preparedness for policy consensus led to media legislation driven along political party lines. Relevant legal provisions that determine how the board members are selected, and consequently, how the management is appointed, foil those provisions which demand that RTK pursue an independent editorial policy. Instead, as Miftari shows, RTK has a quasi-clientelist approach to programming and is subject to a conflict of interest. There is not a good chance that editorial independence of the public broadcaster can be guaranteed as the selection of board members, and consequently senior management appointments within RTK is done according to the affiliation with political parties. In addition, civil society representatives hardly have a chance to enter the board. The political play around RTK takes place without civil society.

PSM in Kosovo is presently in a precarious situation as insecure funding (see below) and a politically influenced management without independent control are serious shortcomings. It is an open question if a consensus can emerge within the political elite to understand that a depoliticized public service broadcaster is in everyone's interest, or if RTK moves closer to becoming a state broadcaster, meaning that it will lose influence, credibility, and ratings, thus steadily undermining itself down the road. A third possibility Miftari envisages is that RTK remains a powerful medium but still fully dependent on state funding with the consequences of lacking independence from politics. As the inception of PSB in Kosovo did not come hand in hand with higher levels of democratization, Miftari argues that the continued selective appropriation of the principles and guidelines that drive the rationale behind public broadcasting in the consolidated democracies have yielded a hybrid-model of PSB. He claims that the consolidation of public broadcasting service requires a certain threshold of democratization level to be passed in a given state, and this will take time and money for solid funding of PSM.

The example of Montenegro shows once again how the engagement of the international community that was not backed by local politicians failed to build a sustainable PSM (see Chapter 6 by Ružić in this volume). While the legal foundations were thoroughly elaborated, the political elites did not organize public hearings which would have enabled professionals, interested parties, and citizens to debate what was at stake. It happened later with the recent amendments of the law from 2002, but the reputation of PSM being controlled by the government was already established. Political problems are the most salient type of problems of PSB in Montenegro. Although the independence of the public broadcasting service is formally guaranteed, political pressures are exercised through many processes, mainly the appointment of managing staff which results in content inappropriate for public television and a lack of political pluralism throughout the program of PSB. Besides, an unsustainable funding model (see below) and permanent changes of the initially adopted legislation affected the status and operation of the public broadcaster. At least there are public debates about the independence of the public service and its editorial policy, although the recommendations of media professionals are not taken into account. Since the ruling party in Montenegro does not wish to let go of control over the public service, the new management of RTCG is facing numerous problems that hamper the work of the public service broadcaster. But the fact that the public service had positive financial results (see below) for the first time in 2015 gives reason for some optimistic prospects.

Looking at North Macedonia motivates Trpevska and Micevski to give Chapter 7 the promising title "Four Normative Principles for Participatory Public Service Model." Indeed, the broadcasting law of 1997, which was a step to become a member state of the Council of Europe and to envisage the accession process to the EU, created an organization that seemed to live up to the expectations one has towards a public broadcaster. However, the non-implementation of a new funding scheme brought the public broadcaster nearly to a breakdown. A new law that was finalized in 2013 disregarded positive experiences of civil society participation in the policy deliberations and reduced its representation in the supervisory board. Although the broadcasting law stipulates clear provisions concerning independence, diversity, and distinctiveness of the public broadcaster compared to commercial broadcasting, a severe political crisis in 2012 put the impartiality and accountability of the Macedonian PSM into question, revealing that the once formally agreed upon standards of unbiased reporting are burdened by ethnic conflict and the interests of the ethnopolitical elites. Recent developments show that the PSM editorial policy is in a heavy political party grip and that a pro-government bias is a rule.

Trpevska and Micevski identify an inverse process of transforming the public into a "party-political" broadcaster as the idea of the public interest in PSB was hijacked by political powers. PSB in North Macedonia face the challenges of market pressure from the commercial media and the pressing changes brought by the digital era (see below). The authors view the North Macedonian PSB as a clientelist resource that is monopolized and colonized, and excludes others from access to it. They do not expect a trend of democratic transformation and consolidation of the public broadcaster if the current tendency towards authoritarianism continues, as weak political and social institutions hinder the consolidation of PSB. They argue that a solid and stable connection with the citizenry and civil society, which might lead to a "Participatory Public Service Model" would help the PSM to gain its place in a democratic society.

With the stipulation in the media law from 2014, the formal prerequisites for an independent public service broadcaster are given in Serbia (see Chapter 8 by Marko in this volume). This amendment of the former law defined the ground that was laid for PSB by international actors (mainly the EU, CoE, and OSCE) more precisely. The new strategic and legislative framework in Serbia reflects the current principles and policies of the EU, especially regarding competition and state aid regulation. But although institutional safeguards for a functioning institution seemed to be set with the definition and tasks of the Steering Board and the Director-General, these mechanisms do not work in practice, as recent experiences demonstrate the lack of transparency, credibility, and independence in the work of the Steering Board. It neglected its duties in controlling the director, leading to heavy management mistakes and financial irregularities. Hence, the main criticism pertains to the governance of RTS, the lack of universality and plurality, the lack of financial transparency (see below), and the politicized procedure of electing the members of the regulatory body. In addition, the Regulatory Agency for Electronic Media (REM) failed to respect its supervisory duties towards the public broadcaster. The question remains if the newly elected Steering Board in 2016 will fulfill its duties in a more accountable manner.

Marko perceives PSB as an indicator of democratic development in Serbia, although it rarely demonstrated its capacity to be a vital vehicle driving the process of democratization. Again, the hope to come closer to the European Union was an incentive to adopt new media laws and procedures in line with European standards, but the essential change has not been achieved. However, it is an achievement that the structure of the PSB system in Serbia reflects the territorial organization of the state. RTV has an emphasized role in representing diversities with a special focus on national minorities and analyses of PSB content by media experts, which indicates a high level of content diversity, although this does not apply to informative programming, as Marko states. Serbian citizens continue to perceive RTS as reflecting the official government policy. Provisions which guarantee the editorial independence of public service broadcasters in Serbia were not established either in the law or in their internal acts. Still, PSB in Serbia has managed to become a popular media institution.

Comparing the legal dimension of PSM in the Western Balkans, three main factors are determining how stable PSM is. First, there is the involvement of societal representatives in the debate leading to a broadcasting law that plays an important role. Second, the eagerness of the international community and its tendency to impose models that might have been considered positive in different historical and cultural contexts brought no sustainable results. Third, the establishment of procedures of control and accountability must be successful to run an institution that delivers value for money and is managed professionally. These considerations will be examined further with a comparative look at the financial dimensions.

The Financial Dimension

Sufficient funding gives a public broadcaster independence and long-term security for planning and developing program schemes and innovation is the basis of success. In consequence, repeated struggles about funding schemes, the height of allocated funds, and obscure mechanisms of funding are the sources for damages of the reputation of a public broadcaster and often a pretext for political interventions. The mechanisms and procedures of funding, we can assume, are a test of the independence of a public broadcaster, on the one hand, and its professional management, on the other. Such examples of PSB organizations in the Western Balkans are manifold.

Astonishing enough, funding is, according to Bino (see Chapter 2 in this volume), not an issue for Albanian PSM. Its sources are threefold: a license fee, state funding, and advertising. It was possible to increase the income from the license fee to a share of nearly 60% in 2014, which should allow for certain independence from government interventions, while 25% of the budget comes from state funding and only a small amount from advertising and other sources. Nevertheless, inefficiency in collecting the license fees, which is connected to the electricity bill, and decreased funding from the state budget have put financial pressure on the broadcaster. This cannot be outweighed by other income, as non-transparent funding through advertising leads to the situation that the media, especially the public broadcaster, in Albania serves the interest of those who sponsor the adverts rather than that of the public. Big hopes for increased revenues are connected to the digital switchover which is expected to generate more advertising income. If these expectations come true is highly dependent on the success of digital innovation (see Chapter 14 by Broughton Micova and Chapter 15 by Murphy in this volume).

In BiH, the situation is characterized by a lack of funding, unpaid debt to the European Broadcasting Union, and severe disputes on funding along the ethnopolitical cleavages of the country (see Chapter 3 by Ahmetašević and Hadžiristić in this volume). The reason why the public broadcaster is so heavily indebted is that there is no agreement on a model of funding. Since nearly half of the population does not pay the license fee, the formal question of PSB financing dominates the political discussion. The core of the discussion is the question of what amount of funding should go to which of the entities and how much to the central broadcaster. This is linked to the aspect of different advertising incomes as the entities have a different stand on the advertising market. In Republika Srpska, the government tries to get hold of the public broadcaster of the entity by paying for the losses and undermining the already weak independence of RTRS. Thus, the ethnic divisions and competition are reflected in the debate on the allocation of the license fee, not allowing a coherent system that promotes PSB in the country as a whole. At the moment, the funding happens through unclear mechanisms without public control. As a consequence of inefficient license fee collection, funding from advertising is inappropriately high and connected to unfair competition. The unstable situation was aggravated even further as the previous funding system, based on a license fee collected through landline telephone bills, expired in June 2016 and no agreed-upon new system was introduced by the time of finalizing this book.

In contrast to BiH, according to Marko (see Chapter 4 in this volume), funding of public service broadcasting in Croatia is stable and a success story, although as a member of the EU it had to adopt new state aid regulations that halved the commercial incomes for PSB. One factor of the successful system is that there is a regulation that sets the amount of monthly fee to a maximum of 1.5% of the average salary in Croatia, based on statistical data for the previous year. The second factor is the existence of a separate organizational unit, Service for License Fee, as part of the HRT business department. This HRT system for license fee collection is accepted as it is one of the oldest in the region, developed and upgraded during a period of more than five decades. Furthermore, the system is well established and operates with cooperation with law offices, public notaries, and public institutions in the domain of finance. The financial operation of the public broadcaster lives up to standards of good governance. Accordingly, during the last three years, HRT established a more transparent and planned financial operation. HRT managed to operate with an annual profit, with a tendency of continuous growth, increased revenues, and rationalization of its expenditures. A transparent distribution system of the budget generated by the license fee might be a soft factor that supports the acceptance of the license fee as well.

The fate of the public broadcaster in Kosovo as a political hostage is especially obvious when it comes to the debate and the struggle about funding (see Chapter 5 by Miftari in this volume). Between 2003 and 2009 the license fee collected via Kosovo Electric Corporation (KEK) gave the public broadcaster a relatively secure funding and certain independence. But allegations of manipulation of public funds, mismanagement, and overspending, which can be found in a report submitted to the Kosovo Assembly, led to the fact that the public broadcaster came under the direct control of the assembly and the collection of the license fee via Kosovo Electric Corporation was declared as unconstitutional. Although the state funds were supposed to serve only during a transitional period, no solution was found to date to the pressing problem. From the side of the public broadcaster RTK, there were complaints that the United Nations Mission in Kosovo (UNMIK) did not provide support in continuing the collection of the license fee, despite the recommendations of the EBU. All this happened in a situation where Kosovo was still a society in the initial democratization stages and neither the notion of checks and balances nor the sense of a public broadcaster as a common public good were ingrained in the collective understanding of the public. So, it was easy to place RTK under political control while the commercial broadcasters were happy with a weakened competitor. RTK itself gave reasons to its pundits as allegations of lack of transparency, in particular with regards to the use of public funds to purchase programming or services from independent productions or sources that are regarded as clientelist networks of RTK, are often raised. A new law from 2012 promised to find a sustainable solution for the funding of RTK but to date, this has not happened.

Quite a range of the problems of the public broadcaster in Montenegro can be traced back to the inappropriate funding model (see Chapter 6 by Ružić in this volume). The funding law, prescribing a license fee and allowing for additional income from various sources, was taken over from the German example, a market and broadcasting situation very different from the one in Montenegro, which has an extremely small audience and market, thus generating small funds. The license fee was only a functioning model as long as it could be collected via Telekom. But once, Montenegro Telekom was privatized, this mechanism broke down, and the subsequent funding out of the state budget not only was insufficient but brought a greater dependency on the state. At least the fact that the public service since 2015 has had positive financial results, gives reason for some optimistic prospects.

The public service broadcasting in North Macedonia kept its funding model for a long time (see Chapter 7 by Trpevska and Micevski in this volume). The main source of funding for MRT was the broadcasting tax which was legally determined as a public charge. Since the late 1990s, the public broadcaster MRT had been facing financial and organizational problems, which generated a decline of audience share and the erosion of its credibility. Hence, debates on media legislation were largely focused on the improvement of the existing funding model. Nevertheless, the broadcasting tax was maintained when a new Law on Audio and Audiovisual Media Services was adopted in 2013. In September 2017, the new government abolished the broadcasting tax and adopted changes to the Law on Audio and Audiovisual Media Services according to which MRT is now funded from the state budget, thus making it more vulnerable to government interference.

In Serbia, funding, at the first sight did not seem to be a problematic issue, as the public broadcaster RTS had managed to become a popular and attractive media institution and was for a long time based mainly on a license fee as the main funding model, which was accompanied by commercial incomes until 2013 (see Chapter 8 by Marko in this volume). The reasonable audience shares meant that it was attractive for advertisers. The advertising revenue comes dominantly from the public companies and the government institutions, adding to the funds from the state budget. But despite these diverse sources, PSB in Serbia has failed to become financially stable and produces losses. Furthermore, the Anti-Corruption Council complained in 2015 about irregularities in the operation of RTS, claiming that RTS's income is higher than indicated. This illegal operation which persisted and the refusal of the managing director to be open to public scrutiny led to the fact that the license fee was abolished in 2014 and replaced by a tax. Hence, although Serbia had a well appreciated public broadcaster, its reputation was damaged. In consequence, it is even more subject, from 2016 onward, to the danger of direct political interference because of management deficiencies and incompetence.

The overlook of the experiences with different and changing funding models of PSB in the Western Balkans suggests that a stable system that is not altered with every new government best serves the purposes of a public broadcaster that has to compete in a diverse media market. As the market does not provide enough advertising income on the one hand, and would not create a programming content expected from a public broadcaster on the other, and because state funding makes PSB very vulnerable to political interference, a broadcasting tax or a license fee seem to be the most appropriate form of funding. However, the success of such public funding depends on its acceptance by the audiences that depends on transparent procedures and a program that gives the audiences an impression of value for money. In addition, properly set mechanisms of collection and legal enforcement of the collection of the license fee are needed. A further condition sine qua non for a stable financial operation of PSB is professional management that does not give a pretext for any political interference. Where one of these conditions was not given—and this is the case in many Western Balkan countries—public service broadcasters came into difficulties and are struggling to date.

The Technical Dimensions: Capacity for and Implementation of Innovation

Digitization and media convergence are the overall framing conditions under which the young public broadcasters in the Western Balkans must develop. This is, among other sociocultural factors that are not discussed in the previous chapters, a fundamentally different situation in comparison to the creation of public service broadcasters in Western Europe after World War Two. From the beginning of their existence, PSB in the Western Balkans had to compete with commercial broadcasters, a situation that was strengthened by developments of digitization and media convergence. This meant that the public service broadcasters, parallel to their political struggles, had to draw strategies on how to secure their existence in the converging media world. The success of these strategies was dependent, on the one hand, on the consensus with political actors about the strategy and its acceptance by the audiences, and on the other hand, on sound funding for technical innovations. Both conditions were rarely given, as a comparative analysis of the examples of Western Balkan PSB shows.

Looking at the transformation from analog to digital broadcasting and the use of new platforms and technologies the situation in the Western Balkans is quite diverse. Where stable political constellations or external support, mainly in funding, was provided, the switchover could happen more or less smoothly and with informing the citizens about the process and taking their needs into account. This was the case in Croatia. But in most of the studied countries, the move to a digital convergent media system seems to have been taken without consideration of the political and financial prerequisites. In addition, structural and management prerequisites for a successful media convergence are not given: as Chapter 12 by Głowacki demonstrates, the organizational separation into radio, television, and online forms follows separation and fragmentation within a single institution in the majority of case studies. The results of the technical transformation thus are ambivalent. Either the benefits are concentrated only in the hands of commercial entities as in North Macedonia, or the process is halted and does not provide new benefits for the audiences, like in Kosovo or BiH. International aid, like in Serbia or Montenegro, helped at least to move the process forward. It remains to be seen if it is to the advantage of the population.[3]

---

[3]   More details on the technical dimension in Chapter 14 by Broughton Micova and Chapter 15 by Murphy in this volume.

Conclusion and Prospects

The introduction of public service broadcasting in the Western Balkans was mainly initiated by different organizations and institutions of the international community. The formal establishment of PSM institutions on the Western Balkans is now fulfilled, but it is the question of whether they were successfully given life and a real meaning for the formation of opinion and the societal discourse in the public sphere and civil society.

Given the misuse of the state media and the biased information that fueled much of the conflicts during the 1990s and early 2000s, it is understandable that those with the power to change essential structures in the countries of former Yugoslavia tried to influence the restructuring of the media system as much as they could, and as the good examples in history advised. Thus, the implementation of public service broadcasting along the role model of the BBC in post-war Germany might have stood as a lighthouse of successful democratic transformation.

Although this is not the place to compare the historic situation of post-war Germany with the situation in the Western Balkans in the 1990s, it is fair to state that the political, economic, social and cultural situation of both cases is different in many aspects—the most important being a completely different media environment characterized by developing media abundance and a higher degree of competition on the media market than was the case in Germany. More importantly, the transfer of one organizational model to another country without considering the specific situation in that country must fail. The "mimetic transformation" (see Chapter 11 by Lowe in this volume) as a way of achieving approximation to "the West" and how it was conceived by the international community, did not consider how the emergence and stabilization of dual broadcasting systems was achieved in Western Europe in a process of *longue durée*. As Peruško argues (see Chapter 12 in this volume), the international community failed to understand that the context of the whole media and political system influences the possibility for imported models to be successfully applied. Therefore, the reforms in the media sector, especially the construction of PSB, failed, because they are dependent on the consolidation of democracy, the rule of law, and the strength of political institutions.

In addition, the governments of the countries of the Western Balkans were not prepared or willing to take on the effort to build truly independent broadcasters. The ambition to keep hold of a powerful thought instrument to influence the public opinion was, and is, too strong; the struggle to control the performance of public service broadcasting and to make it a tool of vested interests rather than the public interest has been too overt. It is not surprising that PSM in the Western Balkans, consequently, does not enjoy the amount of attention and appreciation by the audiences as was hoped-for by those working on the implementation of PSB.

Moreover, the introduction of PSM—its structure, controlling bodies, and the respective laws—happened under near total exclusion of the public sphere. Consultations with the whole spectrum of political actors—political parties, professionals, civil society, and others—did not take place. This might be due to time pressure, or simply to ignorance concerning the nature of PSM having its *raison d'être* in being of the public, for the public, and by the public. Audiences in the Western Balkans have experienced state broadcasters and their weak performance before the phase of media reform; afterward, they embraced the possibilities of the modern commercialized media environment very quickly. This context would have made it necessary to make the introduction of PSM an issue of the society, not only of the political administration and some technocrat experts, and to encourage civil society actors into the building and implementation of the PSB. Lowe (see Chapter 11 in this volume) emphasizes the development of civil society as the essential basis for democracy, and this is true for PSM as well.

Without a general acceptance of the idea of PSM in the public, it was not possible in most of the countries in the Western Balkans to guarantee stable funding of the public broadcasters. Either the license fee model did not work, or the funding from the state budget made the broadcasters vulnerable to political pressure, or the PSMs were left to the pressures of the market. In each of these cases, the management of the public broadcasters did not have the amount of financial security that is necessary for sustainable program planning, and could not implement the innovations that are required to guarantee viable and vital public service media for the future. The impact of the amount of funding on the lack of innovation is obvious, but there are significant structural barriers to adopting the public broadcasters of the Western Balkans to the digital mediascape.

However, even if taking inventory of PSM in the Western Balkans cannot come to an effulgent final assessment, we can give some scenarios under which the prospects of the public broadcasters might improve. A marginalization of PSM is the danger if the financial resources or the remit will remain or get further reduced, which will result in a loss of impact on the market. If PSM's role is diminished to the correction of market failures, or, if PSM tasks are assigned to commercial media through "de-institutionalization" of PSM, PSM will shrink in its significance for the public sphere. This will especially be the case if the close links between politicians and private media groups remain pertinent.

Even worse is the scenario in which PSM will be de-institutionalized radically. This might occur if there is a continued lack of funding, or the unwillingness to reform the PSM where necessary. When the state is in crisis and does not secure the existing conditions for PSM, the strong competition makes PSM a vulnerable player, and audiences, due to poor PSM performance, will turn away from the public broadcasters. As a consequence, PSM will become irrelevant and may disappear.

The role of the state is particularly important in the third scenario, which is the instrumentalization of PSM. If the government controls PSM and uses it as a propaganda machine, the already observed democratic deficiencies in regulating

PSM might become severe, and the erosion of public trust and the regression to state broadcasting is a possibility.

In the most optimistic scenario, PSM will be transformed through a substantial democratization process. Through external and internal pressure, it will adopt democratic standards and contribute to media freedom and pluralism in close relationship with the developing civil society. At best, an increased trust by the public and a better reach and audience share will result in a better contribution to democratization and society. As some politicians may lose interest in PSM that they cannot influence, the stable legal foundation and the strong links to civil society become ever more important.

The following requirements to safeguard PSM in the Western Balkans are essential:

- Structures in management and supervision, which guarantee autonomy and independence in management and programming;
- Participation of representatives of civil society in the supervising bodies and a vital dialogue with the public on their expectation towards PSM, its performance and shortcomings;
- Funding that is stable and foreseeable, and not dependent on changing political majorities and opportunities;
- A legal framework that allows PSM to make full use of the convergent media technologies to transmit its content on any possible platforms.

Given the pressures of the market and the convergent mediascape, the international competition, and the changing audience habits, the requirements for the prospects of PSM in the Western Balkans are in principle the same as those pertinent to any public service media in democratic countries. In this broader picture, necessities for PSM in the Western Balkans are similar to those of PSM general, as they are elaborated in studies by the Council of Europe (2012a; 2012b), Suárez Candel (2012), EBU (2015), Krichels and Holmes (2013), and Maijanen (2017), who looked at the importance of managing change and potential shifts in PSM leadership. What is specific for PSM in the Western Balkans is that they enter the paths to the future from a much worse starting position than those in Western Europe. Given that the international community bears quite an amount of responsibility for the state of PSM in the Western Balkans, and since the EU should have a prominent interest in safeguarding PSM in its member states and its partnering countries, it is fair to conclude this inventory of PSM in the Western Balkans with the statement that the EU and its member states should work hard to safeguard the future of public service media in the region.

References

Council of Europe. 2012a. *Declaration of the Committee of Ministers on Public Service Media Governance.* Accessed May 5, 2020. https://wcd.coe.int /ViewDoc. jsp?id=1908241.

——. 2012b. *Recommendation CM/Rec(2012)1 of the Committee of Ministers to Member States on Public Service Media Governance.* Accessed May 5, 2020. https://wcd.coe. int/ViewDoc.jsp?id=1908265.

European Broadcasting Union. 2015. *Vision 2020: Connect, Grow and Influence.* Geneva: EBU. https://www.ebu.ch/files/live/sites/ebu/files/Publications/EBU-Vision2020-Connect_EN.pdf.

Jakubowicz, Karol. 2004. "Ideas in Our Heads: Introduction of PSB as Part of Media System Change in Central and Eastern Europe." *European Journal of Communication* 19, no. 1 (March): 53–74.

Krichels, Ted, and Stephen Holmes. 2013. *Public Media Models of the Future* Accessed May 5, 2020. https://current.org/wp-content/uploads/2014/01/Models-of-the-Future-report.pdf.

Maijanen, Päivi. 2017. "The Blessing and Curse of Being Public: Managing Change in Public Service Media in Finland." In *Public Service Media Renewal: Adaptation to Digital Network Challenges,* edited by Michał Głowacki and Alicja Jaskiernia, 193–212. Frankfurt am Main: Peter Lang.

Reporters Without Borders and BIRN Albania. n.d. *Media Ownership Monitor Albania: The Albanian Radio Television (RTSH).* Accessed May 5, 2020. http://albania. momrsf.org/en/owners/companies/detail/company/company/show/the-albanian-radio-television-rtsh/.

Suárez Candel, Roberto. 2012. *Adapting Public Service to the Multiplatform Scenario: Challenges, Opportunities and Risks.* Hamburg: Hans-Bredow-Institut. https:// www.hans-bredow-institut.de/uploads/media/Publikationen/cms/media /6bb5e-44fb23771beca285fcd4a1bbd5979db4560.pdf.

List of Contributors

Nidžara Ahmetašević is a scholar and journalist from Bosnia and Herzegovina. She was a fellow with the Alliance for Historical Dialogue and Accountability at Columbia University.

Péter Bajomi-Lázár is Professor of Mass Communication at the Budapest Business School University of Applied Sciences, Hungary.

Blerjana Bino is a researcher of media studies and co-founder of the Center for Science and Innovation for Development, Albania.

Sally Broughton Micova is Lecturer in Communications Policy and Politics at the University of East Anglia, Norwich, England.

Laia Castro Herrero is Senior Research and Teaching Associate at the Department of Communication and Media Research, University of Zurich, Switzerland, and Lecturer at Universitat Internacional de Catalunya, Barcelona.

Gregory Ferrell Lowe is Director of the Communication Program, Northwestern University in Qatar.

Michał Głowacki is a researcher at the Faculty of Journalism, Information and Book Studies, University of Warsaw, Poland.

Tea Hadžiristić is a researcher and policy analyst at Infrastructure Canada.

Tarik Jusić is Lecturer and Guarantor of the study program at the School of Communication and Media, University of New York in Prague, Czech Republic.

Davor Marko is Balkans program manager at Thomson Foundation in Belgrade, Serbia, and research fellow at the Centre for Media, Data and Society, Central European University.

Igor Micevski is PhD candidate in Political Sociology, Faculty of Philosophy, University Ss. Cyril and Methodius, and a Researcher at the Research Institute on Social Development (RESIS), Skopje, North Macedonia.

Naser Miftari is Assistant Professor at the Department of Journalism, University of Prishtina, Kosovo.

Marko Milosavljević is Associate Professor of Journalism at the Faculty of Social Sciences, Research Centre for the Terminology of Social Sciences and Journalism, University of Ljubljana, Slovenia.

Kenneth Murphy is a lecturer in Media/Communications at the School of Media, Technological University Dublin, Ireland.

Zrinjka Peruško is Professor of Media Sociology and Communication at the Faculty of Political Science, University of Zagreb, Croatia.

Melita Poler Kovačič is Professor of Journalism at the Faculty of Social Sciences, University of Ljubljana, Slovenia.

Manuel Puppis is Professor at the Department of Communication and Media Research (DCM), University of Fribourg, Switzerland.

Nataša Ružić is Associate Professor at the Faculty of Political Science, University of Montenegro.

Barbara Thomass is Professor at the Institute for Media Research, Ruhr-Universität Bochum, Germany.

Snežana Trpevska is an expert in media policy and researcher at the Research Institute on Social Development (RESIS), Skopje, North Macedonia.

Index

CPSIA information can be obtained
at www.ICGtesting.com
Printed in the USA
JSHW041105200721
17060JS00001B/59

9 789633 864012